I'll never put out graphic novels two months in a row ever again. Here's *World Trigger* volume 8.

—Daisuke Ashihara, 2014

Daisuke Ashihara began his manga career at the age of 27 when his manga *Room 303* won second place in the 75th Tezuka Awards. His first series, *Super Dog Rilienthal*, began serialization in *Weekly Shonen Jump* in 2009. *World Trigger* is his second serialized work in *Weekly Shonen Jump*. He is also the author of several shorter works, including the one-shots *Super Dog Rilienthal*, *Trigger Keeper* and *Elite Agent Jin*.

WORLD TRIGGER VOL. 8
SHONEN JUMP Manga Edition

STORY AND ART BY DAISUKE ASHIHARA

Translation/Lillian Olsen
Touch-Up Art & Lettering/Annaliese Christman
Design/Sam Elzway
Weekly Shonen Jump Editor/Hope Donovan
Graphic Novel Editor/Marlene First

WORLD TRIGGER © 2013 by Daisuke Ashihara/SHUEISHA Inc.
All rights reserved.
First published in Japan in 2013 by SHUEISHA Inc., Tokyo.
English translation rights arranged by SHUEISHA Inc.

The stories, characters and incidents mentioned
in this publication are entirely fictional.

Printed in the U.S.A.

Published by VIZ Media, LLC
P.O. Box 77010
San Francisco, CA 94107

10 9 8 7 6 5 4 3 2 1
First printing, January 2016

www.viz.com

PARENTAL ADVISORY
WORLD TRIGGER is rated T for Teen and is
recommended for ages 13 and up. This volume
contains fantasy violence.
ratings.viz.com

THE WORLD'S
MOST POPULAR MANGA
SHONEN JUMP
www.shonenjump.com

SHONEN JUMP MANGA EDITION

WORLD TRIGGER 8

DAISUKE ASHIHARA

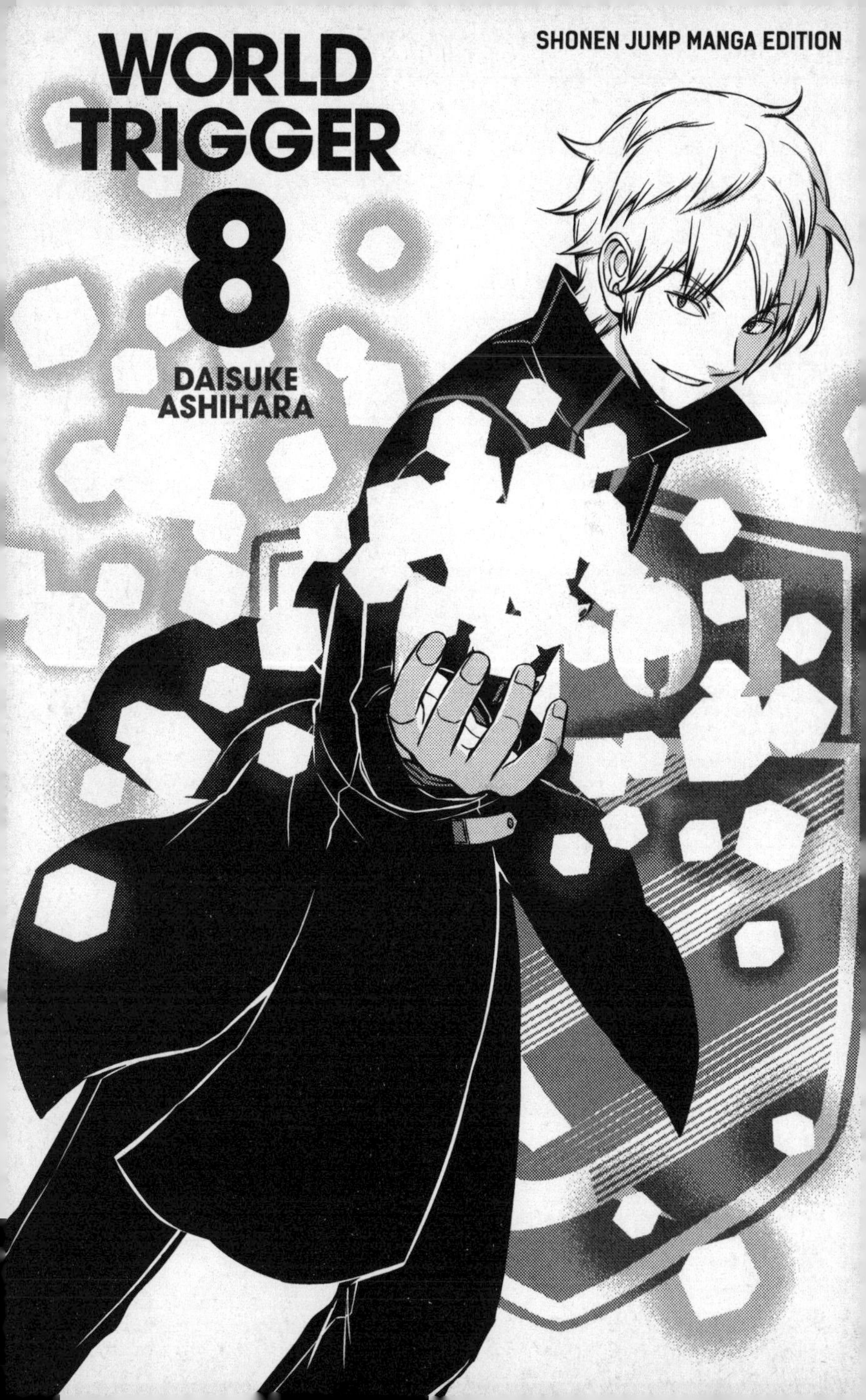

WORLD TRIGGER DATA BASE

on NEIGHBOR

nvaders from another dimension that enter Mikado City through Gates. Most "Neighbors" here are Trion soldiers built for war. The Neighbors who actually live on the other side of the Gates are human, like Yuma.

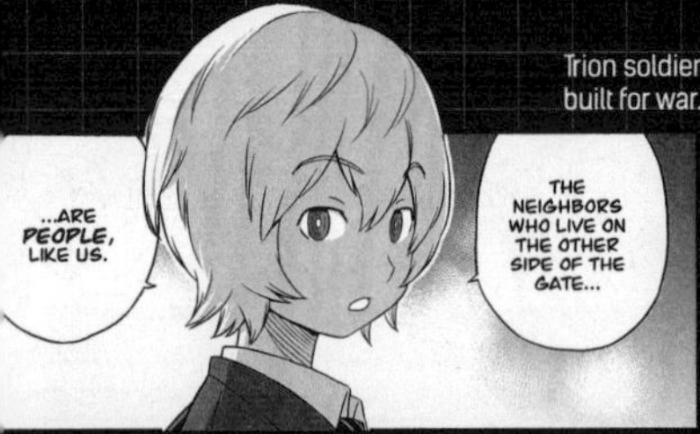
THE NEIGHBORS WHO LIVE ON THE OTHER SIDE OF THE GATE...
...ARE PEOPLE, LIKE US.

Trion soldier built for war.

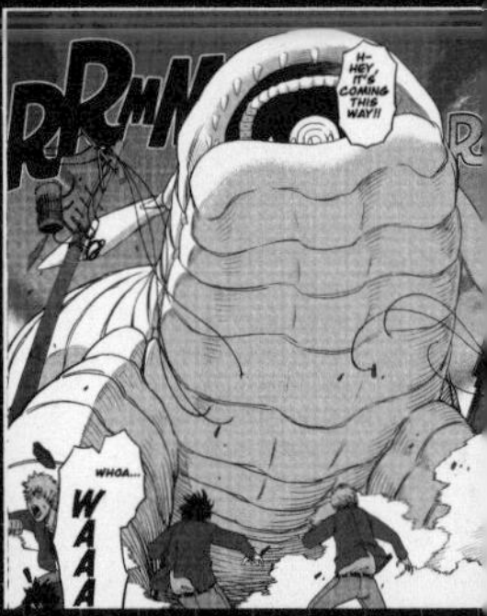
H-HEY, IT'S COMING THIS WAY!!
RRMN
WHOA...
WAAA

AFTOKRATOR

he largest military nation in the Neighbor world, eported to have seven Black Triggers 13 years go. They are invading Earth to kidnap people vith Trion abilities.

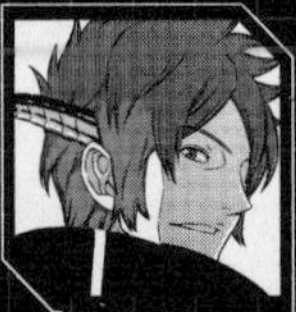
HYREIN

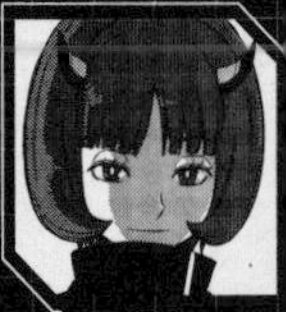
MIRA

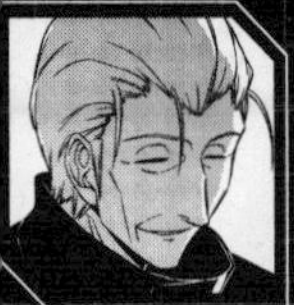
VIZA

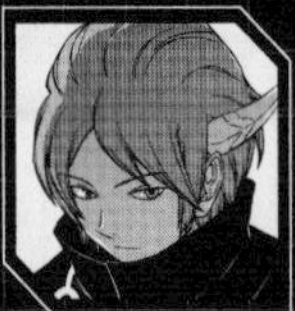
HYUSE

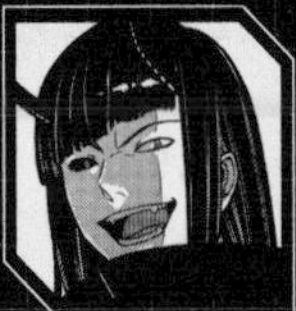
ENEDORA

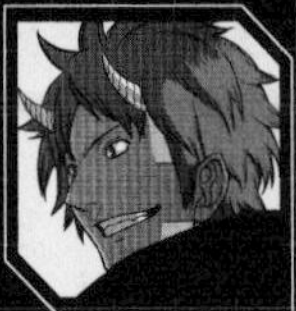
RANBANEIN

(withdrawn)

Horns

Aftokrator produces humans with exceptional Trion abilities by implanting Trigger-equipped Trion receptors into their heads. A horned person's fighting abilities far exceed those of a normal Trigger user's. Some horns are compatible with Black Triggers, which turn the horns black.

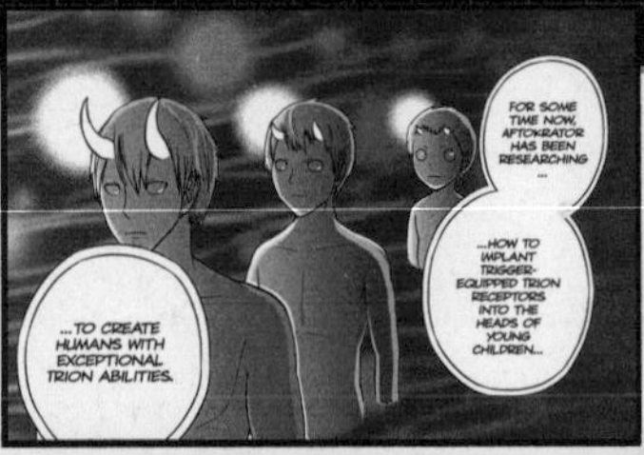
FOR SOME TIME NOW, AFTOKRATOR HAS BEEN RESEARCHING...
...HOW TO IMPLANT TRIGGER-EQUIPPED TRION RECEPTORS INTO THE HEADS OF YOUNG CHILDREN...
...TO CREATE HUMANS WITH EXCEPTIONAL TRION ABILITIES.

BORDER

An agency founded to protect the city's peace from Neighbors. Agents are classified as follows: C-Rank for trainees, B-Rank for main forces, A-Rank for elites and S-Rank for those with Black Triggers. A-Rank squads get to go on away missions to Neighbor worlds.

Resistance

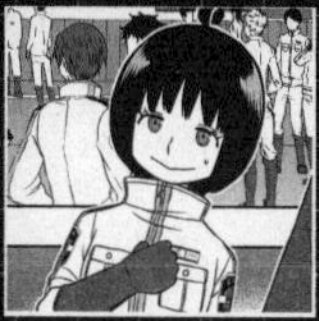

C-Rank: Chika

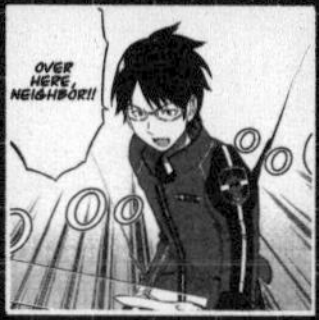
OVER HERE, NEIGHBOR!!

B-Rank: Osamu

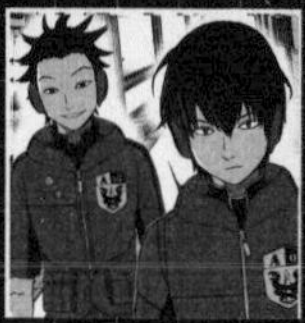

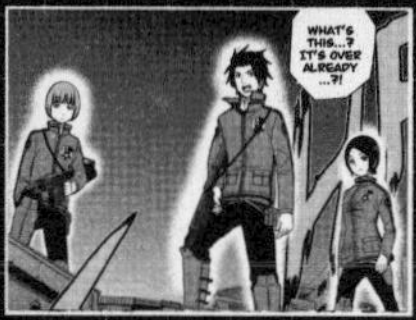
WHAT'S THIS...? IT'S OVER ALREADY ...?!

A-Rank: Arashiyama Squad, Miwa Squad

Trigger

A technology created by Neighbors to manipulate Trion. Used mainly as weapons, Triggers come in various types. Border classifies them into three groups: Attacker, Gunner, and Sniper.

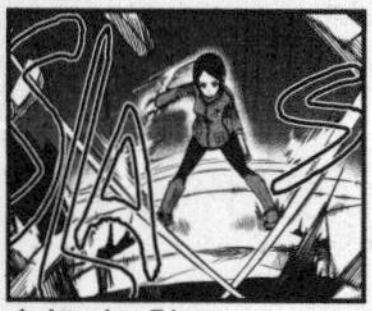

▲ Attacker Trigger

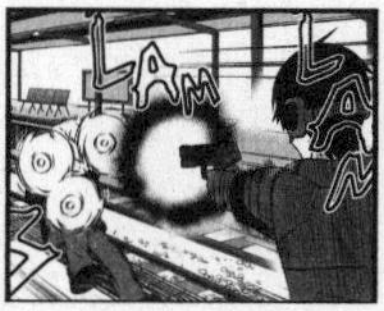

▲ Gunner Trigger

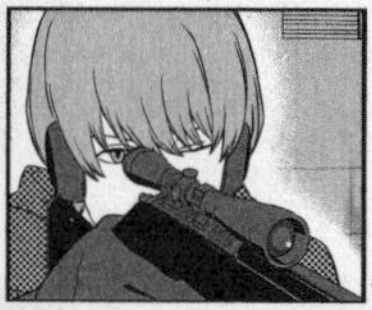

◀ Sniper Trigger

Black Trigger

A special Trigger created when a skilled user pours their entire life force and Trion into a Trigger. Outperforms regular Triggers, but the user must be compatible with the personality of the creator, meaning only a few people can use any given Black Trigger.

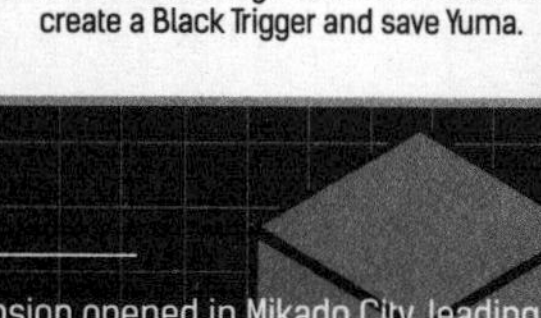
I'LL SAVE YOU.
YUGO...
...CREATED A BLACK TRIGGER TO SAVE YUMA.

▲ Yuma's father Yugo sacrificed his life to create a Black Trigger and save Yuma.

STORY

About four years ago, a Gate connecting to another dimension opened in Mikado City, leading to the appearance of invaders called Neighbors. After the establishment of the Border Defense Agency, people were able to return to their normal lives.

Osamu Mikumo is a junior high student who meets Yuma Kuga, a Neighbor. Yuma is targeted for capture by Border, but Tamakoma Branch agent Yuichi Jin steps in to help. He convinces Yuma to join Border instead, then gives his Black Trigger to HQ in exchange for Yuma's enlistment. Now Osamu, Yuma and Osamu's friend Chika work toward making A-Rank together.

Another large-scale Neighbor attack on Mikado City begins. Humanoid Neighbors take notice of Chika's powerful Trion levels, closing in while Osamu and the others try to hold out against continous attacks from the Trion soldiers. Their horns signify that they are from Aftokrator. The agents face off with the formidable Humanoid Neighbors, but then one of them forces his way into Border Headquarters! What will happen now?!

WORLD TRIGGER CHARACTERS

TAMAKOMA BRANCH

Understanding toward Neighbors. Considered divergent from Border's main philosophy.

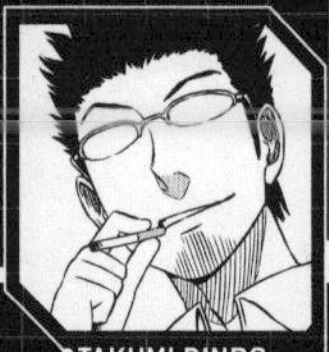

TAKUMI RINDO

Tamakoma Branch Director

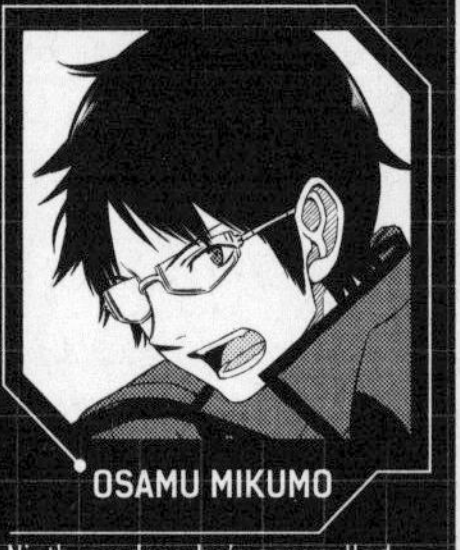

OSAMU MIKUMO

Ninth-grader who's compelled to help those in trouble. B-Rank Border agent.

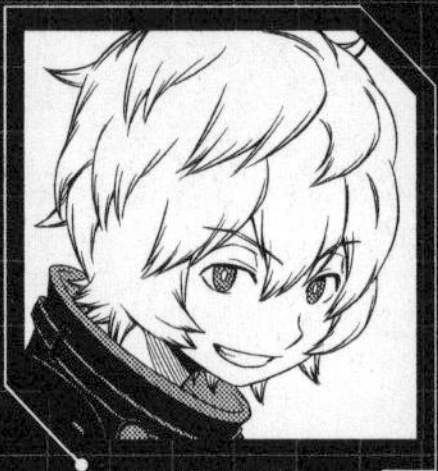

YUMA KUGA

A Neighbor who carries a Black Trigger.

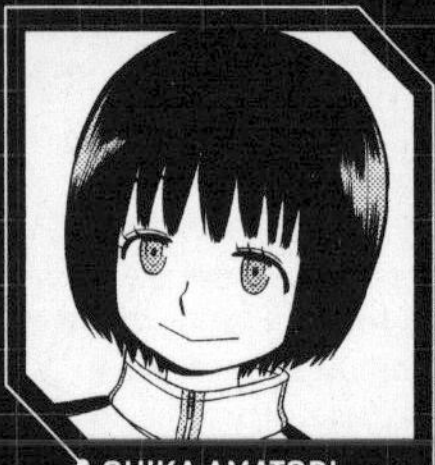

CHIKA AMATORI

Osamu's childhood friend. She has high Trion levels.

TAMAKOMA-1

Tamakoma's A-Rank squad.

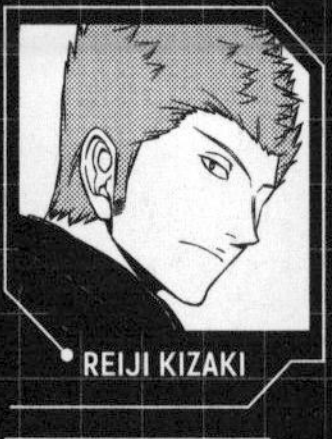

REIJI KIZAKI

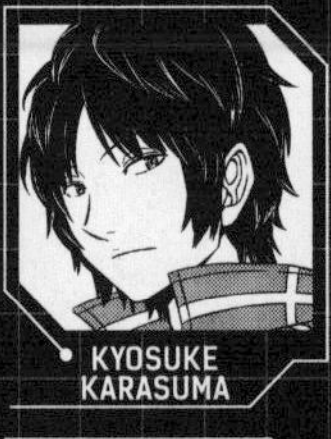

KYOSUKE KARASUMA

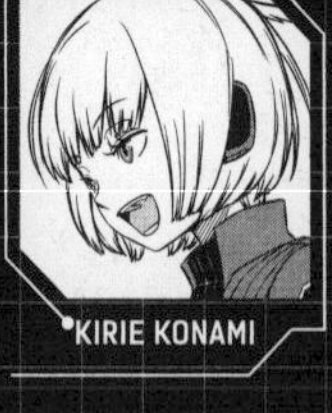

KIRIE KONAMI

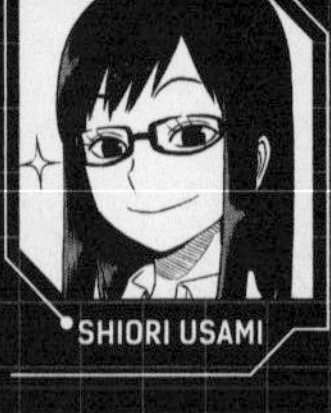

SHIORI USAMI

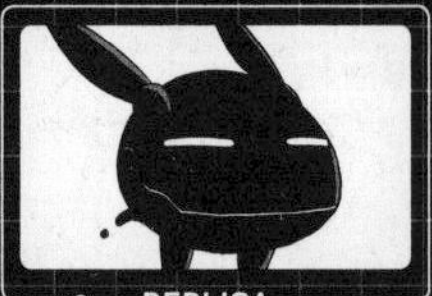

REPLICA

Yuma's chaperone.

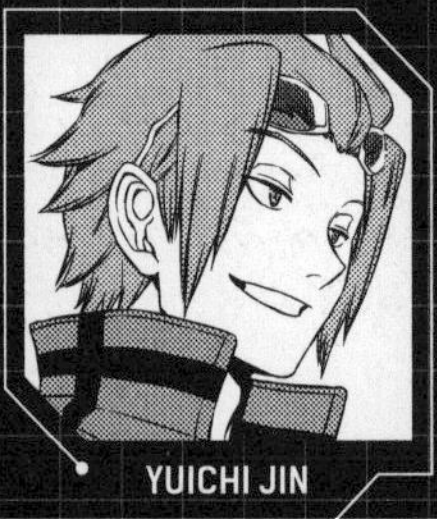

YUICHI JIN

Former S-Rank Black Trigger user. His Side Effect lets him see the future.

BORDER HQ

A-RANK AGENTS

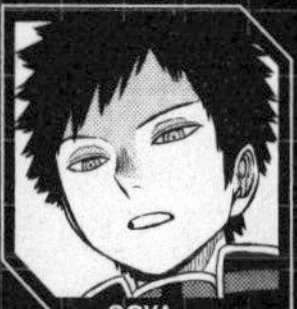
SOYA KAZAMA

Captain, A-Rank #3 Squad, Attacker

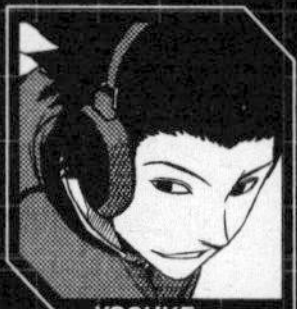
YOSUKE YONEYA

A-Rank #7 Miwa Squad Attacker

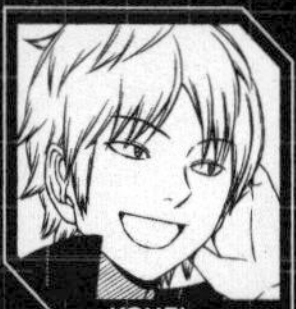
KOHEI IZUMI

A-Rank #1 Tachikawa Squad Shooter

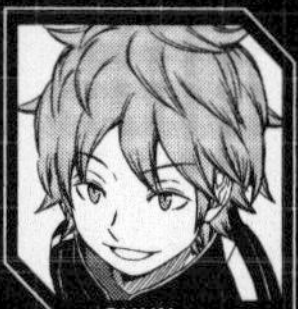
SHUN MIDORIKAWA

A-Rank #4 Kusakabe Squad Attacker

SUWA SQUAD

HQ's B-Rank #10 Squad. Captain Suwa was cubified by a Rabit.

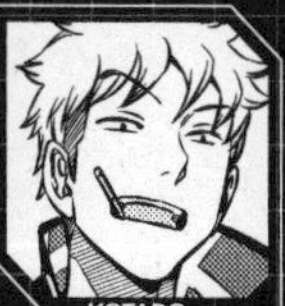
KOTARO SUWA

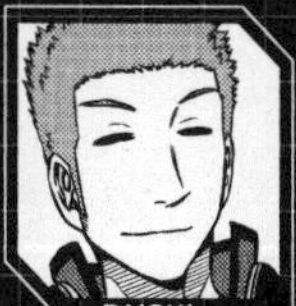
DAICHI TSUTSUMI

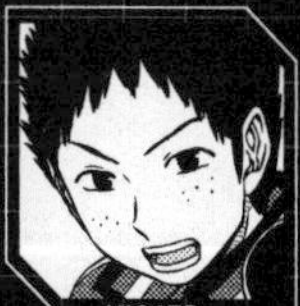
HISATO SASAMORI

BORDER SENIOR OFFICERS

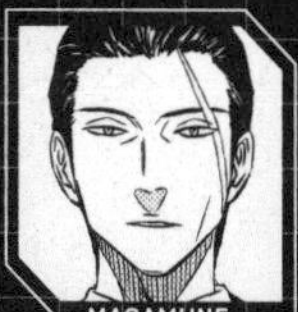
MASAMUNE KIDO

HQ Commander

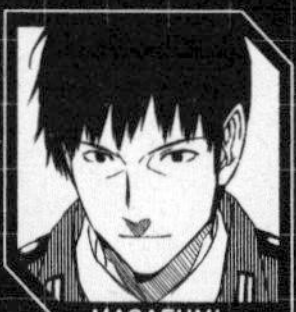
MASAFUMI SHINODA

HQ Director, Defense Force Commander

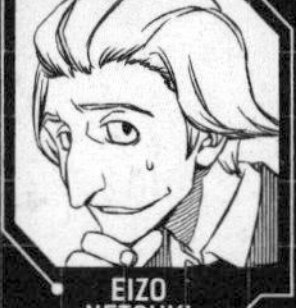
EIZO NETSUKI

PR Director

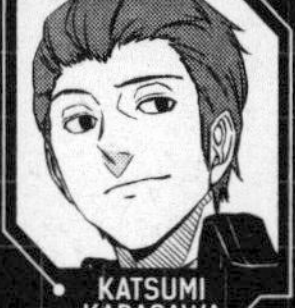
KATSUMI KARASAWA

Business Director

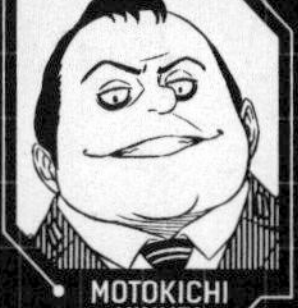
MOTOKICHI KINUTA

R&D Director

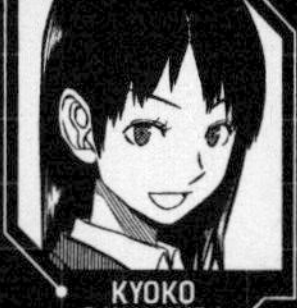
KYOKO SAWAMURA

HQ Assistant Director

C-RANK TRAINEE

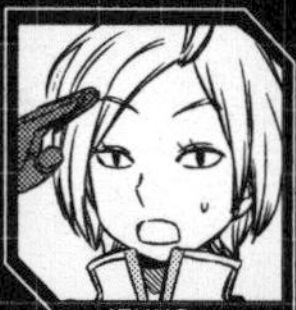
IZUHO NATSUME

Aspiring sniper and Chika's friend.

WORLD TRIGGER

CONTENTS

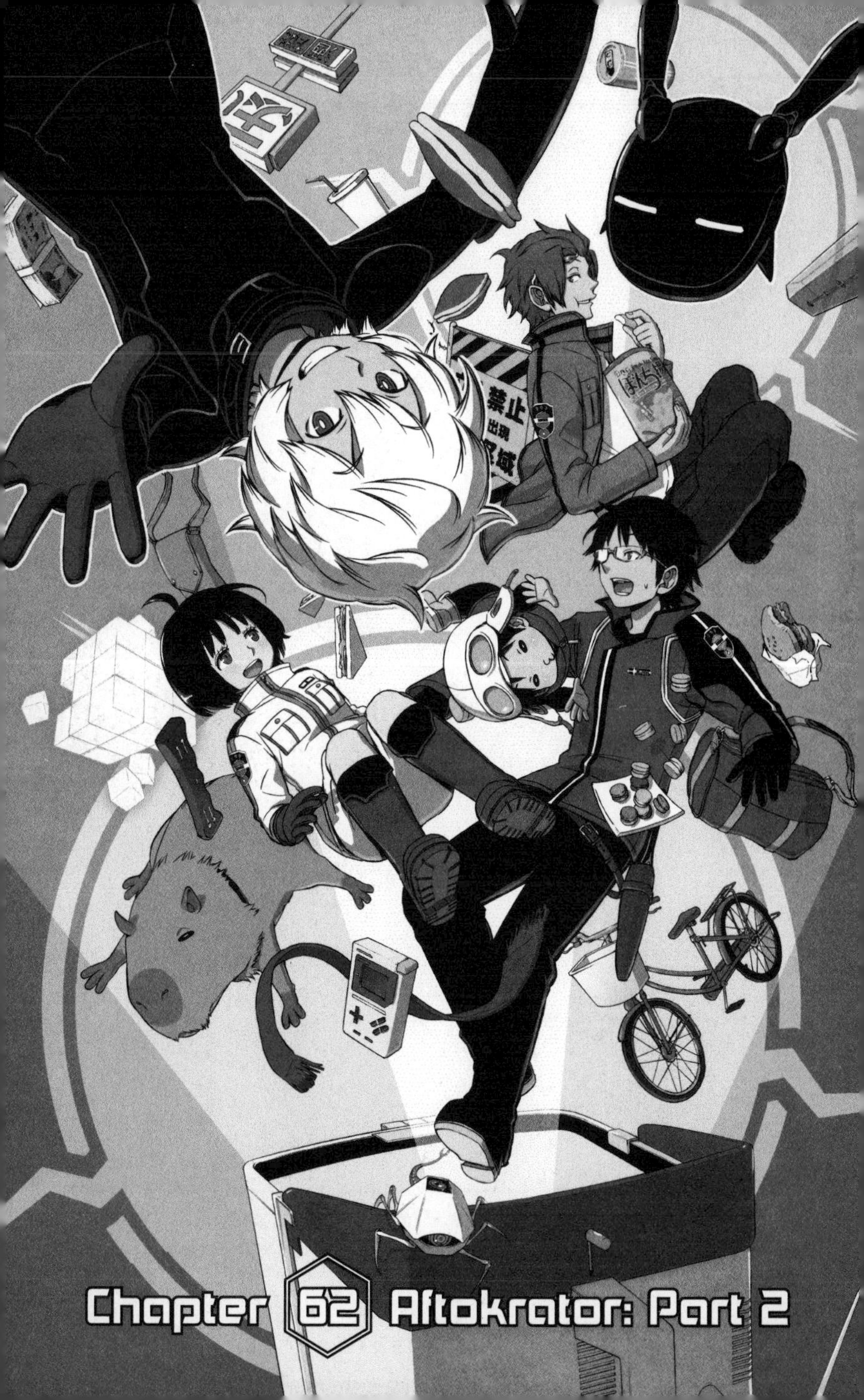

Chapter 62 Aftokrator: Part 2

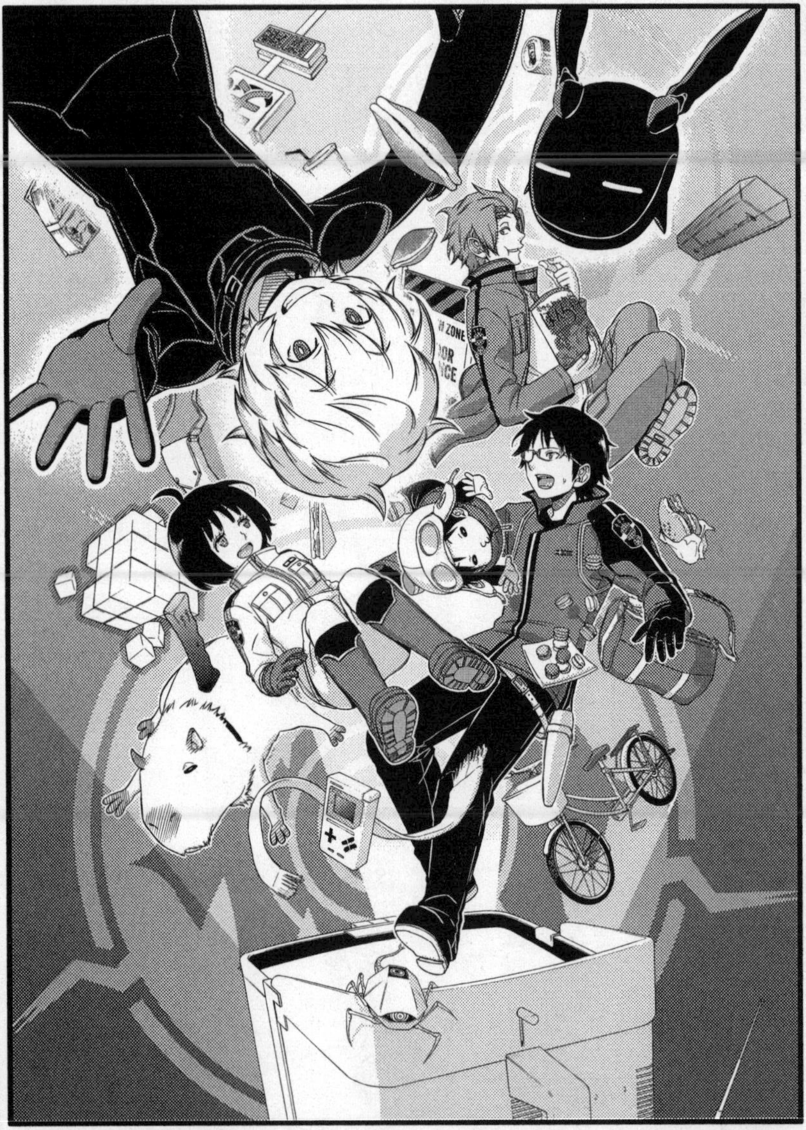

N ZONE
DOR
NCE

■ 2014 *Weekly Shonen Jump* issue 27 center color page (10th time)

I made this more cheerful than usual because this was the color page commemorating the anime. Look closely and you can see a wad of cash floating around. There's also a Gameboy-shaped Trion measuring instrument built by Shiori. I feel like I made Chika 30 percent cuter than usual, so I'm quite satisfied.

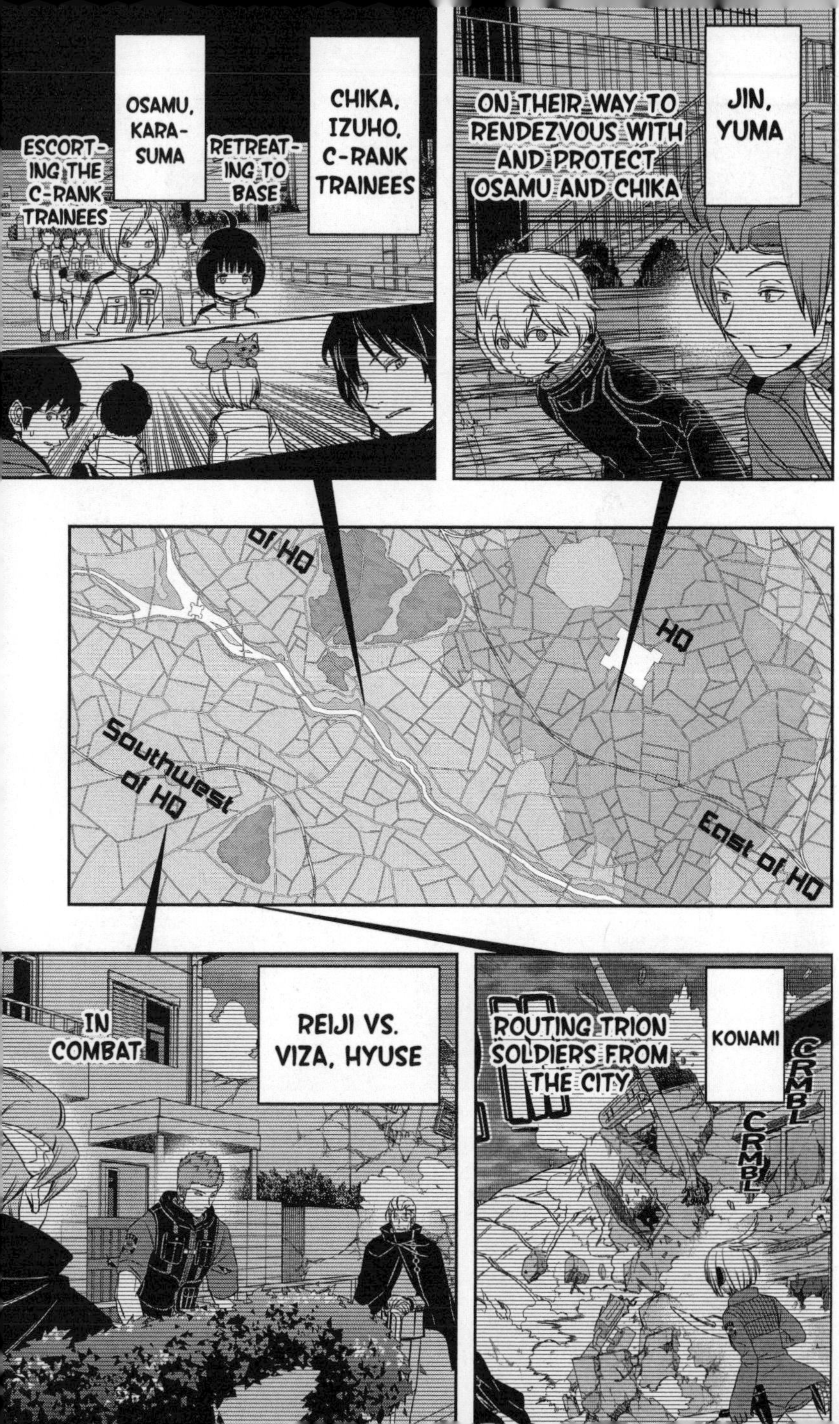
JIN, YUMA
ON THEIR WAY TO RENDEZVOUS WITH AND PROTECT OSAMU AND CHIKA
CHIKA, IZUHO, C-RANK TRAINEES
RETREAT-ING TO BASE
OSAMU, KARA-SUMA
ESCORT-ING THE C-RANK TRAINEES
HQ
of HQ
East of HQ
Southwest of HQ
KONAMI
ROUTING TRION SOLDIERS FROM THE CITY
CRMBL
CRMBL
REIJI VS. VIZA, HYUSE
IN COMBAT

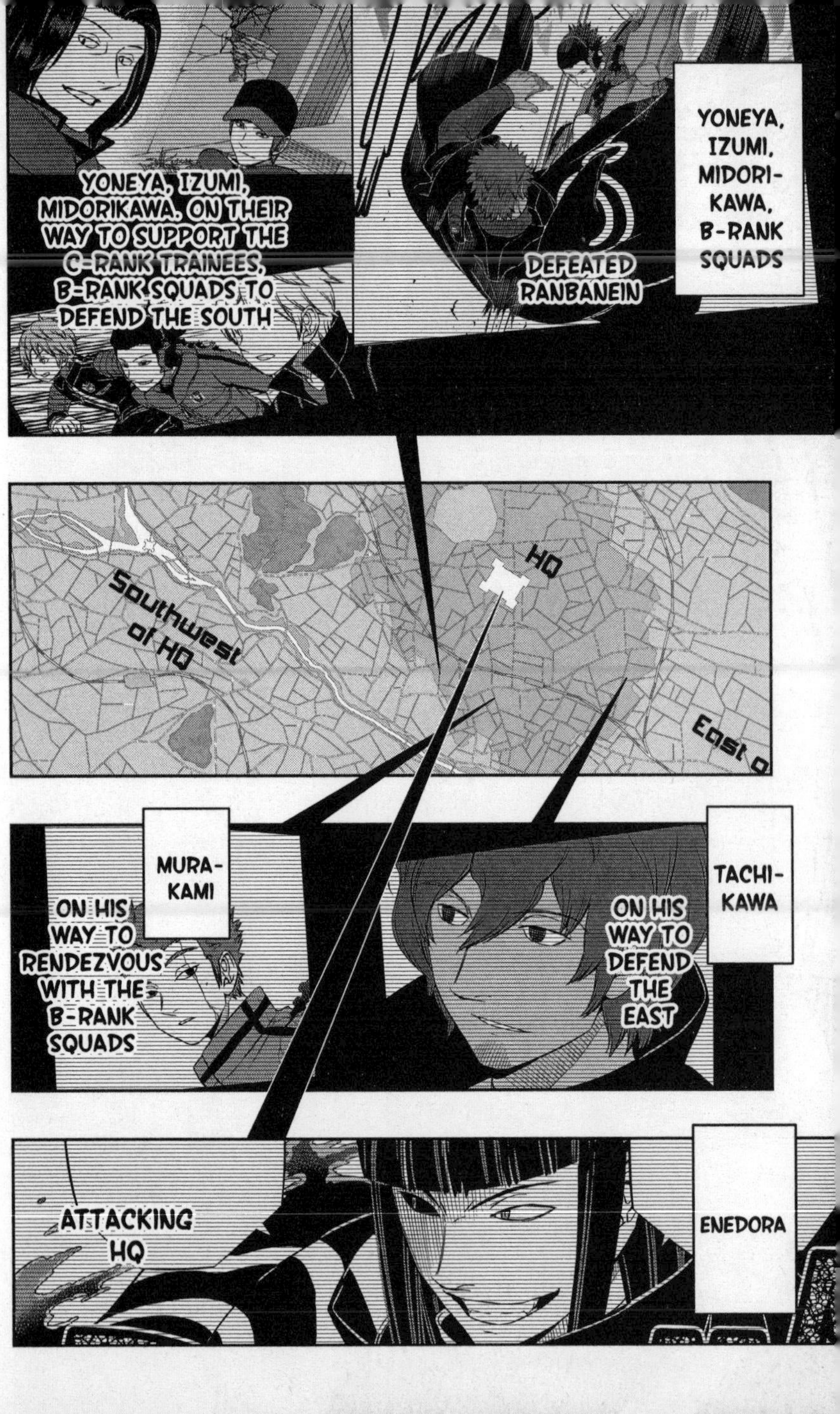
YONEYA, IZUMI, MIDORI-KAWA, B-RANK SQUADS
DEFEATED RANBANEIN
YONEYA, IZUMI, MIDORIKAWA. ON THEIR WAY TO SUPPORT THE C-RANK TRAINEES, B-RANK SQUADS TO DEFEND THE SOUTH
HQ
Southwest of HQ
East o
TACHI-KAWA
ON HIS WAY TO DEFEND THE EAST
MURA-KAMI
ON HIS WAY TO RENDEZVOUS WITH THE B-RANK SQUADS
ENEDORA
ATTACKING HQ

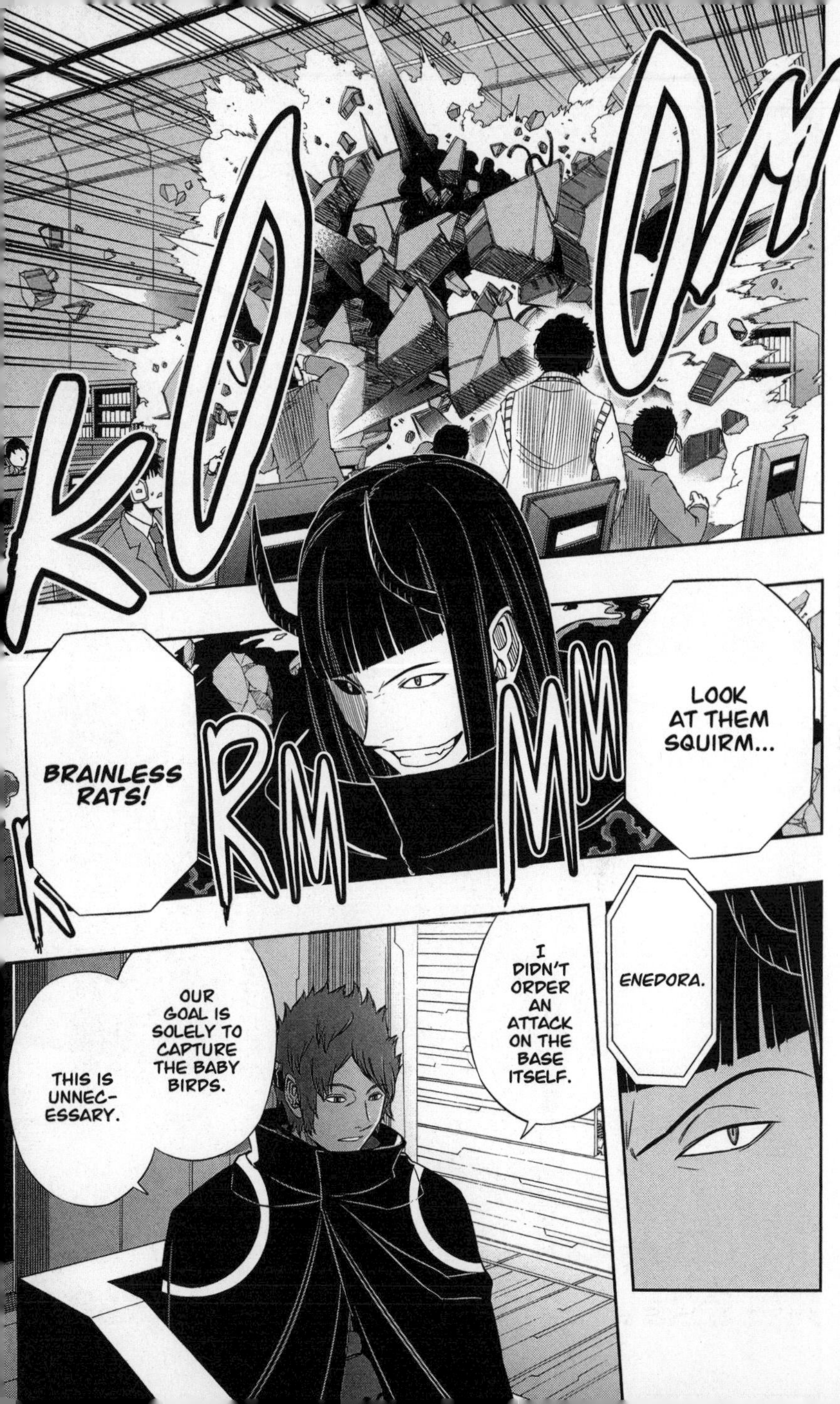
KOOM
LOOK AT THEM SQUIRM...
RMMM
BRAINLESS RATS!
ENEDORA.
I DIDN'T ORDER AN ATTACK ON THE BASE ITSELF.
OUR GOAL IS SOLELY TO CAPTURE THE BABY BIRDS.
THIS IS UNNEC-ESSARY.

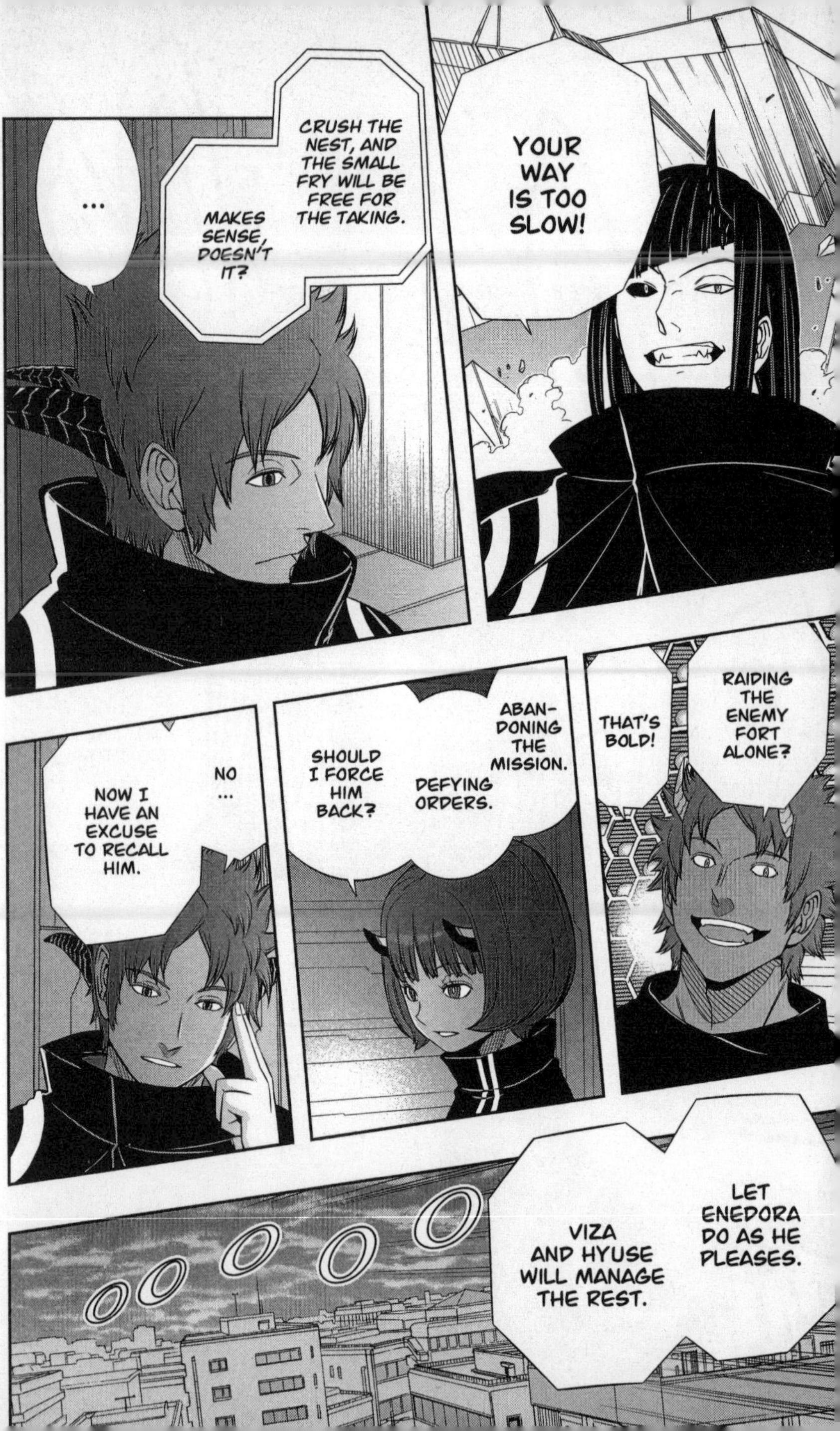
YOUR WAY IS TOO SLOW!
CRUSH THE NEST, AND THE SMALL FRY WILL BE FREE FOR THE TAKING.
MAKES SENSE, DOESN'T IT?
...
RAIDING THE ENEMY FORT ALONE?
THAT'S BOLD!
ABANDONING THE MISSION.
DEFYING ORDERS.
SHOULD I FORCE HIM BACK?
NO ...
NOW I HAVE AN EXCUSE TO RECALL HIM.
LET ENEDORA DO AS HE PLEASES.
VIZA AND HYUSE WILL MANAGE THE REST.

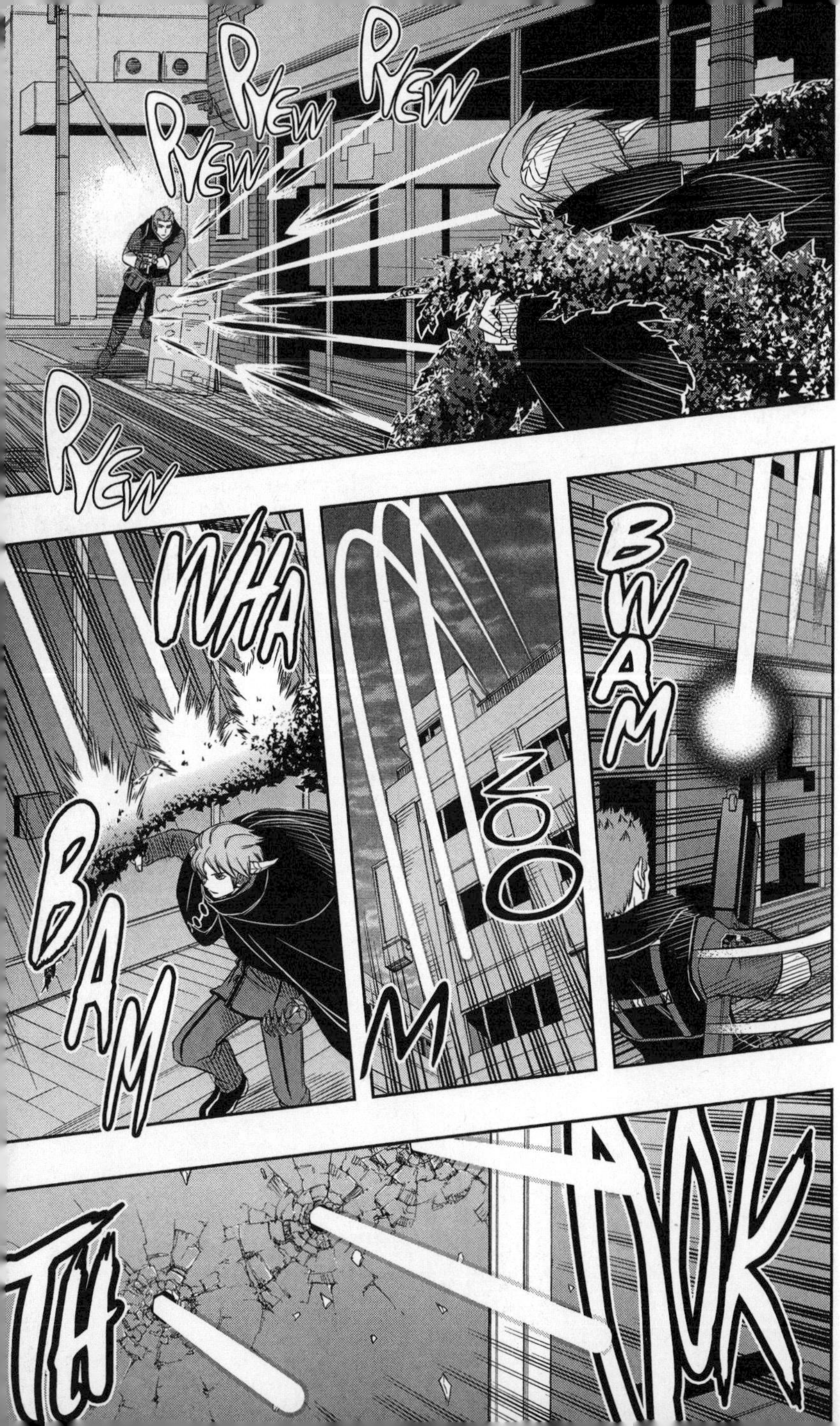
PYEW
PYEW
PYEW
PYEW
BWAM
ZOOM
WHA
BAM
TH
ACK

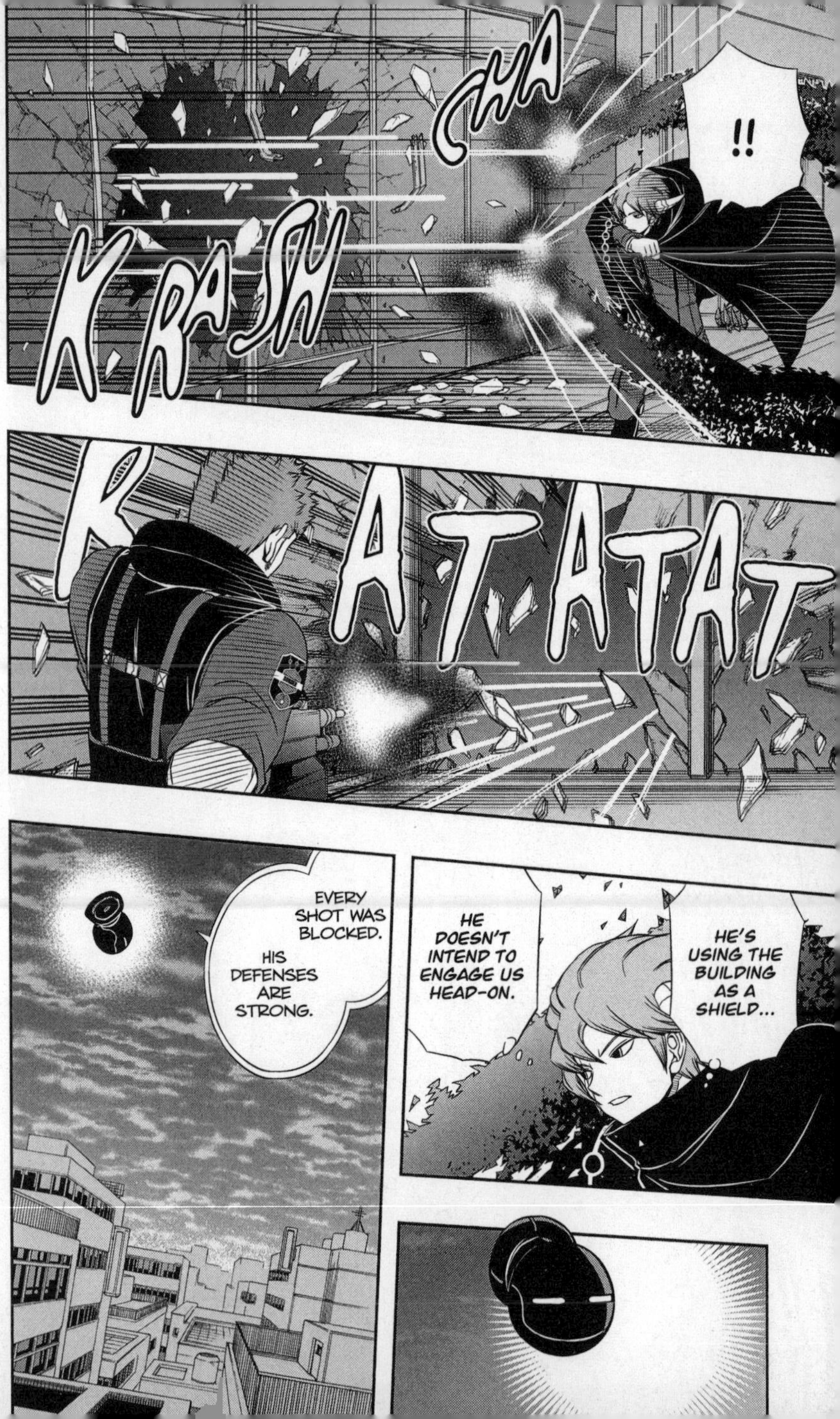
!!
KRASH
CHA
KATATAT
HE'S USING THE BUILDING AS A SHIELD...
HE DOESN'T INTEND TO ENGAGE US HEAD-ON.
EVERY SHOT WAS BLOCKED.
HIS DEFENSES ARE STRONG.

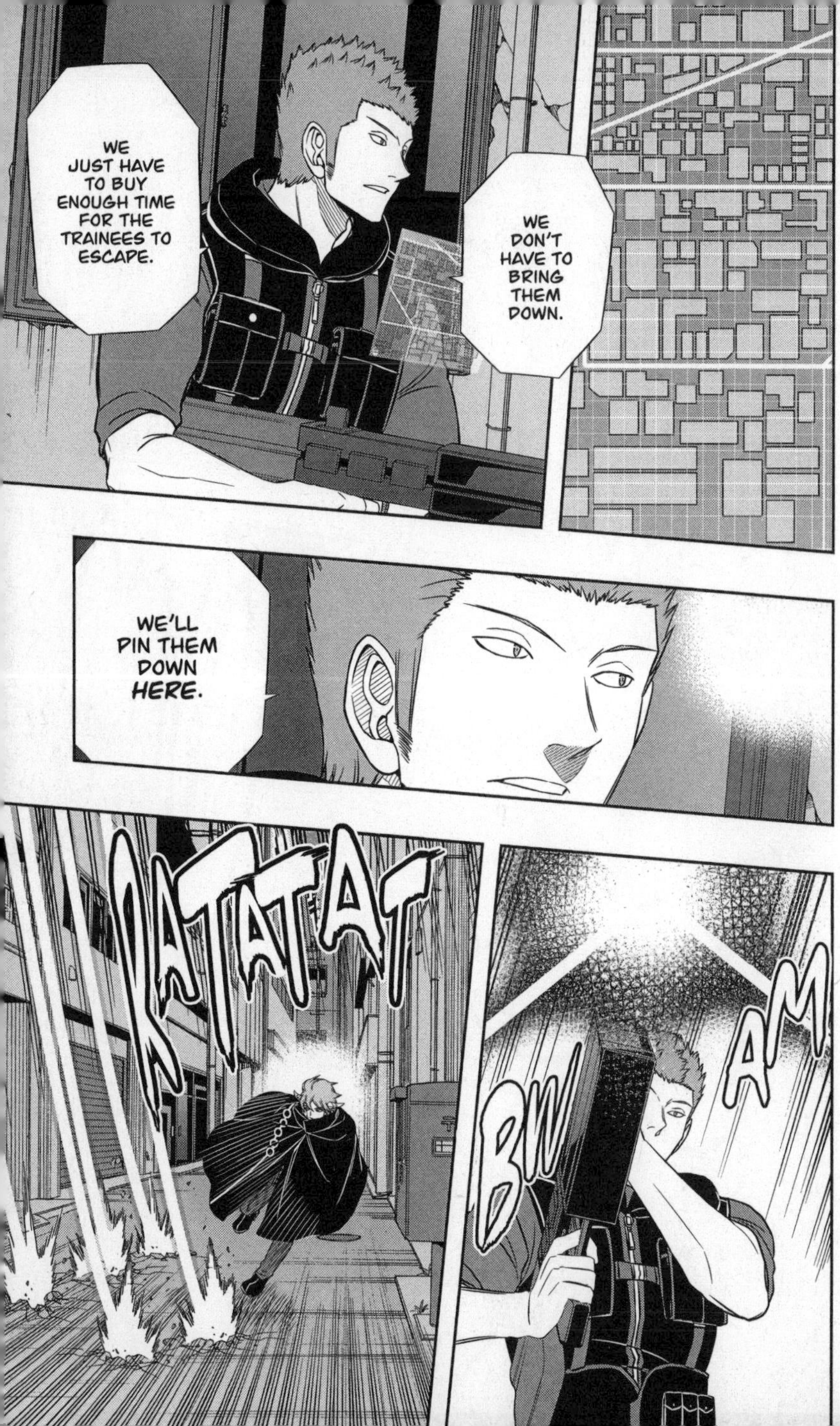
WE DON'T HAVE TO BRING THEM DOWN.
WE JUST HAVE TO BUY ENOUGH TIME FOR THE TRAINEES TO ESCAPE.
WE'LL PIN THEM DOWN HERE.
BWAM
RATATAT

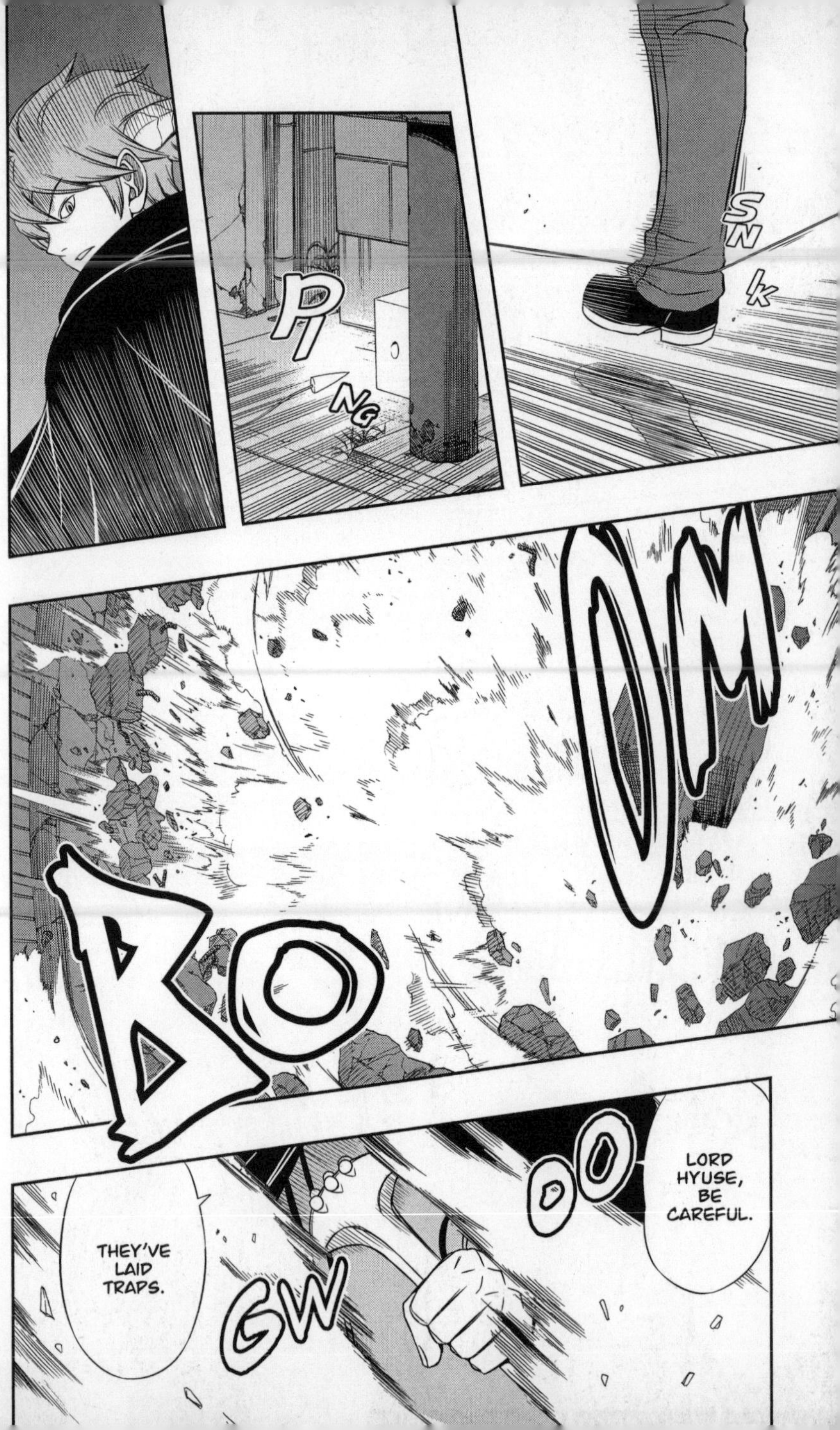
SNK
PING
BOOOM
LORD HYUSE, BE CAREFUL.
GWOO
THEY'VE LAID TRAPS.

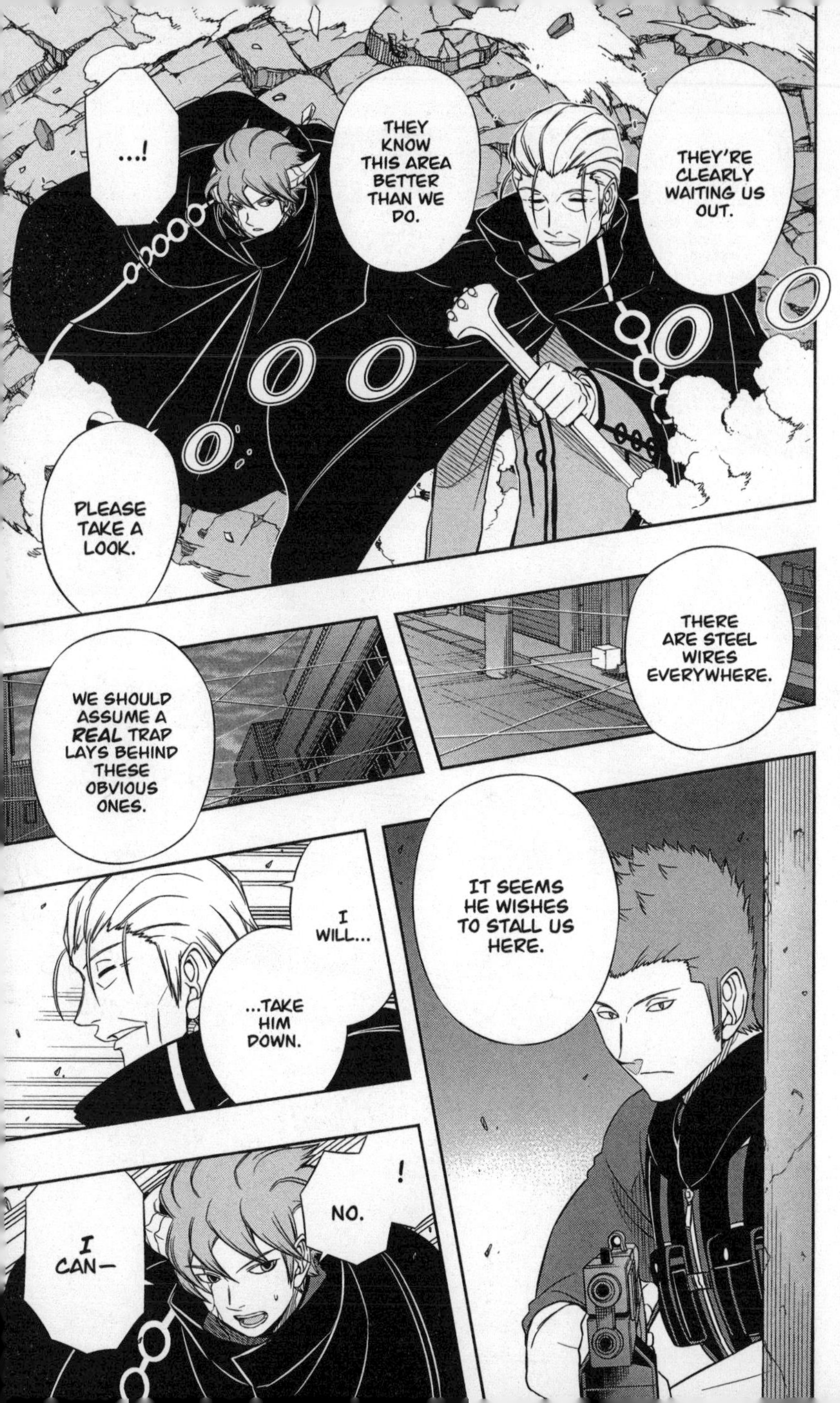
THEY'RE CLEARLY WAITING US OUT.
THEY KNOW THIS AREA BETTER THAN WE DO.
...!
PLEASE TAKE A LOOK.
THERE ARE STEEL WIRES EVERYWHERE.
WE SHOULD ASSUME A **REAL** TRAP LAYS BEHIND THESE OBVIOUS ONES.
IT SEEMS HE WISHES TO STALL US HERE.
I WILL...
...TAKE HIM DOWN.
!
NO.
I CAN—

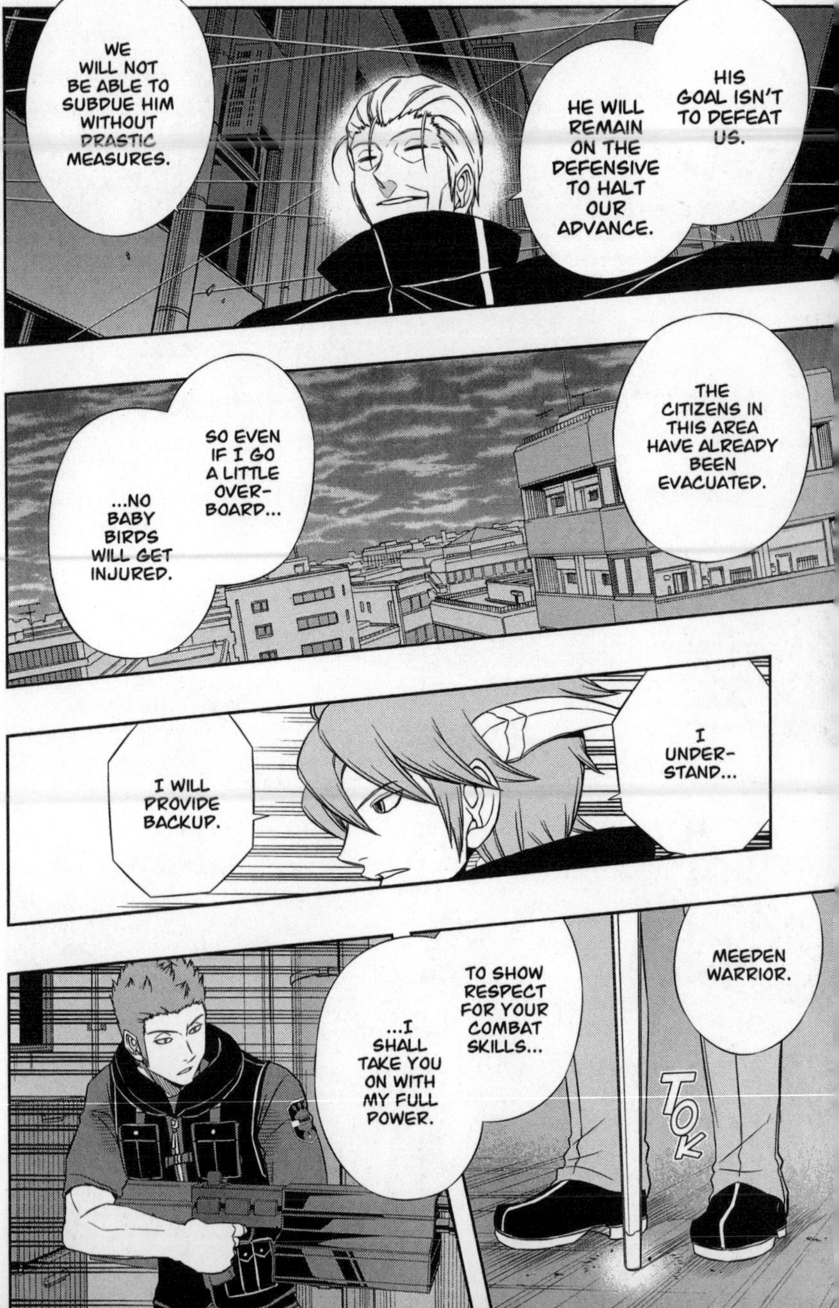
HIS GOAL ISN'T TO DEFEAT US.
HE WILL REMAIN ON THE DEFENSIVE TO HALT OUR ADVANCE.
WE WILL NOT BE ABLE TO SUBDUE HIM WITHOUT DRASTIC MEASURES.
THE CITIZENS IN THIS AREA HAVE ALREADY BEEN EVACUATED.
SO EVEN IF I GO A LITTLE OVER-BOARD...
...NO BABY BIRDS WILL GET INJURED.
I UNDER-STAND...
I WILL PROVIDE BACKUP.
MEEDEN WARRIOR.
TOK
TO SHOW RESPECT FOR YOUR COMBAT SKILLS...
...I SHALL TAKE YOU ON WITH MY FULL POWER.

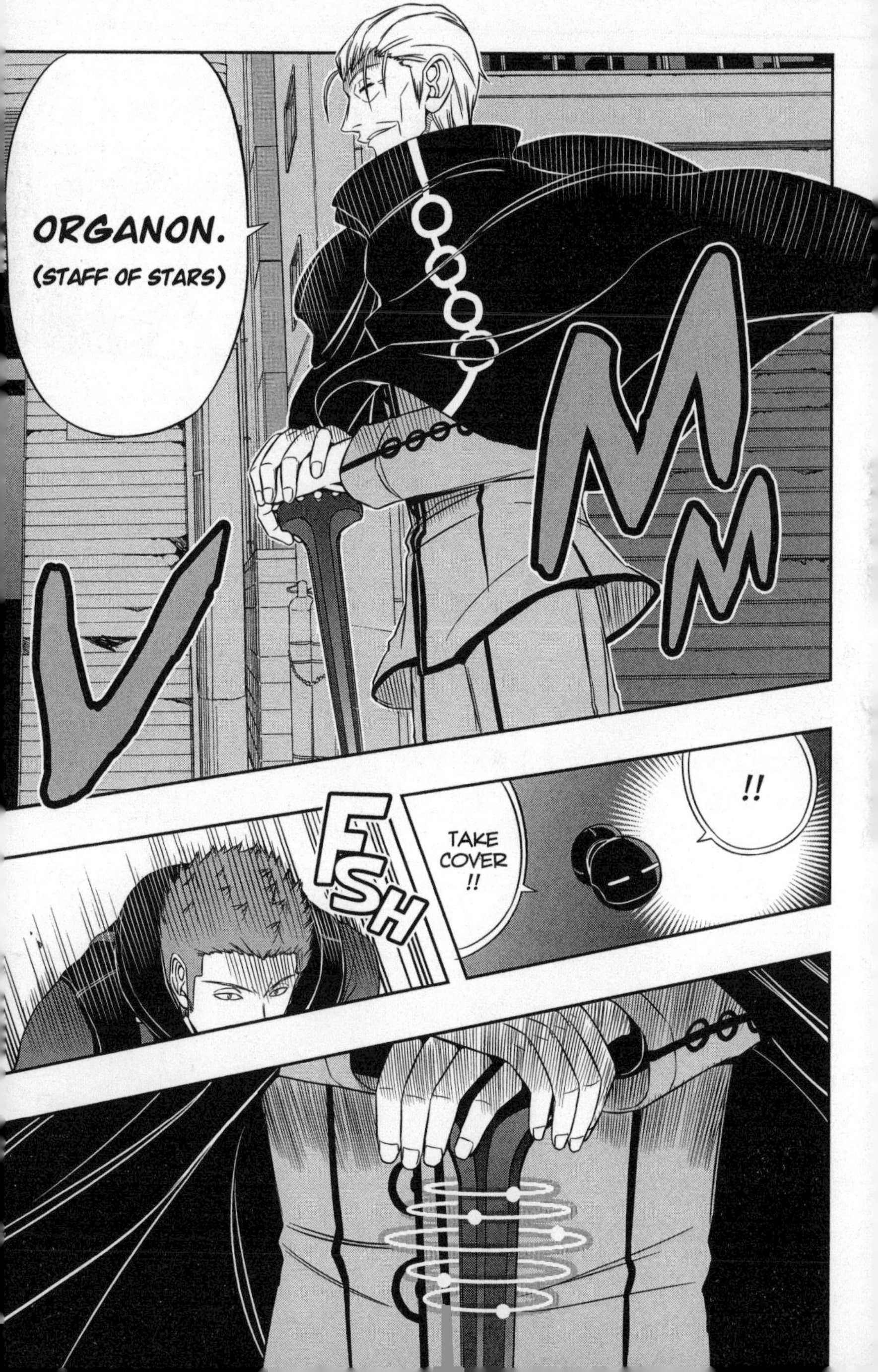

ORGANON.
(STAFF OF STARS)
VMM
!!
TAKE COVER !!
FSH

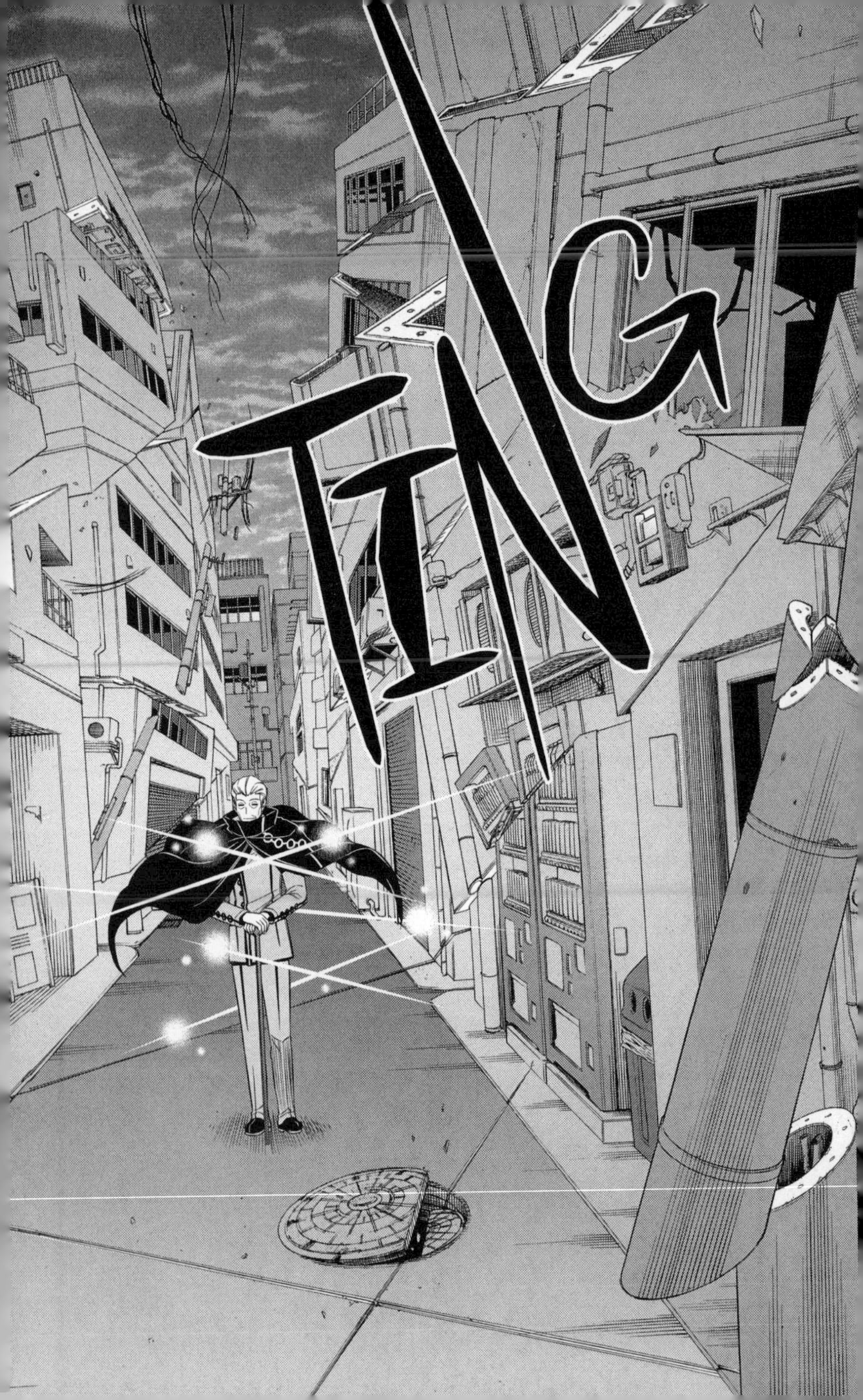
TING

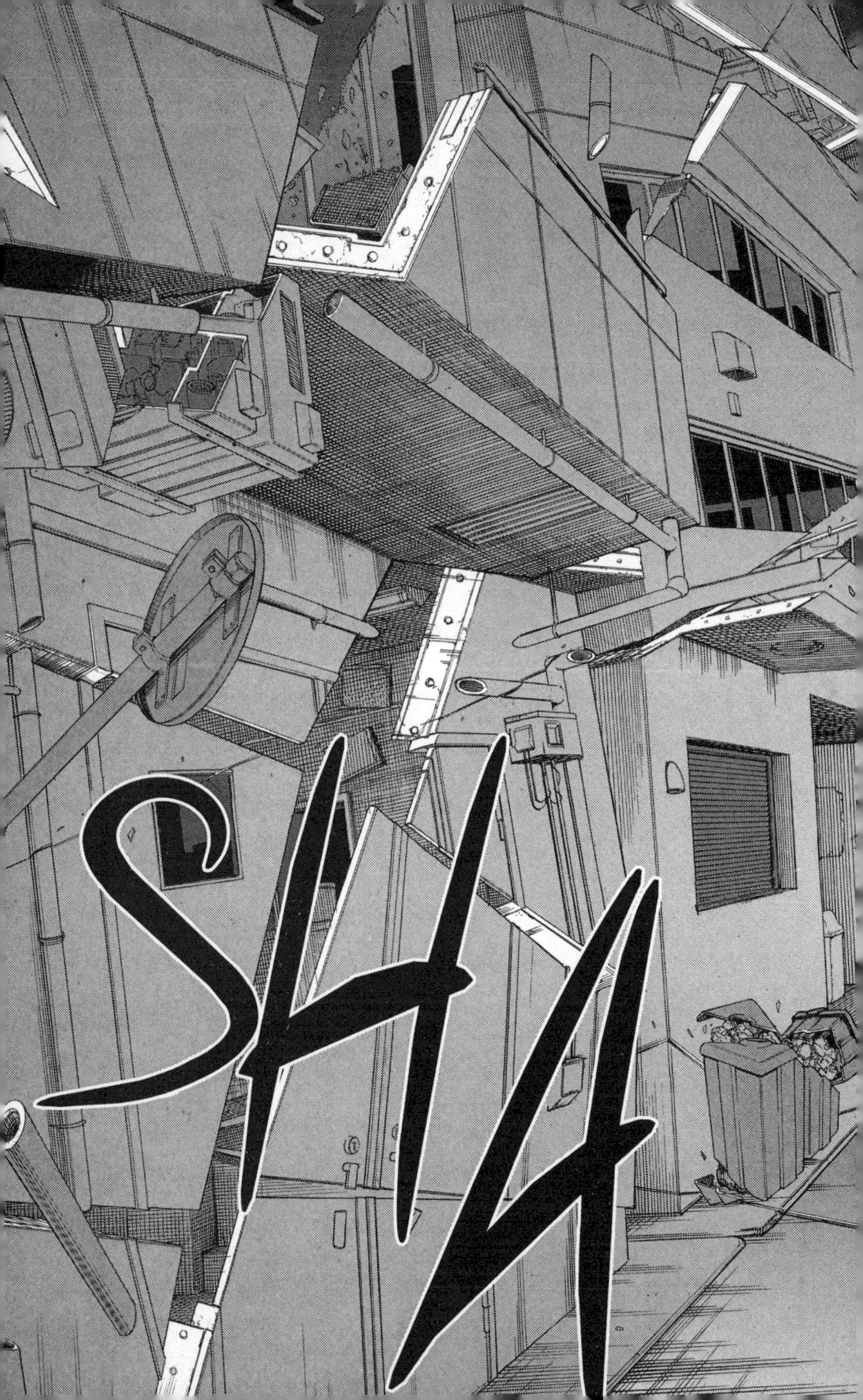
SHA

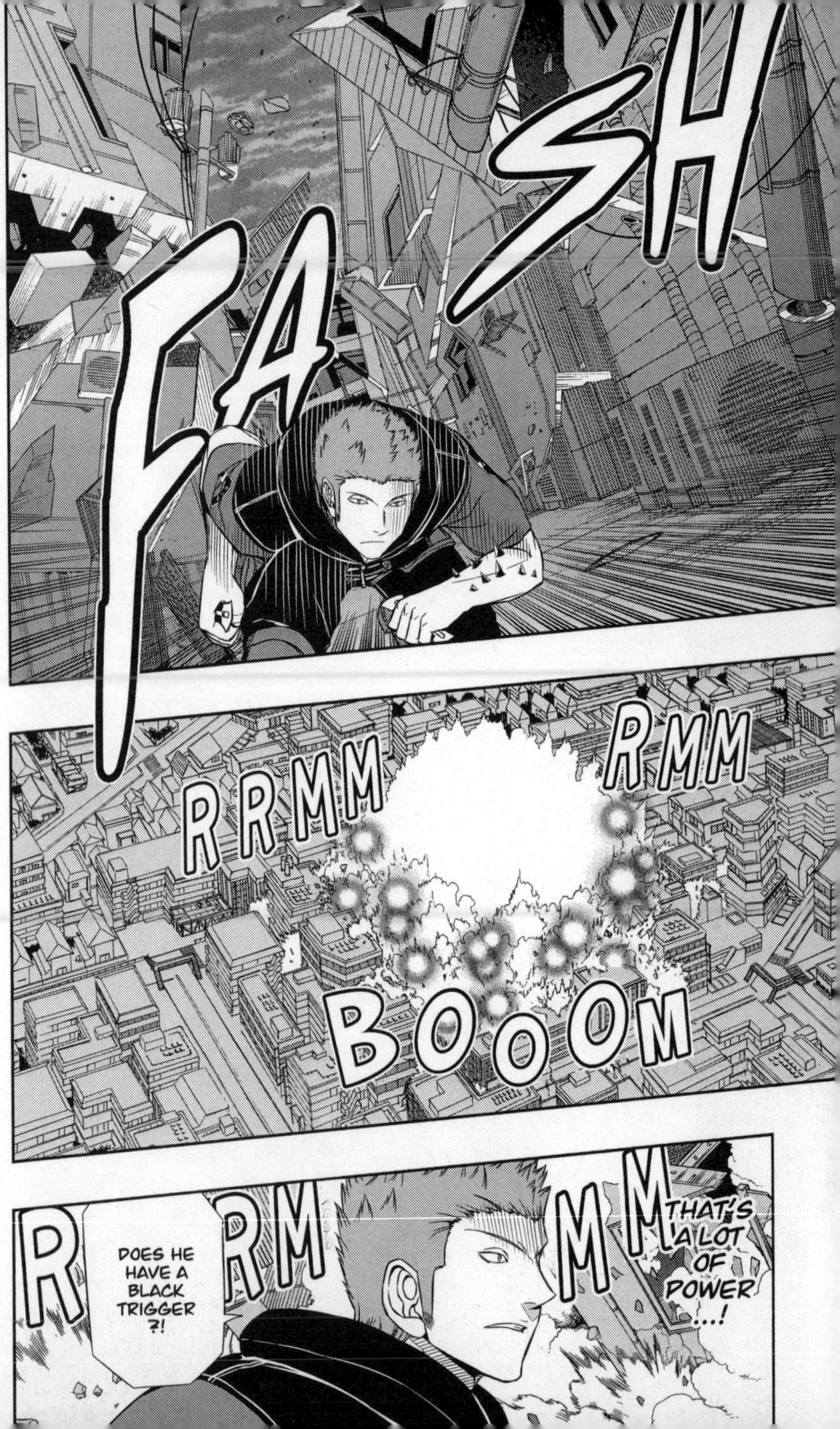
FASH
RRMM
RMM
BOOOM
MM
THAT'S A LOT OF POWER...!
RRM
DOES HE HAVE A BLACK TRIGGER?!

Anythink Bennett

495 7th Street
Bennett, CO 80102
303-405-3231

Date: 8/11/2022 Time: 6:00:25 PM

Items checked out this session: 1

Title: World Trigger, Vol. 8 / Ashihara, Daisuke
Barcode: 33021028802699
Due Date: 09/01/2022

Page 1 of 1

... where anything is possible.

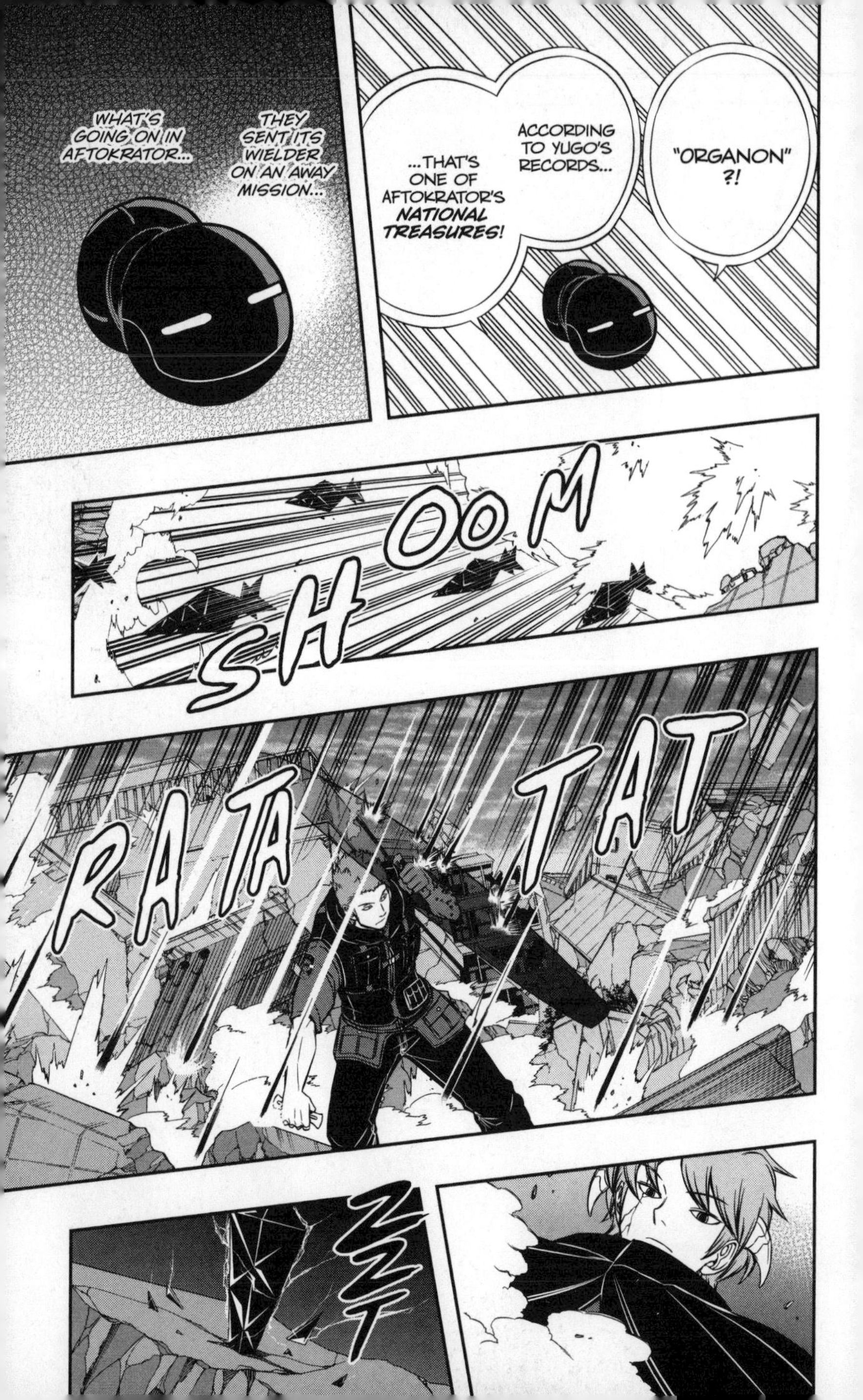
"ORGANON" ?!
ACCORDING TO YUGO'S RECORDS...
...THAT'S ONE OF AFTOKRATOR'S *NATIONAL TREASURES!*
THEY SENT ITS WIELDER ON AN AWAY MISSION...
WHAT'S GOING ON IN AFTOKRATOR...
SHOOM
RATATAT
ZZZT

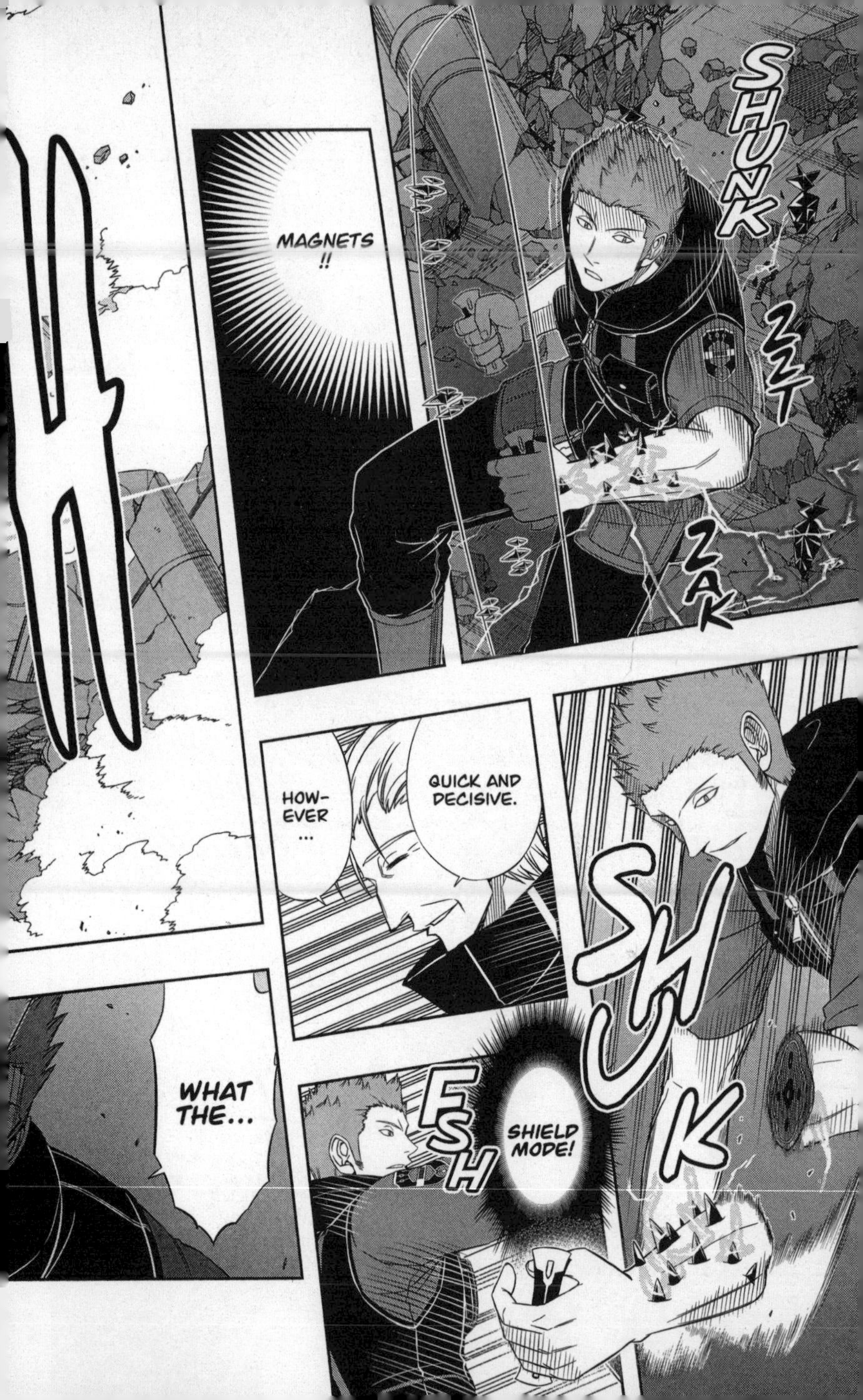
SHUNK
ZZZT
ZAK
MAGNETS !!
SHUK
QUICK AND DECISIVE.
HOW-EVER ...
SHIELD MODE!
FSH
WHAT THE...

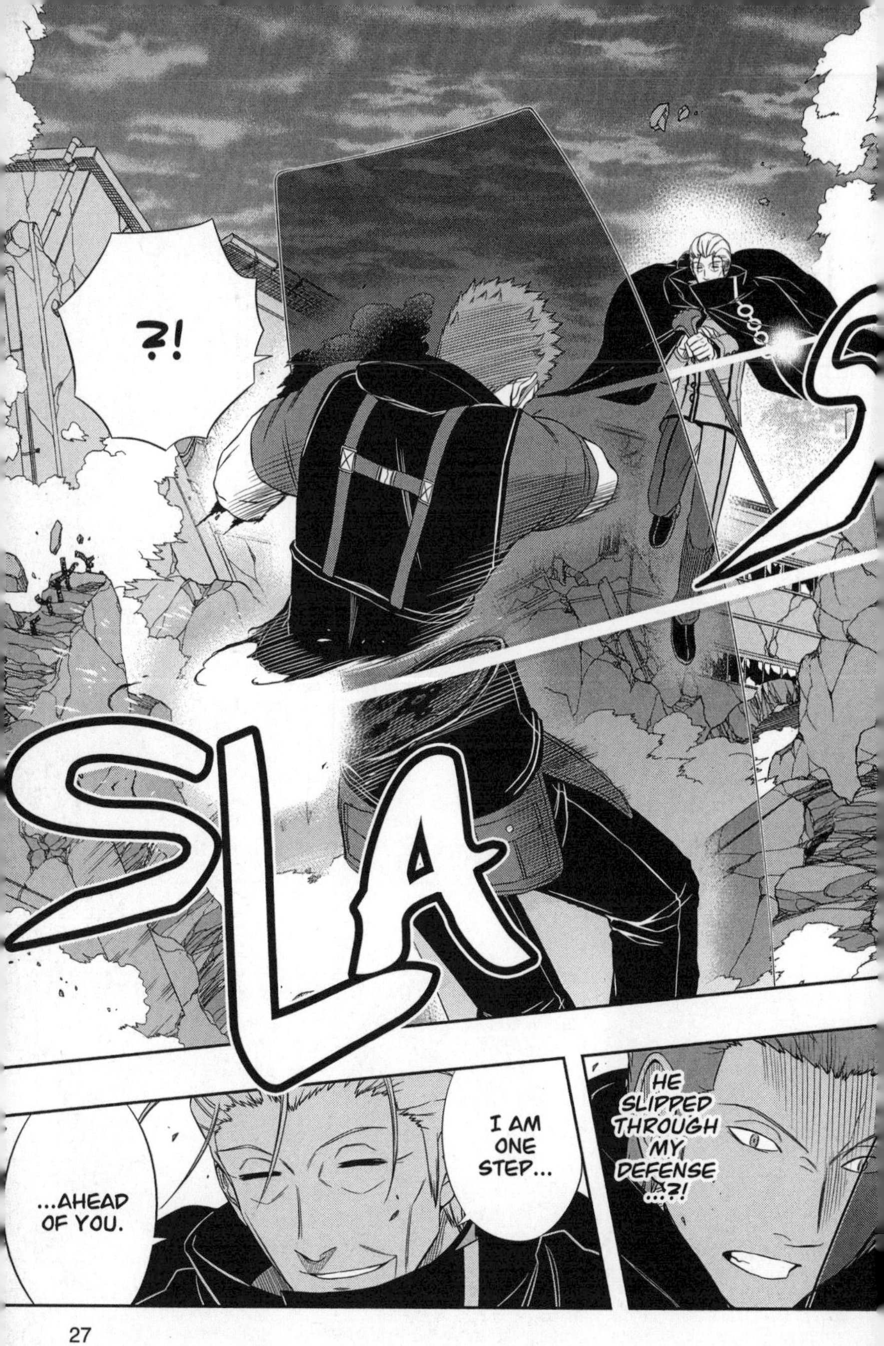
?!
SLA
S
HE SLIPPED THROUGH MY DEFENSE ...?!
I AM ONE STEP...
...AHEAD OF YOU.

First Popularity Poll Contest Results

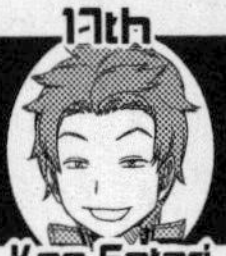
17th

Ken Satori
■ Average face

*Results were announced in the opening color pages of Chapter 63 in Weekly Shonen Jump.

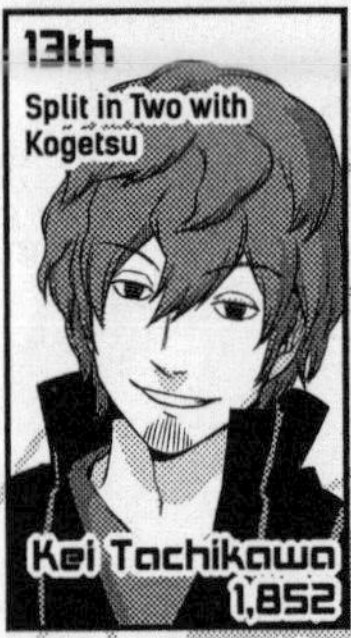
13th
Split in Two with Kogetsu
Kei Tachikawa
1,852

■ Did eating mochi help him or hurt him?

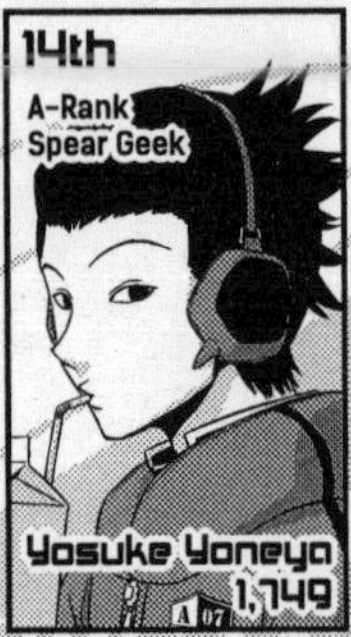
14th
A-Rank Spear Geek
Yosuke Yoneya
1,749

■ Popularity shoots up when he interacts with Osamu and Yuma.

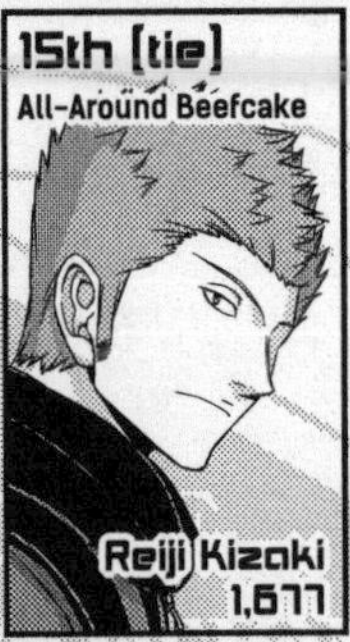
15th (tie)
All-Around Beefcake
Reiji Kizaki
1,677

■ Punching a Rabit bumped him up into the picture section.

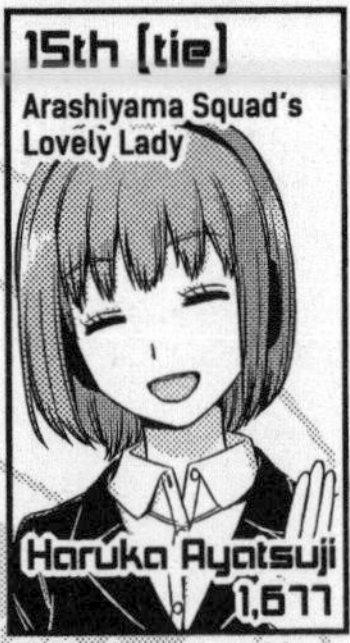
15th (tie)
Arashiyama Squad's Lovely Lady
Haruka Ayatsuji
1,677

■ She has a lot of fans.

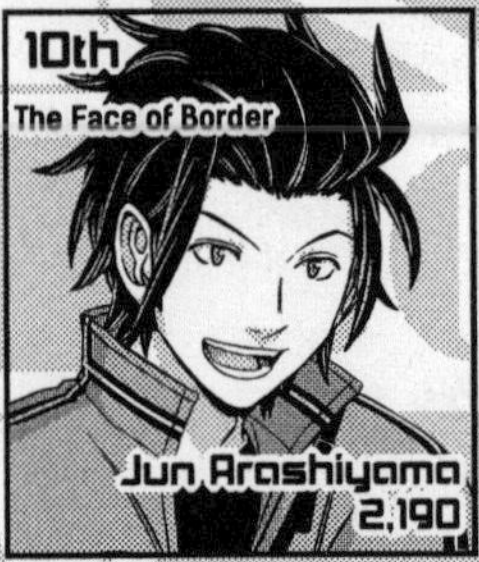
10th
The Face of Border
Jun Arashiyama
2,190

■ People who voted for him **get** it. He's great.

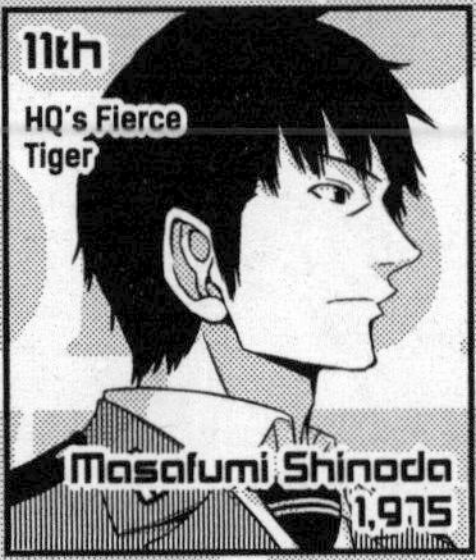
11th
HQ's Fierce Tiger
Masafumi Shinoda
1,975

■ Top among the senior officers. He looks **good** here.

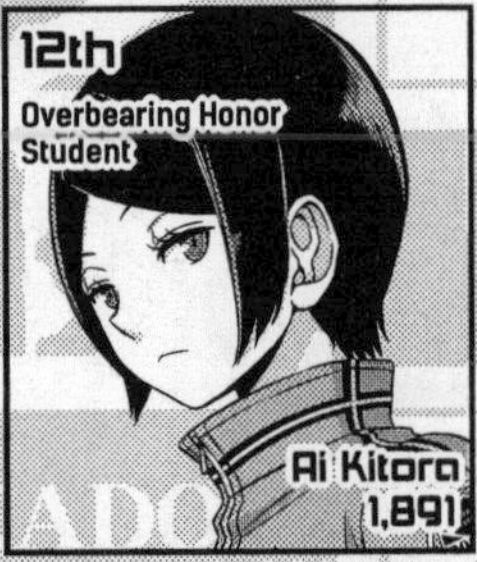
12th
Overbearing Honor Student
Ai Kitora
1,891

■ She got cubed right before the voting. Did that affect the result?

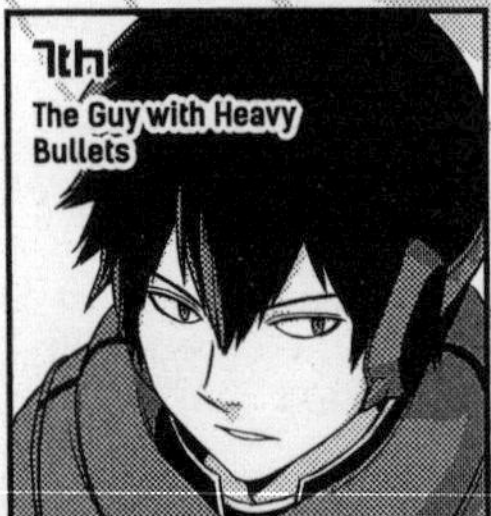
7th
The Guy with Heavy Bullets
Shuji Miwa
2,823

■ This ranking is based without him having any victories. Sister complex for the win.

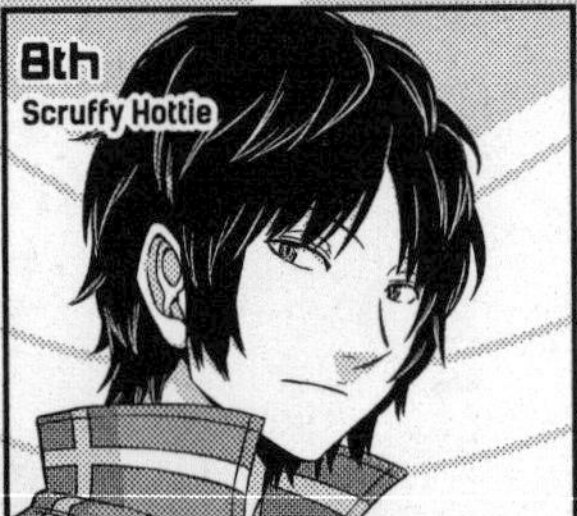
8th
Scruffy Hottie
Kyosuke Karasuma
2,372

■ This ranking is based without him having any battles. Hottie for the win.

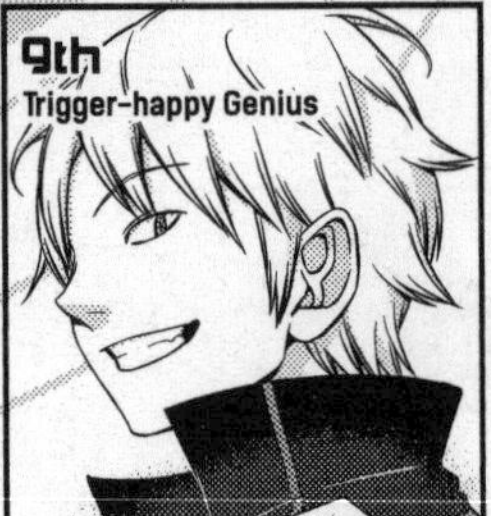
9th
Trigger-happy Genius
Kohei Izumi
2,294

■ This ranking is based solely on the fight over the Black Trigger. Genius for the win.

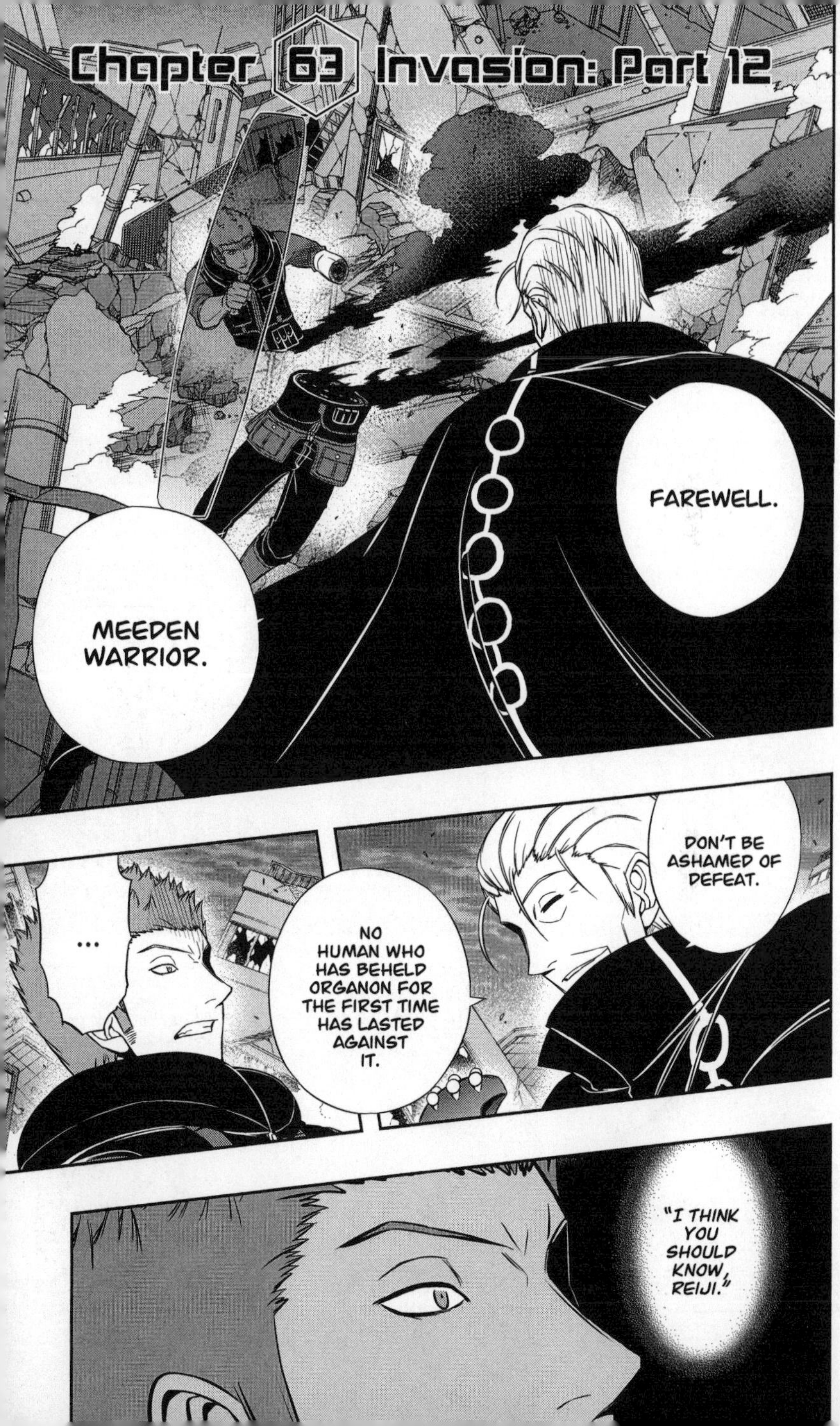
Chapter 63 Invasion: Part 12
FAREWELL.
MEEDEN WARRIOR.
DON'T BE ASHAMED OF DEFEAT.
NO HUMAN WHO HAS BEHELD ORGANON FOR THE FIRST TIME HAS LASTED AGAINST IT.
...
"I THINK YOU SHOULD KNOW, REIJI."

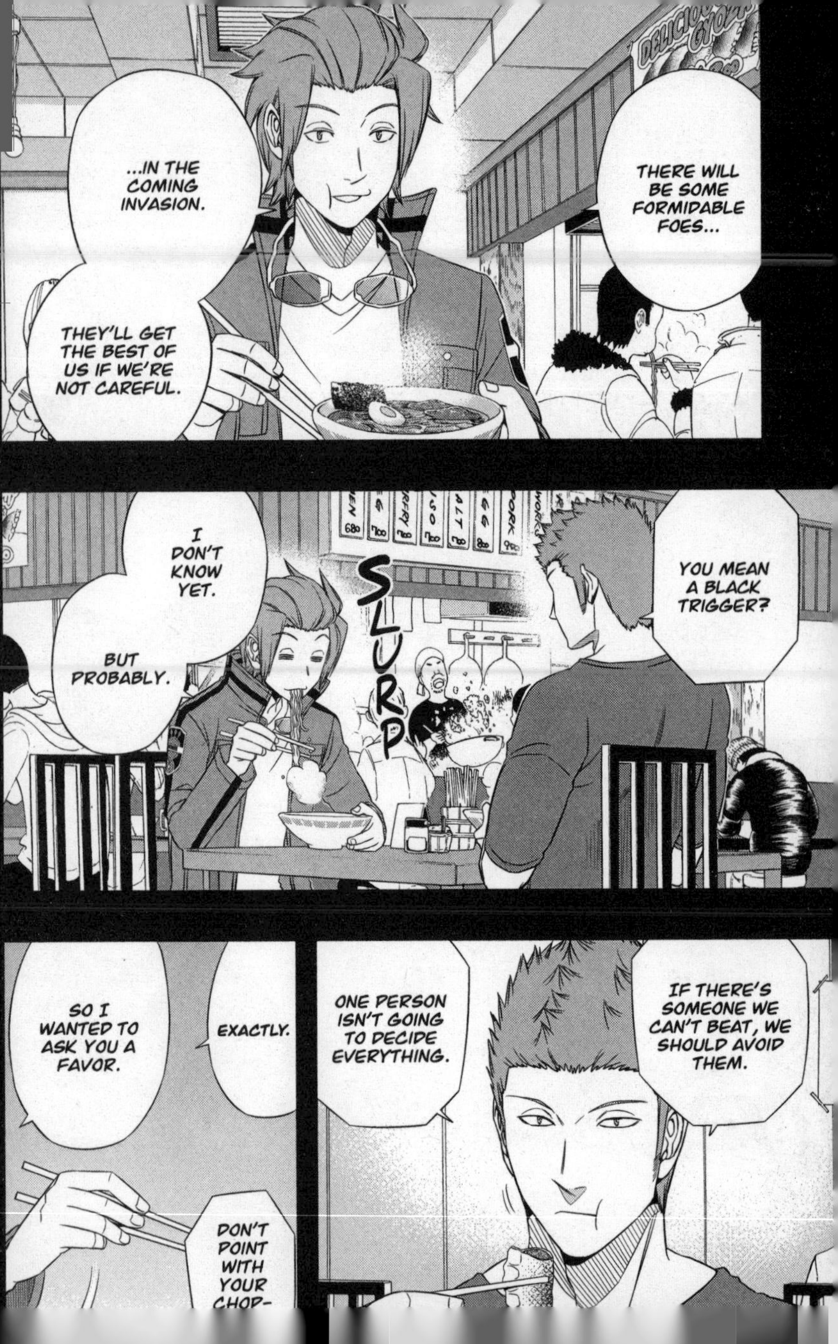
THERE WILL BE SOME FORMIDABLE FOES...
...IN THE COMING INVASION.
THEY'LL GET THE BEST OF US IF WE'RE NOT CAREFUL.
YOU MEAN A BLACK TRIGGER?
I DON'T KNOW YET.
BUT PROBABLY.
SLURP
IF THERE'S SOMEONE WE CAN'T BEAT, WE SHOULD AVOID THEM.
ONE PERSON ISN'T GOING TO DECIDE EVERYTHING.
EXACTLY.
SO I WANTED TO ASK YOU A FAVOR.
DON'T POINT WITH YOUR CHOP-

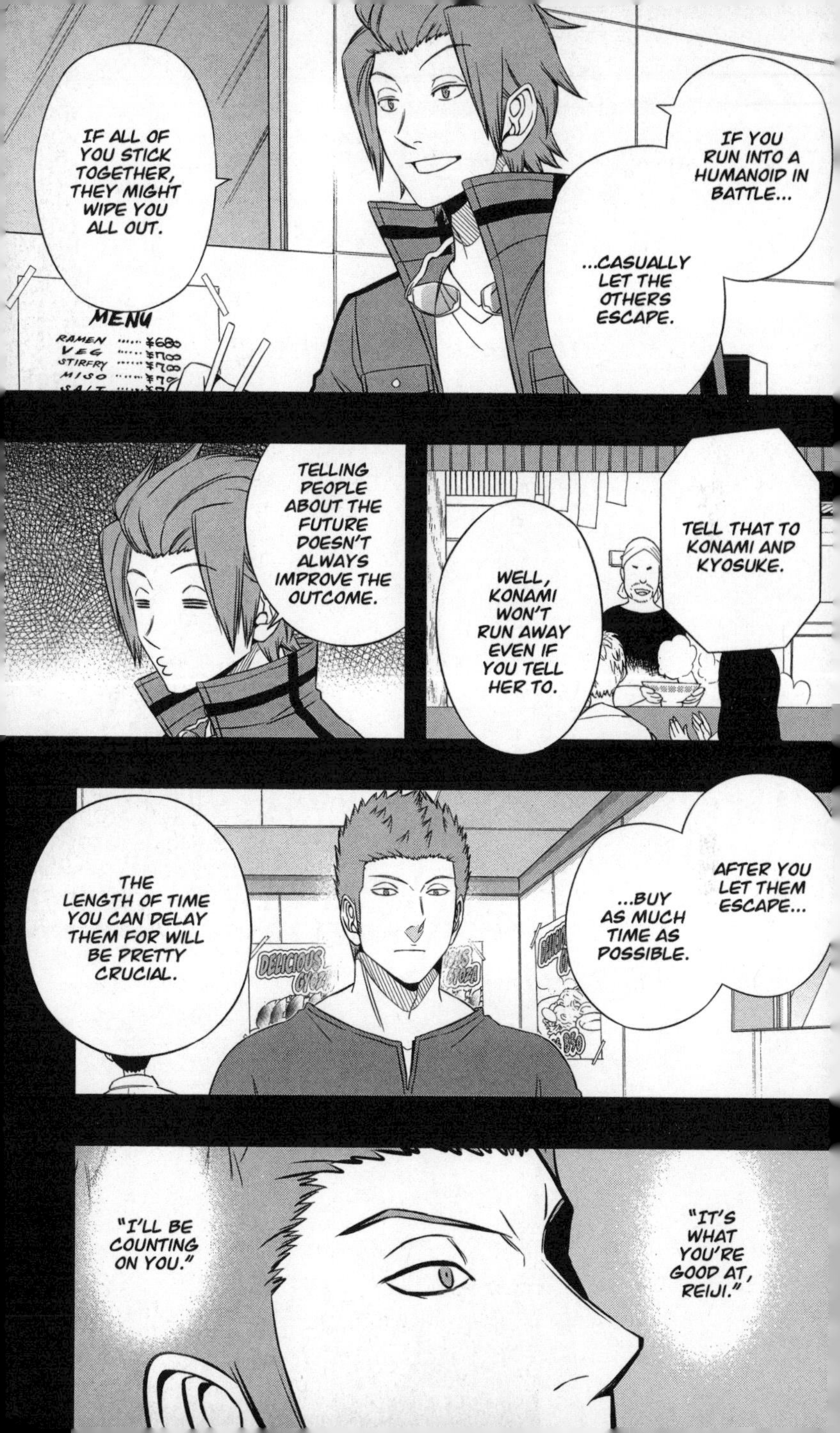
IF YOU RUN INTO A HUMANOID IN BATTLE...
...CASUALLY LET THE OTHERS ESCAPE.
IF ALL OF YOU STICK TOGETHER, THEY MIGHT WIPE YOU ALL OUT.
MENU
RAMEN ······ ¥680
VEG ······ ¥700
STIRFRY ······ ¥700
MISO
TELL THAT TO KONAMI AND KYOSUKE.
WELL, KONAMI WON'T RUN AWAY EVEN IF YOU TELL HER TO.
TELLING PEOPLE ABOUT THE FUTURE DOESN'T ALWAYS IMPROVE THE OUTCOME.
AFTER YOU LET THEM ESCAPE...
...BUY AS MUCH TIME AS POSSIBLE.
THE LENGTH OF TIME YOU CAN DELAY THEM FOR WILL BE PRETTY CRUCIAL.
DELICIOUS GYOZA
"IT'S WHAT YOU'RE GOOD AT, REIJI."
"I'LL BE COUNTING ON YOU."

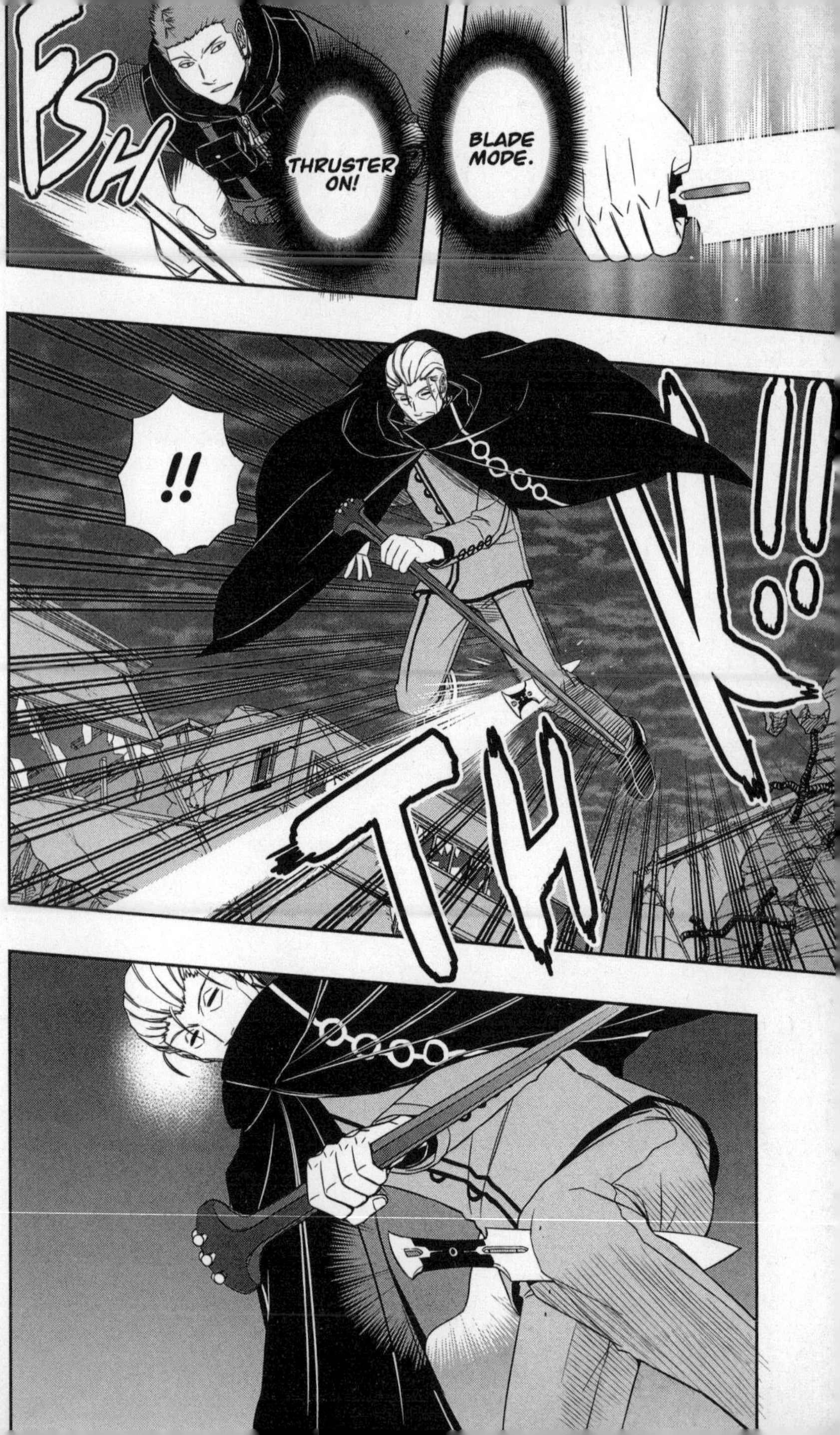
BLADE MODE.
THRUSTER ON!
FSH
!!
THK!!

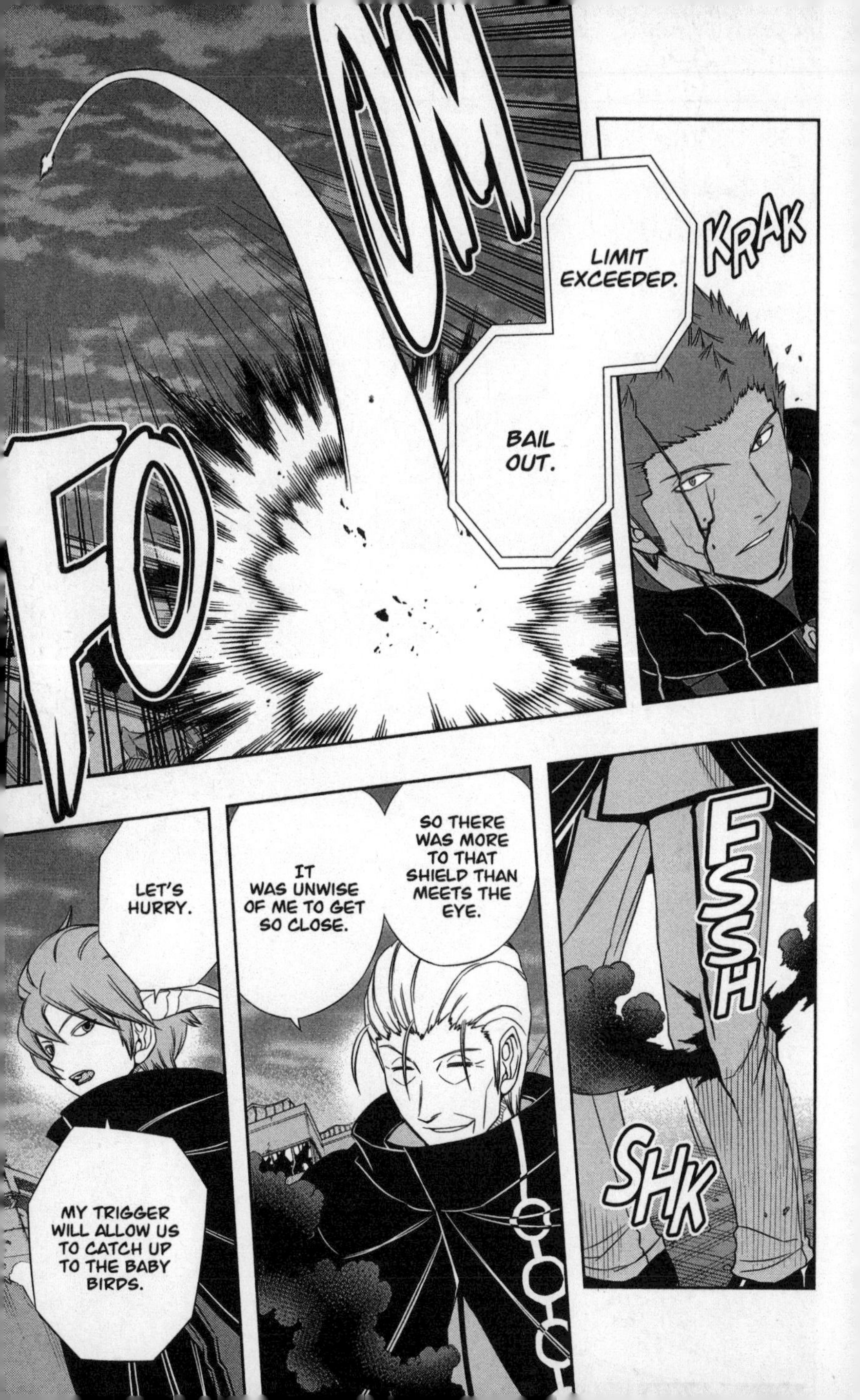
KRAK
LIMIT EXCEEDED.
BAIL OUT.
FOOM
FSSH
SHK
SO THERE WAS MORE TO THAT SHIELD THAN MEETS THE EYE.
IT WAS UNWISE OF ME TO GET SO CLOSE.
LET'S HURRY.
MY TRIGGER WILL ALLOW US TO CATCH UP TO THE BABY BIRDS.

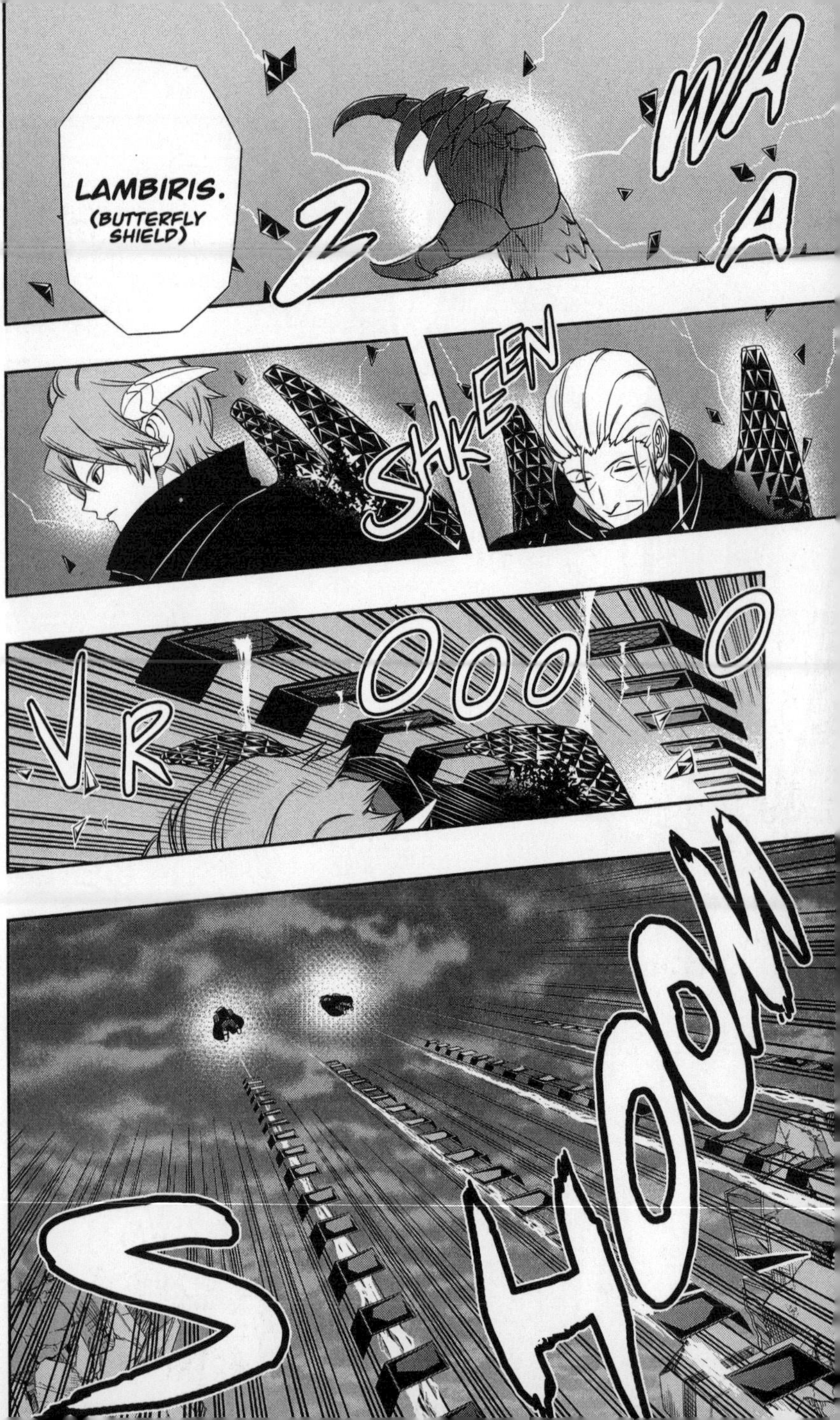
ZWAA
LAMBIRIS.
(BUTTERFLY SHIELD)
SHKEEN
VROOOOO
SHOOM

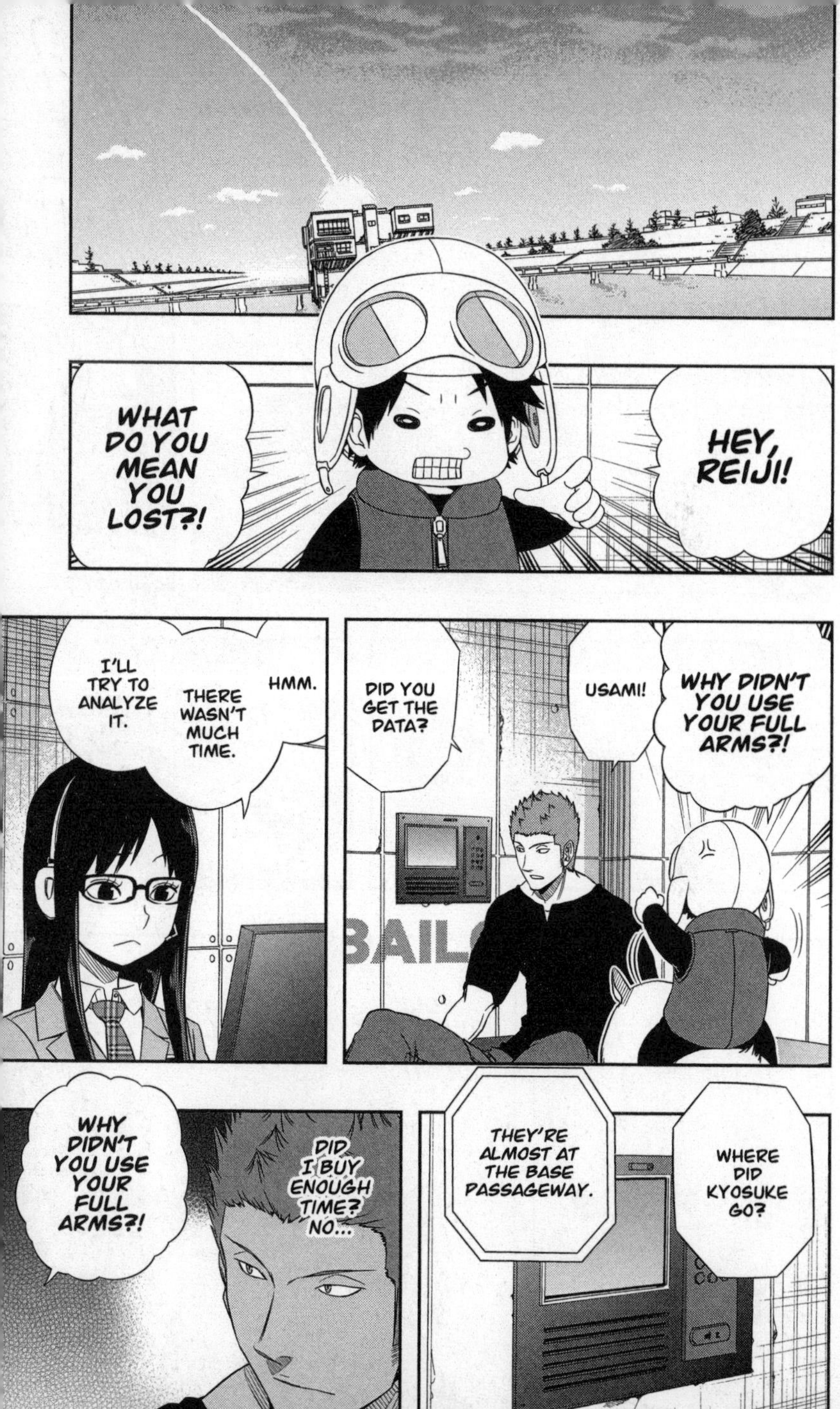
HEY, REIJI!
WHAT DO YOU MEAN YOU LOST?!
WHY DIDN'T YOU USE YOUR FULL ARMS?!
USAMI!
DID YOU GET THE DATA?
HMM.
THERE WASN'T MUCH TIME.
I'LL TRY TO ANALYZE IT.
WHERE DID KYOSUKE GO?
THEY'RE ALMOST AT THE BASE PASSAGEWAY.
DID I BUY ENOUGH TIME? NO...
WHY DIDN'T YOU USE YOUR FULL ARMS?!

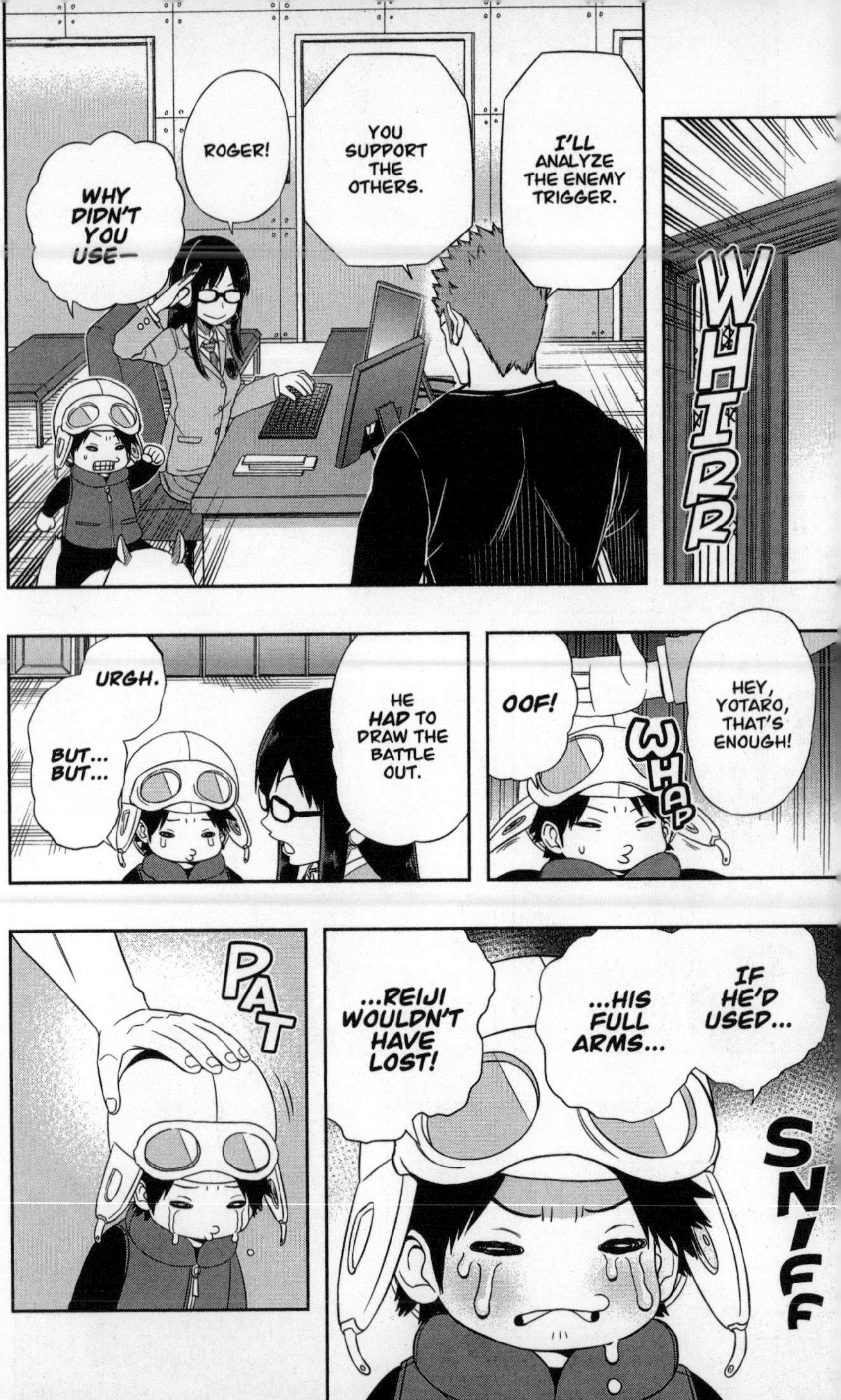
WHIRR
I'LL ANALYZE THE ENEMY TRIGGER.
YOU SUPPORT THE OTHERS.
ROGER!
WHY DIDN'T YOU USE—
HEY, YOTARO, THAT'S ENOUGH!
WHAP
OOF!
HE HAD TO DRAW THE BATTLE OUT.
URGH.
BUT... BUT...
IF HE'D USED...
...HIS FULL ARMS...
...REIJI WOULDN'T HAVE LOST!
SNIFF
PAT

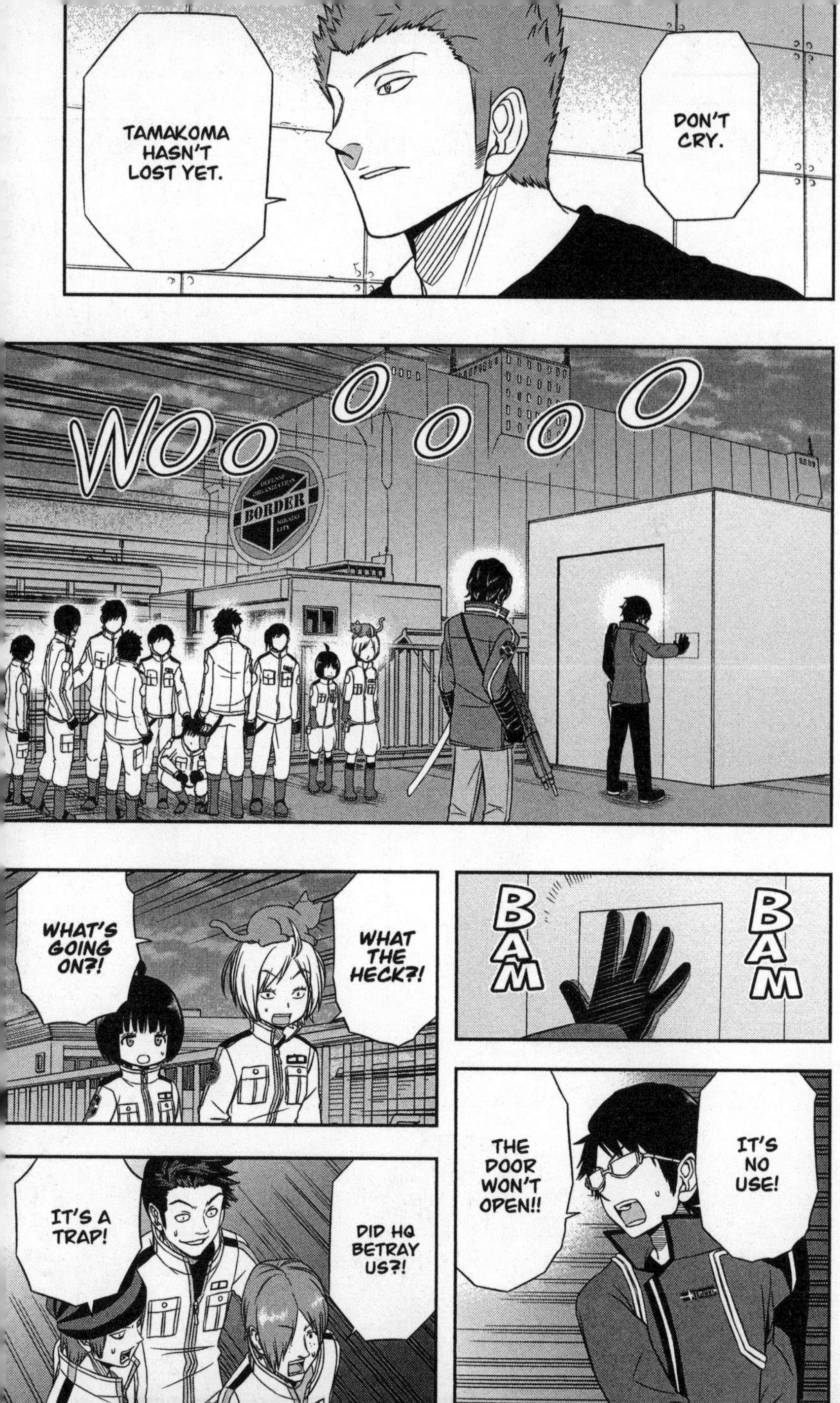
DON'T CRY.
TAMAKOMA HASN'T LOST YET.
WOOOOOOO
DEFENSE ORGANIZATION
BORDER
MIKADO CITY
BAM BAM
WHAT THE HECK?!
WHAT'S GOING ON?!
IT'S NO USE!
THE DOOR WON'T OPEN!!
DID HQ BETRAY US?!
IT'S A TRAP!

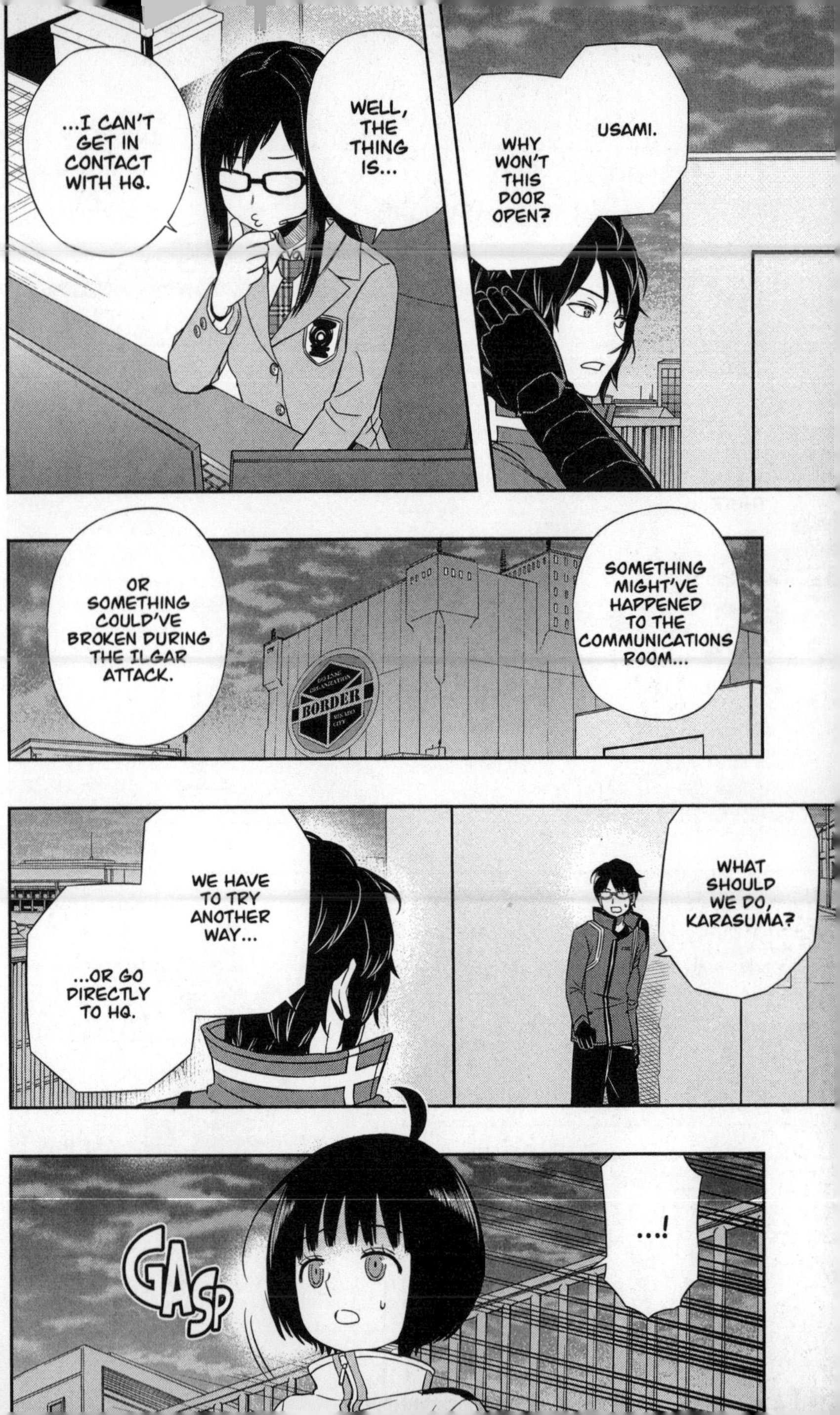
USAMI.
WHY WON'T THIS DOOR OPEN?
WELL, THE THING IS...
...I CAN'T GET IN CONTACT WITH HQ.
SOMETHING MIGHT'VE HAPPENED TO THE COMMUNICATIONS ROOM...
BORDER
OR SOMETHING COULD'VE BROKEN DURING THE ILGAR ATTACK.
WHAT SHOULD WE DO, KARASUMA?
WE HAVE TO TRY ANOTHER WAY...
...OR GO DIRECTLY TO HQ.
...!
GASP

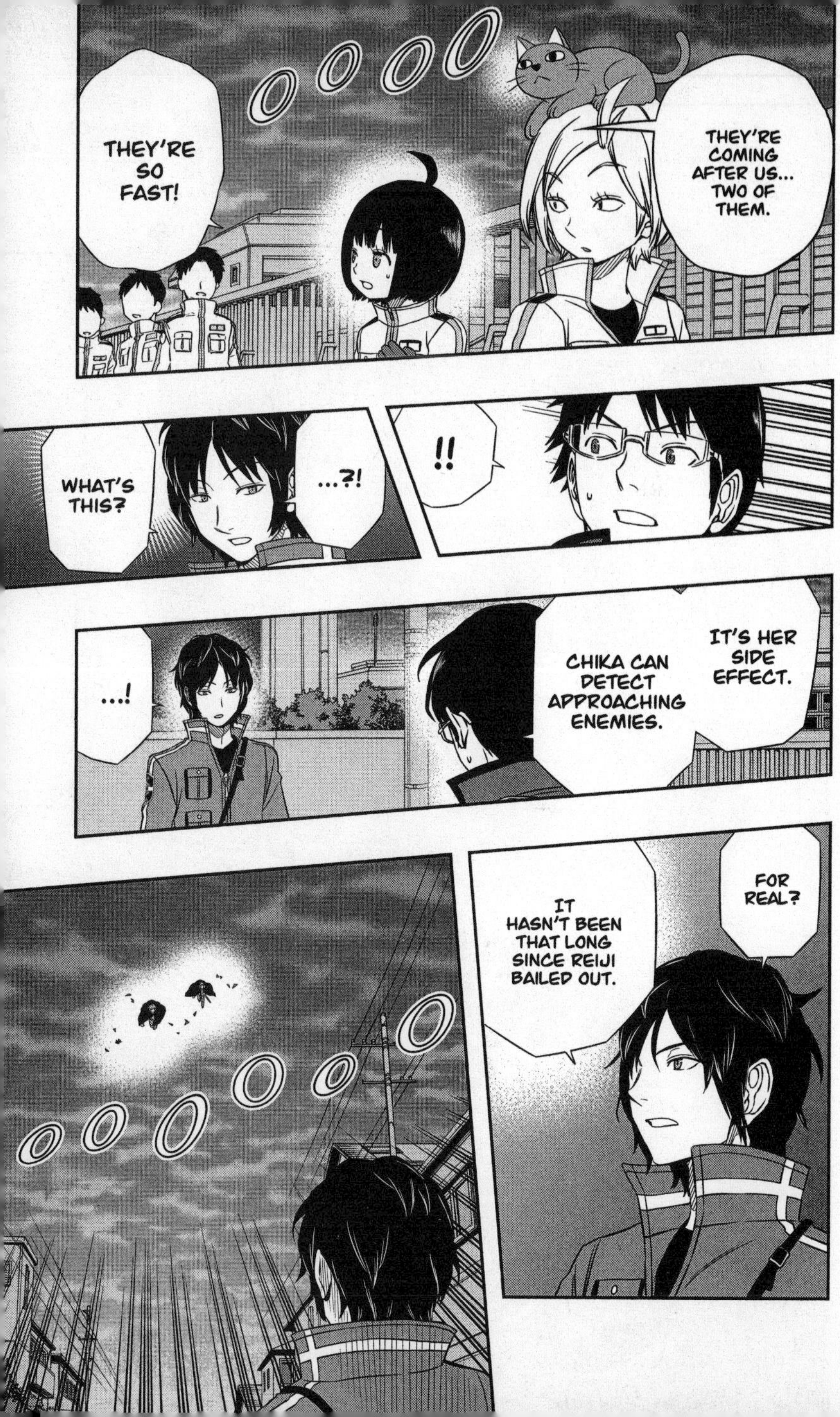
THEY'RE COMING AFTER US... TWO OF THEM.
THEY'RE SO FAST!
!!
...?!
WHAT'S THIS?
IT'S HER SIDE EFFECT.
CHIKA CAN DETECT APPROACHING ENEMIES.
...!
FOR REAL?
IT HASN'T BEEN THAT LONG SINCE REIJI BAILED OUT.

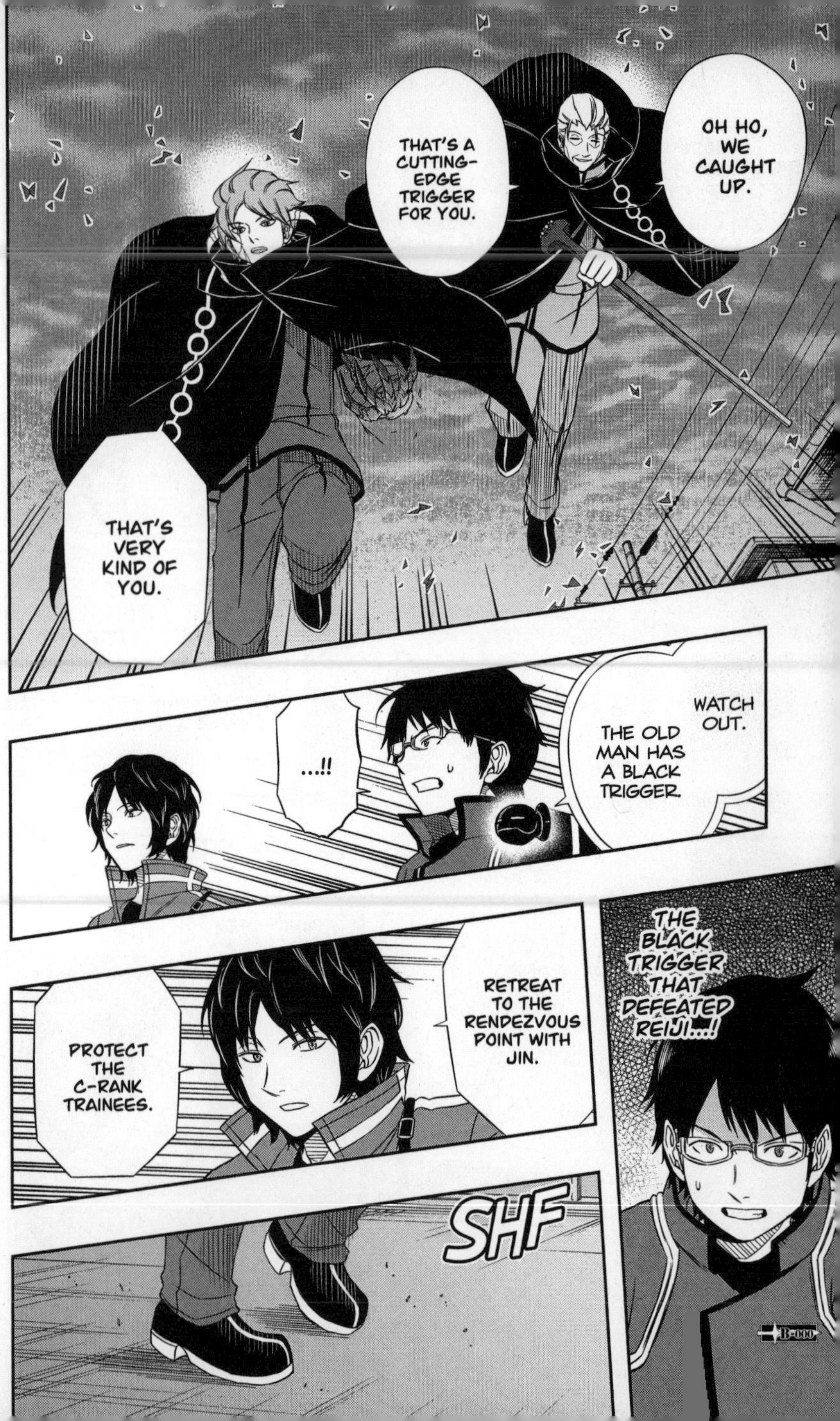
OH HO, WE CAUGHT UP.
THAT'S A CUTTING-EDGE TRIGGER FOR YOU.
THAT'S VERY KIND OF YOU.
WATCH OUT.
THE OLD MAN HAS A BLACK TRIGGER.
...!!
THE BLACK TRIGGER THAT DEFEATED REIJI...!
RETREAT TO THE RENDEZVOUS POINT WITH JIN.
PROTECT THE C-RANK TRAINEES.
SHF

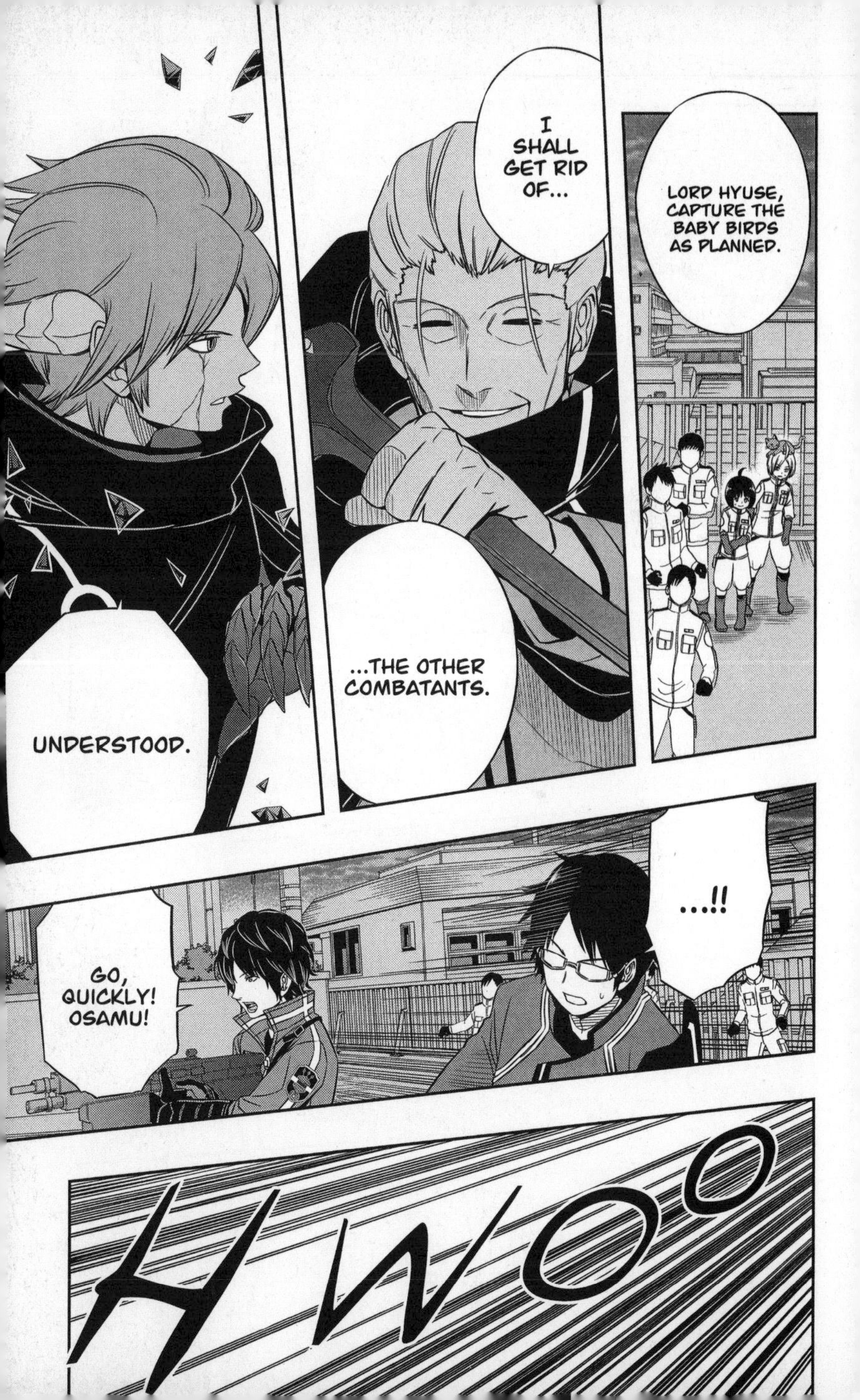
LORD HYUSE, CAPTURE THE BABY BIRDS AS PLANNED.
I SHALL GET RID OF...
...THE OTHER COMBATANTS.
UNDERSTOOD.
...!!
GO, QUICKLY! OSAMU!
HWOO

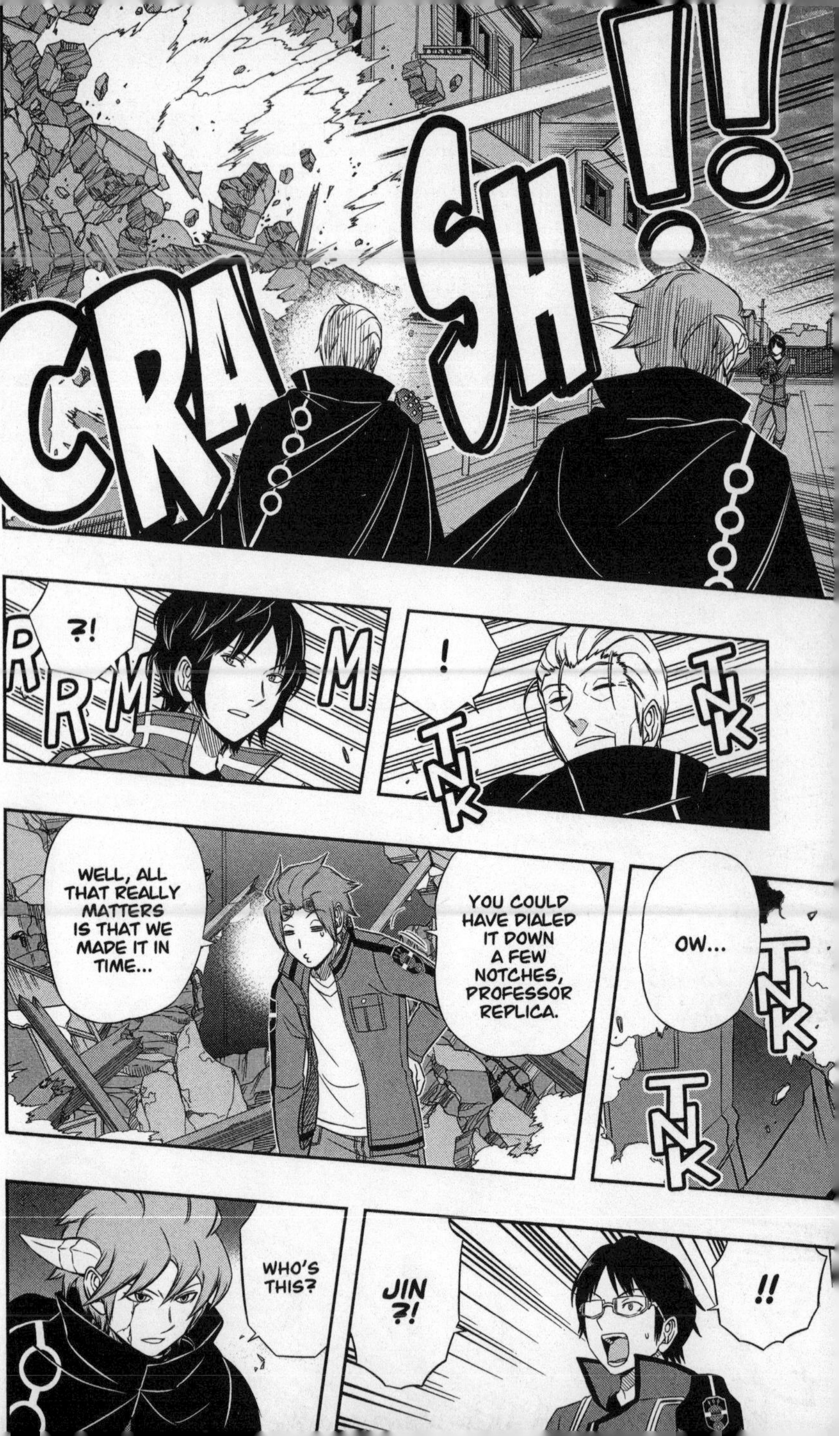
CRASH!!
!
TNK
TNK
?!
RRMMM
OW...
TNK
TNK
YOU COULD HAVE DIALED IT DOWN A FEW NOTCHES, PROFESSOR REPLICA.
WELL, ALL THAT REALLY MATTERS IS THAT WE MADE IT IN TIME...
!!
JIN?!
WHO'S THIS?

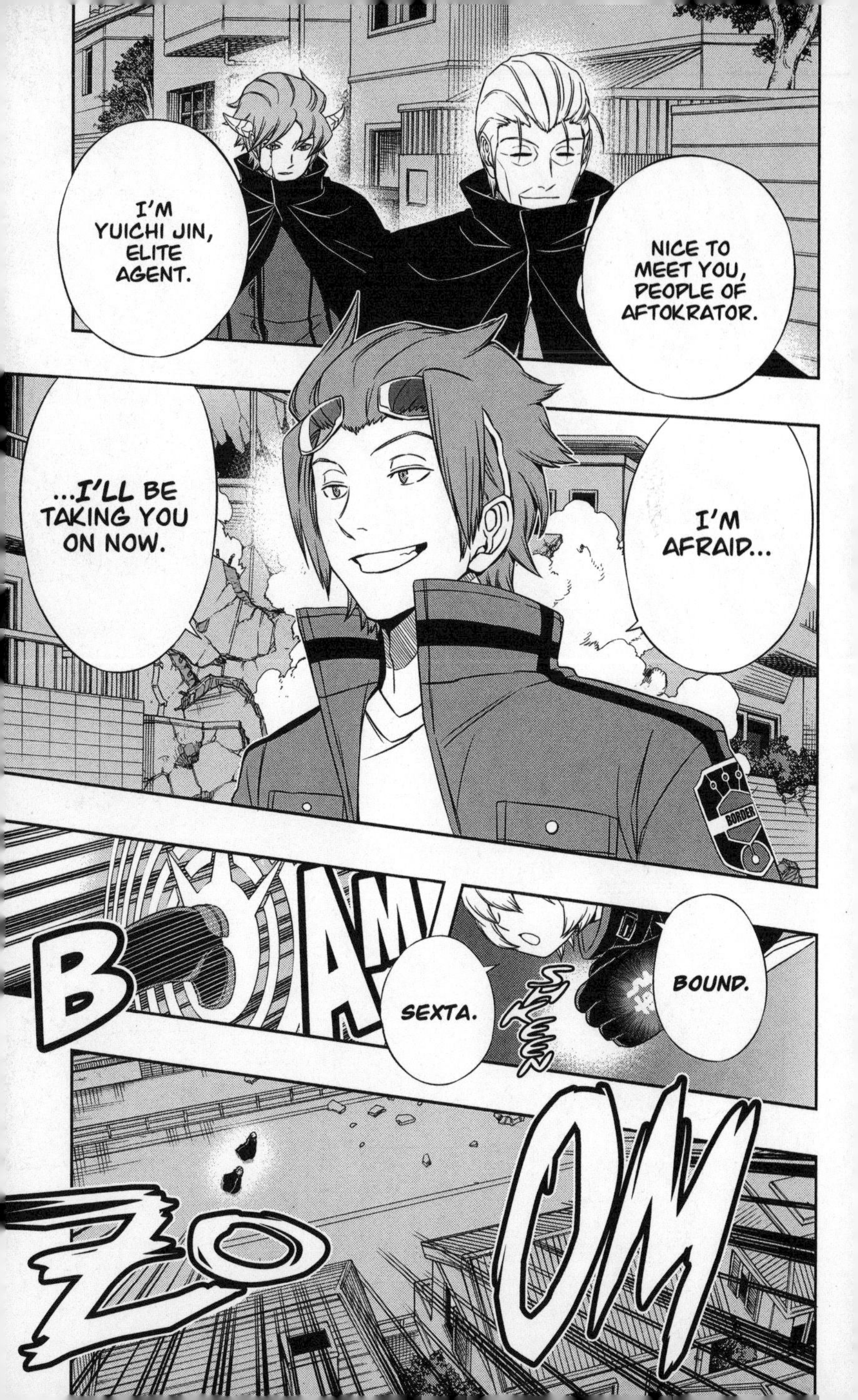
NICE TO MEET YOU, PEOPLE OF AFTOKRATOR.
I'M YUICHI JIN, ELITE AGENT.
I'M AFRAID...
...I'LL BE TAKING YOU ON NOW.
BOUND.
SEXTA.
ZOOM

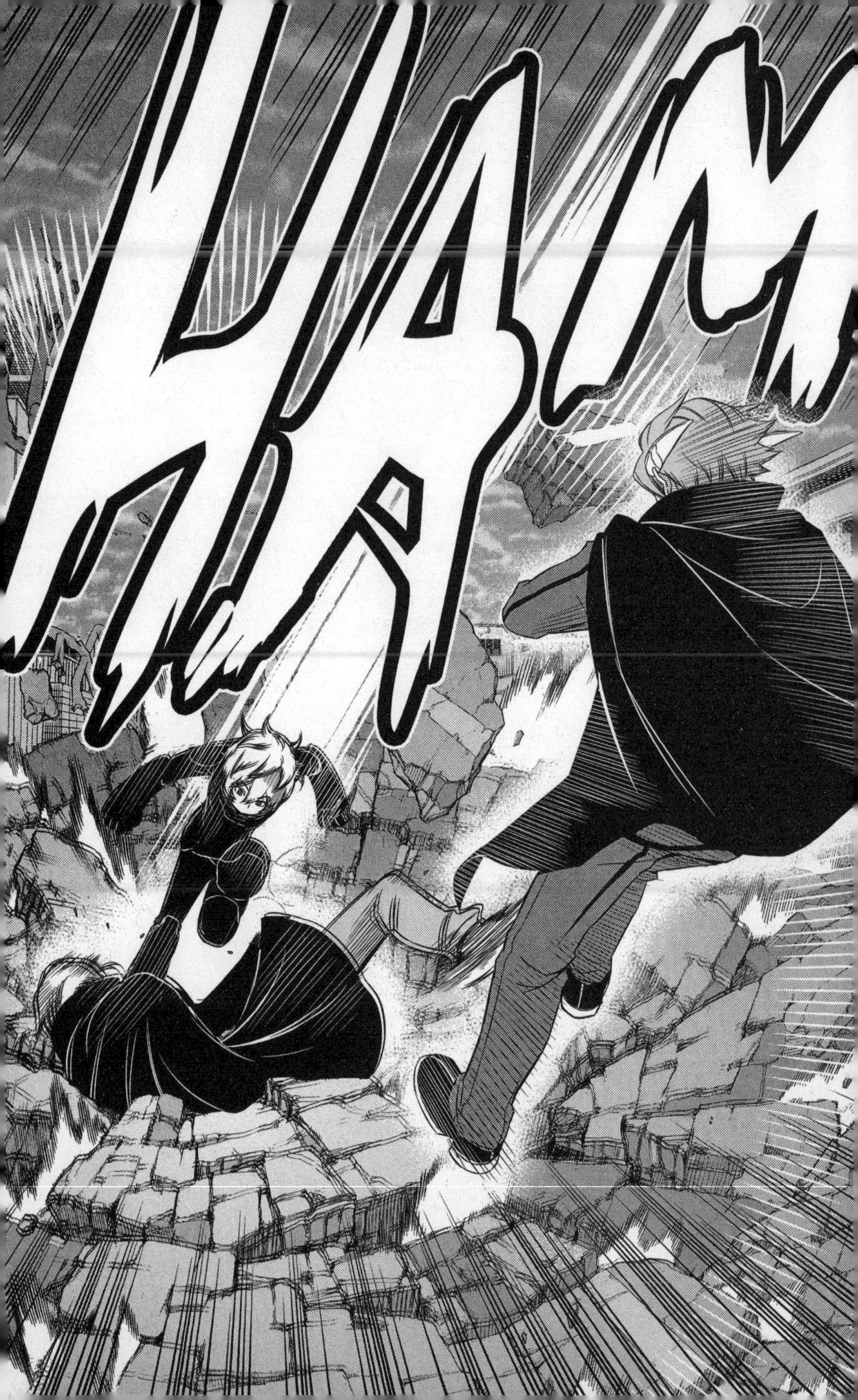

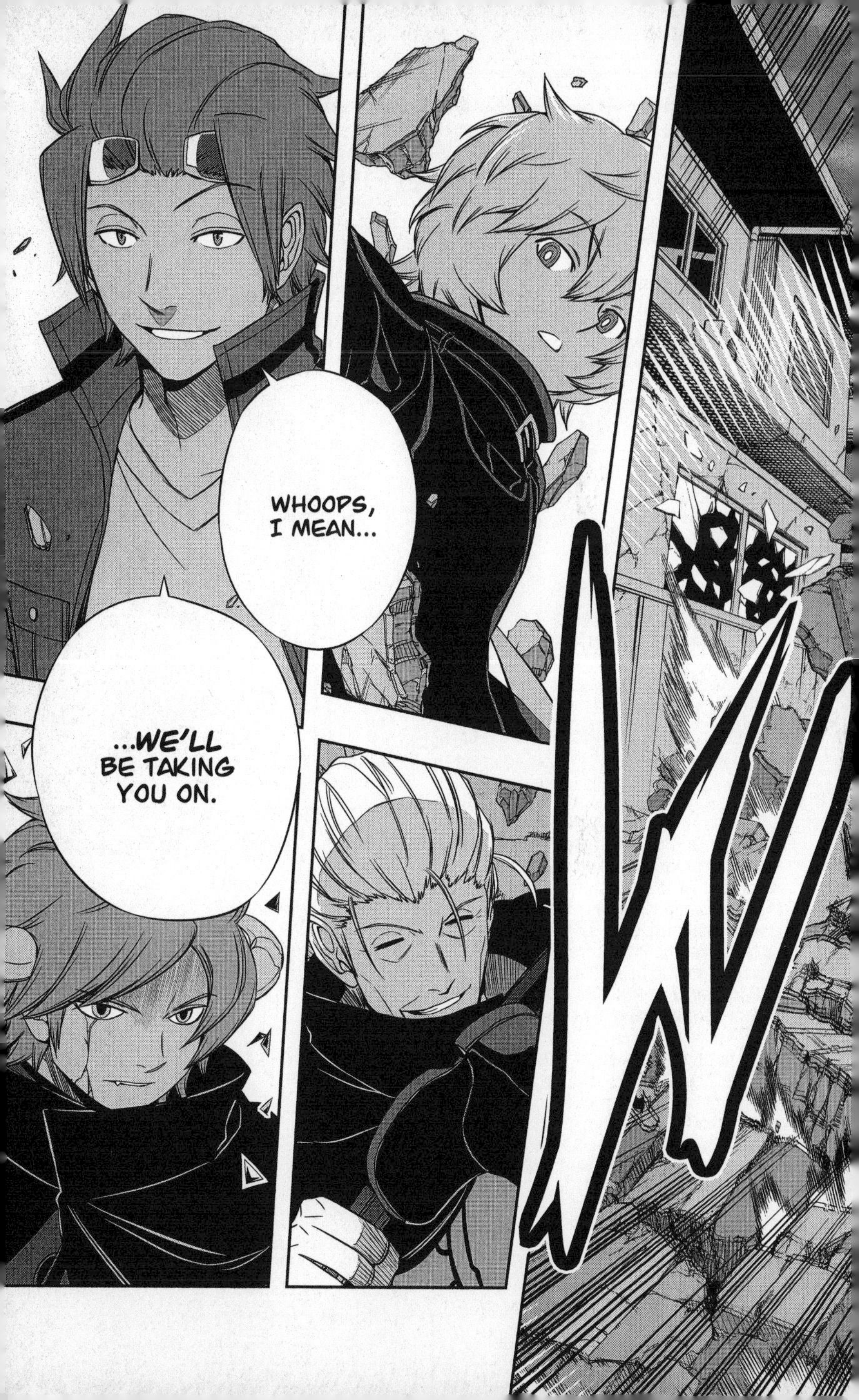
W
WHOOPS, I MEAN...
...WE'LL BE TAKING YOU ON.

First Popularity Poll Contest Results (continued)

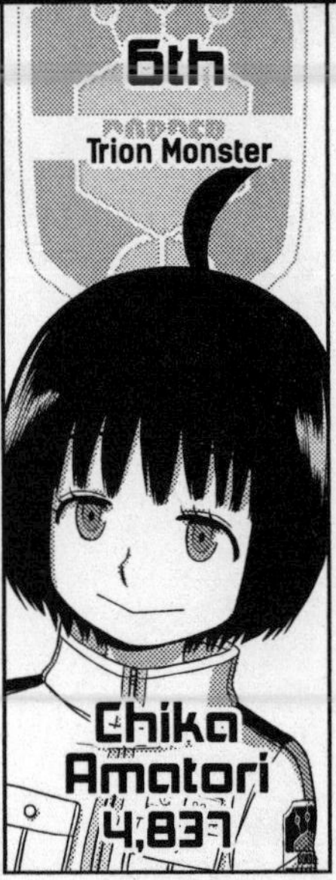
6th
Trion Monster
Chika
Amatori
4,837

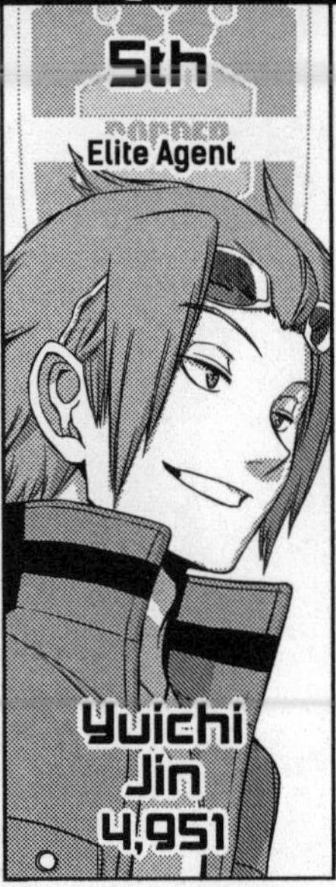
5th
Elite Agent
Yuichi
Jin
4,951

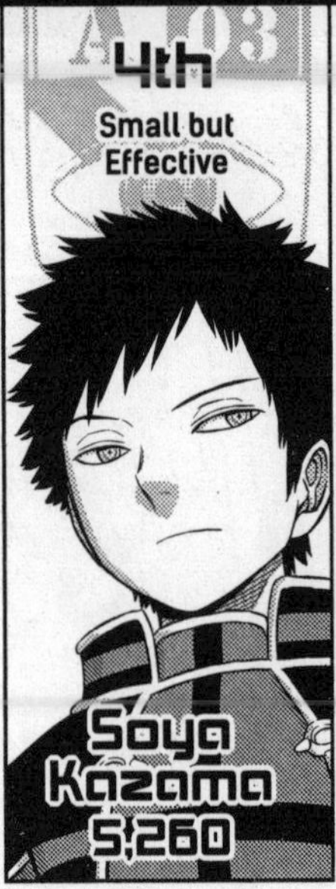
4th
Small but
Effective
Soya
Kazama
5,260

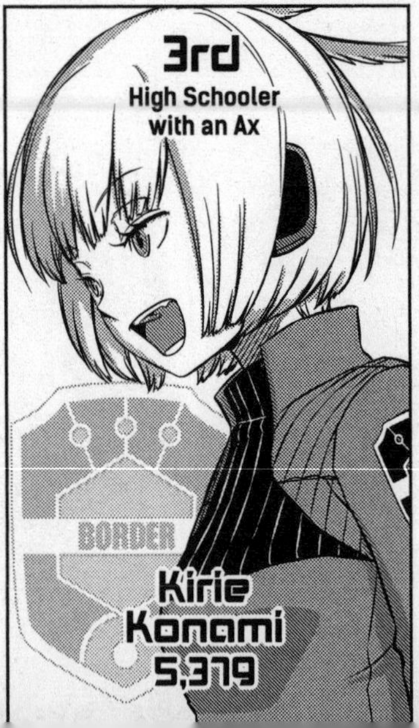
3rd
High Schooler
with an Ax
BORDER
Kirie
Konami
5,379

■Konami's 3rd! Kazama's 4th! That was a surprise since I was sure that Jin would be in the top three. I get the feeling that there were more votes from passionate fans for Konami and Kazama, rather than Jin simply getting fewer votes. Maybe the fact that Jin took a backseat after the fight over the Black Trigger also affected the results.

I was happy that Chika ranked sixth. It was only by a narrow margin after Jin. Chika got the most votes for "second most favorite character," paired with either Osamu or Yuma. Tamakoma-2 are such good friends with each other.

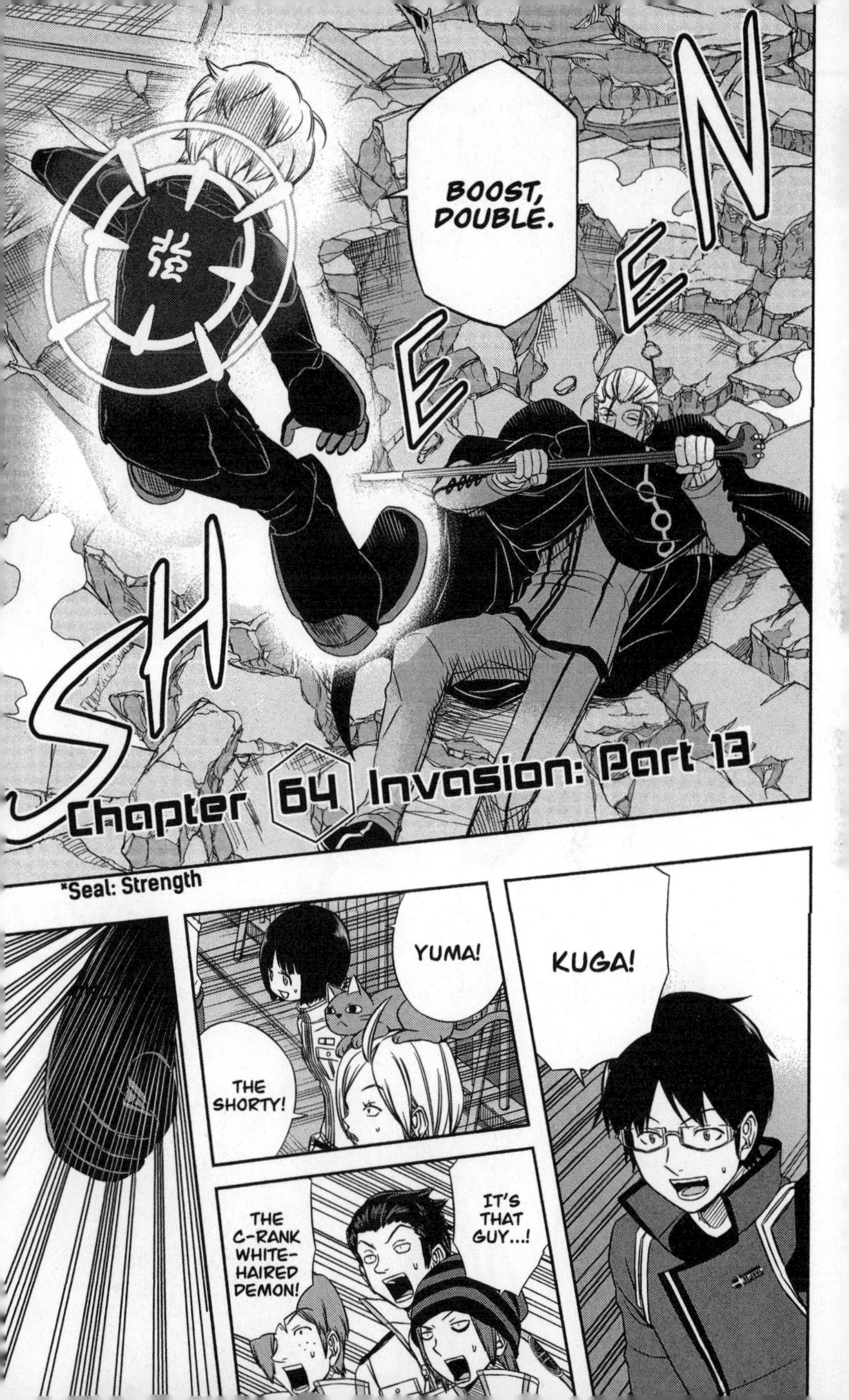
BOOST, DOUBLE.
SHEEN
Chapter 64 Invasion: Part 13
*Seal: Strength
KUGA!
YUMA!
THE SHORTY!
IT'S THAT GUY...!
THE C-RANK WHITE-HAIRED DEMON!

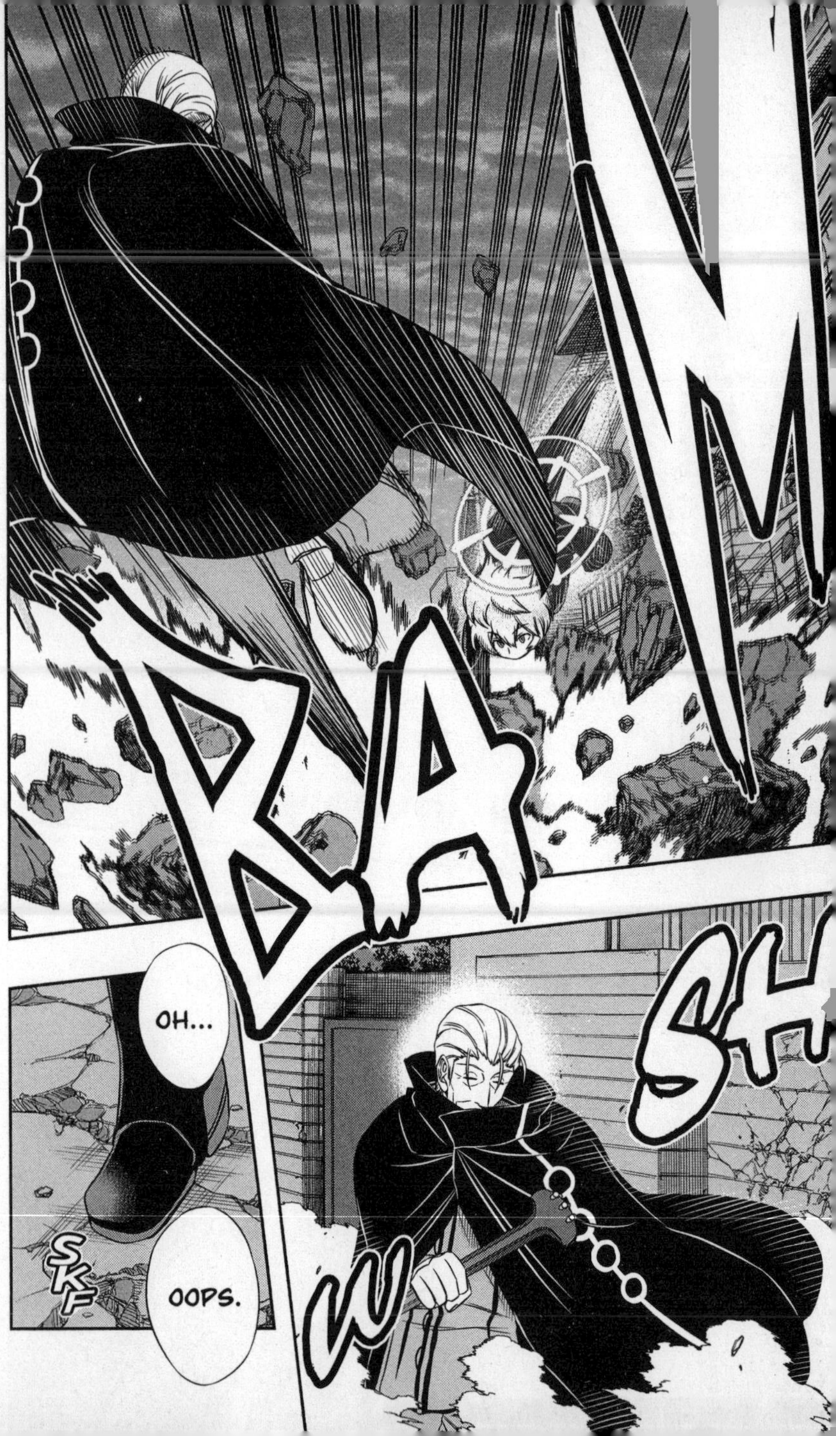
BAM
OH...
OOPS.
SKF

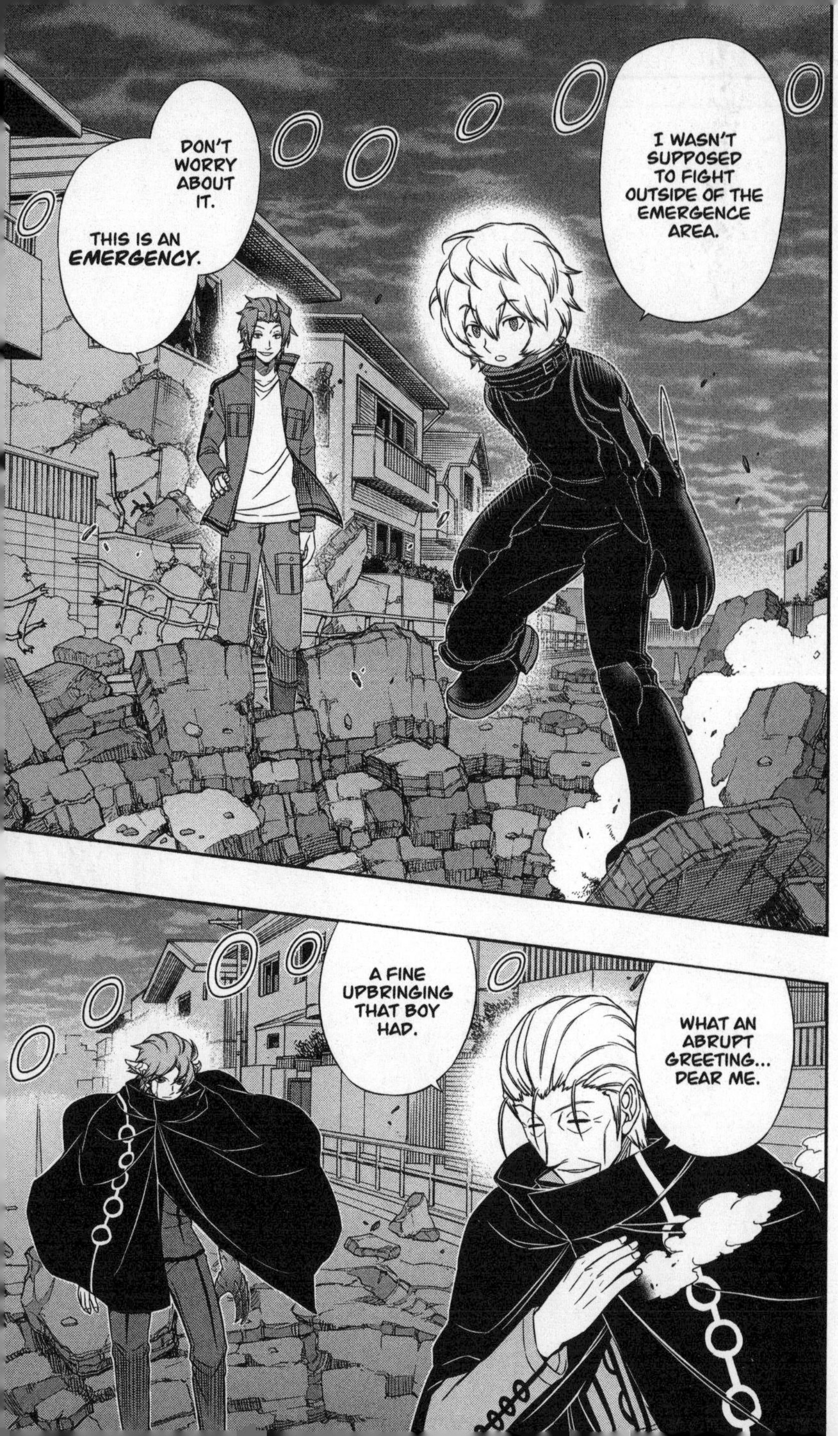
I WASN'T SUPPOSED TO FIGHT OUTSIDE OF THE EMERGENCE AREA.
DON'T WORRY ABOUT IT.
THIS IS AN EMERGENCY.
WHAT AN ABRUPT GREETING... DEAR ME.
A FINE UPBRINGING THAT BOY HAD.

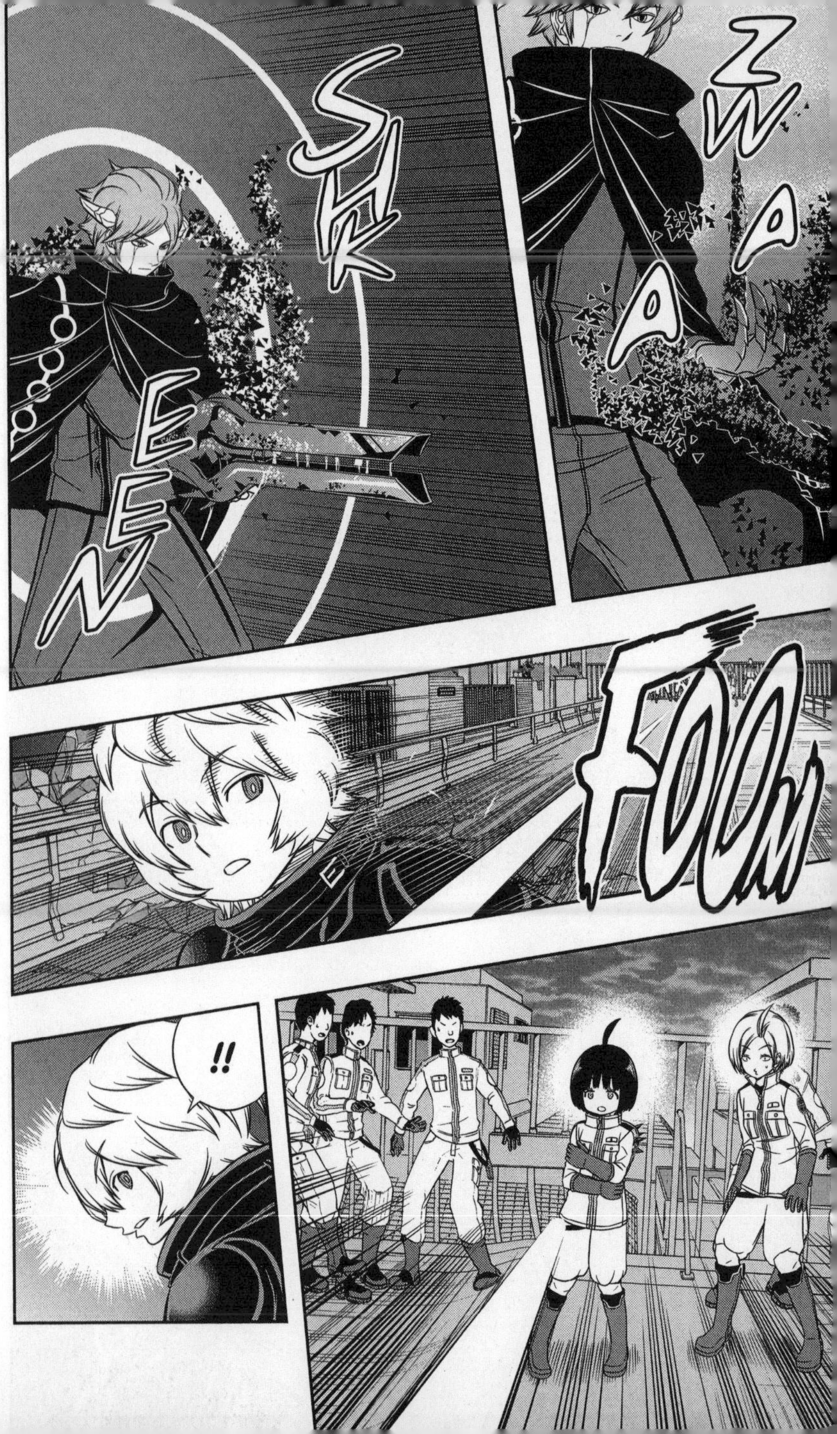
ZWAA
SHK
EEN
FOOM
!!

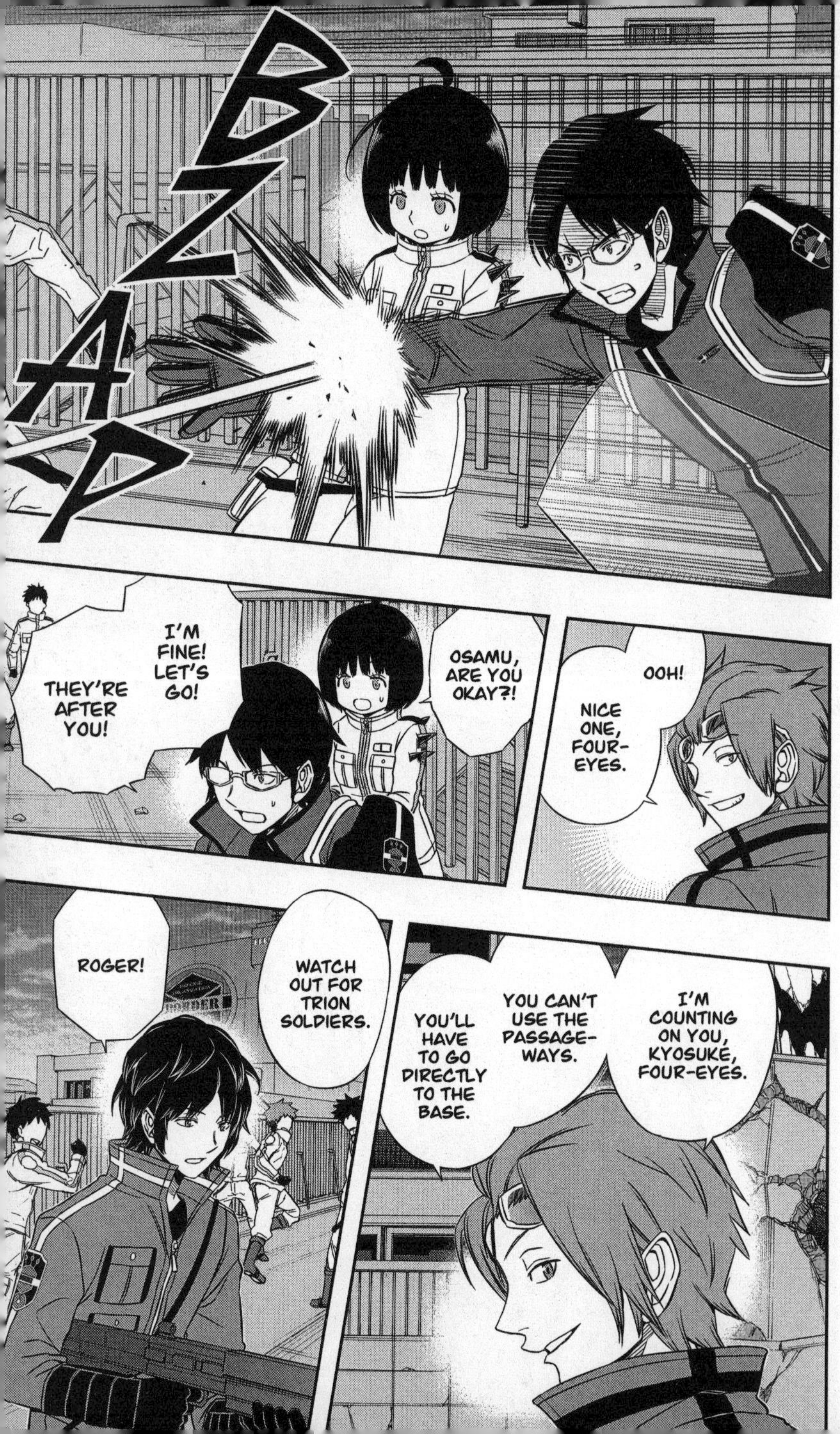
BZAP
OOH!
NICE ONE, FOUR-EYES.
OSAMU, ARE YOU OKAY?!
I'M FINE! LET'S GO!
THEY'RE AFTER YOU!
I'M COUNTING ON YOU, KYOSUKE, FOUR-EYES.
YOU CAN'T USE THE PASSAGE-WAYS.
YOU'LL HAVE TO GO DIRECTLY TO THE BASE.
WATCH OUT FOR TRION SOLDIERS.
ROGER!
BORDER

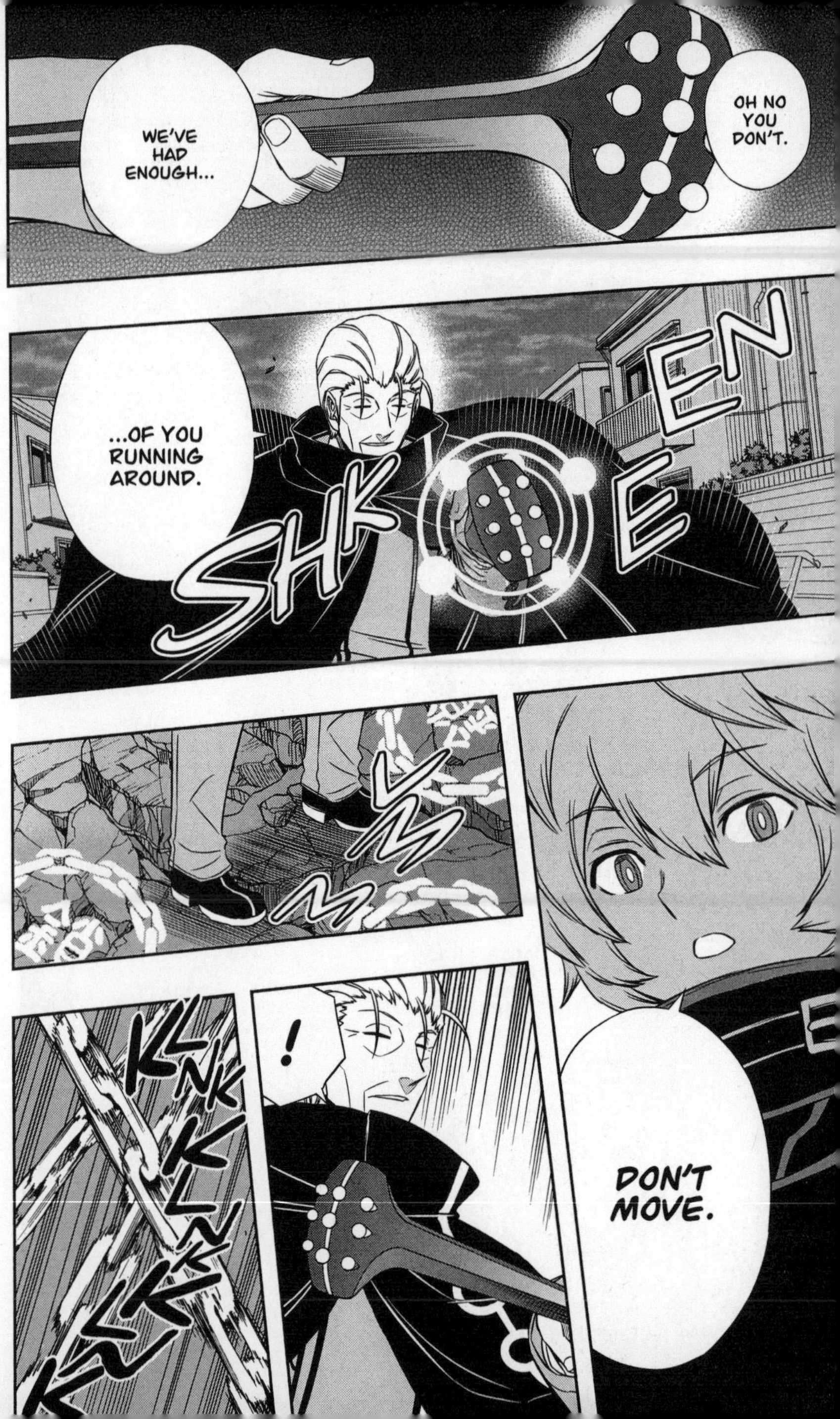
OH NO YOU DON'T.
WE'VE HAD ENOUGH...
...OF YOU RUNNING AROUND.
SHKEEN
DON'T MOVE.
MMM
!
KLNK KLNK KLNK

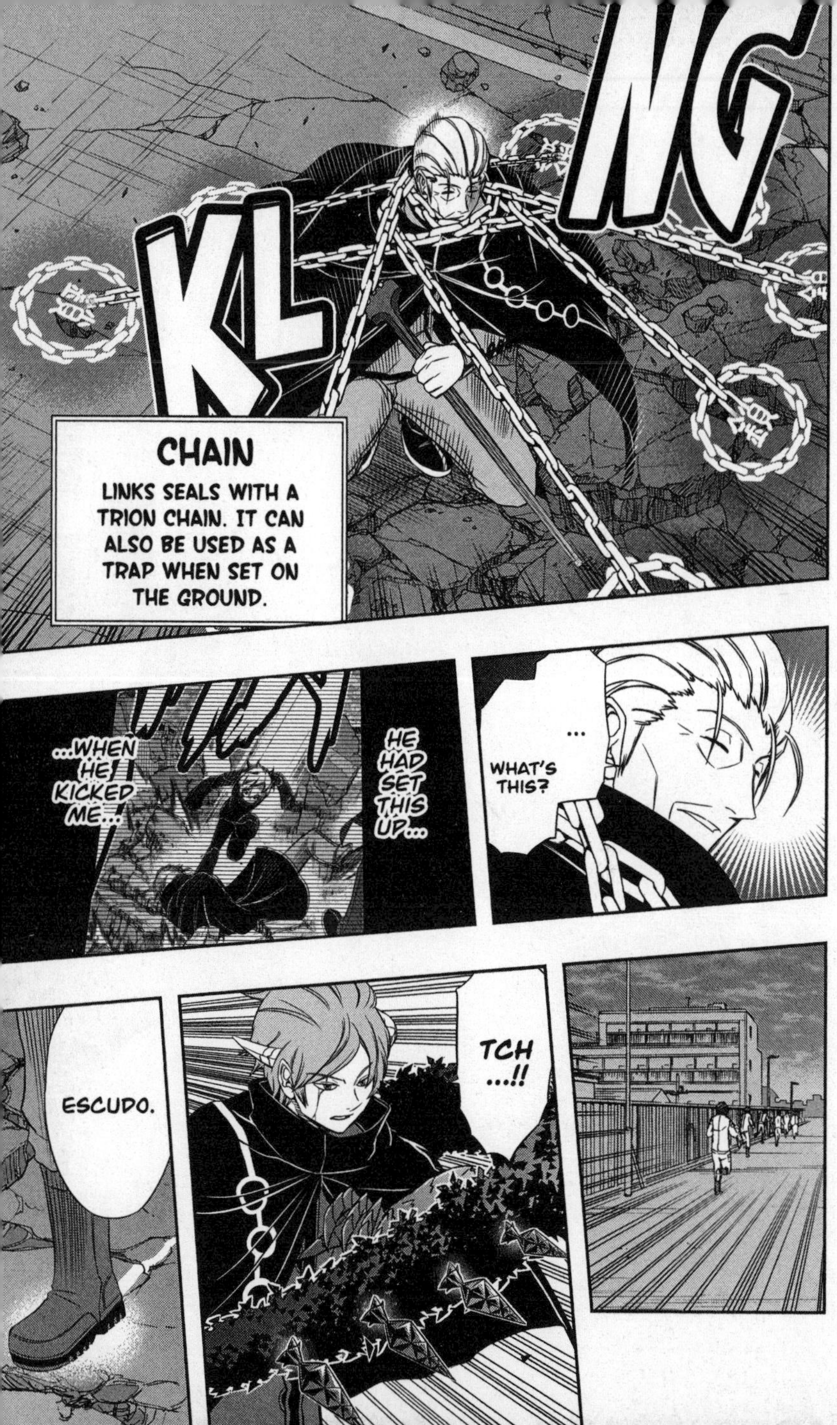
KL
NG
CHAIN
LINKS SEALS WITH A TRION CHAIN. IT CAN ALSO BE USED AS A TRAP WHEN SET ON THE GROUND.
...
WHAT'S THIS?
HE HAD SET THIS UP...
...WHEN HE KICKED ME...
TCH ...!!
ESCUDO.

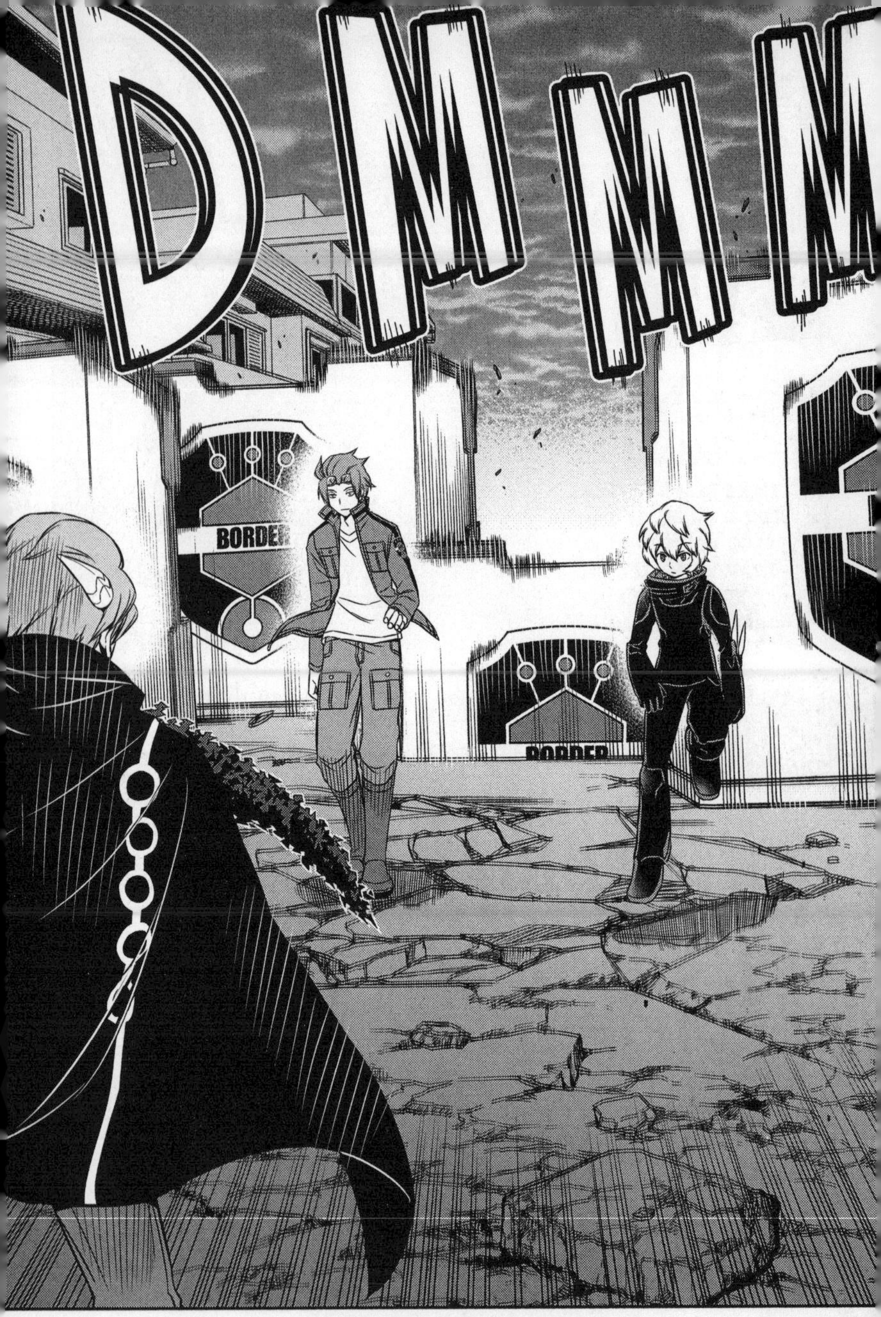
DMMM
BORDER
BORDER

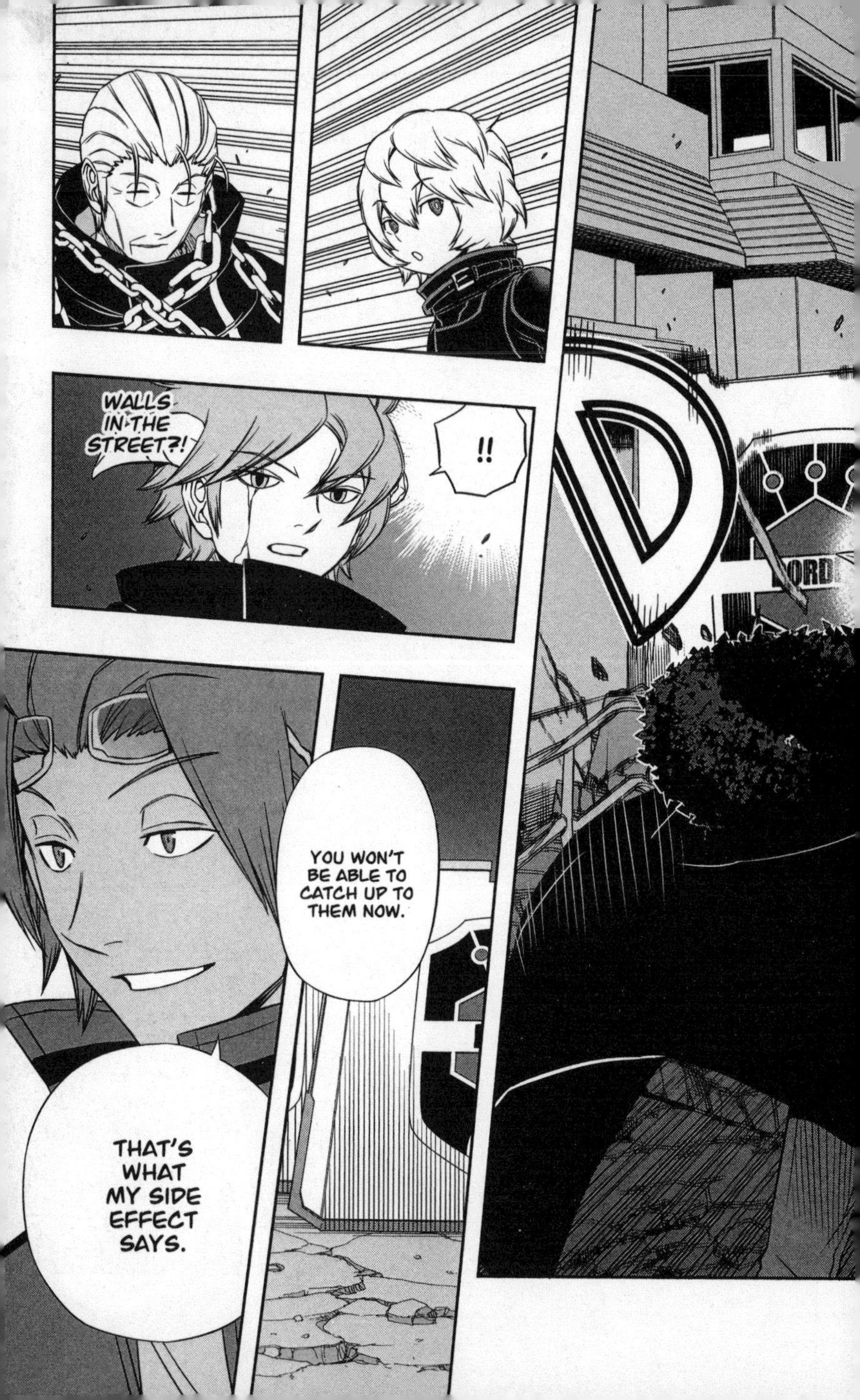
!!
WALLS IN THE STREET?!
YOU WON'T BE ABLE TO CATCH UP TO THEM NOW.
THAT'S WHAT MY SIDE EFFECT SAYS.

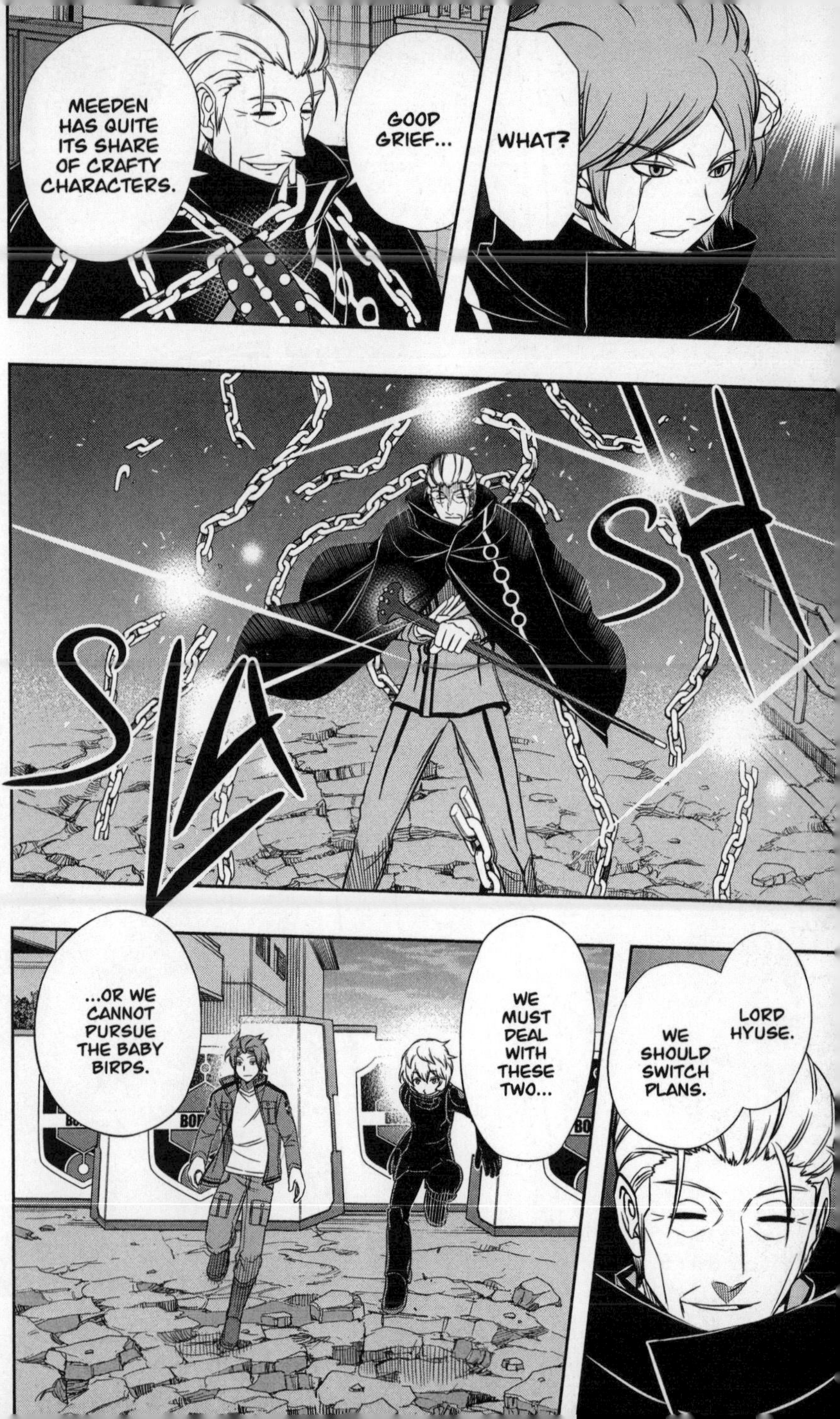
WHAT?
GOOD GRIEF...
MEEDEN HAS QUITE ITS SHARE OF CRAFTY CHARACTERS.
LORD HYUSE.
WE SHOULD SWITCH PLANS.
WE MUST DEAL WITH THESE TWO...
...OR WE CANNOT PURSUE THE BABY BIRDS.

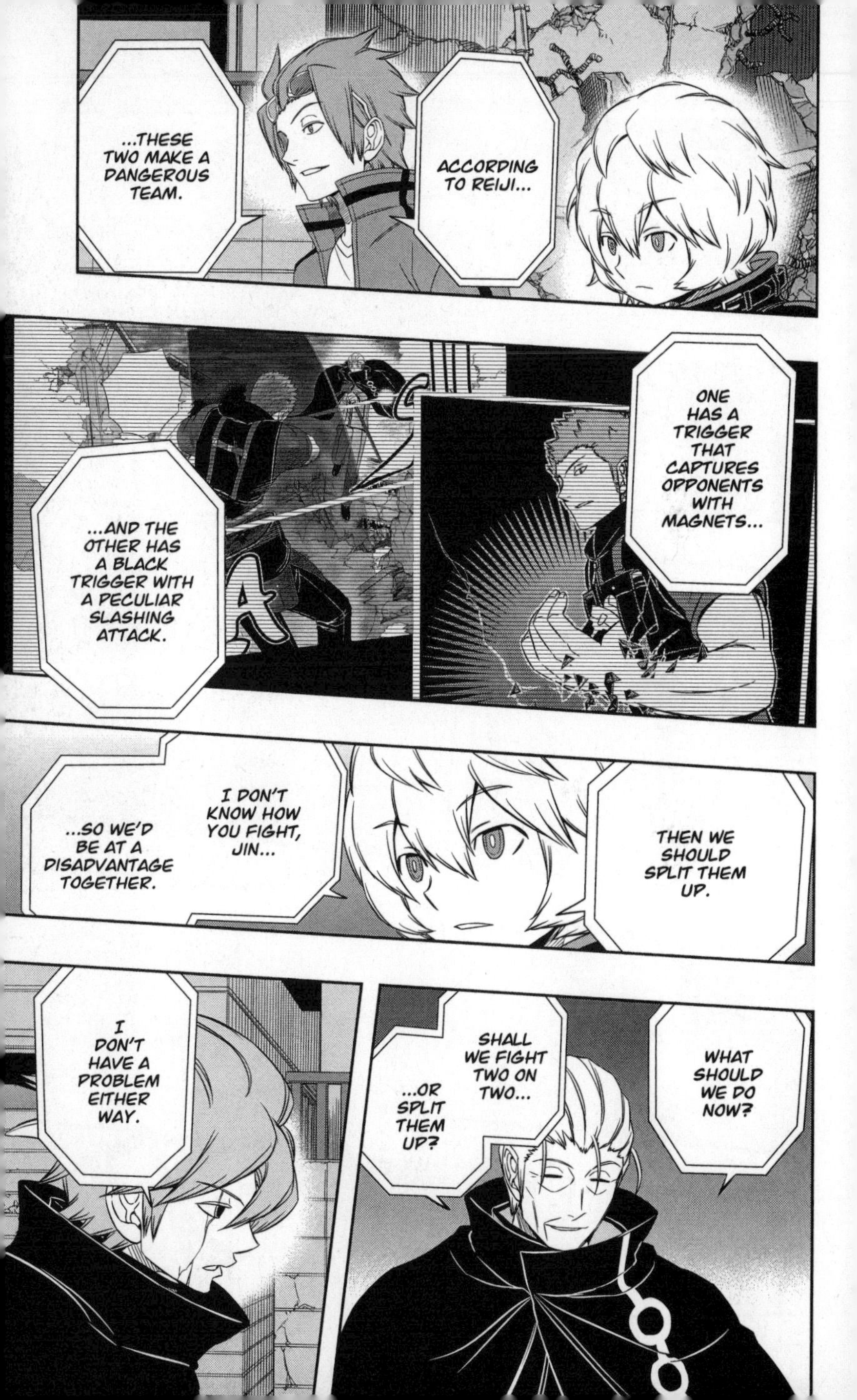
ACCORDING TO REIJI...
...THESE TWO MAKE A DANGEROUS TEAM.
ONE HAS A TRIGGER THAT CAPTURES OPPONENTS WITH MAGNETS...
...AND THE OTHER HAS A BLACK TRIGGER WITH A PECULIAR SLASHING ATTACK.
I DON'T KNOW HOW YOU FIGHT, JIN...
...SO WE'D BE AT A DISADVANTAGE TOGETHER.
THEN WE SHOULD SPLIT THEM UP.
WHAT SHOULD WE DO NOW?
SHALL WE FIGHT TWO ON TWO...
...OR SPLIT THEM UP?
I DON'T HAVE A PROBLEM EITHER WAY.

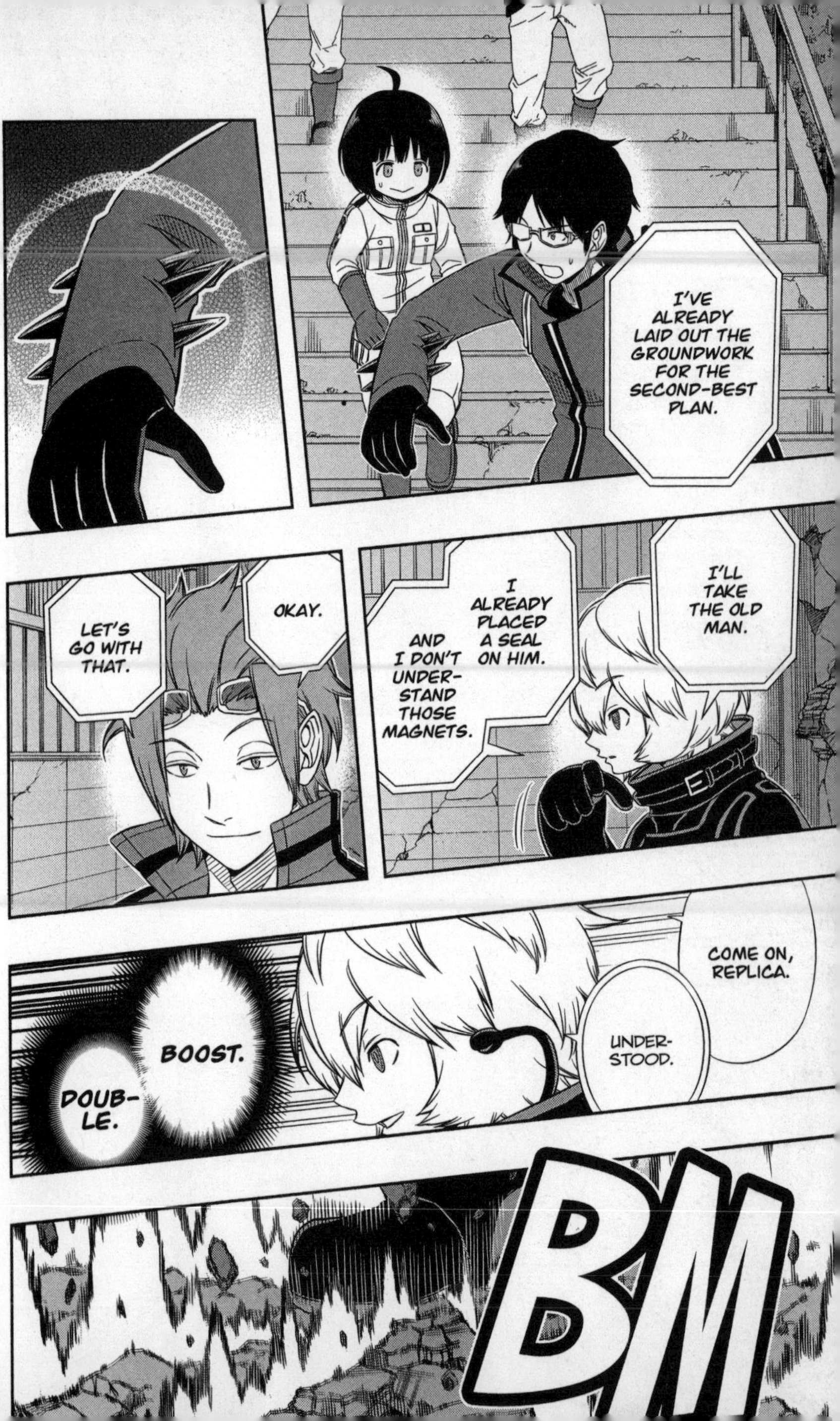
I'VE ALREADY LAID OUT THE GROUNDWORK FOR THE SECOND-BEST PLAN.
I'LL TAKE THE OLD MAN.
I ALREADY PLACED A SEAL ON HIM.
AND I DON'T UNDER-STAND THOSE MAGNETS.
OKAY.
LET'S GO WITH THAT.
COME ON, REPLICA.
UNDER-STOOD.
BOOST.
DOUB-LE.
BM

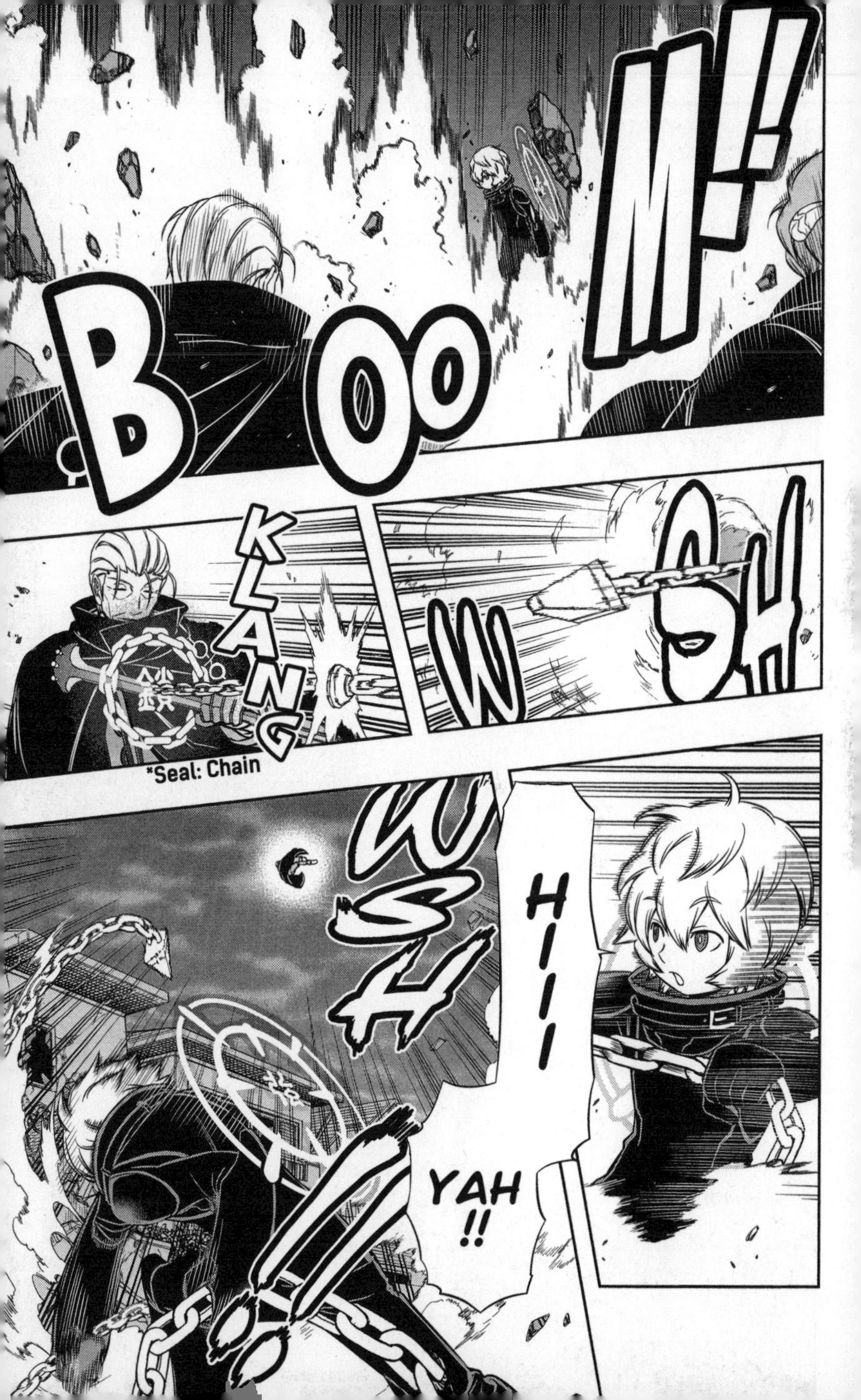
BOOM!!
WSH
KLANG
*Seal: Chain
HIII
YAH!!
WSH

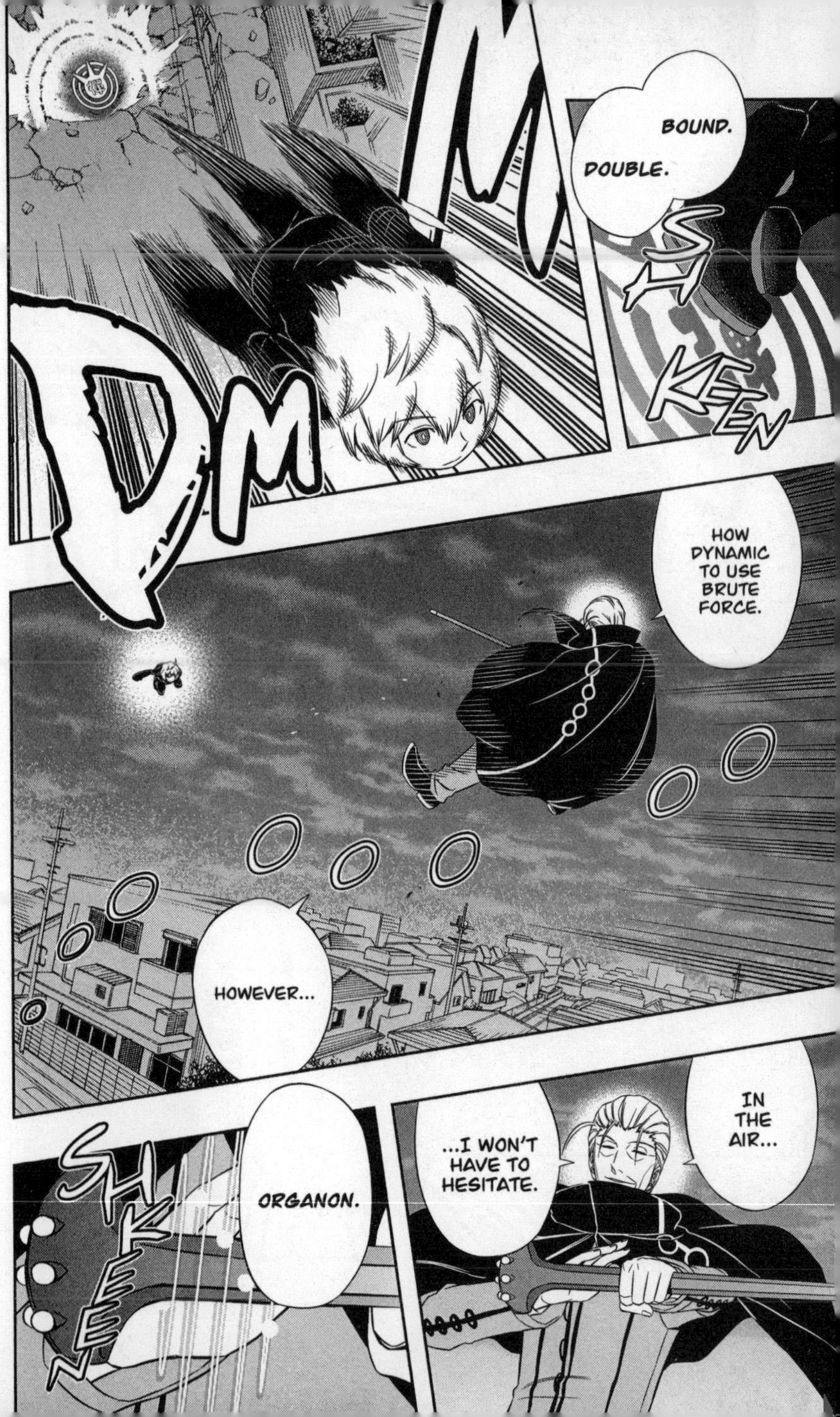
BOUND.
DOUBLE.
SHKEEN
HOW DYNAMIC TO USE BRUTE FORCE.
HOWEVER...
IN THE AIR...
...I WON'T HAVE TO HESITATE.
ORGANON.

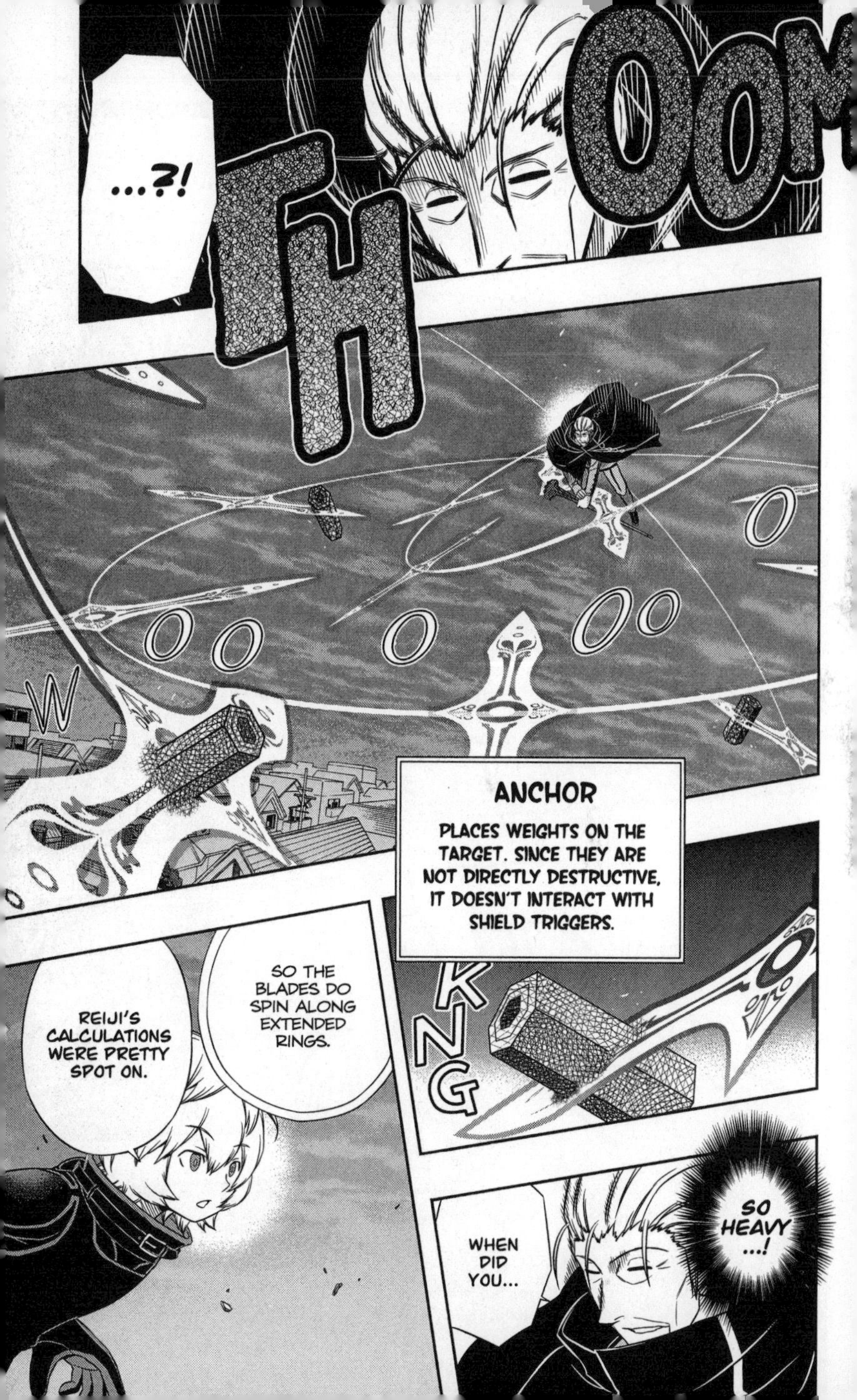

THOOM
...?!
W
ANCHOR
PLACES WEIGHTS ON THE TARGET. SINCE THEY ARE NOT DIRECTLY DESTRUCTIVE, IT DOESN'T INTERACT WITH SHIELD TRIGGERS.
KNG
SO HEAVY ...!
WHEN DID YOU...
SO THE BLADES DO SPIN ALONG EXTENDED RINGS.
REIJI'S CALCULATIONS WERE PRETTY SPOT ON.

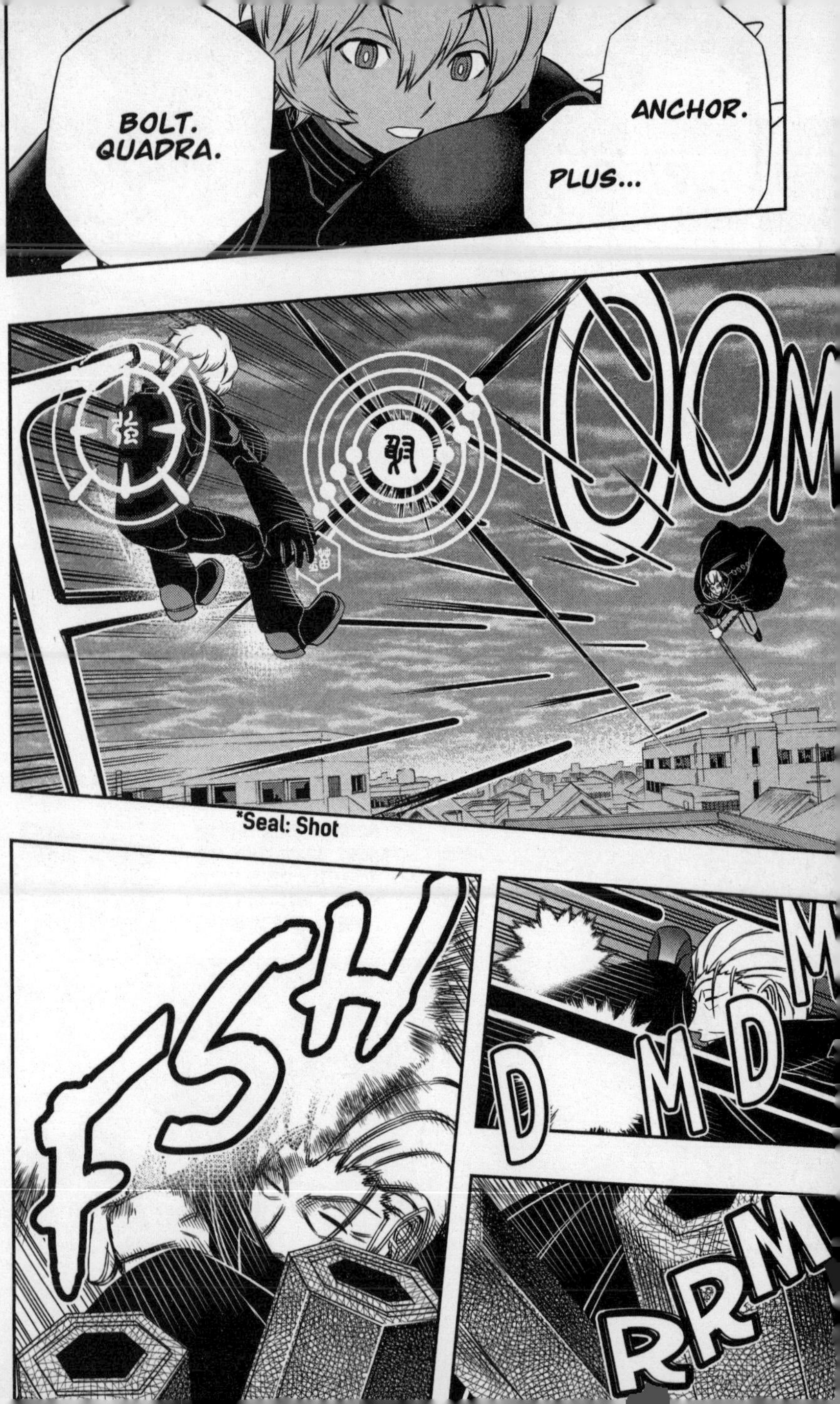
ANCHOR.
PLUS...
BOLT.
QUADRA.
OOM
*Seal: Shot
DMDMM
RRM
FSH

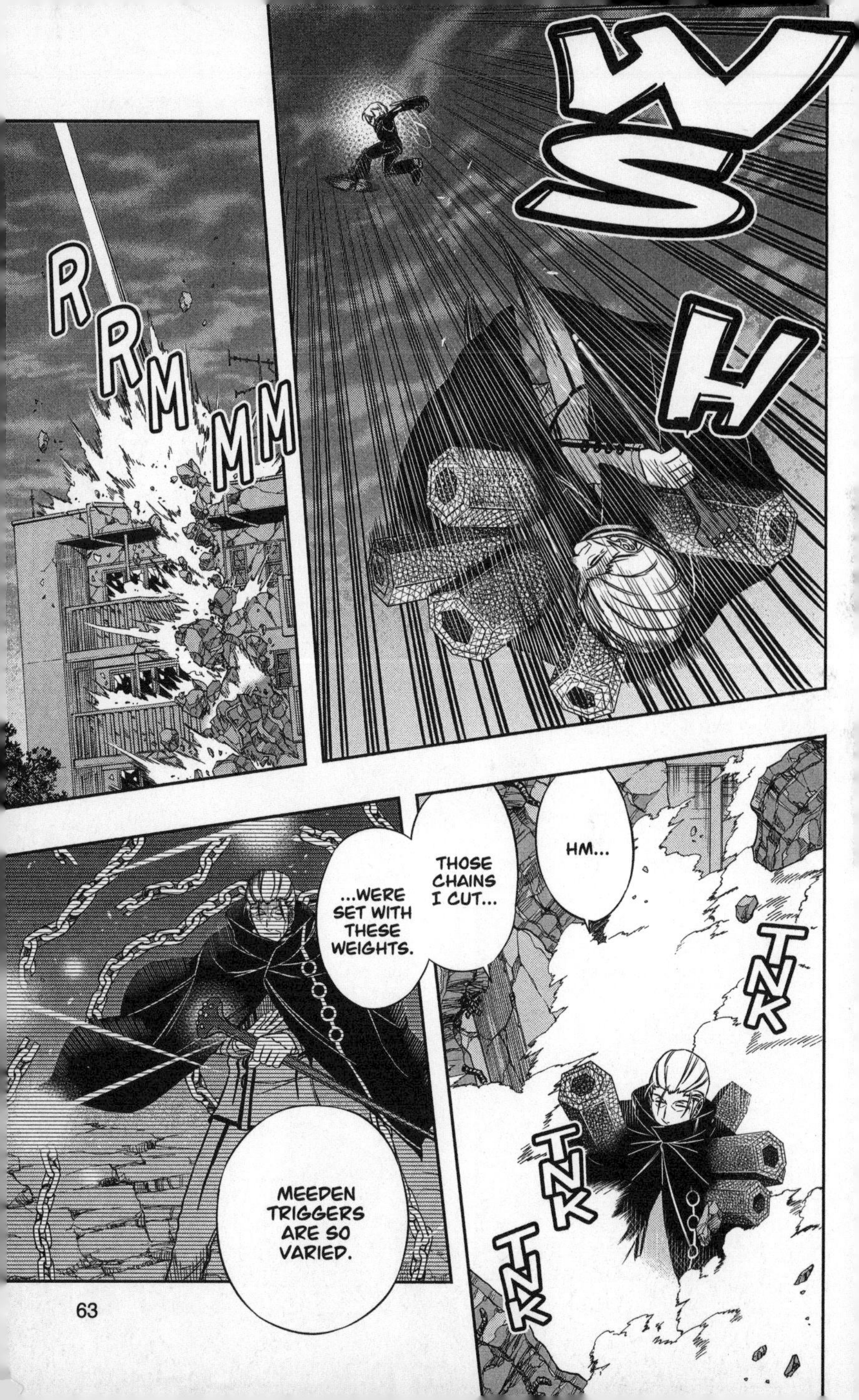
WSH
RRMMMM
HM...
THOSE CHAINS I CUT...
...WERE SET WITH THESE WEIGHTS.
TNK
TNK
TNK
MEEDEN TRIGGERS ARE SO VARIED.

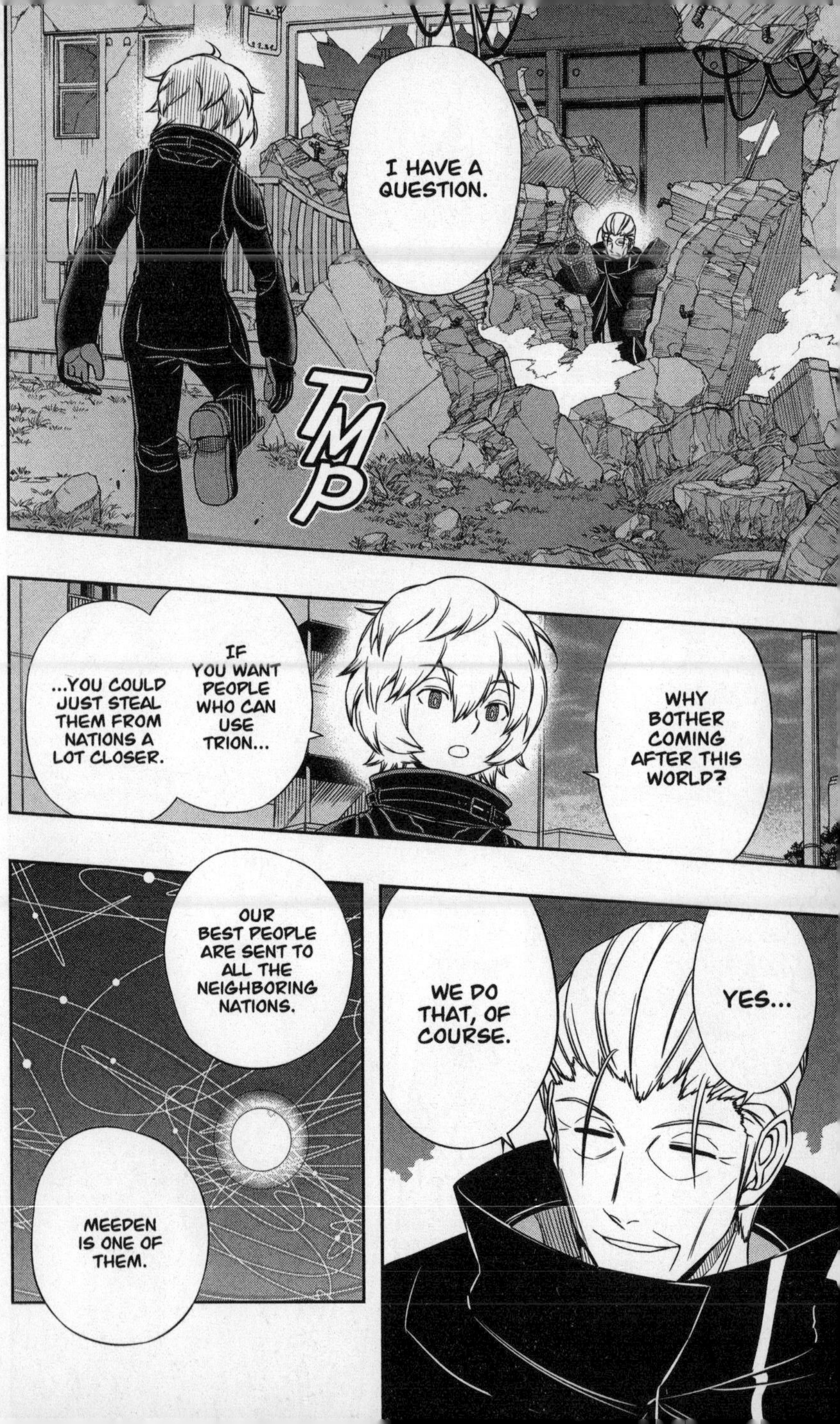
I HAVE A QUESTION.
TMP
WHY BOTHER COMING AFTER THIS WORLD?
IF YOU WANT PEOPLE WHO CAN USE TRION...
...YOU COULD JUST STEAL THEM FROM NATIONS A LOT CLOSER.
YES...
WE DO THAT, OF COURSE.
OUR BEST PEOPLE ARE SENT TO ALL THE NEIGHBORING NATIONS.
MEEDEN IS ONE OF THEM.

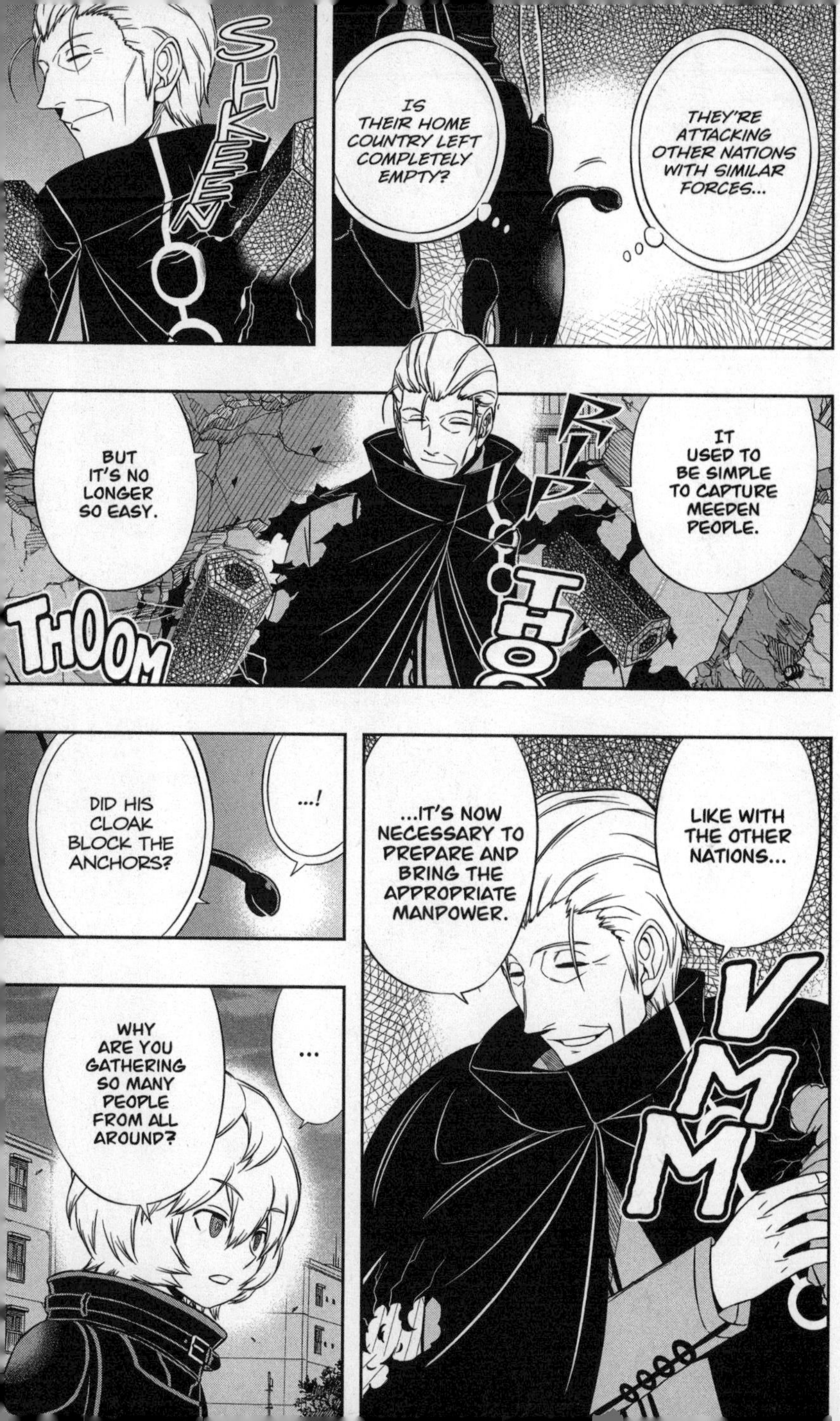
THEY'RE ATTACKING OTHER NATIONS WITH SIMILAR FORCES...
IS THEIR HOME COUNTRY LEFT COMPLETELY EMPTY?
SHKEEN
RIP
IT USED TO BE SIMPLE TO CAPTURE MEEDEN PEOPLE.
THO
BUT IT'S NO LONGER SO EASY.
THOOM
LIKE WITH THE OTHER NATIONS...
...IT'S NOW NECESSARY TO PREPARE AND BRING THE APPROPRIATE MANPOWER.
VMM
...!
DID HIS CLOAK BLOCK THE ANCHORS?
...
WHY ARE YOU GATHERING SO MANY PEOPLE FROM ALL AROUND?

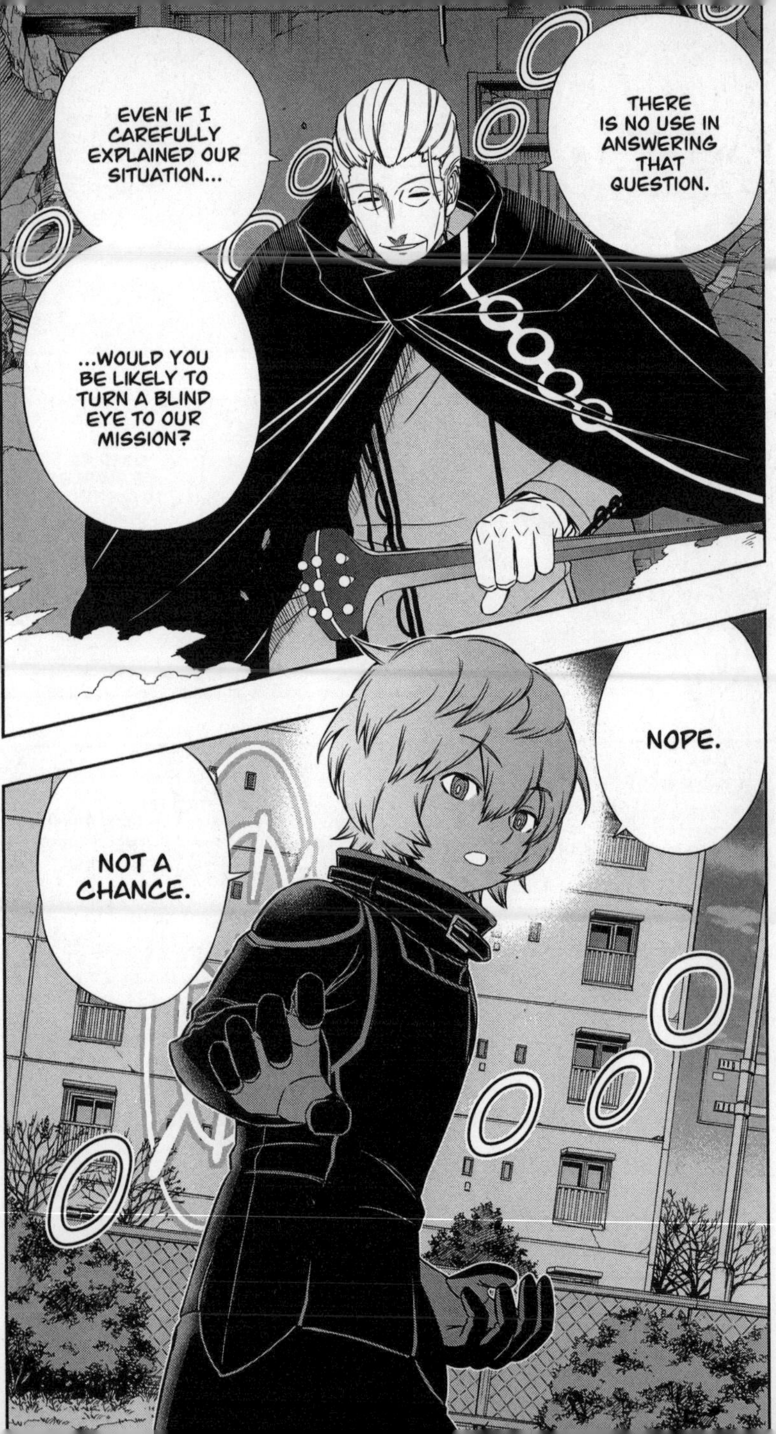
THERE IS NO USE IN ANSWERING THAT QUESTION.
EVEN IF I CAREFULLY EXPLAINED OUR SITUATION...
...WOULD YOU BE LIKELY TO TURN A BLIND EYE TO OUR MISSION?
NOPE.
NOT A CHANCE.

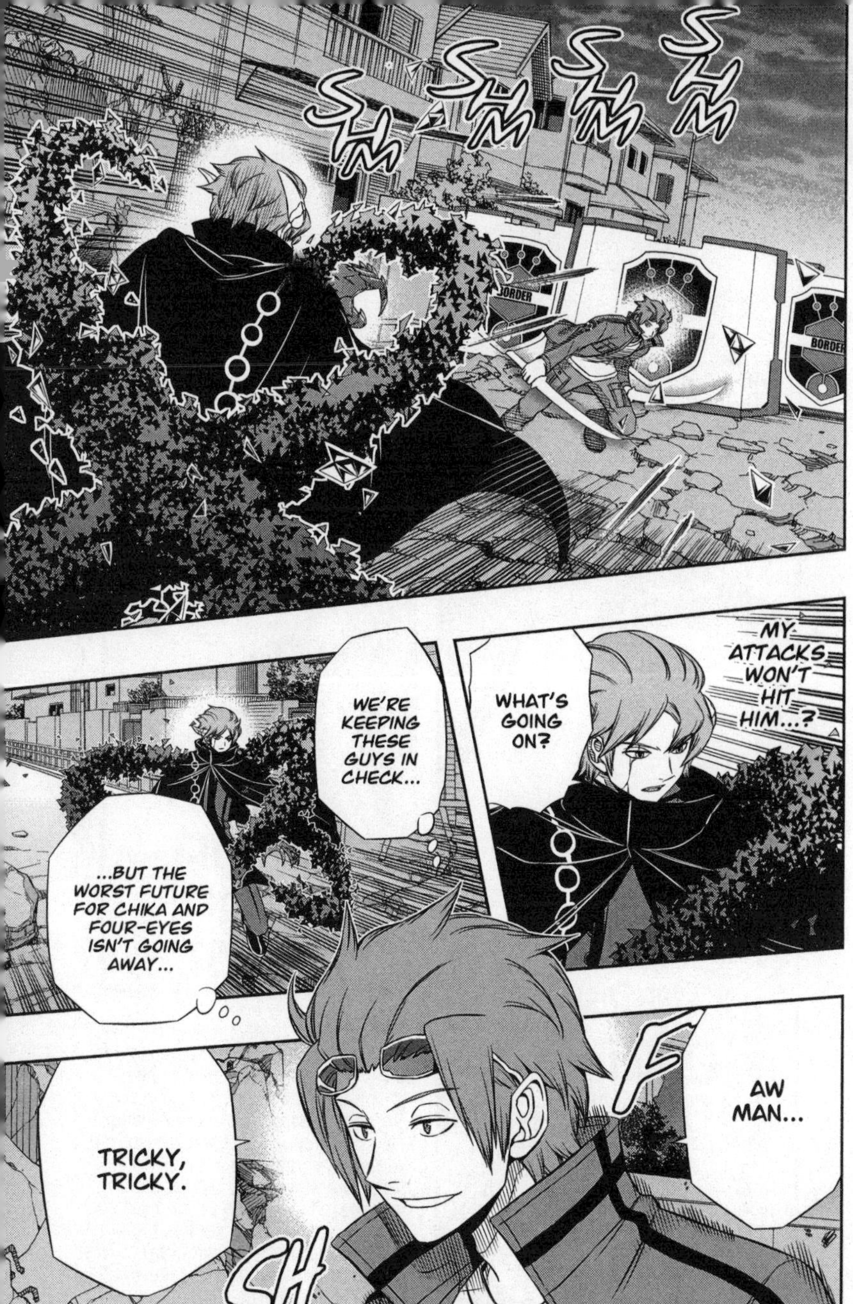
SHM
SHM
SHM
SHM
MY ATTACKS WON'T HIT HIM...?
WHAT'S GOING ON?
WE'RE KEEPING THESE GUYS IN CHECK...
...BUT THE WORST FUTURE FOR CHIKA AND FOUR-EYES ISN'T GOING AWAY...
F
AW MAN...
TRICKY, TRICKY.
SH

First Popularity Poll Contest Results (continued)

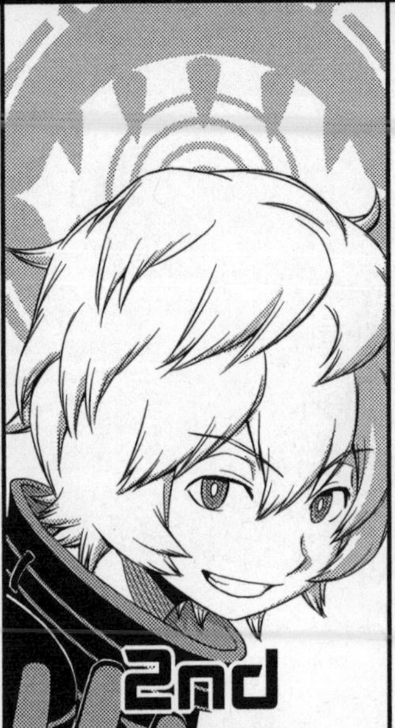
2nd
Transient Black Trigger
Yuma Kuga
5,561

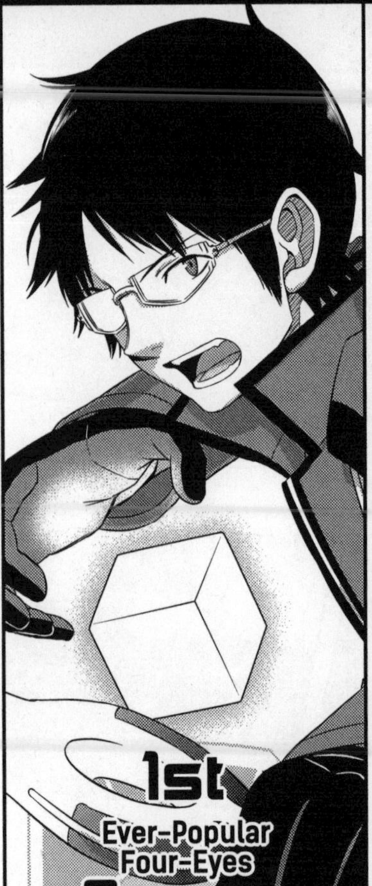
1st
Ever-Popular Four-Eyes
Osamu Mikumo
6,646

■Osamu's in first!
The fact that the weak character who gives it his all got first place goes to show what kind of manga *World Trigger* is. Osamu got the most votes for "favorite character" by a huge margin. Yuma got equally many votes for favorite and second favorite, landing him overall in second place. It reflects who he is as a character too. Yuma and Osamu being top two was the best outcome for me. I couldn't feel luckier.

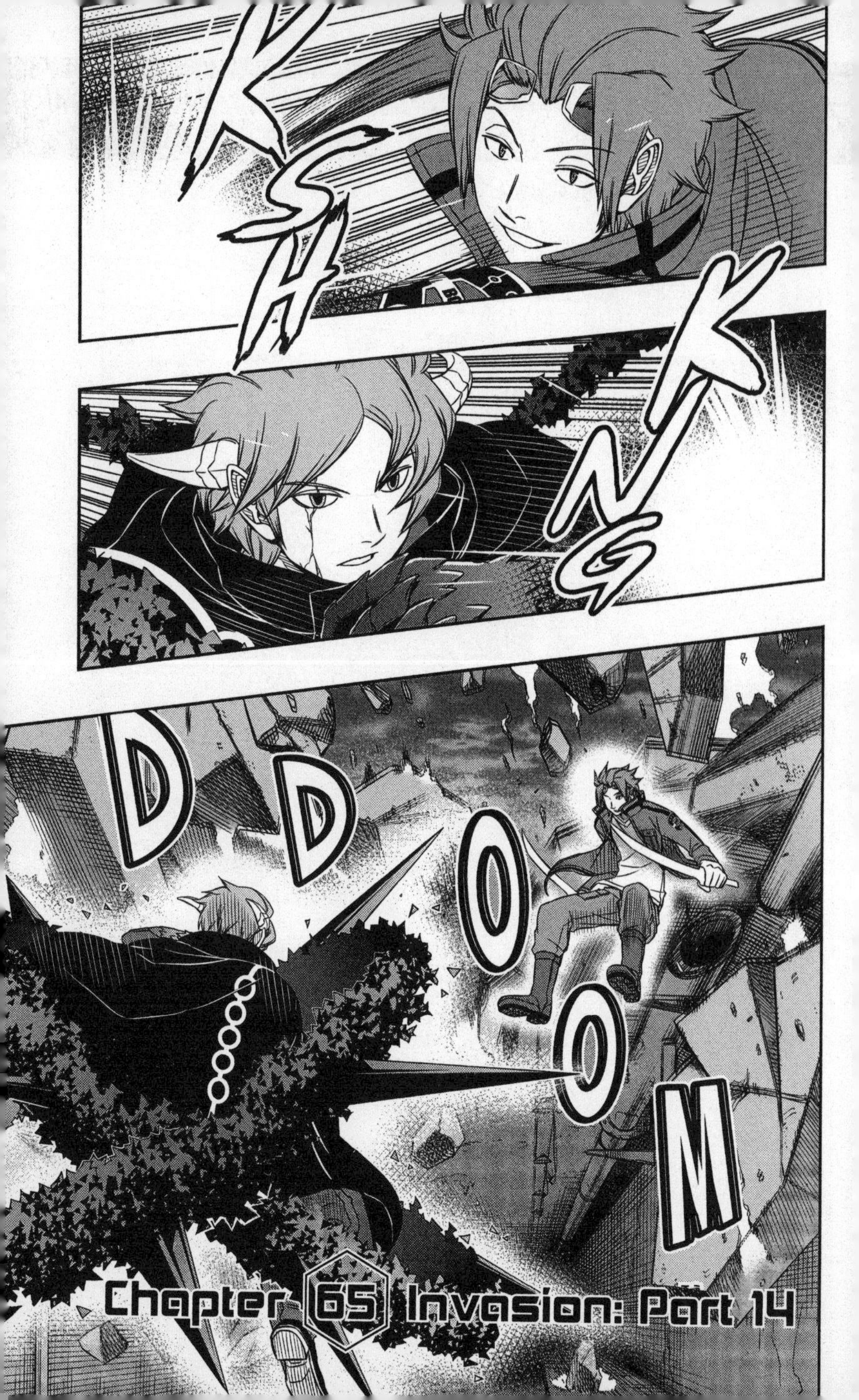
KSH
KNG
DDOOOM
Chapter 65 Invasion: Part 14

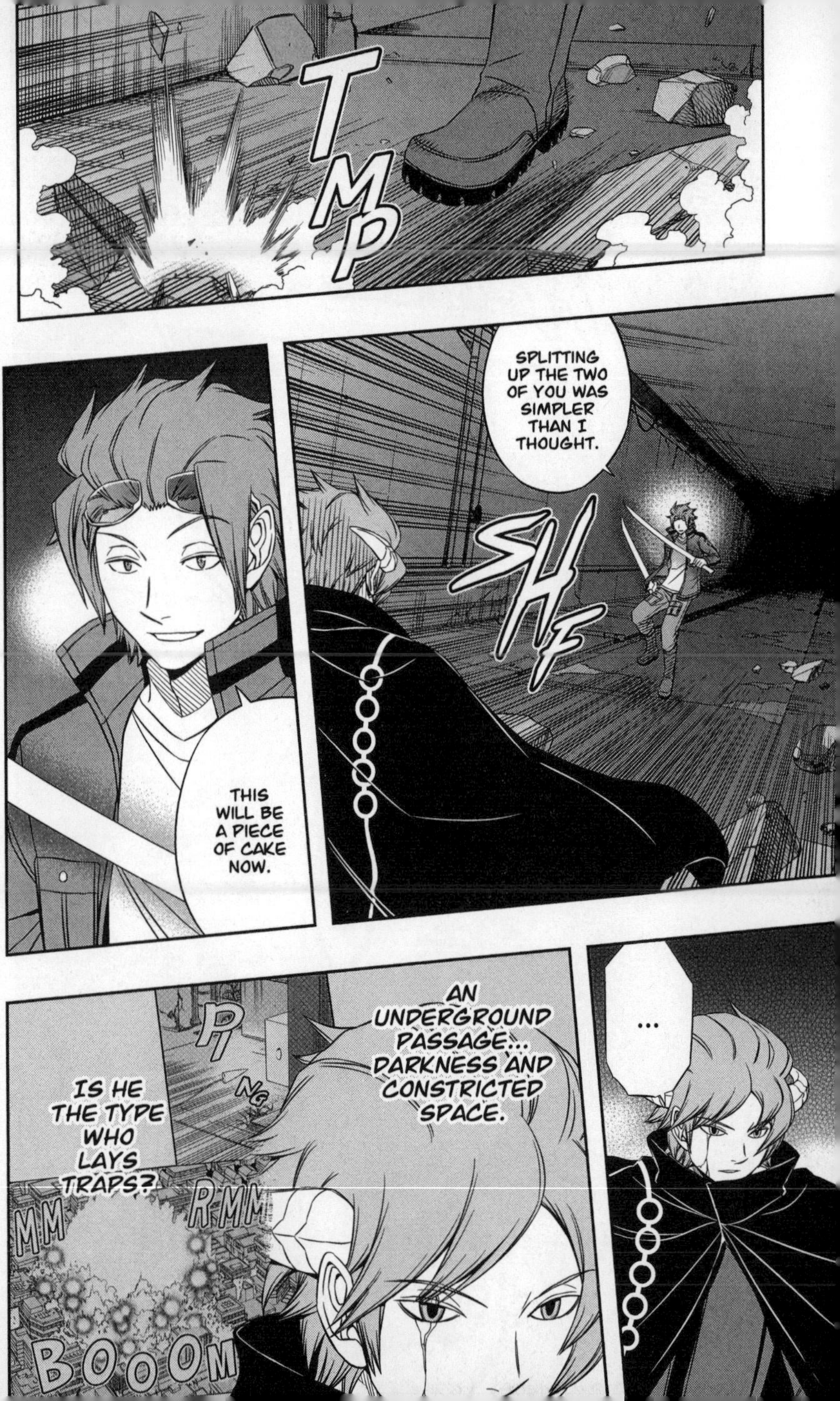
TMP
SPLITTING UP THE TWO OF YOU WAS SIMPLER THAN I THOUGHT.
SHF
THIS WILL BE A PIECE OF CAKE NOW.
...
AN UNDERGROUND PASSAGE... DARKNESS AND CONSTRICTED SPACE.
PING
IS HE THE TYPE WHO LAYS TRAPS?
RMMMM
BOOOOM

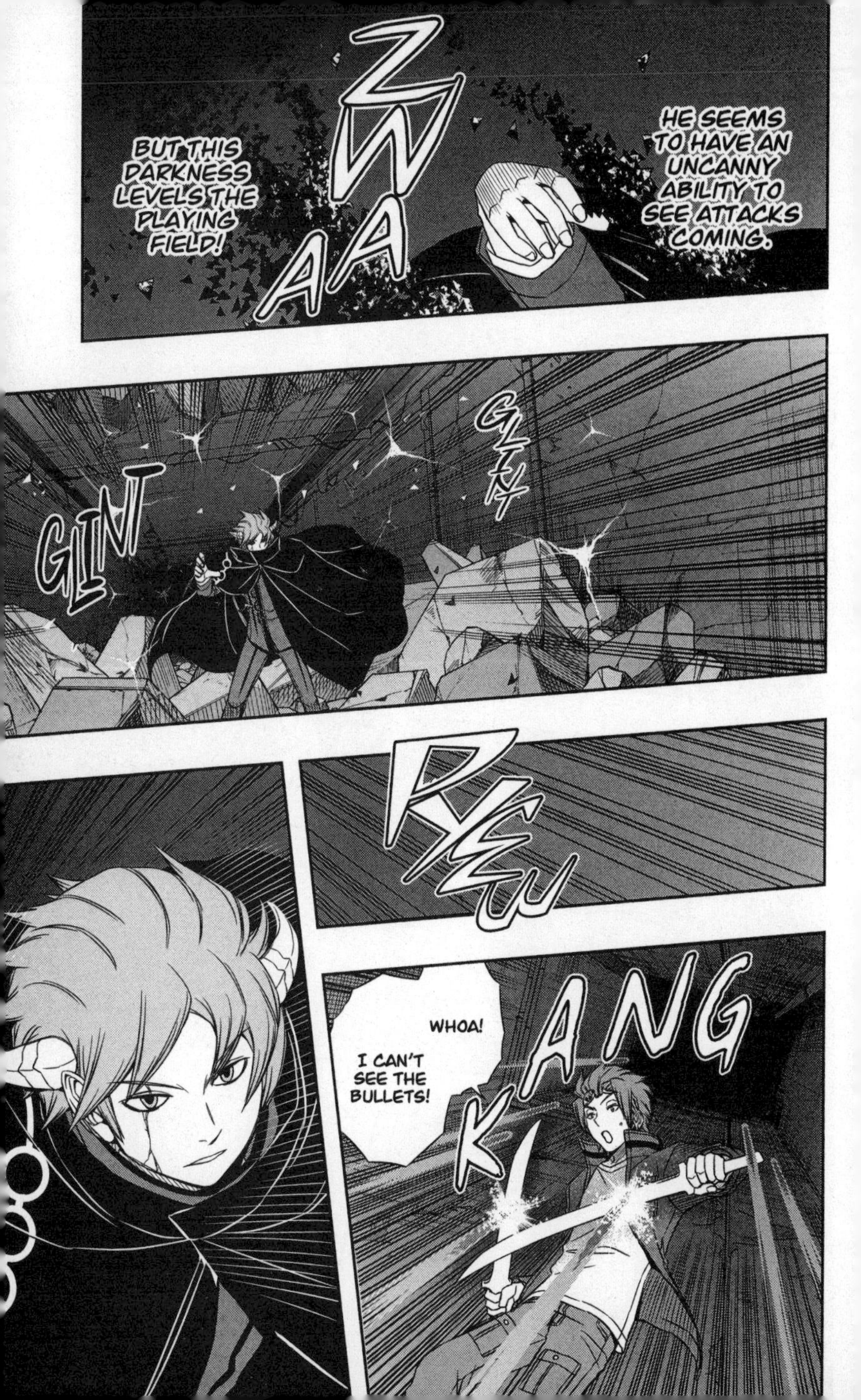
HE SEEMS TO HAVE AN UNCANNY ABILITY TO SEE ATTACKS COMING.
ZWAA
BUT THIS DARKNESS LEVELS THE PLAYING FIELD!
GLINT
GLINT
PYEW
KANG
WHOA!
I CAN'T SEE THE BULLETS!

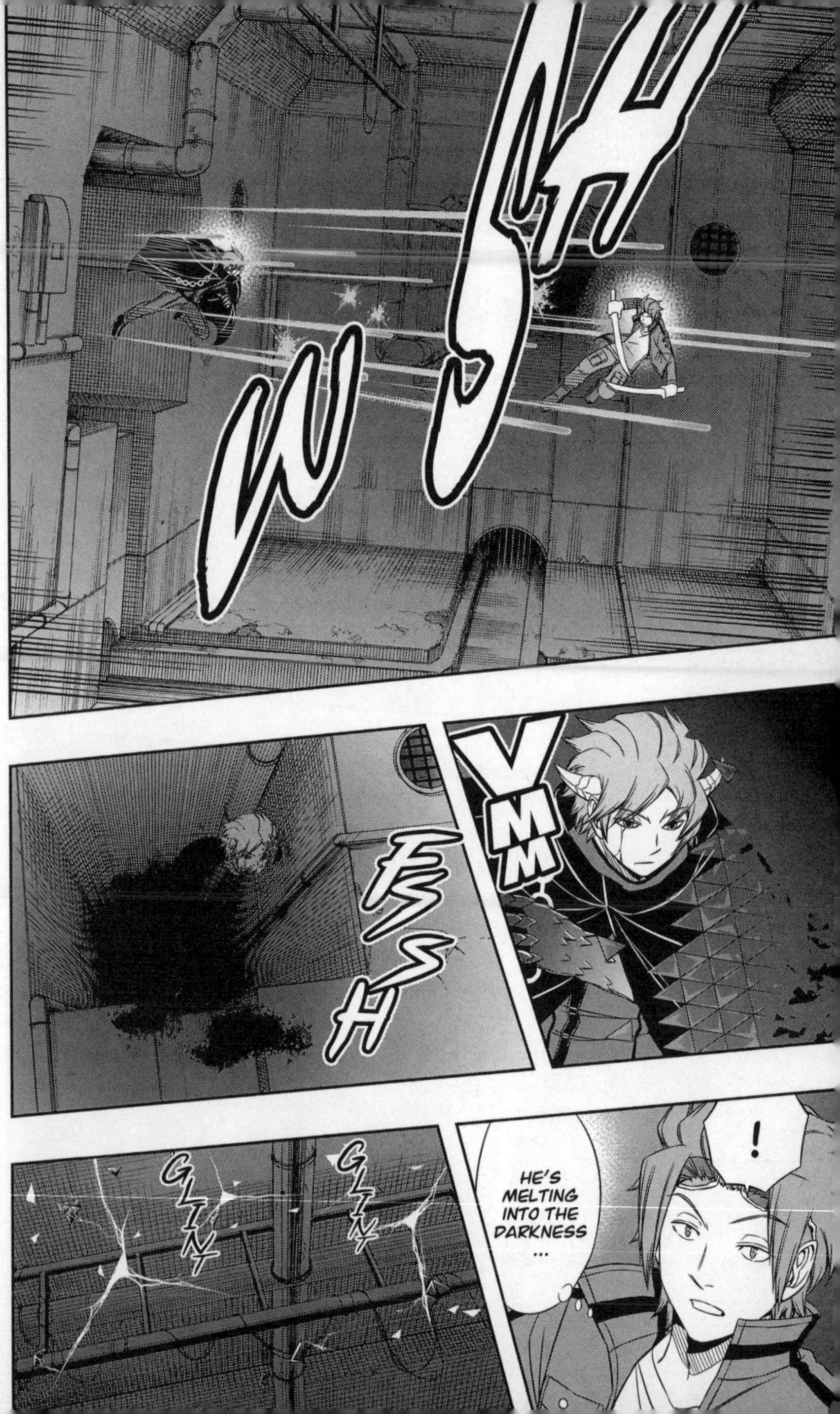
WSH
VMM
FSSH
!
HE'S MELTING INTO THE DARKNESS ...
GLINT
GLINT

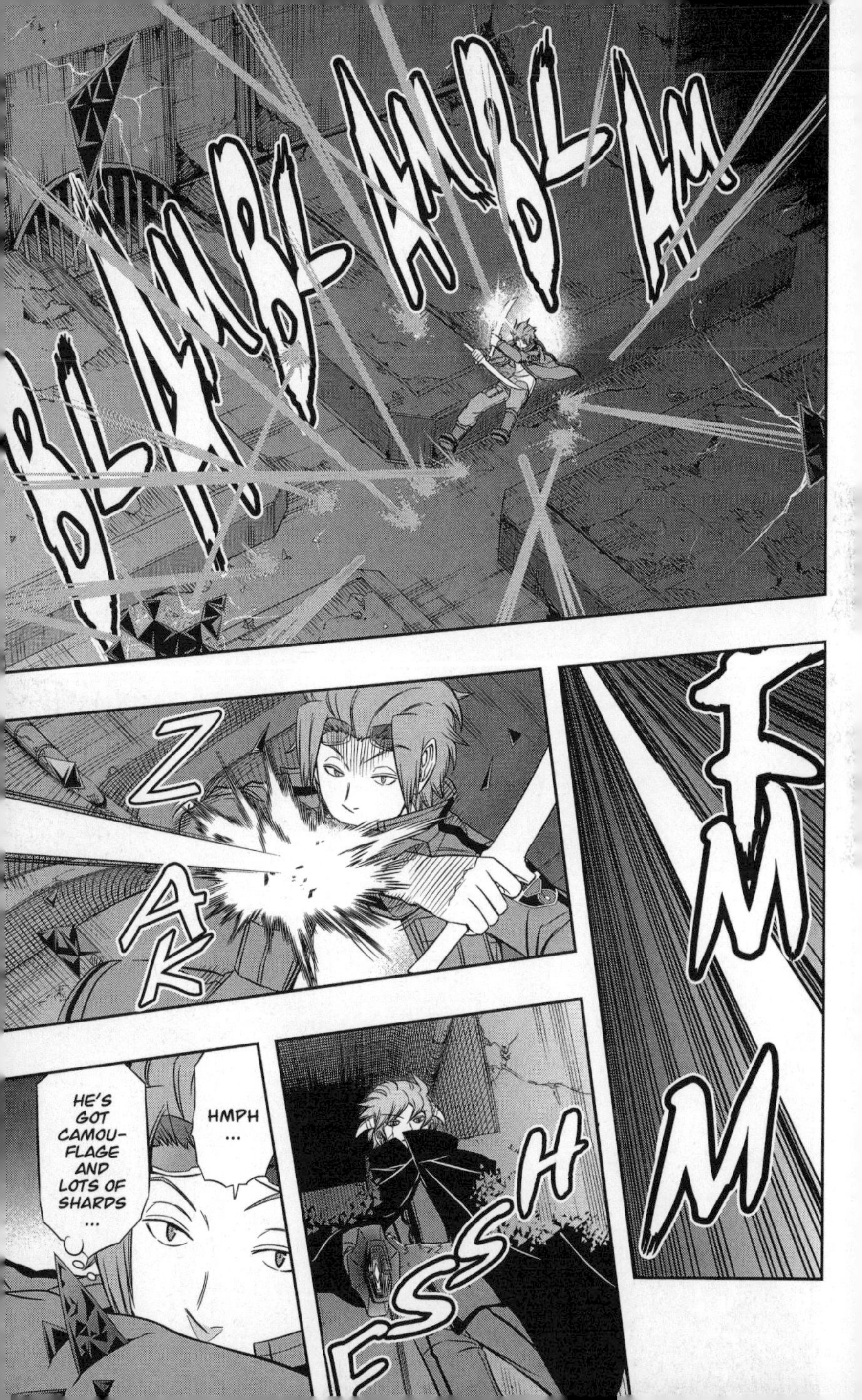
BLAM BLAM BLAM BLAM
FMM
ZAK
FSSH
HMPH...
HE'S GOT CAMOUFLAGE AND LOTS OF SHARDS...

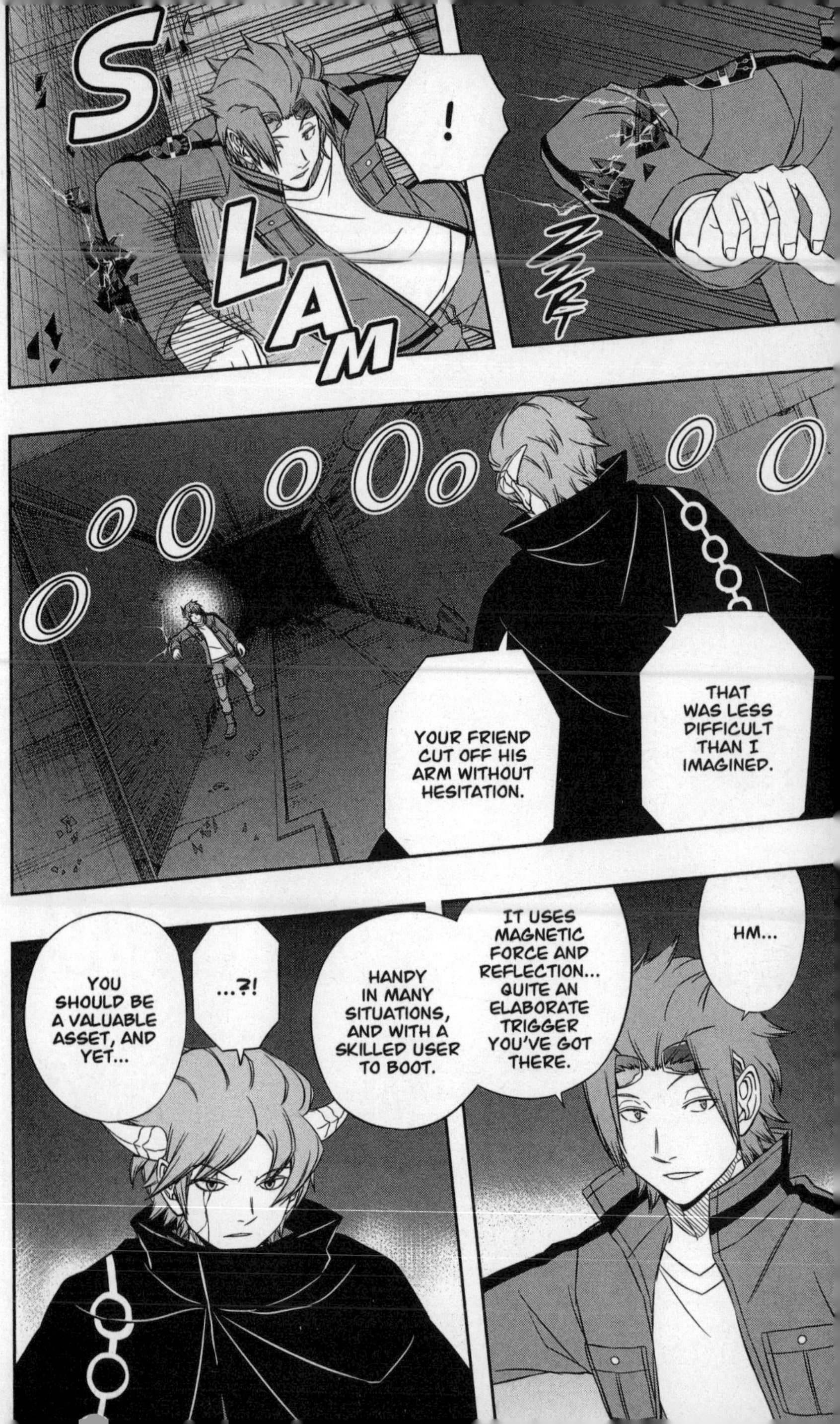
ZZZT
!
SLAM
OOOOOOOO
THAT WAS LESS DIFFICULT THAN I IMAGINED.
YOUR FRIEND CUT OFF HIS ARM WITHOUT HESITATION.
HM...
IT USES MAGNETIC FORCE AND REFLECTION... QUITE AN ELABORATE TRIGGER YOU'VE GOT THERE.
HANDY IN MANY SITUATIONS, AND WITH A SKILLED USER TO BOOT.
...?!
YOU SHOULD BE A VALUABLE ASSET, AND YET...

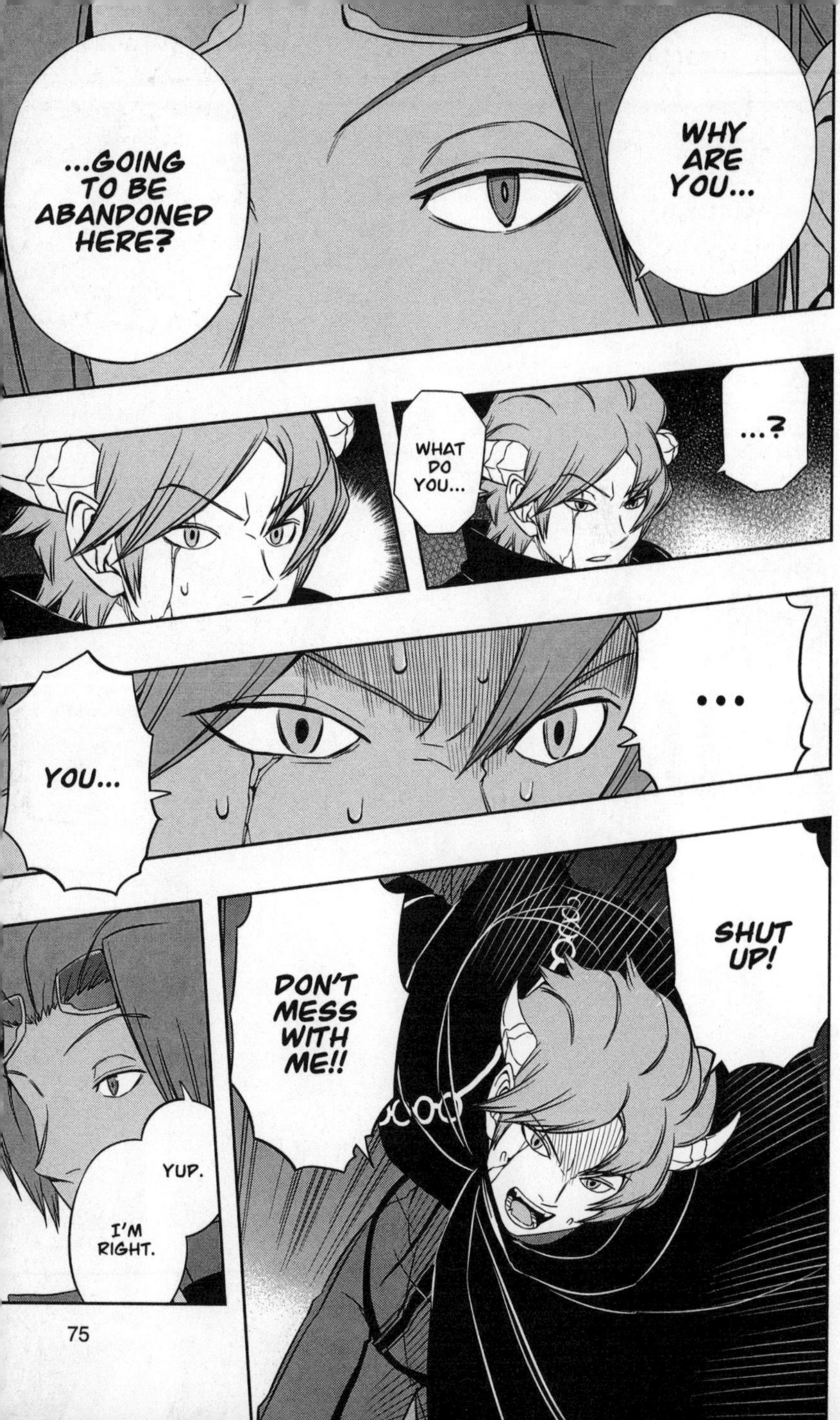
WHY ARE YOU...
...GOING TO BE ABANDONED HERE?
...?
WHAT DO YOU...
...
YOU...
SHUT UP!
DON'T MESS WITH ME!!
YUP.
I'M RIGHT.

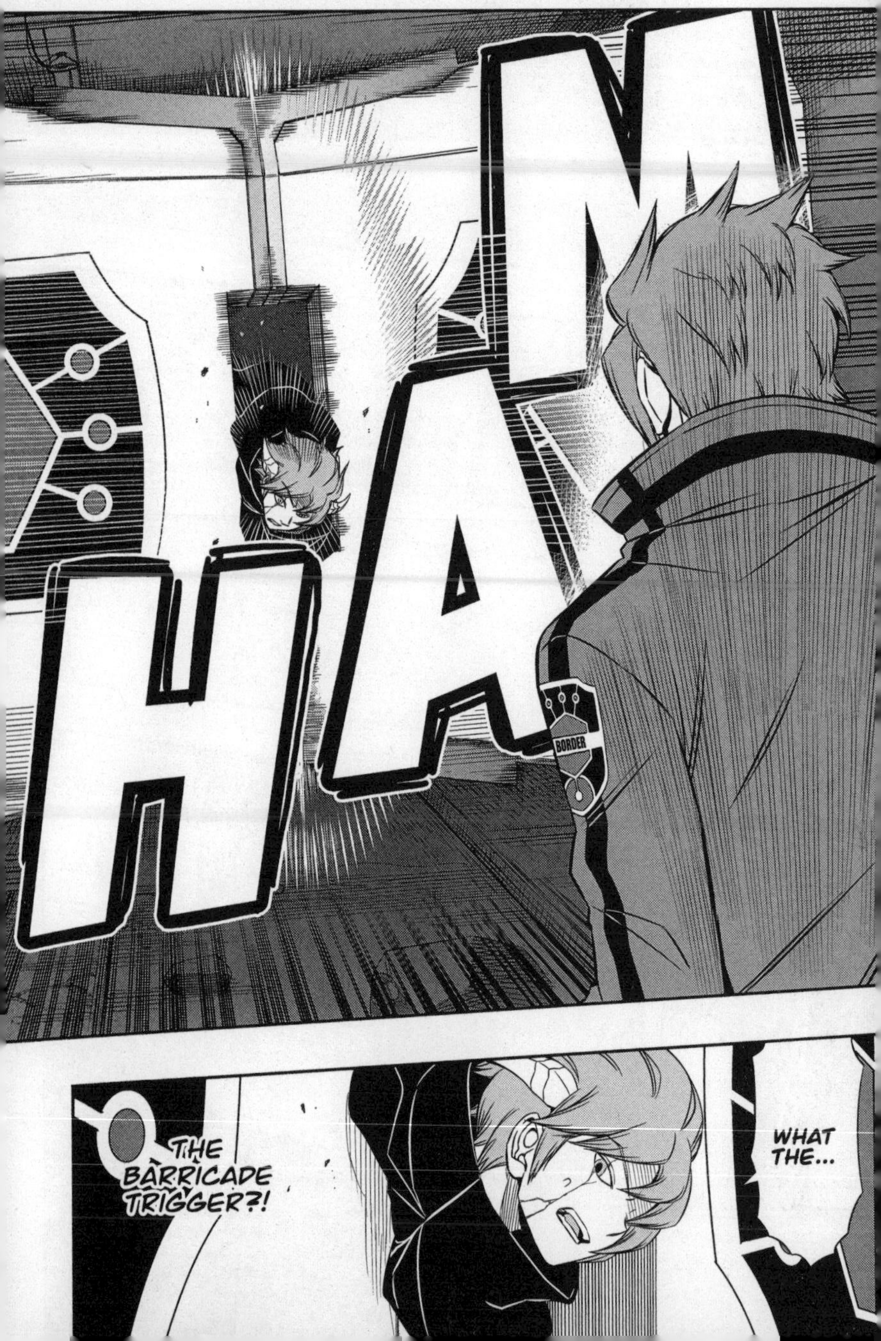
HAM
WHAT THE...
THE BARRICADE TRIGGER?!

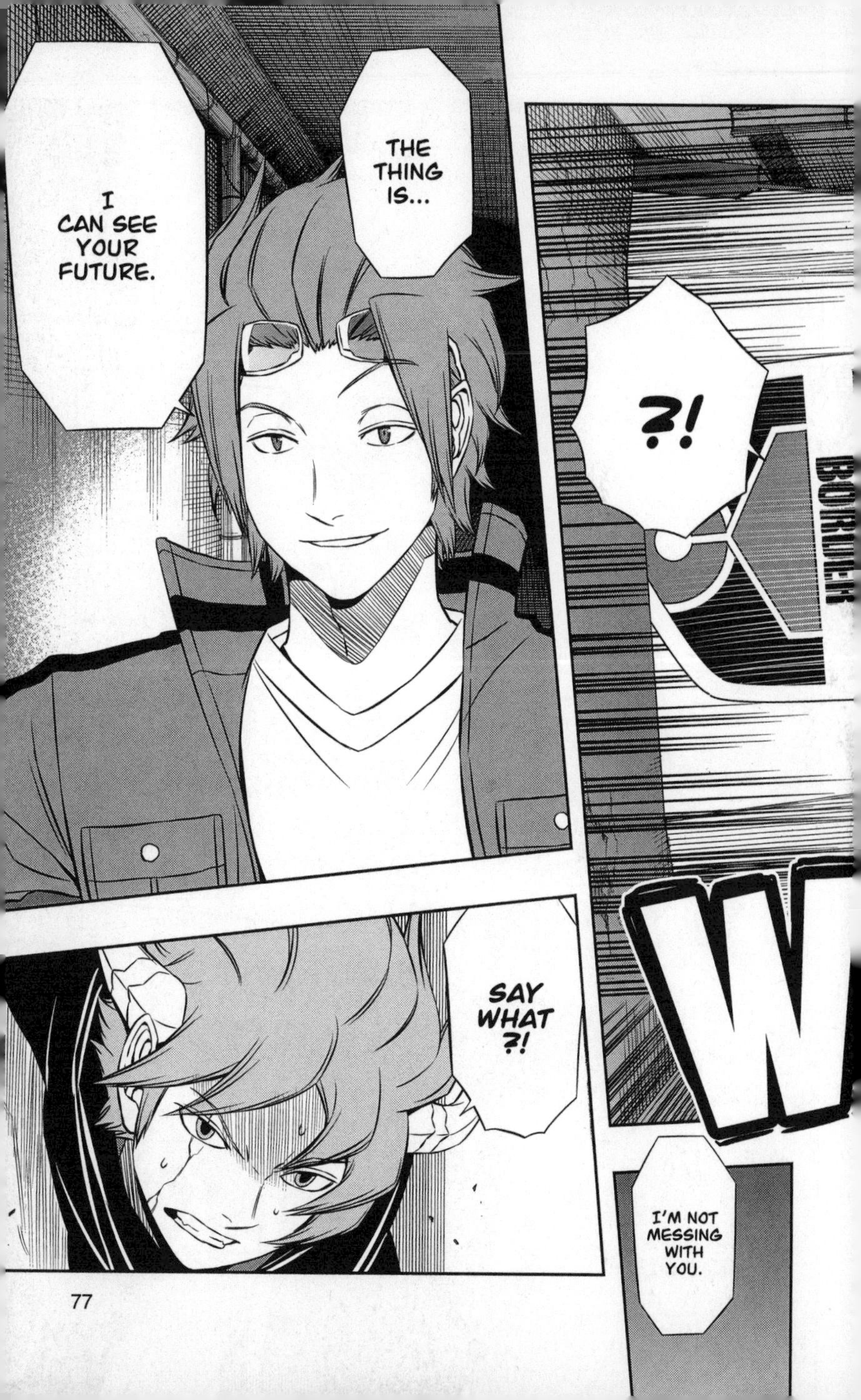
THE THING IS...
I CAN SEE YOUR FUTURE.
SAY WHAT ?!
?!
BORDER
I'M NOT MESSING WITH YOU.

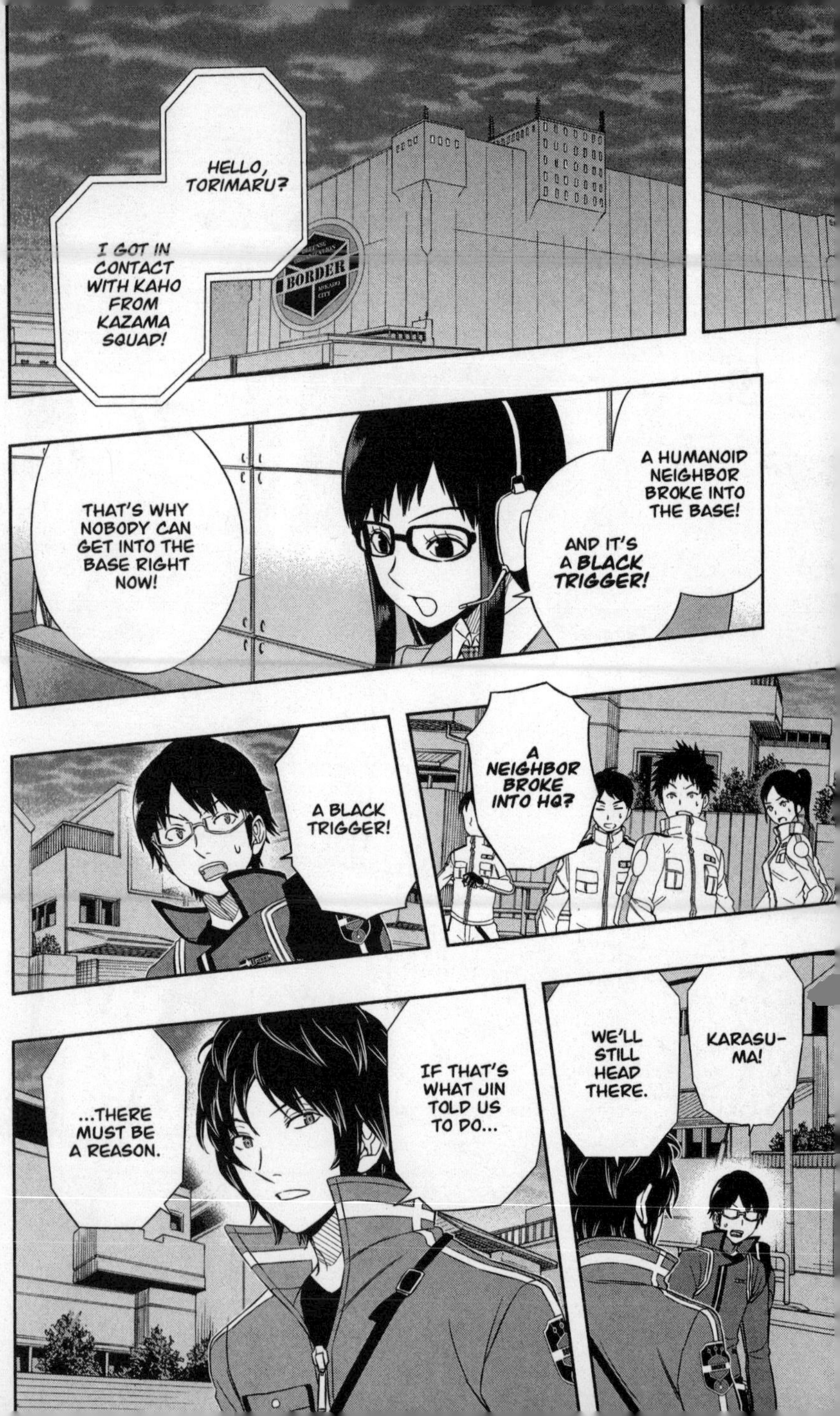
HELLO, TORIMARU?
I GOT IN CONTACT WITH KAHO FROM KAZAMA SQUAD!
BORDER
A HUMANOID NEIGHBOR BROKE INTO THE BASE!
AND IT'S A BLACK TRIGGER!
THAT'S WHY NOBODY CAN GET INTO THE BASE RIGHT NOW!
A NEIGHBOR BROKE INTO HQ?
A BLACK TRIGGER!
KARASU-MA!
WE'LL STILL HEAD THERE.
IF THAT'S WHAT JIN TOLD US TO DO...
...THERE MUST BE A REASON.

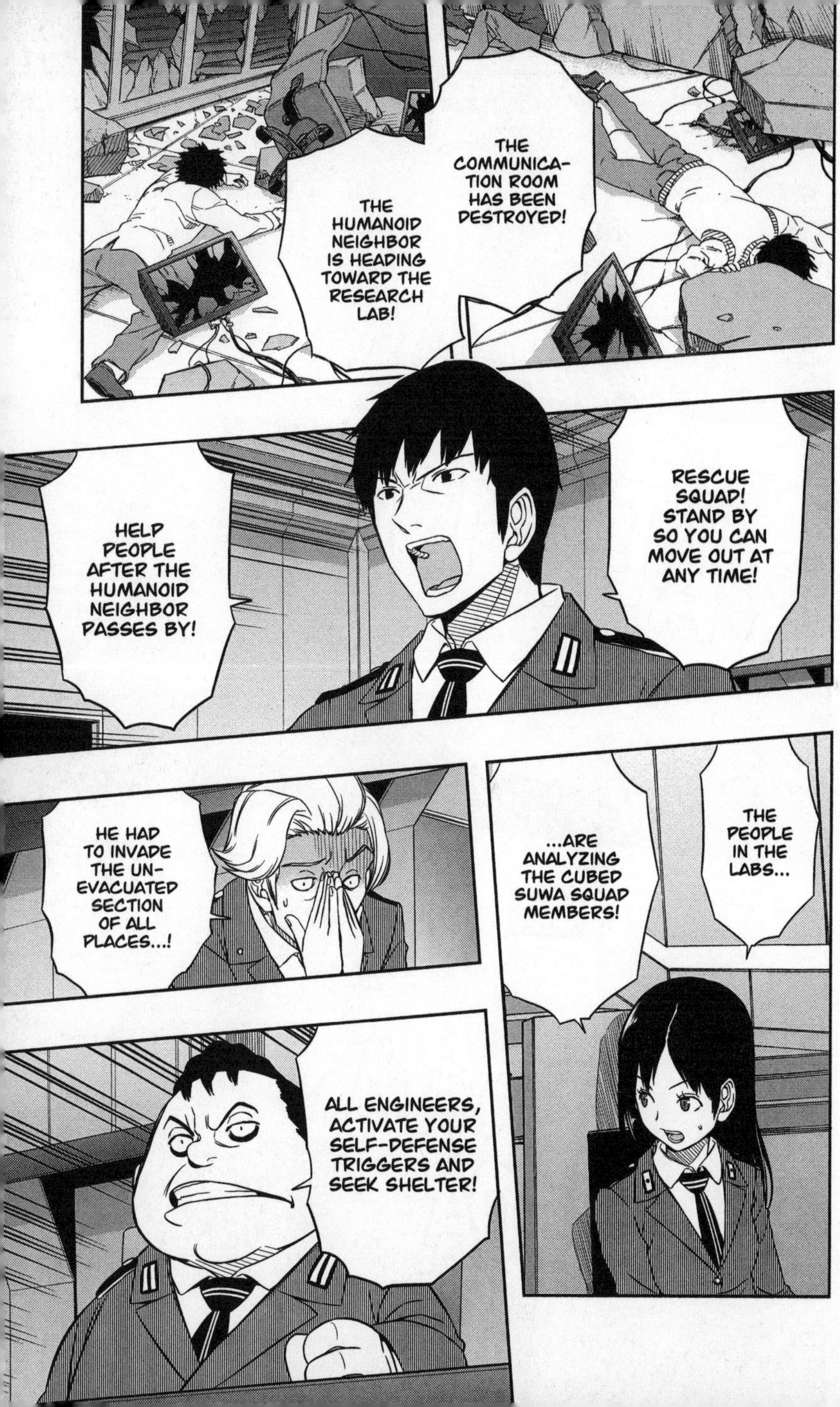
THE COMMUNICA-TION ROOM HAS BEEN DESTROYED!
THE HUMANOID NEIGHBOR IS HEADING TOWARD THE RESEARCH LAB!
RESCUE SQUAD! STAND BY SO YOU CAN MOVE OUT AT ANY TIME!
HELP PEOPLE AFTER THE HUMANOID NEIGHBOR PASSES BY!
THE PEOPLE IN THE LABS...
...ARE ANALYZING THE CUBED SUWA SQUAD MEMBERS!
HE HAD TO INVADE THE UN-EVACUATED SECTION OF ALL PLACES...!
ALL ENGINEERS, ACTIVATE YOUR SELF-DEFENSE TRIGGERS AND SEEK SHELTER!

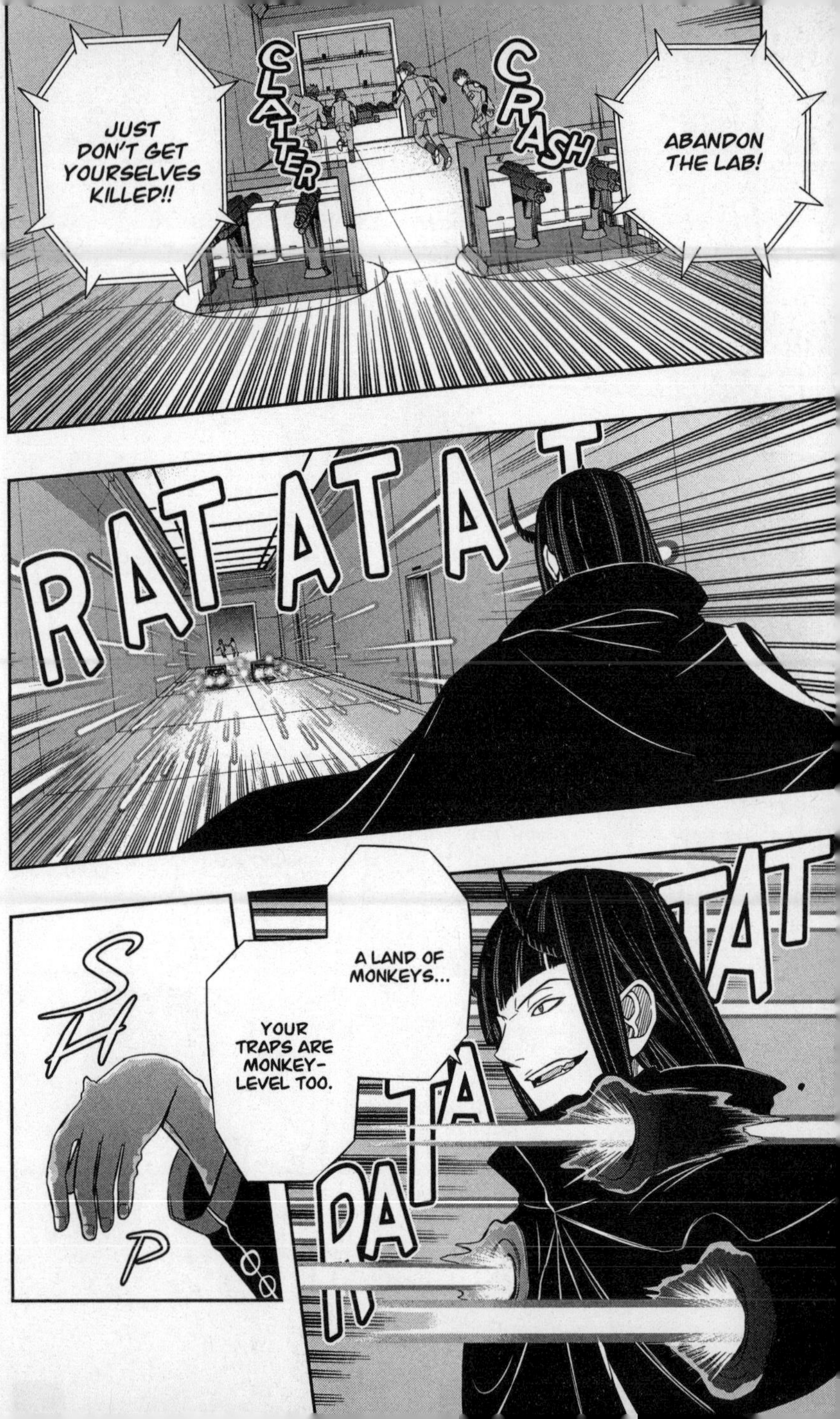
ABANDON THE LAB!
CRASH
CLATTER
JUST DON'T GET YOURSELVES KILLED!!
RAT AT AT
TAT
A LAND OF MONKEYS...
YOUR TRAPS ARE MONKEY-LEVEL TOO.
TA
DA
SHP

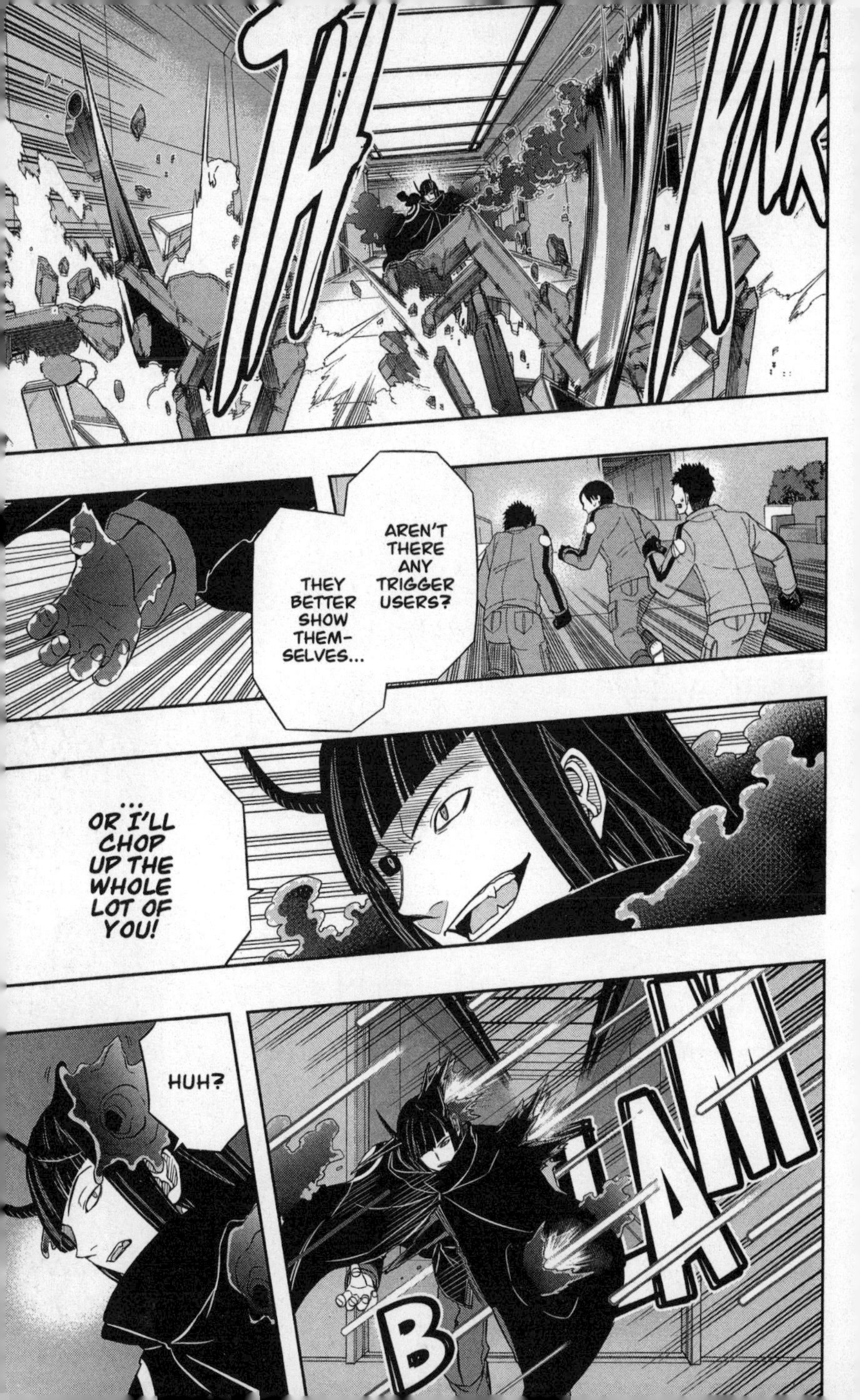
AREN'T THERE ANY TRIGGER USERS?
THEY BETTER SHOW THEM-SELVES...
...OR I'LL CHOP UP THE WHOLE LOT OF YOU!
HUH?

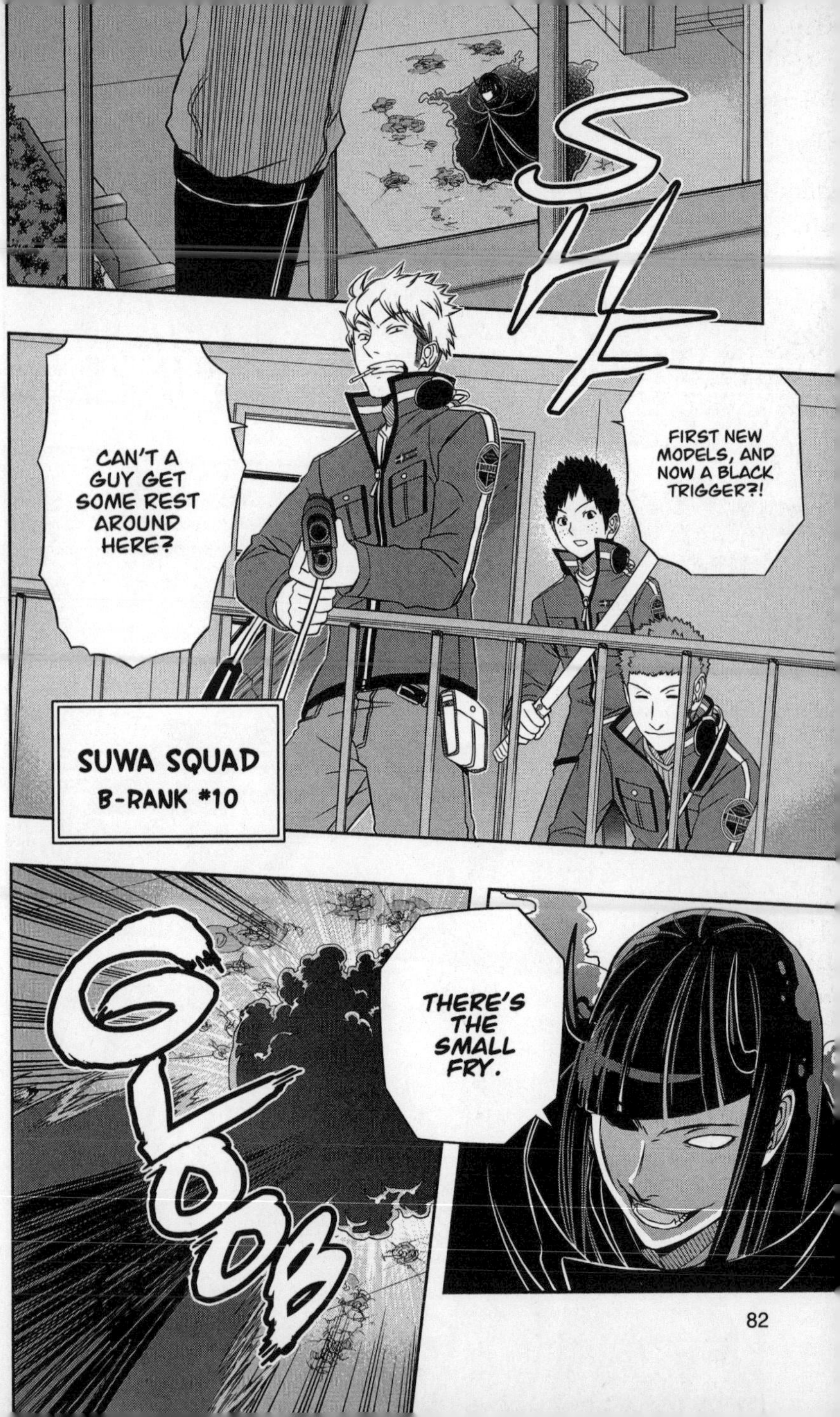
SHF
FIRST NEW MODELS, AND NOW A BLACK TRIGGER?!
CAN'T A GUY GET SOME REST AROUND HERE?
SUWA SQUAD
B-RANK #10
THERE'S THE SMALL FRY.
GLOOB

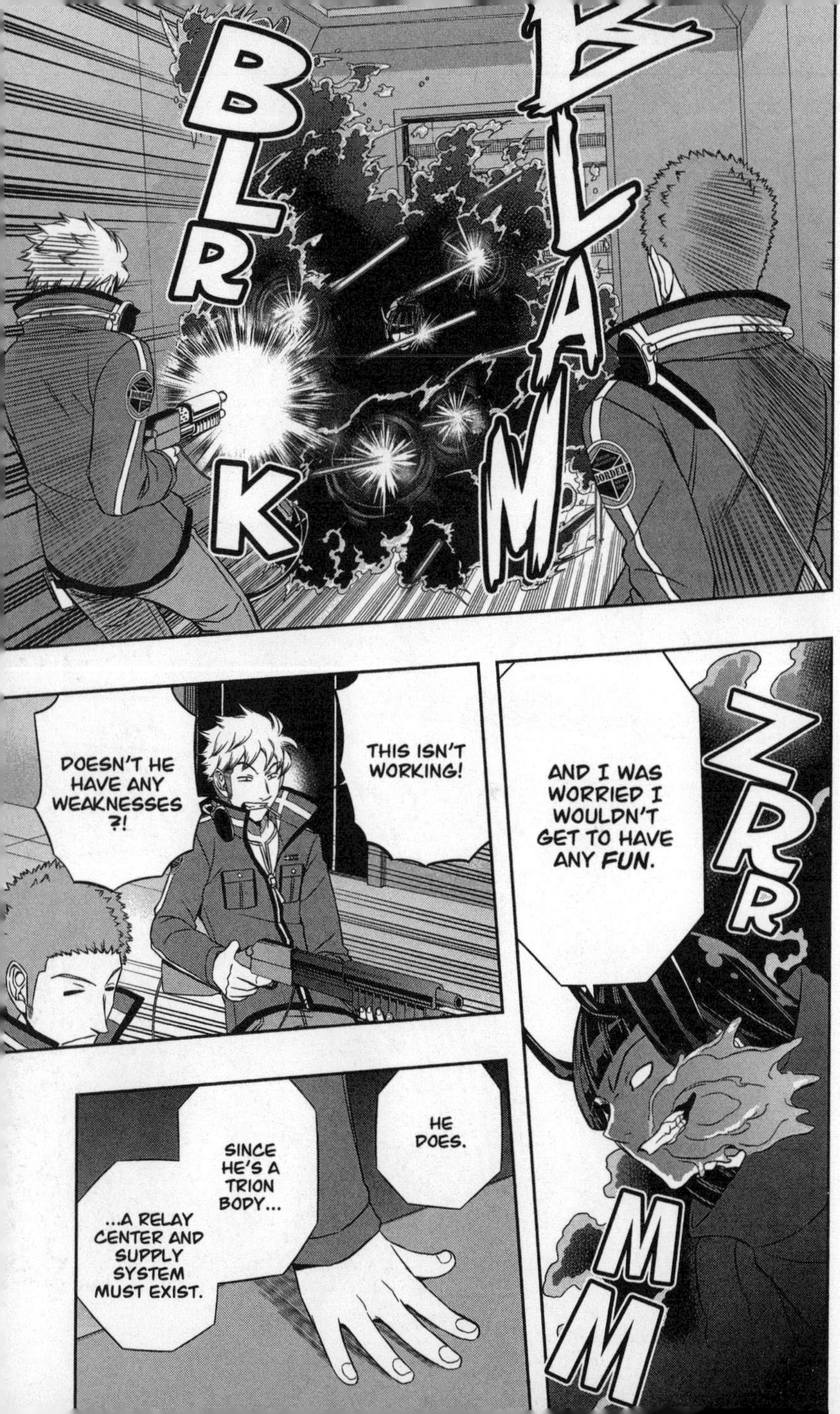
BLAM
BLRK
ZRR
AND I WAS WORRIED I WOULDN'T GET TO HAVE ANY FUN.
MM
THIS ISN'T WORKING!
DOESN'T HE HAVE ANY WEAKNESSES?!
HE DOES.
SINCE HE'S A TRION BODY...
...A RELAY CENTER AND SUPPLY SYSTEM MUST EXIST.

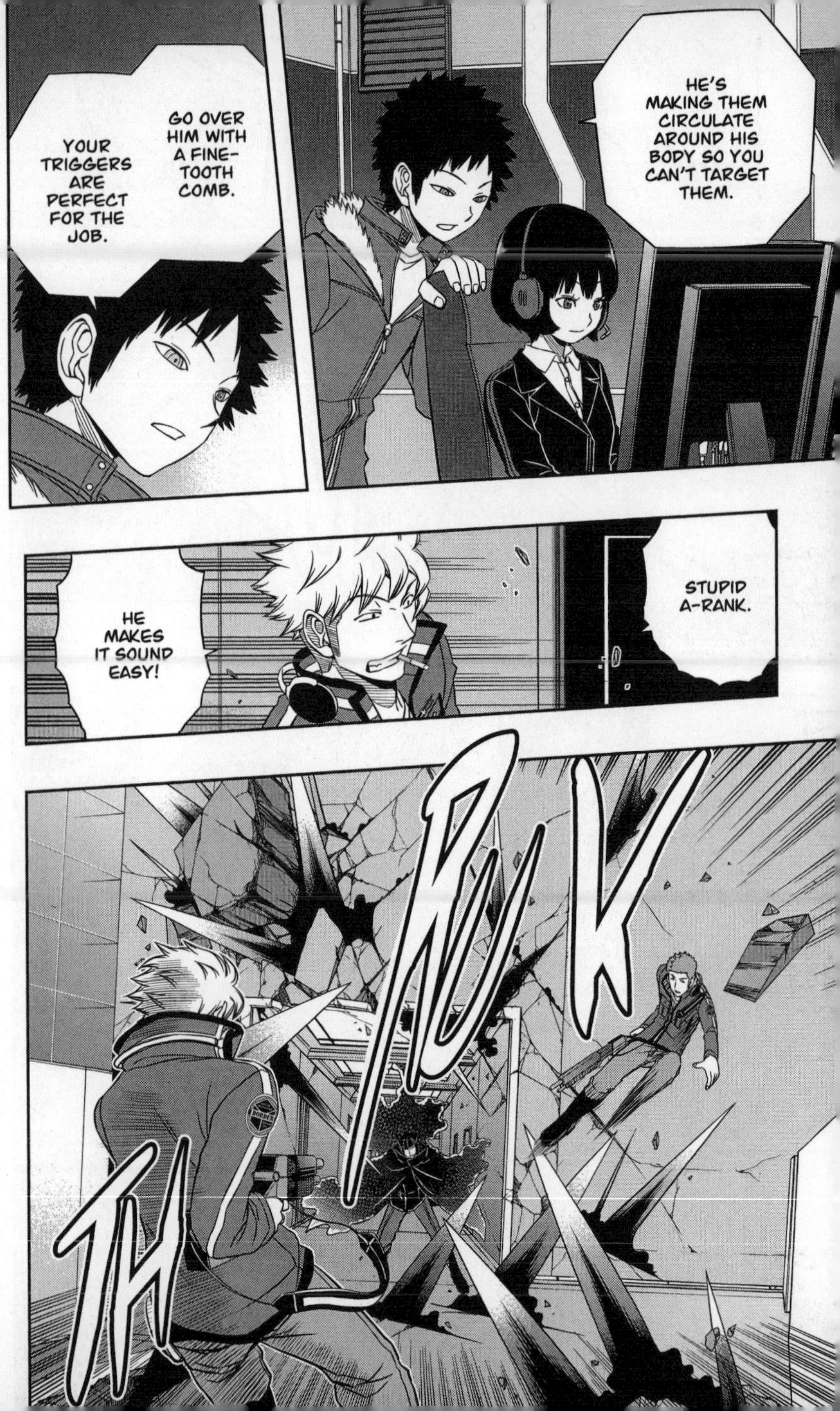
HE'S MAKING THEM CIRCULATE AROUND HIS BODY SO YOU CAN'T TARGET THEM.
GO OVER HIM WITH A FINE-TOOTH COMB.
YOUR TRIGGERS ARE PERFECT FOR THE JOB.
STUPID A-RANK.
HE MAKES IT SOUND EASY!

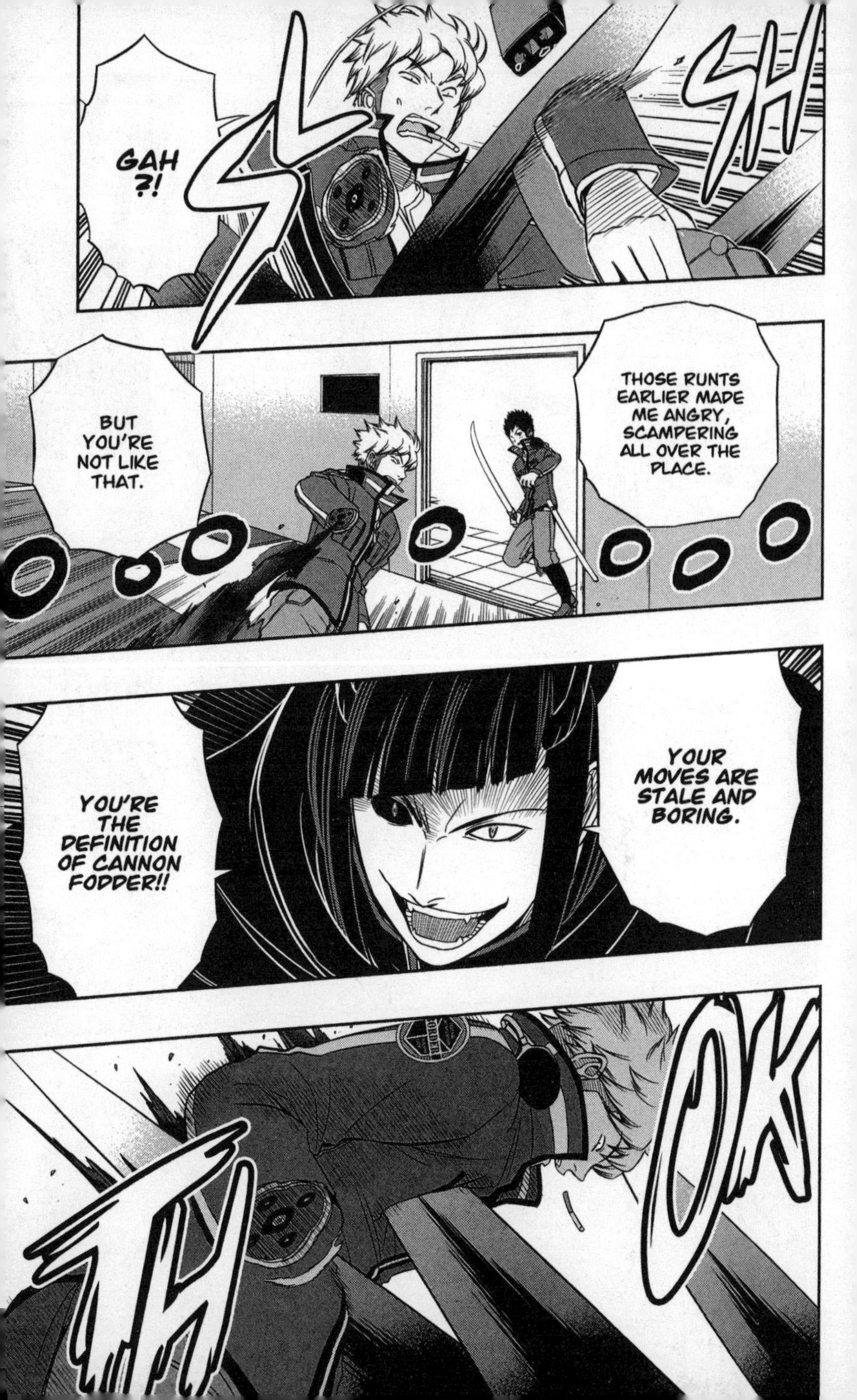
SH
GAH ?!
SL
THOSE RUNTS EARLIER MADE ME ANGRY, SCAMPERING ALL OVER THE PLACE.
BUT YOU'RE NOT LIKE THAT.
YOUR MOVES ARE STALE AND BORING.
YOU'RE THE DEFINITION OF CANNON FODDER!!
OK
TH

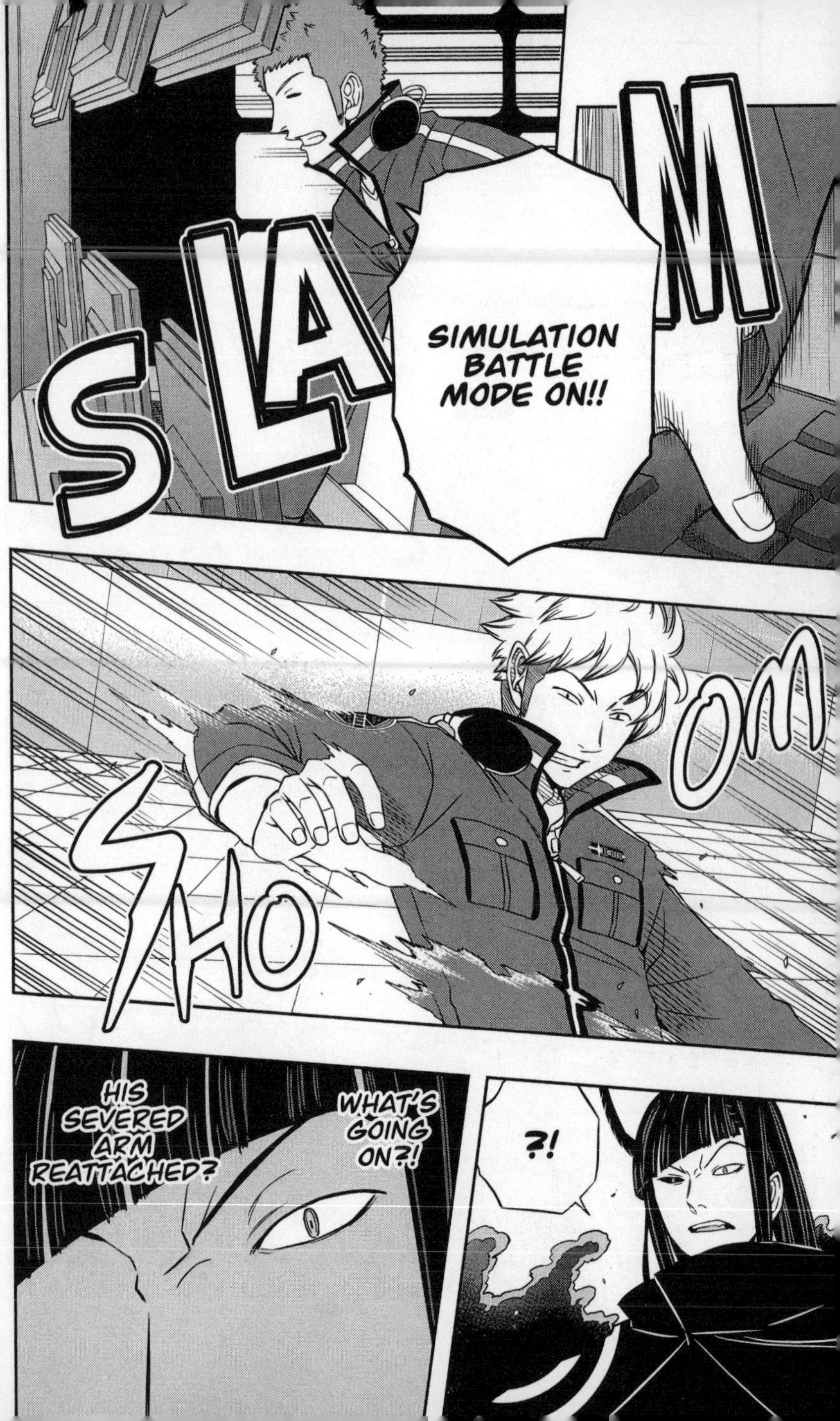
SLAM
SIMULATION BATTLE MODE ON!!
SHOOM
?!
WHAT'S GOING ON?!
HIS SEVERED ARM REATTACHED?

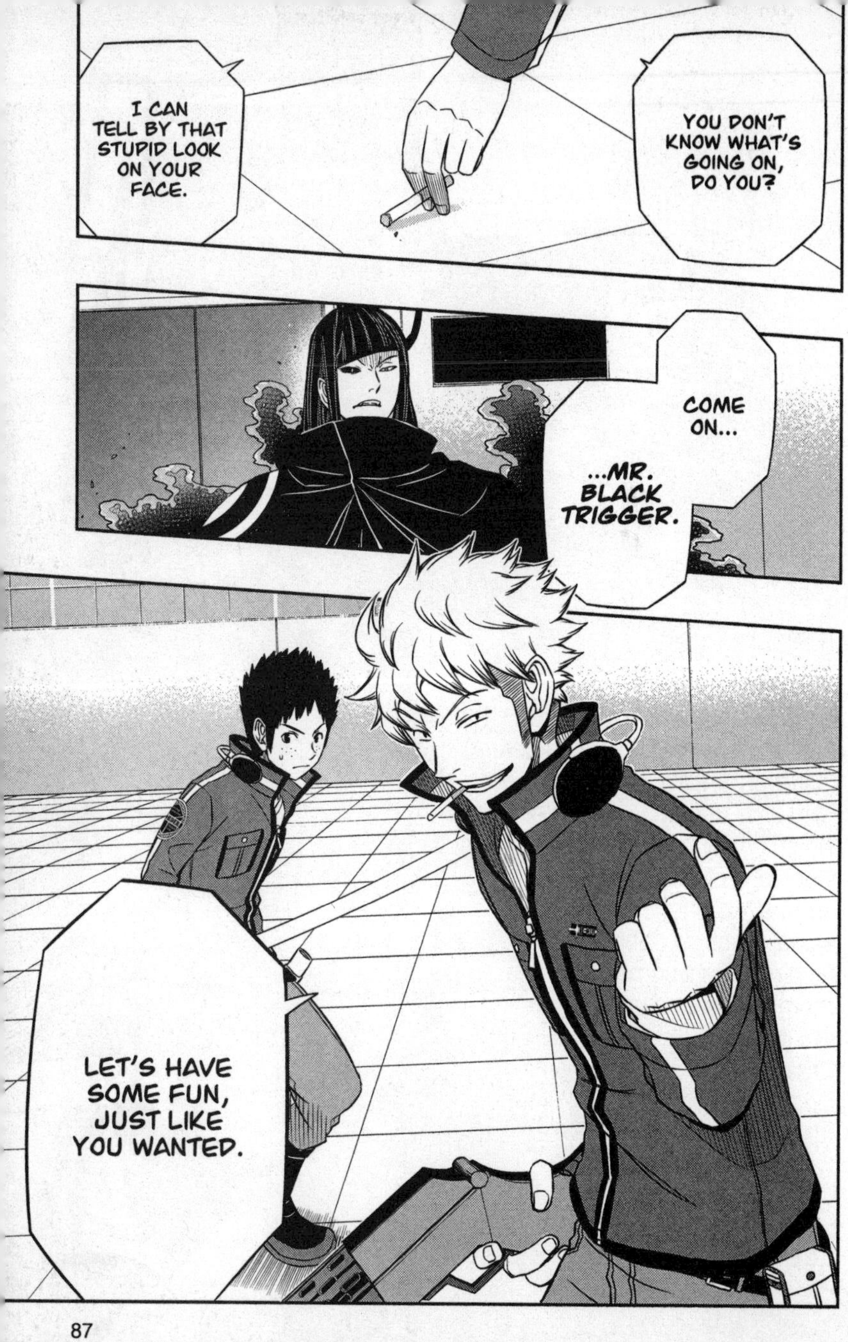
YOU DON'T KNOW WHAT'S GOING ON, DO YOU?
I CAN TELL BY THAT STUPID LOOK ON YOUR FACE.
COME ON...
...MR. BLACK TRIGGER.
LET'S HAVE SOME FUN, JUST LIKE YOU WANTED.

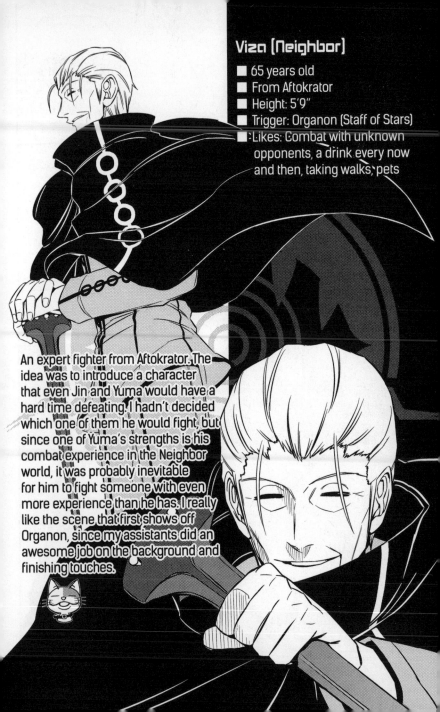

Viza (Neighbor)

- 65 years old
- From Aftokrator
- Height: 5'9"
- Trigger: Organon (Staff of Stars)
- Likes: Combat with unknown opponents, a drink every now and then, taking walks, pets

An expert fighter from Aftokrator. The idea was to introduce a character that even Jin and Yuma would have a hard time defeating. I hadn't decided which one of them he would fight, but since one of Yuma's strengths is his combat experience in the Neighbor world, it was probably inevitable for him to fight someone with even more experience than he has. I really like the scene that first shows off Organon, since my assistants did an awesome job on the background and finishing touches.

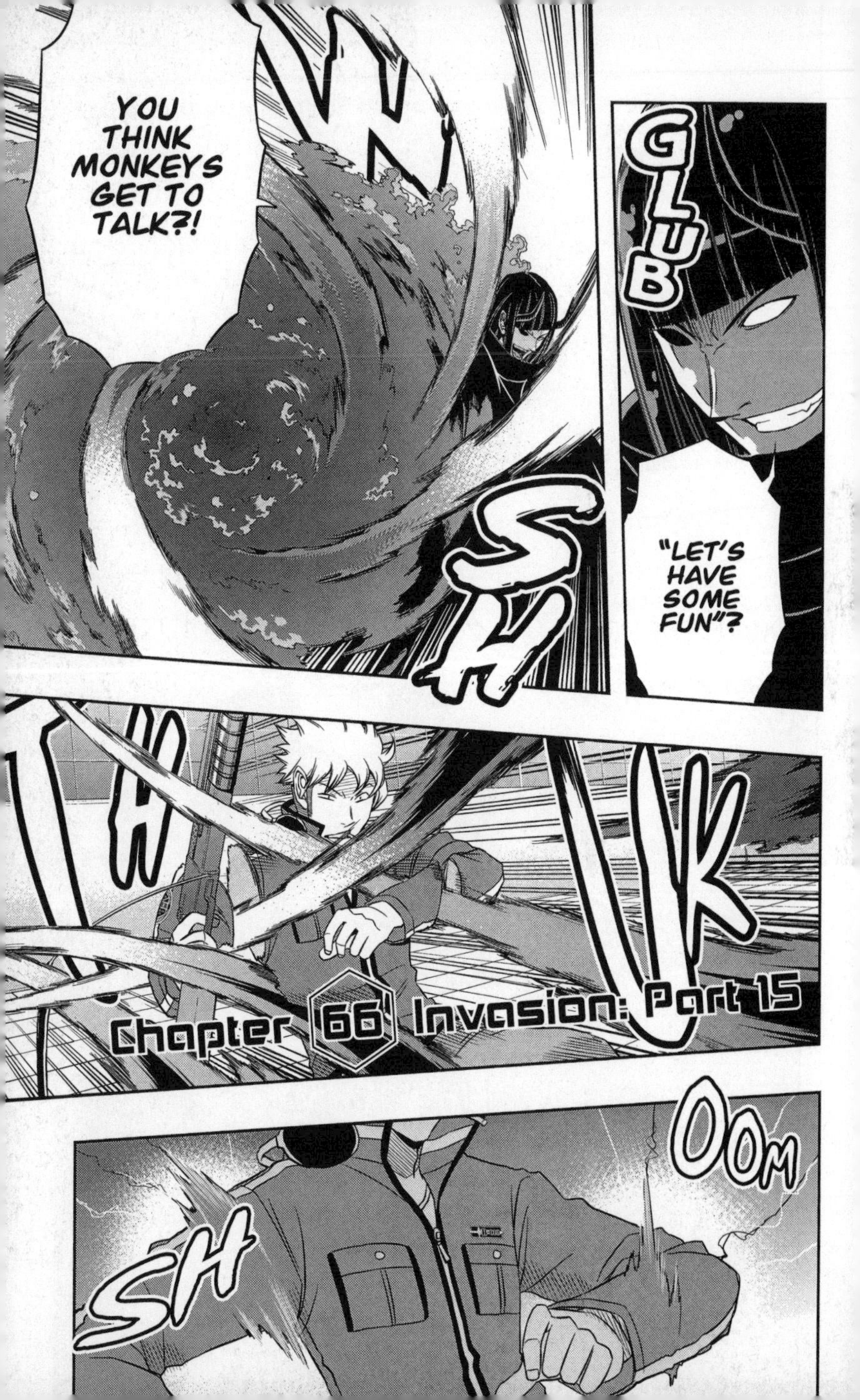

GLUB
"LET'S HAVE SOME FUN"?
YOU THINK MONKEYS GET TO TALK?!
SH
Chapter 66 Invasion: Part 15
OOM
SH

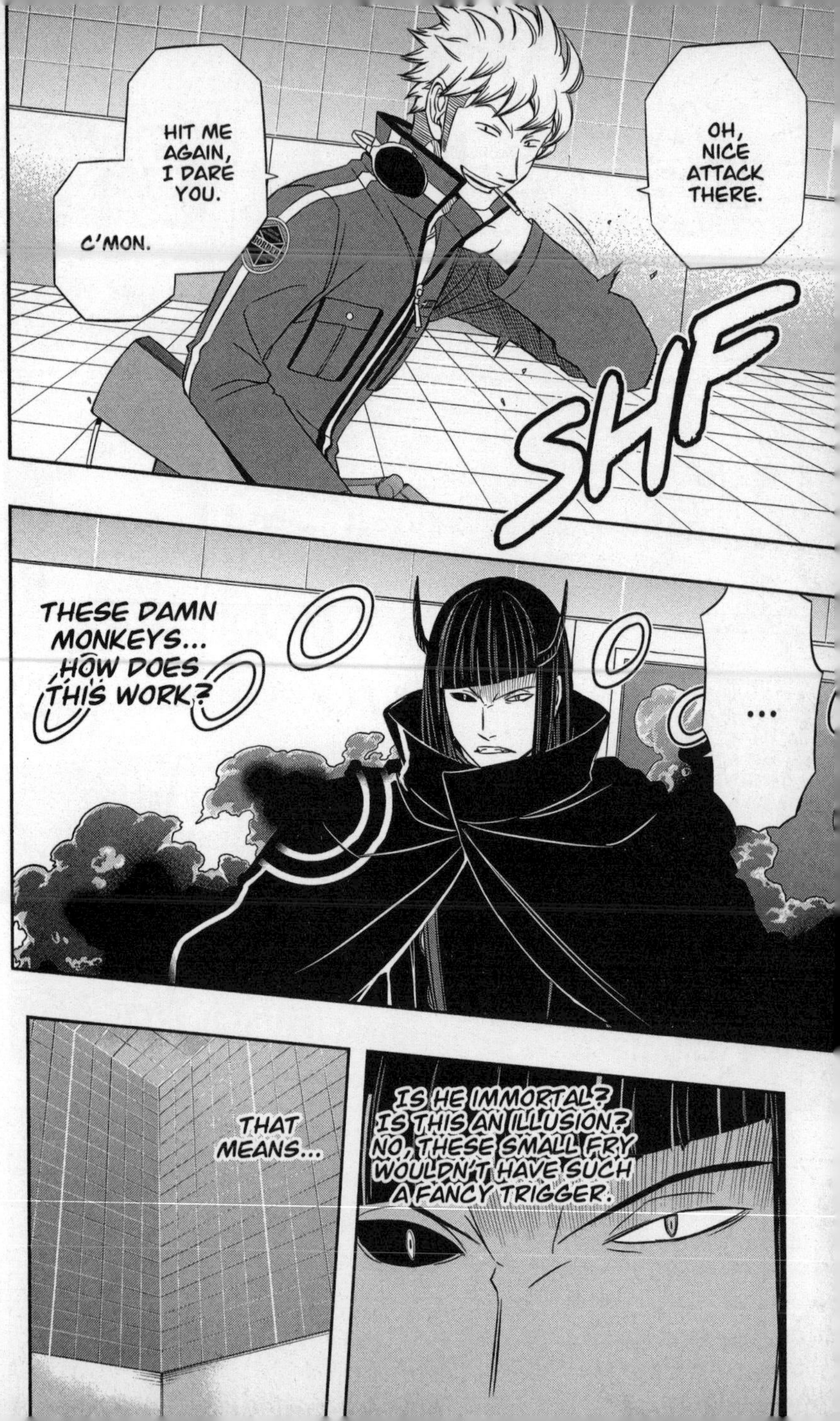
OH, NICE ATTACK THERE.
HIT ME AGAIN, I DARE YOU.
C'MON.
SHF
...
THESE DAMN MONKEYS... HOW DOES THIS WORK?
IS HE IMMORTAL? IS THIS AN ILLUSION? NO, THESE SMALL FRY WOULDN'T HAVE SUCH A FANCY TRIGGER.
THAT MEANS...

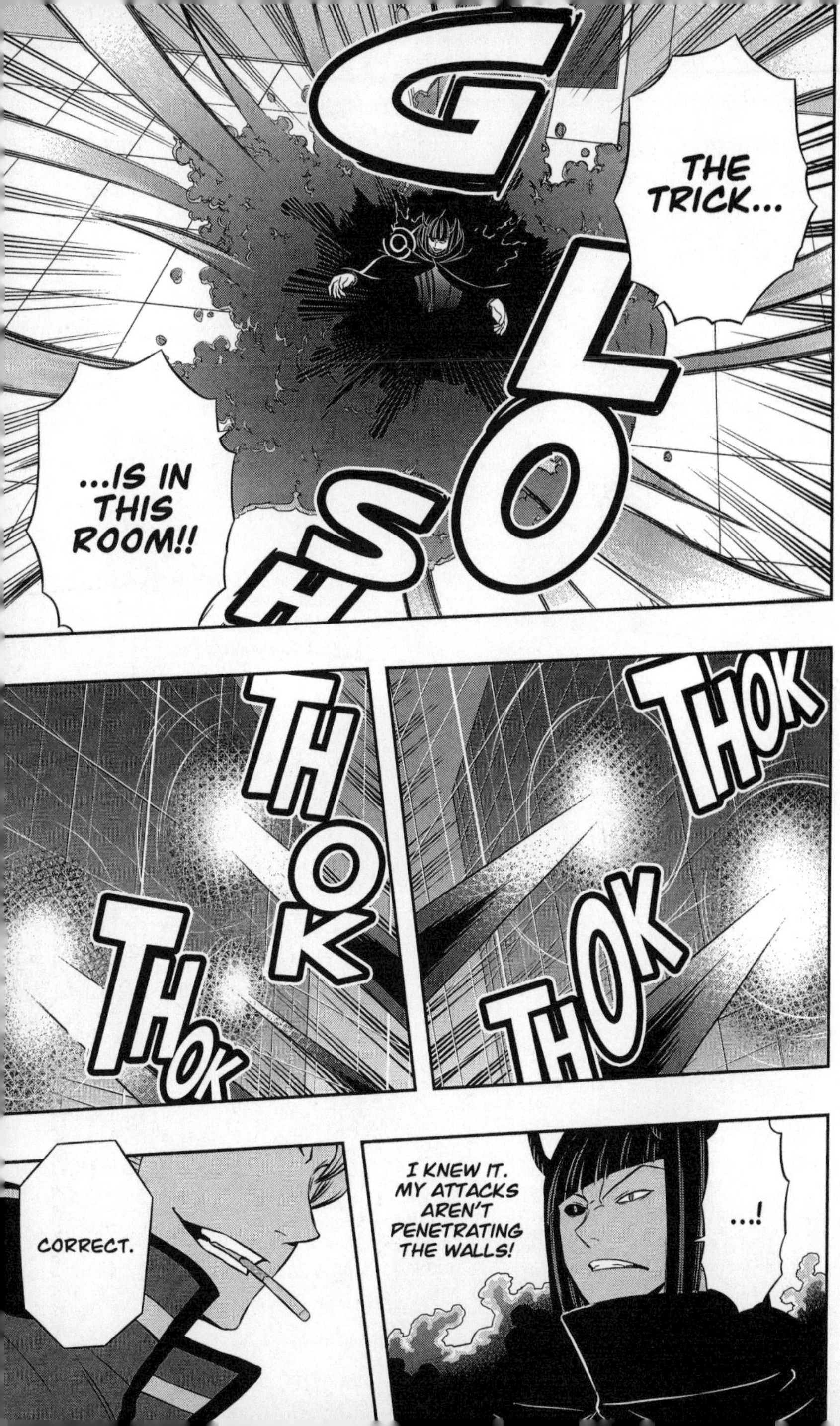
THE TRICK...
GLOSH
...IS IN THIS ROOM!!
THOK
THOK
THOK
THOK
...!
I KNEW IT. MY ATTACKS AREN'T PENETRATING THE WALLS!
CORRECT.

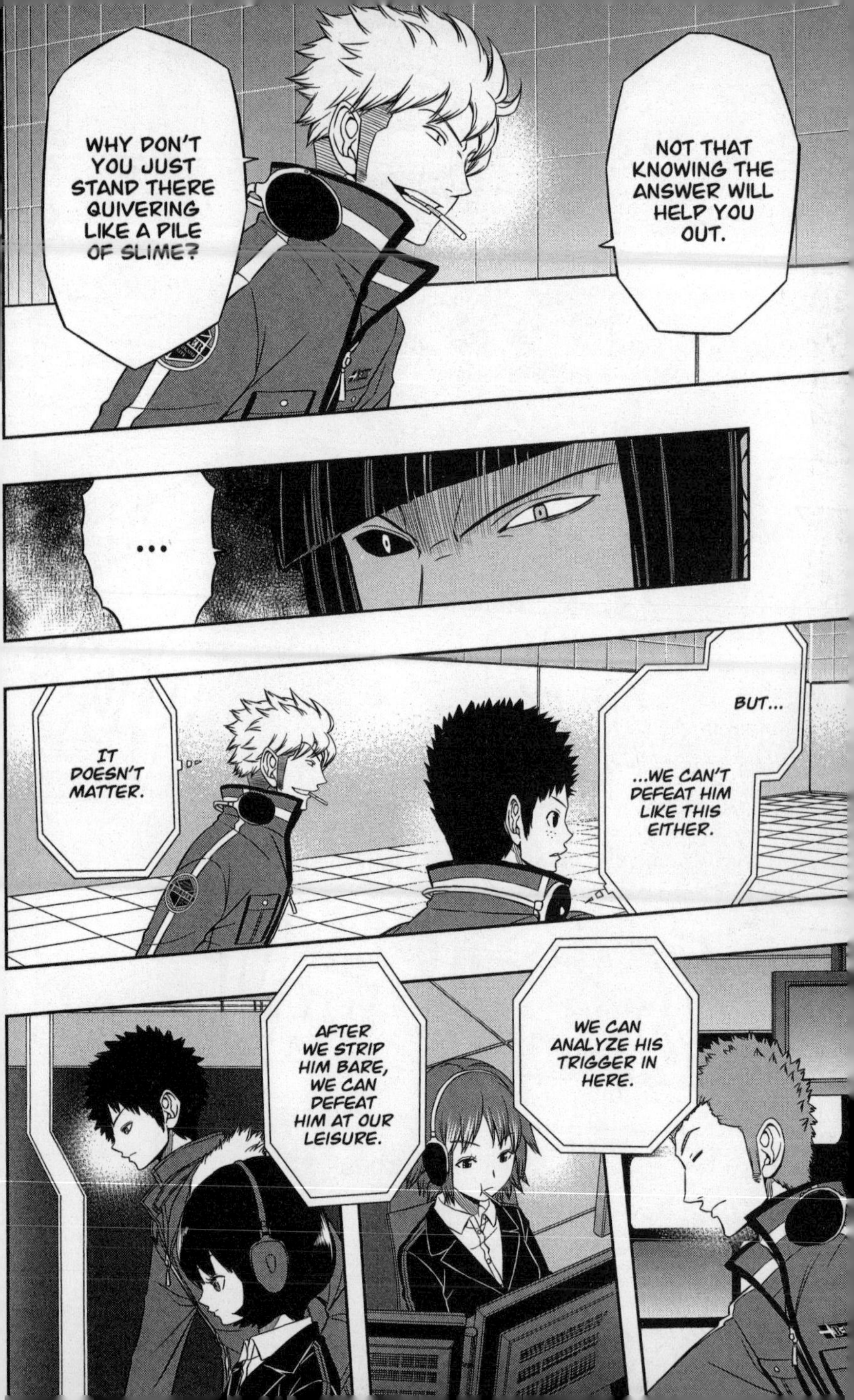
NOT THAT KNOWING THE ANSWER WILL HELP YOU OUT.
WHY DON'T YOU JUST STAND THERE QUIVERING LIKE A PILE OF SLIME?
...
BUT...
...WE CAN'T DEFEAT HIM LIKE THIS EITHER.
IT DOESN'T MATTER.
WE CAN ANALYZE HIS TRIGGER IN HERE.
AFTER WE STRIP HIM BARE, WE CAN DEFEAT HIM AT OUR LEISURE.

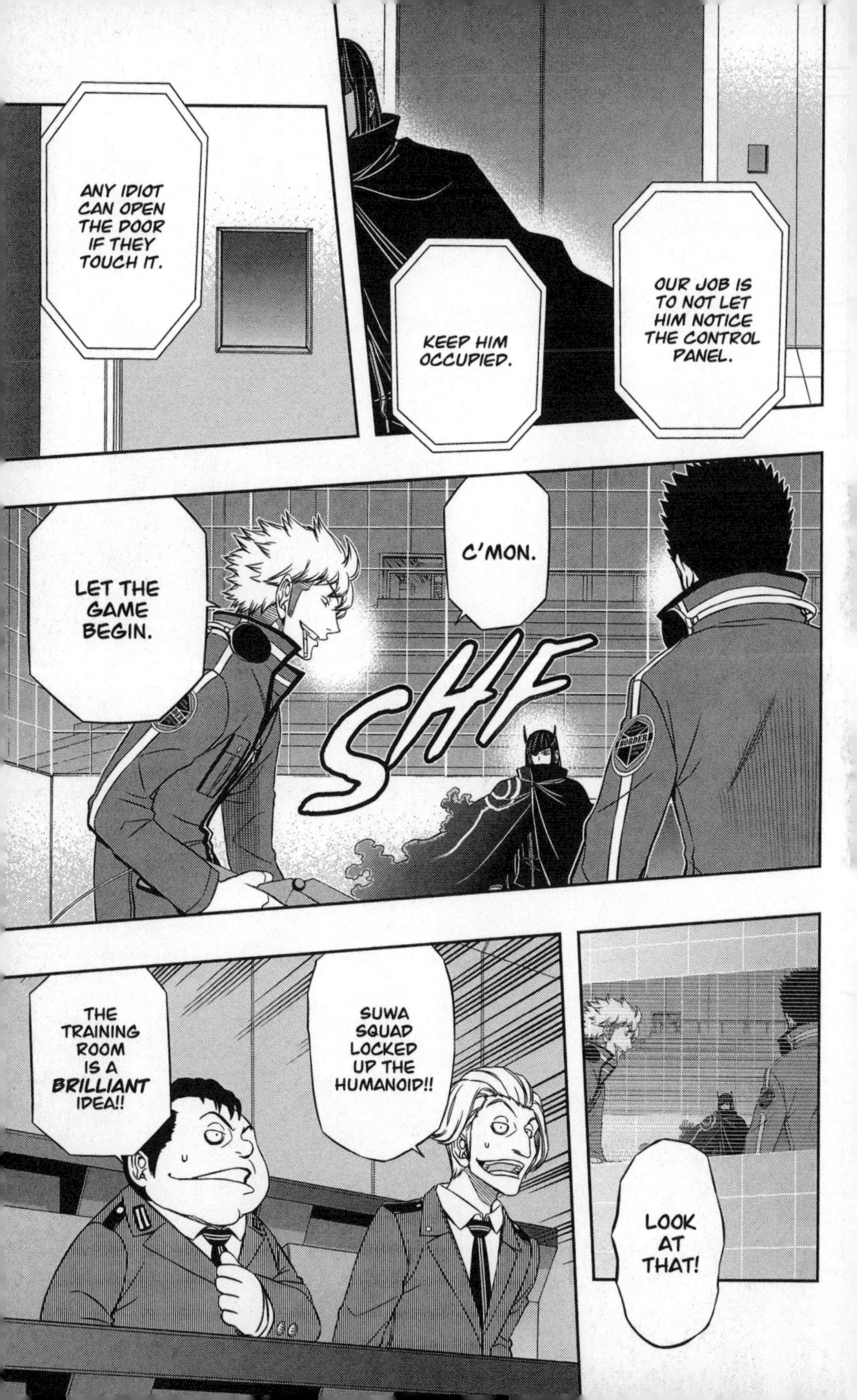
OUR JOB IS TO NOT LET HIM NOTICE THE CONTROL PANEL.
KEEP HIM OCCUPIED.
ANY IDIOT CAN OPEN THE DOOR IF THEY TOUCH IT.
C'MON.
SHF
LET THE GAME BEGIN.
BORDER
LOOK AT THAT!
SUWA SQUAD LOCKED UP THE HUMANOID!!
THE TRAINING ROOM IS A BRILLIANT IDEA!!

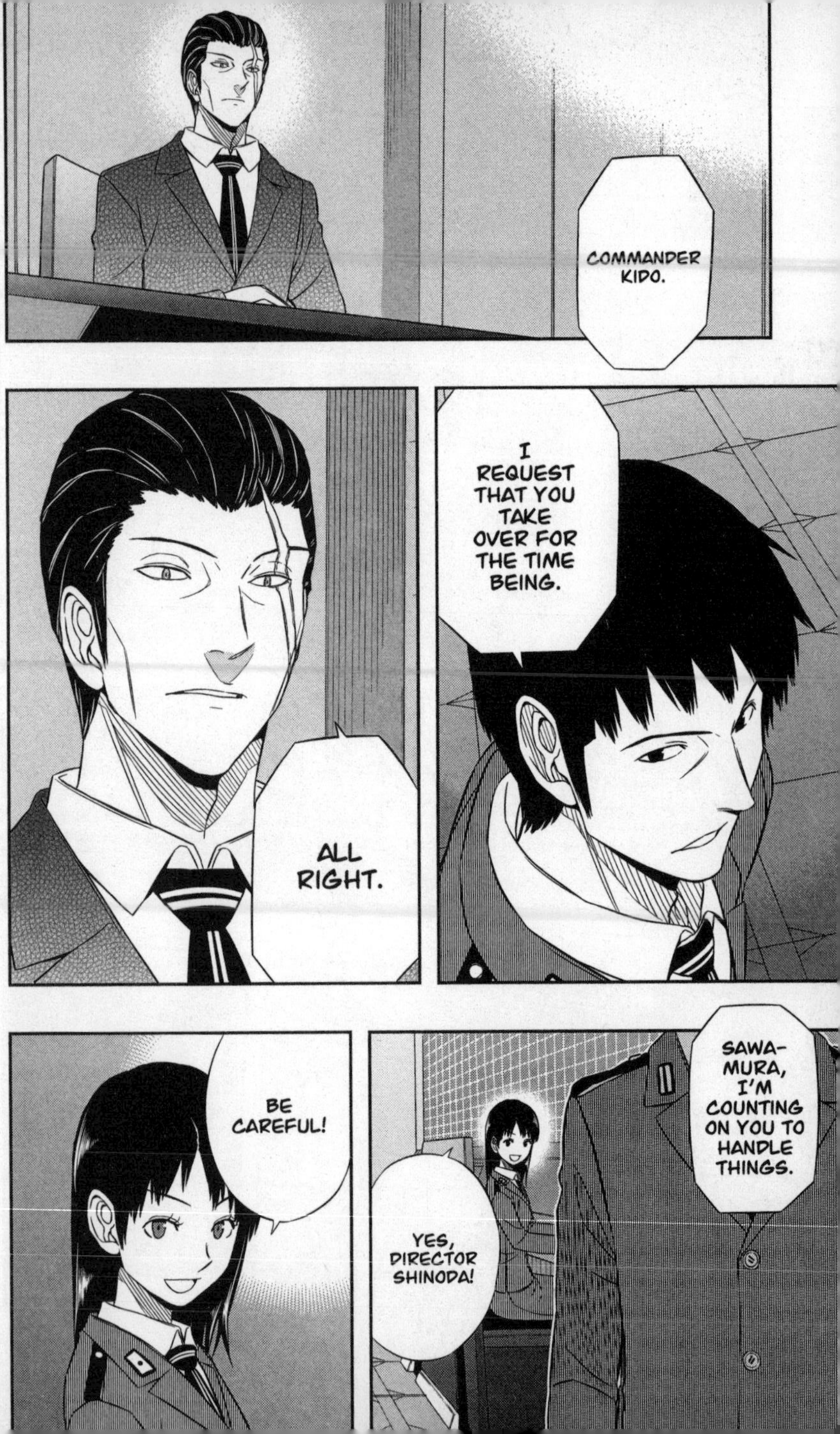
COMMANDER KIDO.
I REQUEST THAT YOU TAKE OVER FOR THE TIME BEING.
ALL RIGHT.
SAWAMURA, I'M COUNTING ON YOU TO HANDLE THINGS.
YES, DIRECTOR SHINODA!
BE CAREFUL!

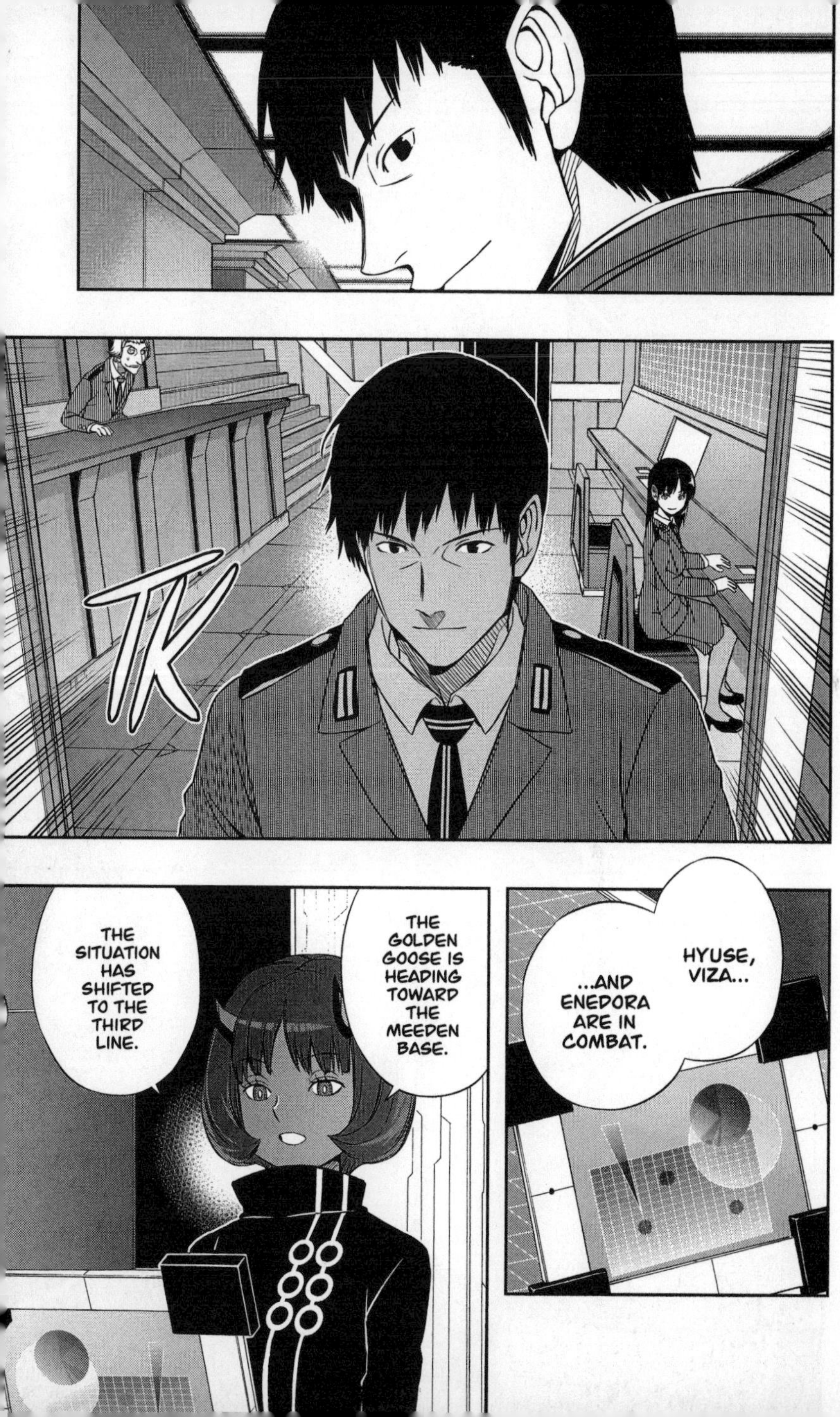
TK
HYUSE, VIZA... ...AND ENEDORA ARE IN COMBAT.
THE GOLDEN GOOSE IS HEADING TOWARD THE MEEDEN BASE.
THE SITUATION HAS SHIFTED TO THE THIRD LINE.

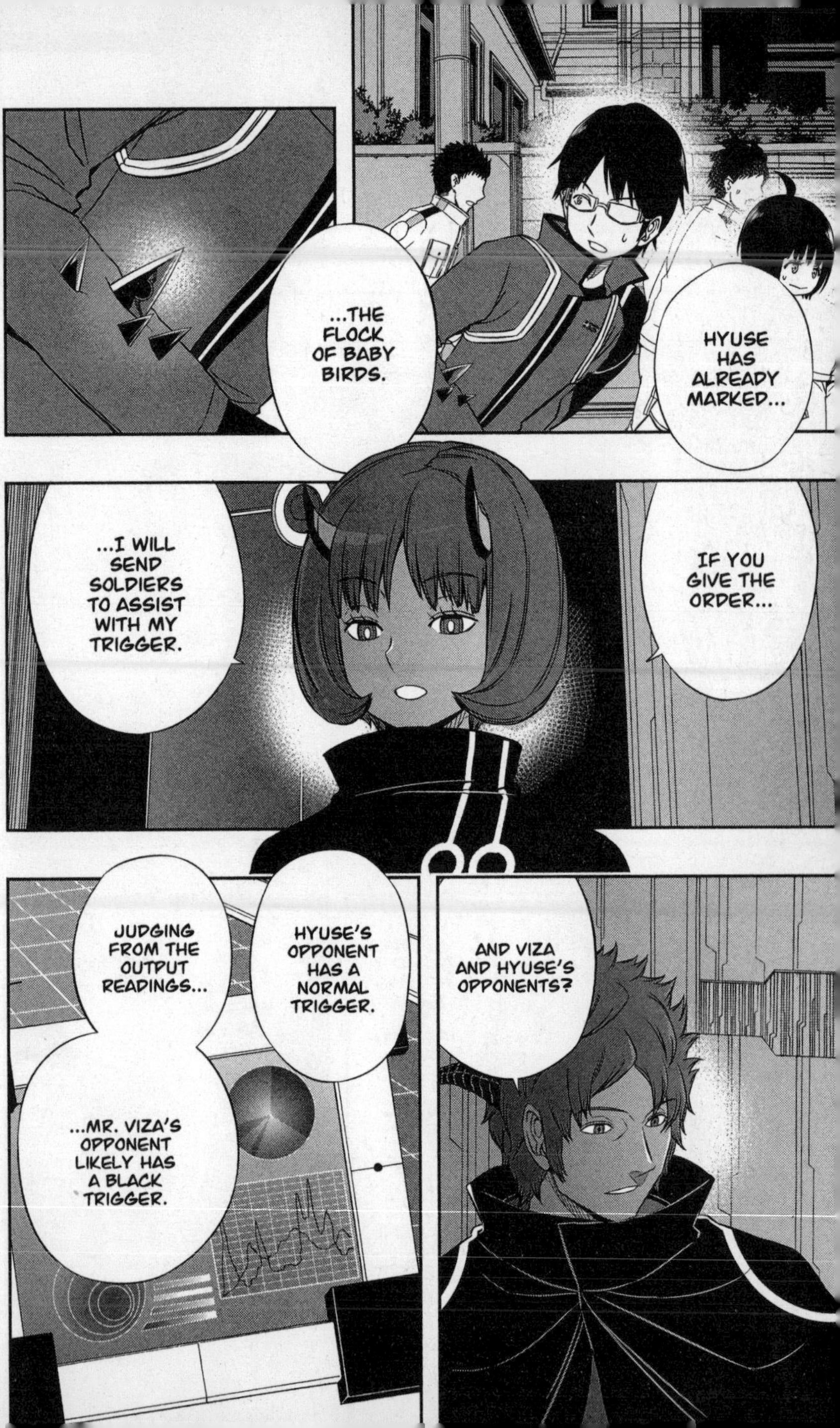
HYUSE HAS ALREADY MARKED...
...THE FLOCK OF BABY BIRDS.
IF YOU GIVE THE ORDER...
...I WILL SEND SOLDIERS TO ASSIST WITH MY TRIGGER.
AND VIZA AND HYUSE'S OPPONENTS?
HYUSE'S OPPONENT HAS A NORMAL TRIGGER.
JUDGING FROM THE OUTPUT READINGS...
...MR. VIZA'S OPPONENT LIKELY HAS A BLACK TRIGGER.

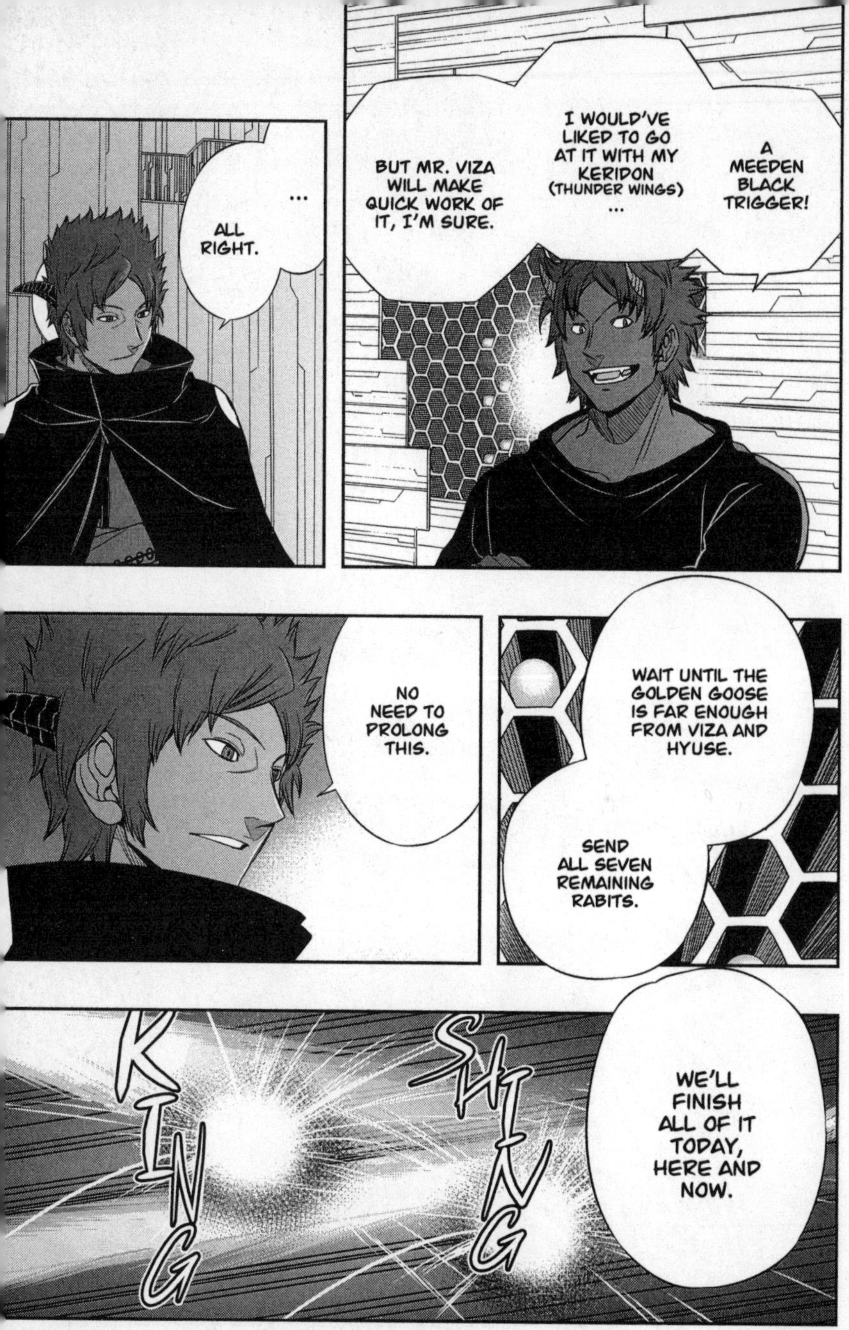
A MEEDEN BLACK TRIGGER!
I WOULD'VE LIKED TO GO AT IT WITH MY KERIDON (THUNDER WINGS) ...
BUT MR. VIZA WILL MAKE QUICK WORK OF IT, I'M SURE.
... ALL RIGHT.
WAIT UNTIL THE GOLDEN GOOSE IS FAR ENOUGH FROM VIZA AND HYUSE.
SEND ALL SEVEN REMAINING RABITS.
NO NEED TO PROLONG THIS.
WE'LL FINISH ALL OF IT TODAY, HERE AND NOW.
SHING
KING

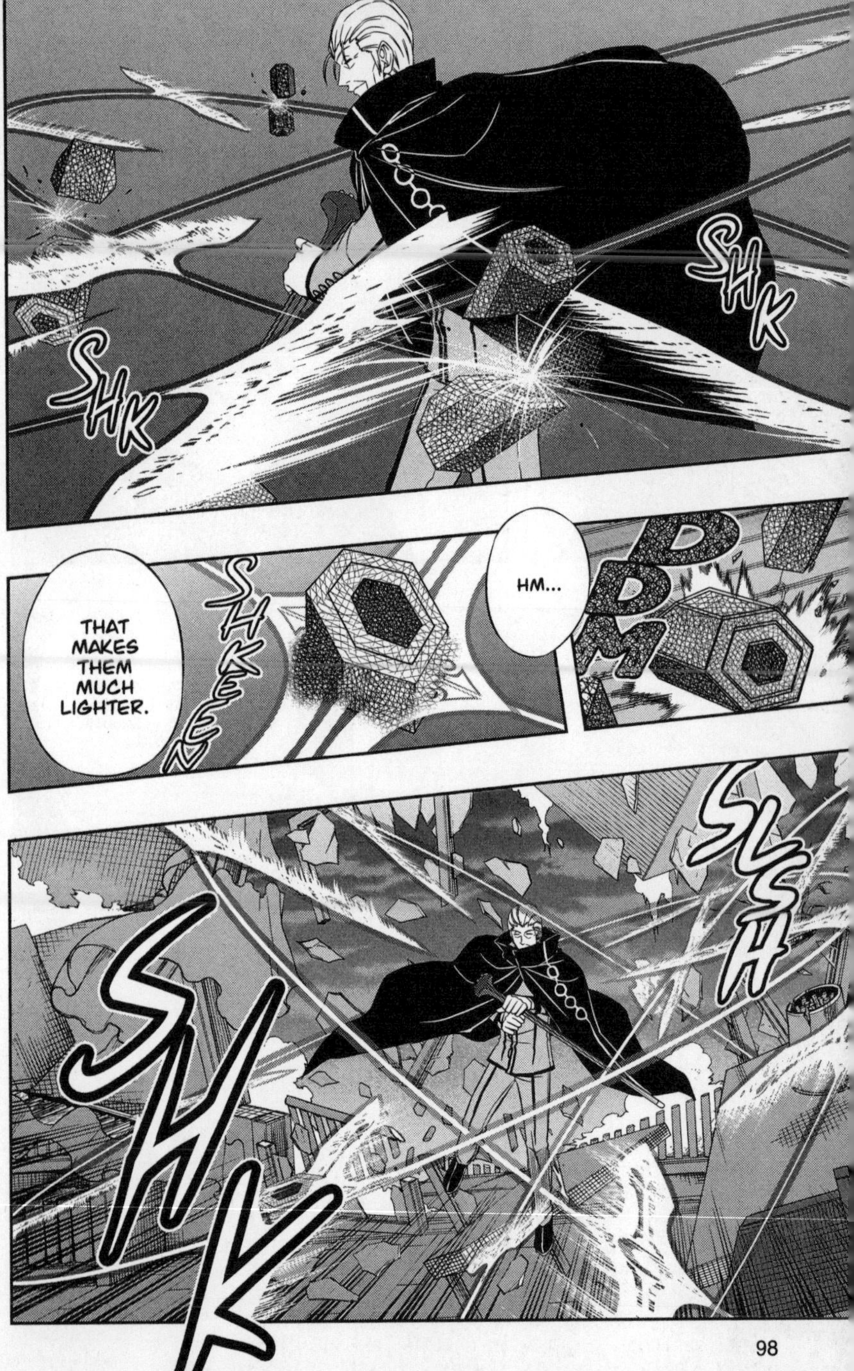
SHK
SHK
HM...
DDM
SHKEEN
THAT MAKES THEM MUCH LIGHTER.
SLSH
SHK

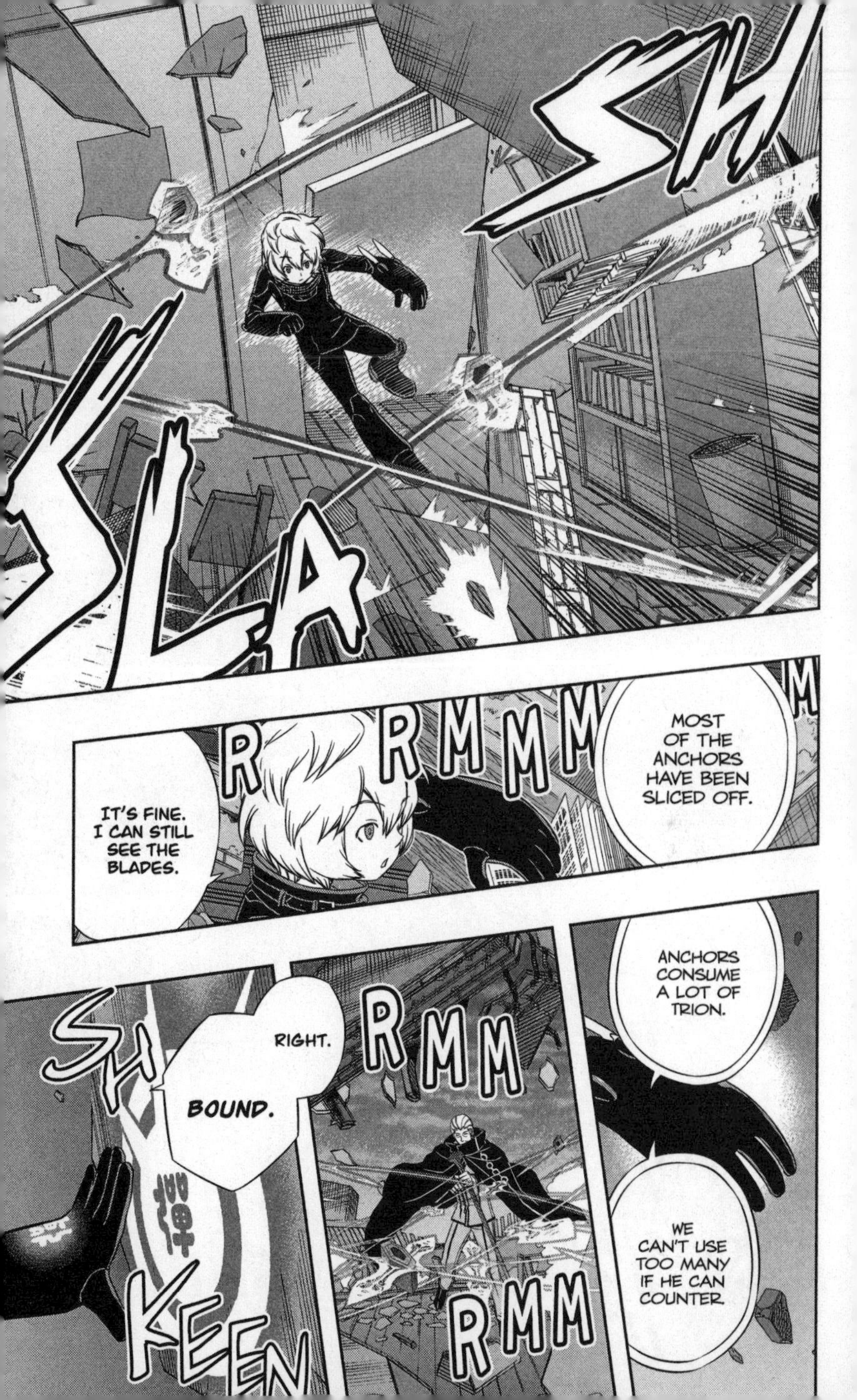
SH
SLA
RMMMMM
MOST OF THE ANCHORS HAVE BEEN SLICED OFF.
IT'S FINE. I CAN STILL SEE THE BLADES.
ANCHORS CONSUME A LOT OF TRION.
WE CAN'T USE TOO MANY IF HE CAN COUNTER
RMM
RMM
RIGHT.
BOUND.
SH
KEEN

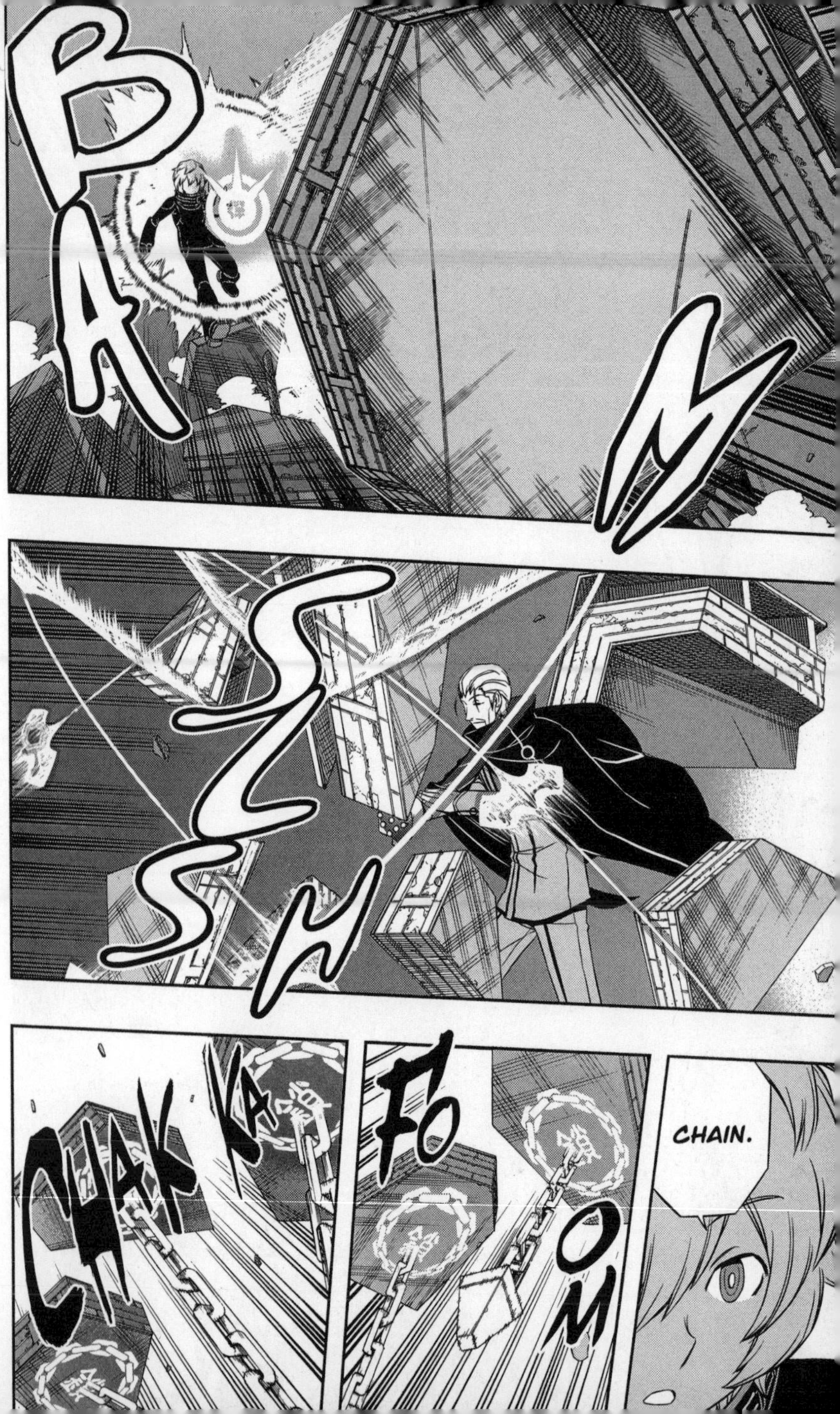
BAM
CHAIN.
FOOM
CHAK
KA

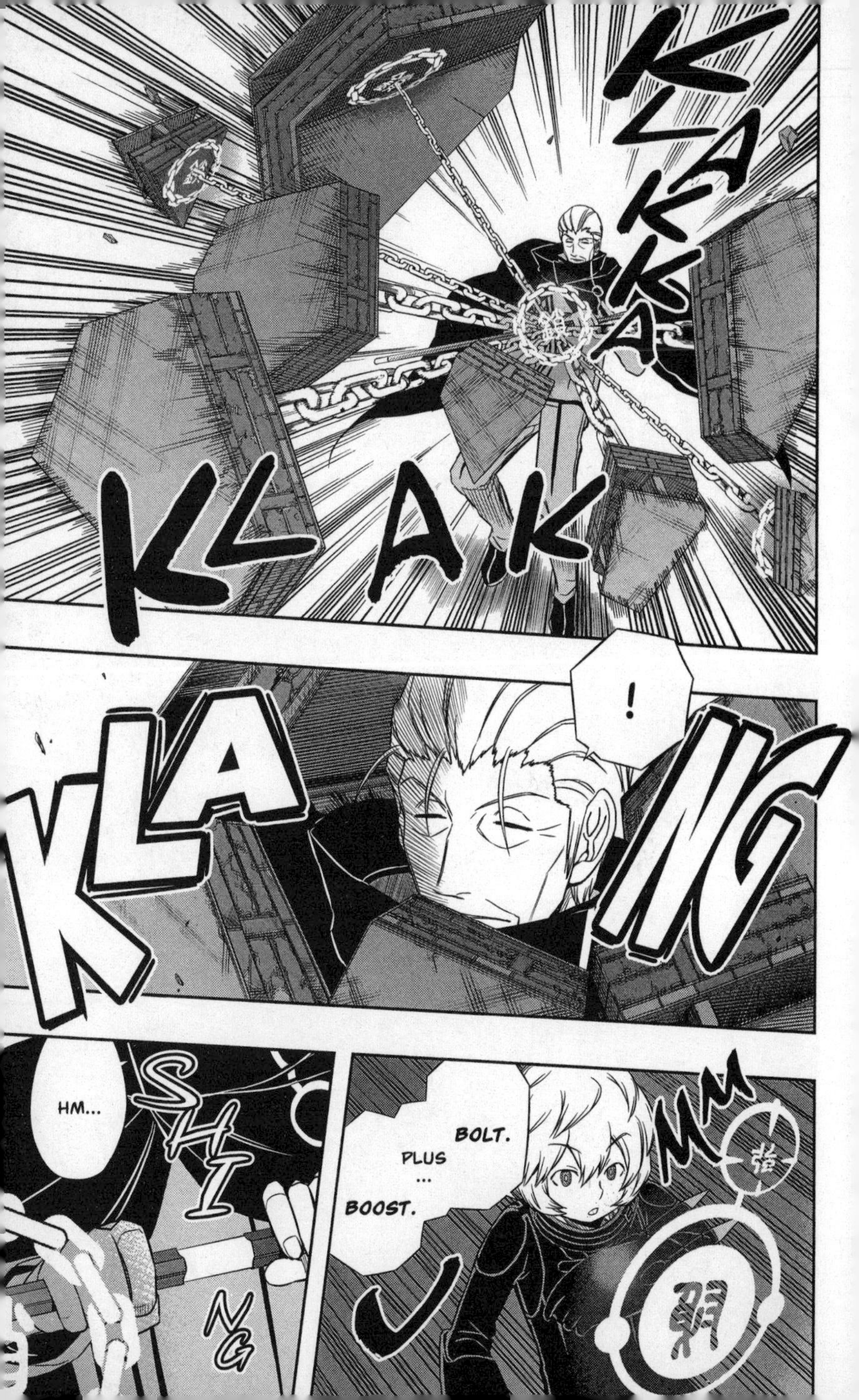
KAKAKA
KLAK
!
KLA
NG
BOLT.
PLUS...
BOOST.
MM
HM...
SHI
NG

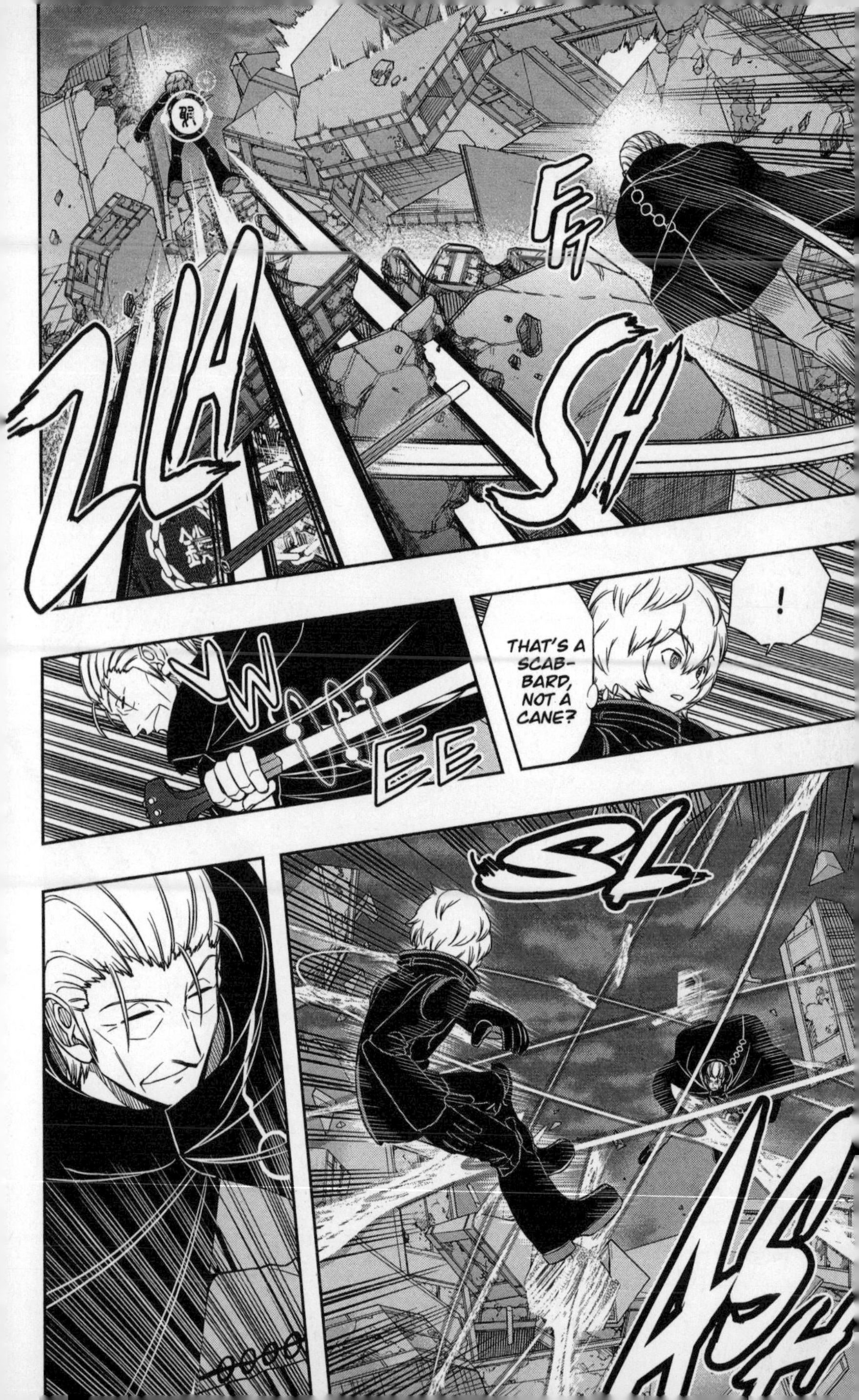
FFT
ZLASH
!
THAT'S A SCAB-BARD, NOT A CANE?
VWEE
SL

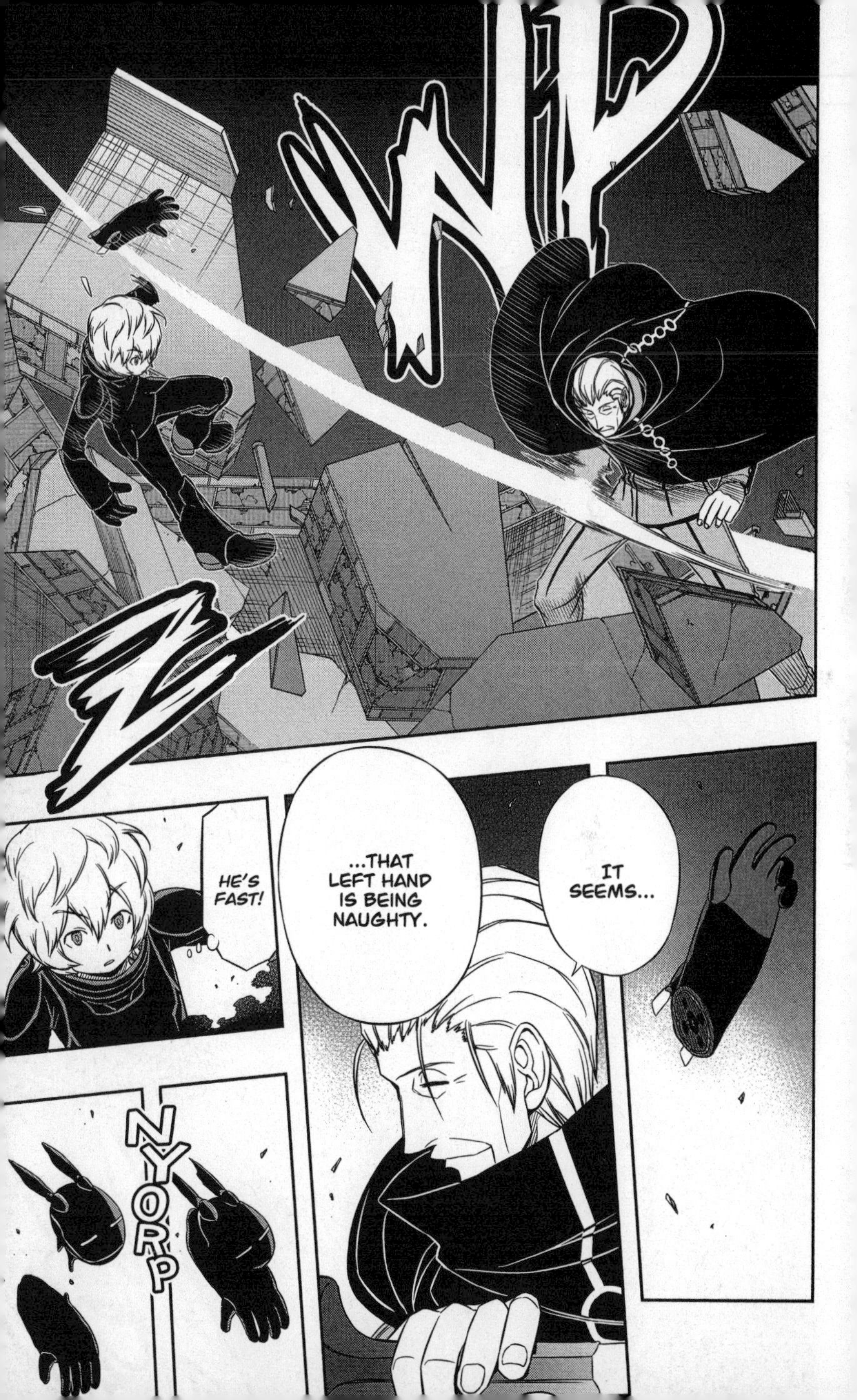
WHIP
IT SEEMS...
...THAT LEFT HAND IS BEING NAUGHTY.
HE'S FAST!
NYORP

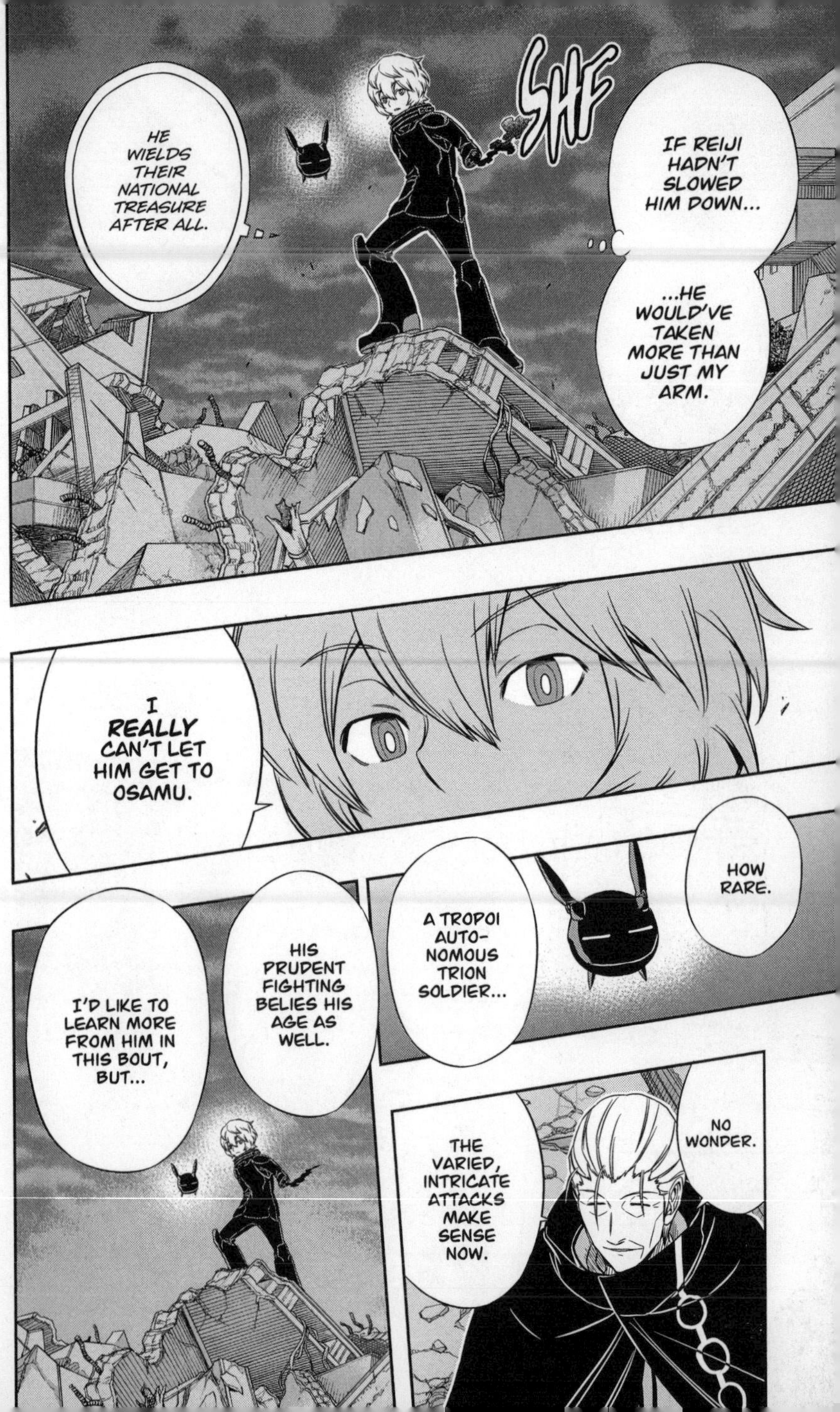
SHF
IF REIJI HADN'T SLOWED HIM DOWN...
...HE WOULD'VE TAKEN MORE THAN JUST MY ARM.
HE WIELDS THEIR NATIONAL TREASURE AFTER ALL.
I **REALLY** CAN'T LET HIM GET TO OSAMU.
HOW RARE.
A TROPOI AUTO-NOMOUS TRION SOLDIER...
NO WONDER.
THE VARIED, INTRICATE ATTACKS MAKE SENSE NOW.
HIS PRUDENT FIGHTING BELIES HIS AGE AS WELL.
I'D LIKE TO LEARN MORE FROM HIM IN THIS BOUT, BUT...

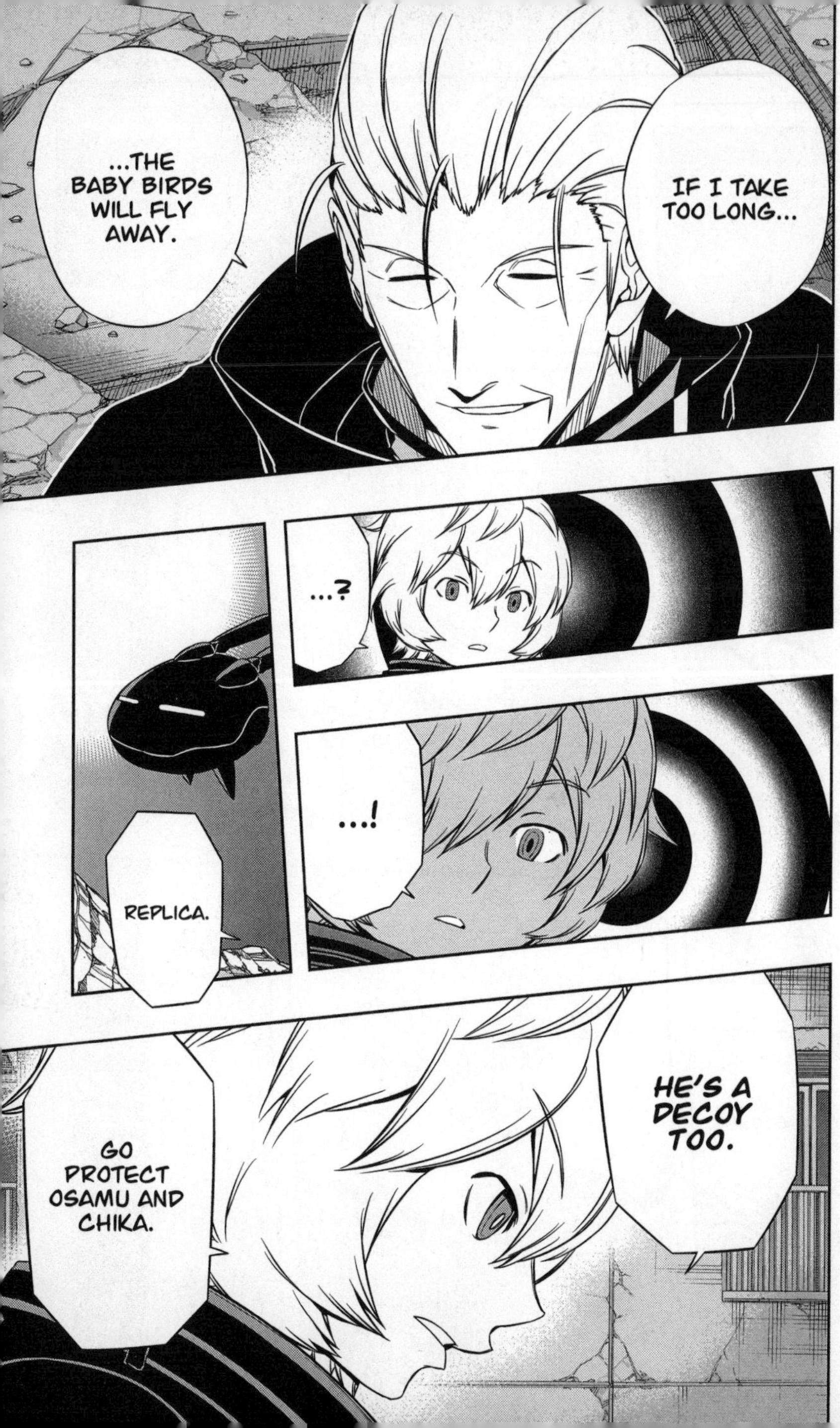
IF I TAKE TOO LONG...
...THE BABY BIRDS WILL FLY AWAY.
...?
...!
REPLICA.
HE'S A DECOY TOO.
GO PROTECT OSAMU AND CHIKA.

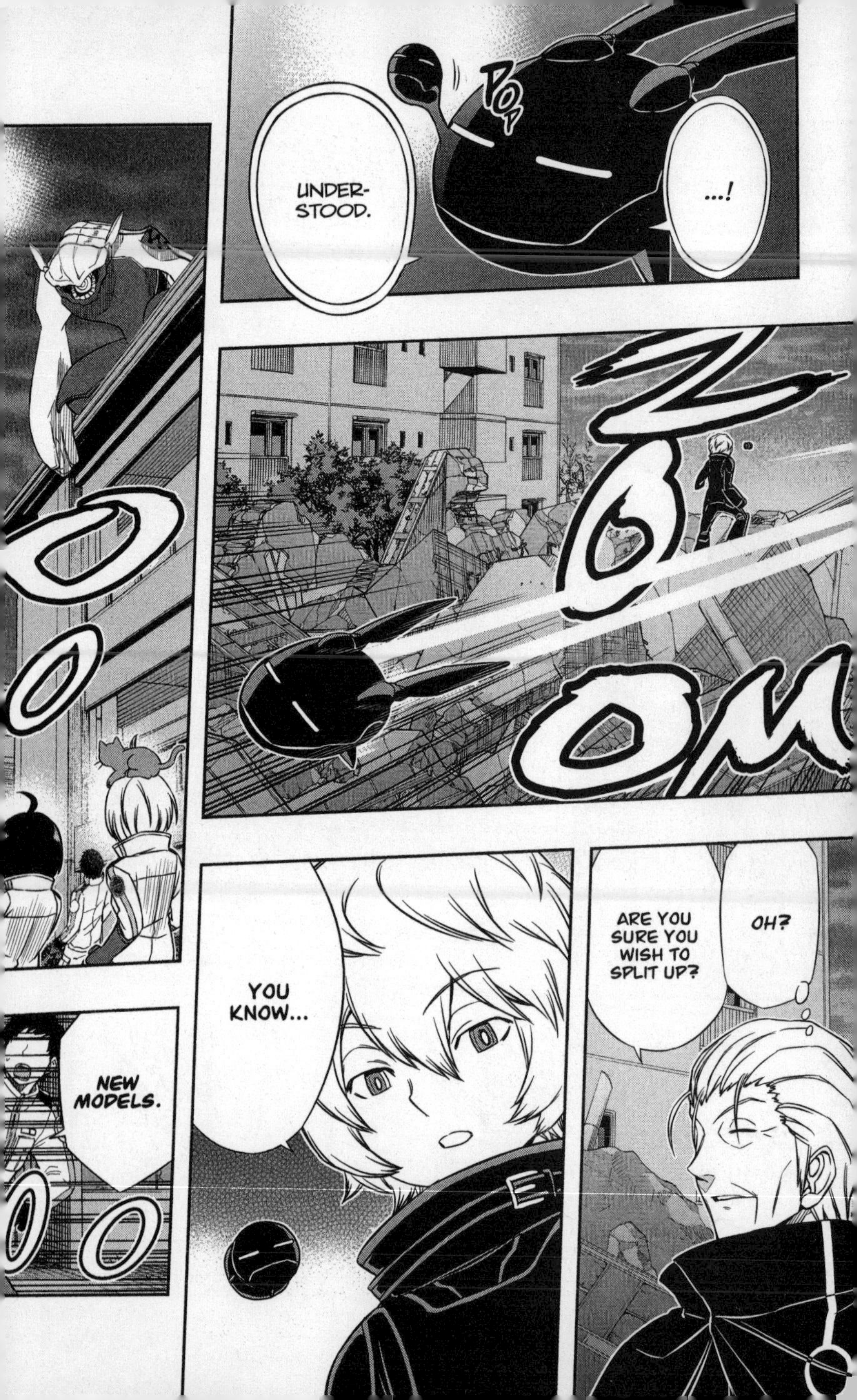
...!
POP
UNDER-STOOD.
ZOOM
OO
OH?
ARE YOU SURE YOU WISH TO SPLIT UP?
YOU KNOW...
NEW MODELS.
OO

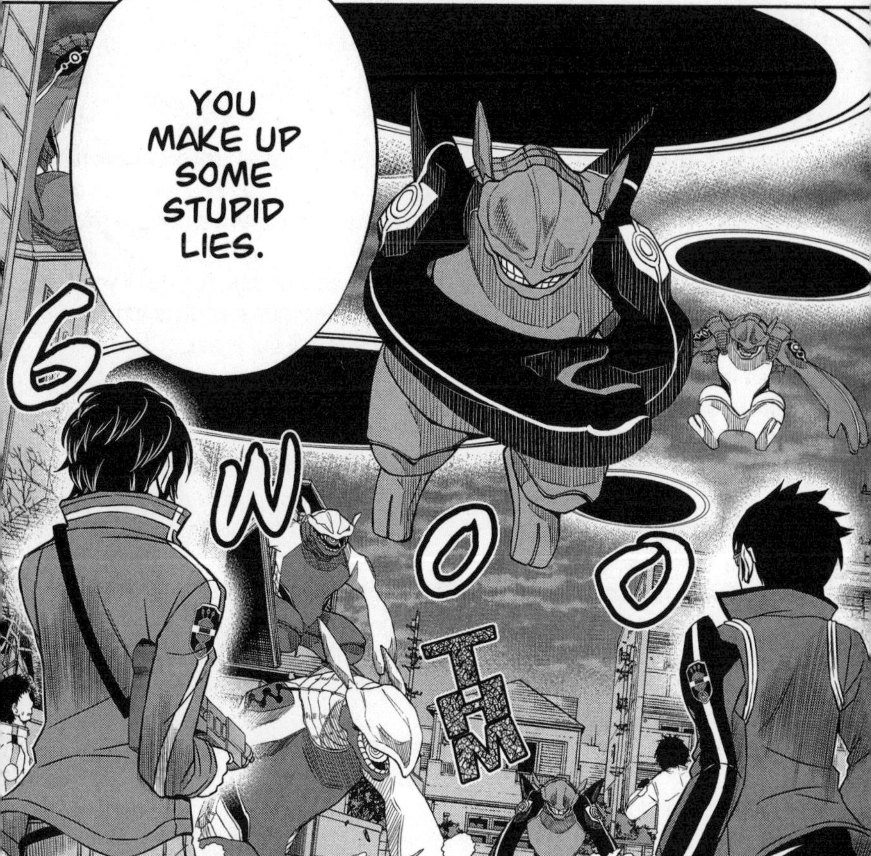
YOU MAKE UP SOME STUPID LIES.
GWOOO
THM
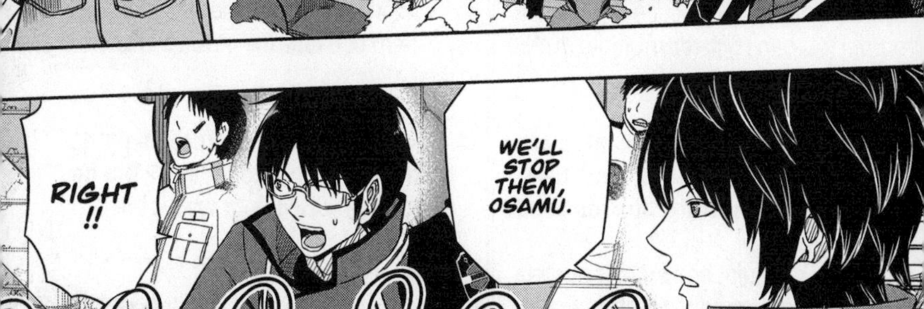
WE'LL STOP THEM, OSAMU.
RIGHT !!

Q&A: Part 6

The questions are getting more hard-core.

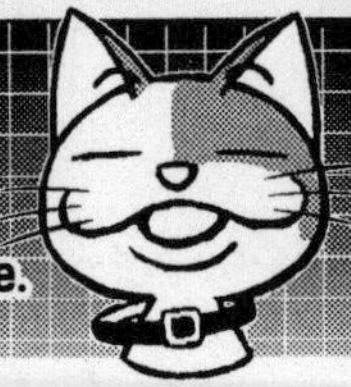

■How heavy is one of Miwa's lead bullets?

About 100kg (220lb). Yuma's Anchor is about twice that.

■What is the relationship between Tsukimi and Tachikawa? (Tachikawa's birthday comes earlier so he's older, isn't he?)

Tsukimi is Tachikawa's childhood friend and mentor when it comes to strategy. It goes Azuma, Tsukimi (and many other pupils) and then Tachikawa.

■The Trion body wears a Border uniform when the Trigger is activated, but are the Trion bodies automatically made wearing a uniform?

The clothing upon Trigger activation can be an outfit specifically chosen by the Agent or can just be the default outfit. You can register multiple outfits of your choosing.

■When Yuma's wounds healed after he was struck by a car, does that mean his Trion body repaired itself?

Yes. Yuma's regular body is less durable than his combat body, but it has a repair function. A regular combat body wouldn't be damaged in a car crash.

■Do Sniper rifles only stay out in gun form, or can they be put away at will? Can one be carried around as a smaller version?

Once guns are out, they stay out. If you "put it away," another gun's worth of Trion must be used to take it out again.

■Can All-Rounders snipe too?

Not really. An All-Rounder is good at close and mid-range combat. The only perfect All-Rounder who can also snipe is Reiji.

■Is Utagawa an Attacker or All-Rounder?

The first editions of the graphic novels (in Japan) have it wrong. He's an All-Rounder.

■Is it important for Snipers to have good eyesight?

Eyesight is perfected for the combat body, so it doesn't matter. People with glasses keep them because the glasses are tied to their identity.

■Is Satori's double-barreled sniping technique highly advanced? Did he need to practice it, or was it his natural talent?

He practiced. Satori pursued firepower and awesomeness to perfect it. But nobody's going to imitate him.

Chapter 67 Invasion: Part 16

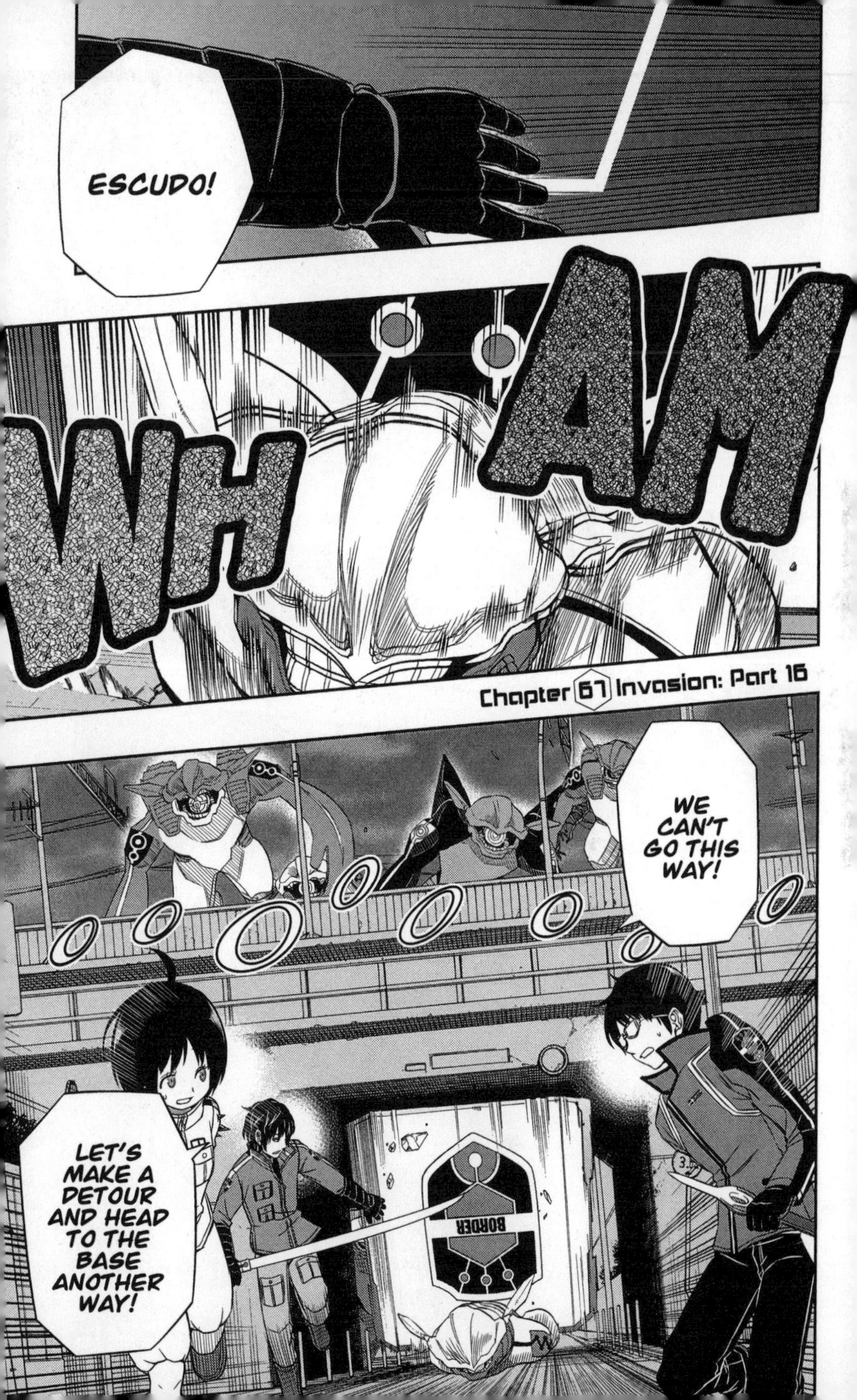
ESCUDO!
WHAM
WE CAN'T GO THIS WAY!
LET'S MAKE A DETOUR AND HEAD TO THE BASE ANOTHER WAY!

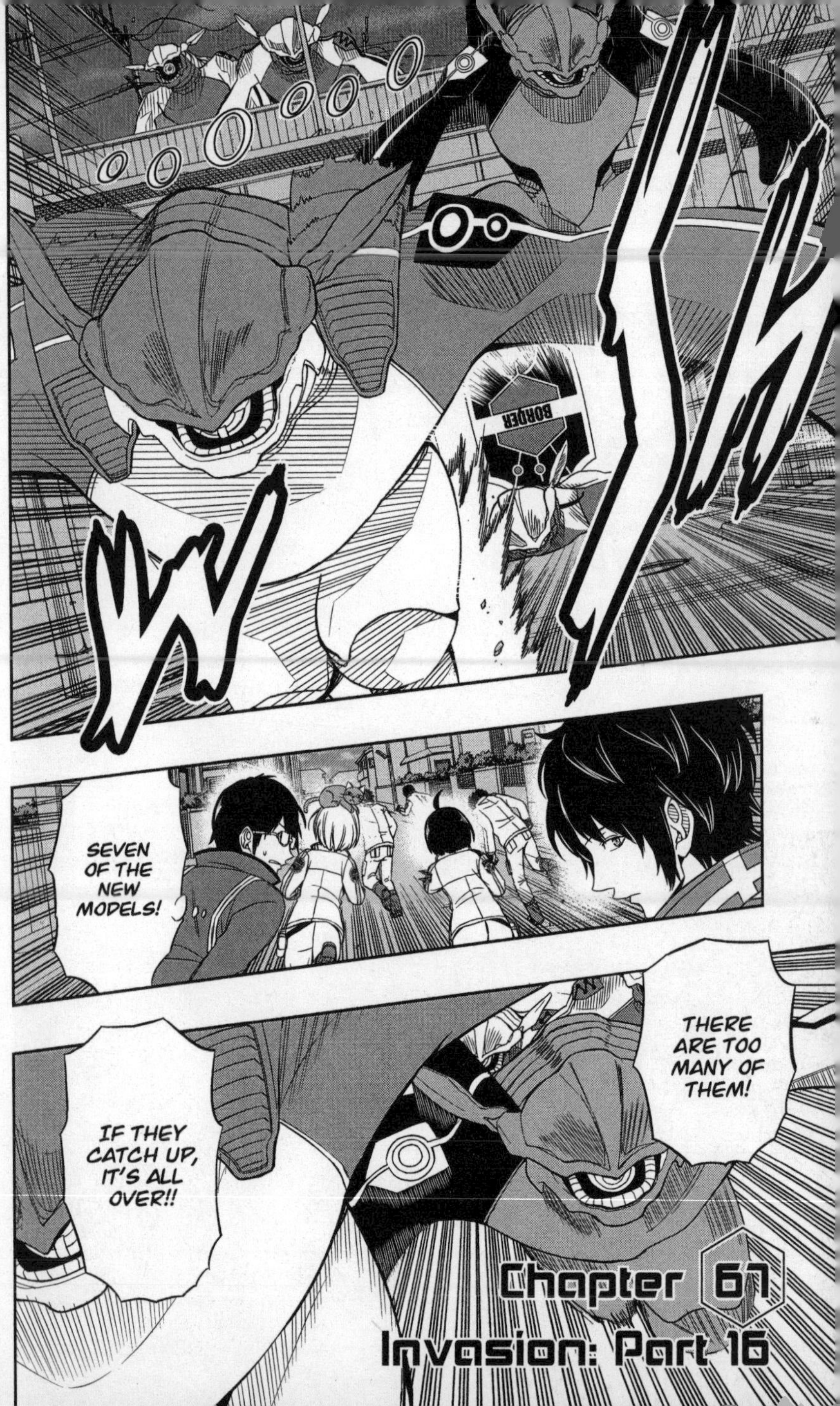
BORDER
SEVEN OF THE NEW MODELS!
THERE ARE TOO MANY OF THEM!
IF THEY CATCH UP, IT'S ALL OVER!!
Chapter 67
Invasion: Part 16

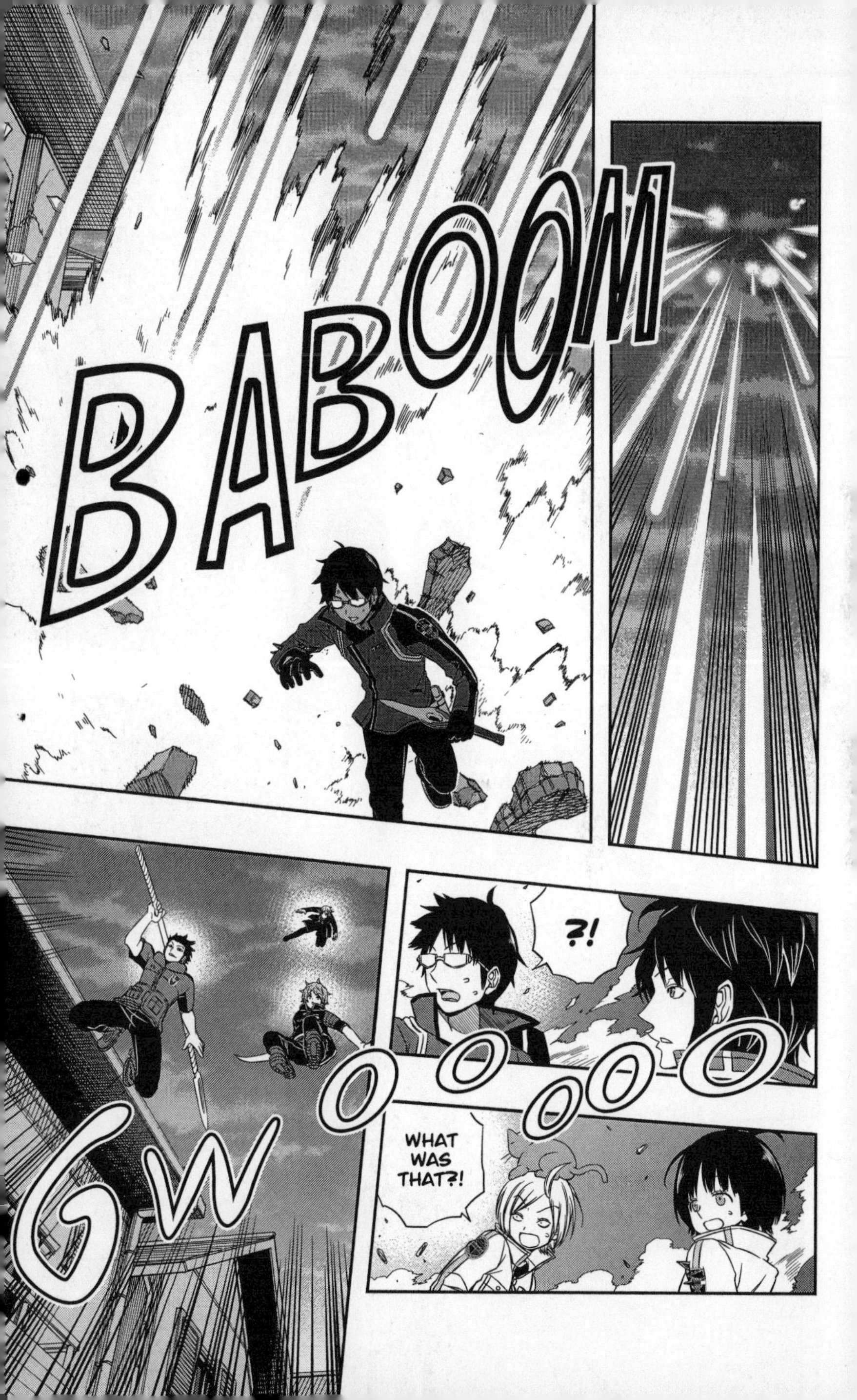
BABOOM
?!
WHAT WAS THAT?!
GWOOOOO

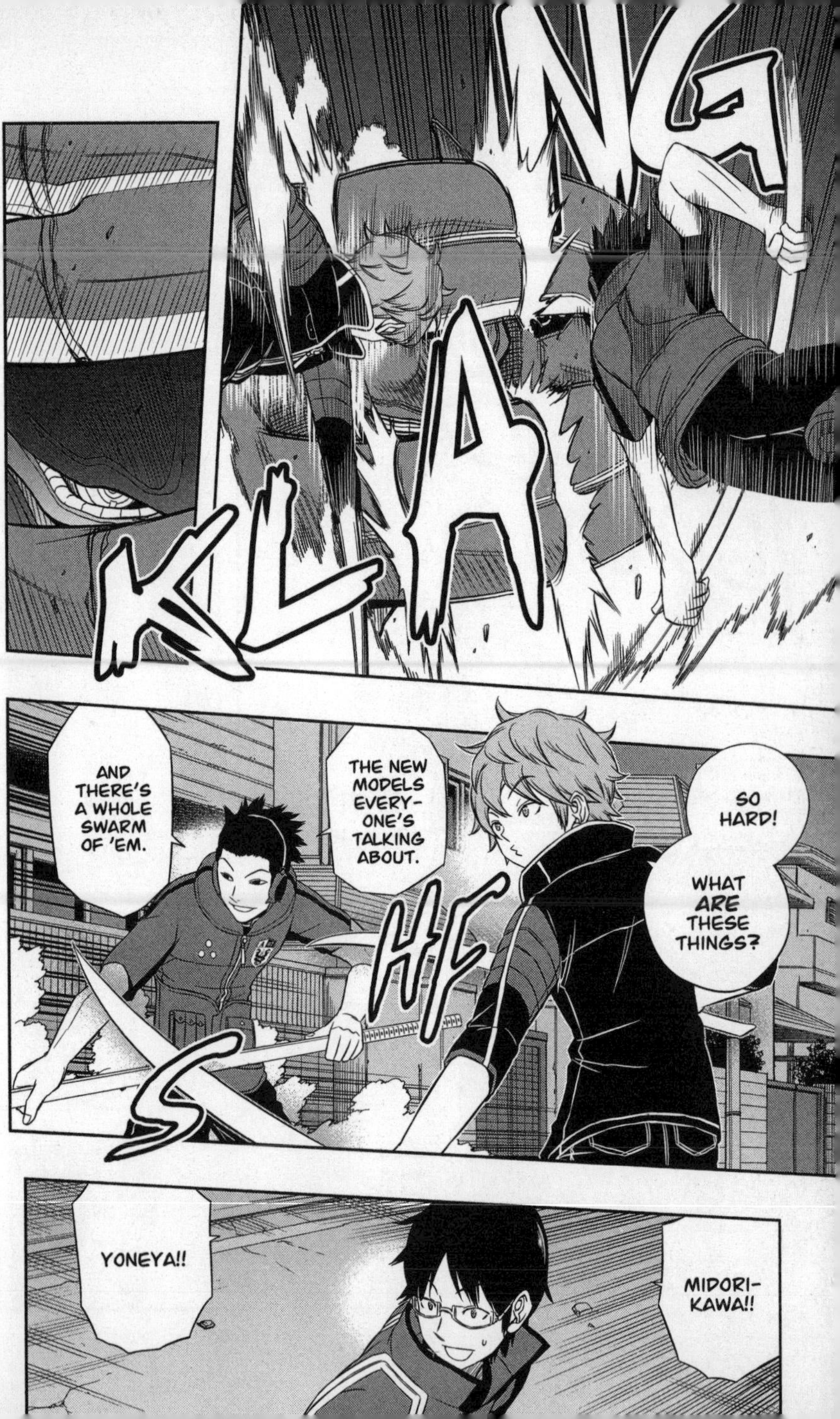
NG
KLA
SO HARD!
WHAT ARE THESE THINGS?
THE NEW MODELS EVERY-ONE'S TALKING ABOUT.
AND THERE'S A WHOLE SWARM OF 'EM.
SHF
MIDORI-KAWA!!
YONEYA!!

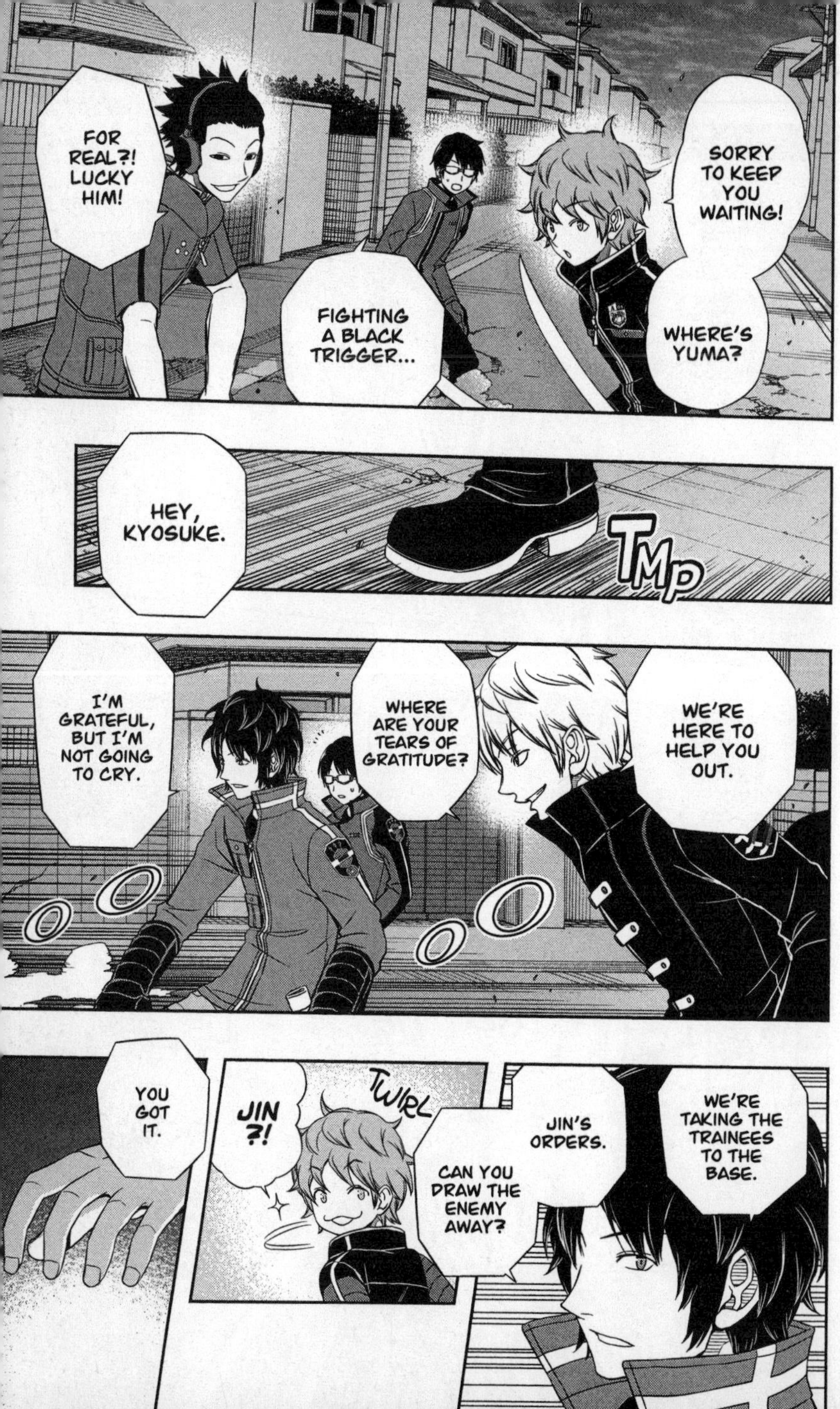
SORRY TO KEEP YOU WAITING!
WHERE'S YUMA?
FIGHTING A BLACK TRIGGER...
FOR REAL?! LUCKY HIM!
TMP
HEY, KYOSUKE.
WE'RE HERE TO HELP YOU OUT.
WHERE ARE YOUR TEARS OF GRATITUDE?
I'M GRATEFUL, BUT I'M NOT GOING TO CRY.
WE'RE TAKING THE TRAINEES TO THE BASE.
JIN'S ORDERS.
CAN YOU DRAW THE ENEMY AWAY?
TWIRL
JIN ?!
YOU GOT IT.

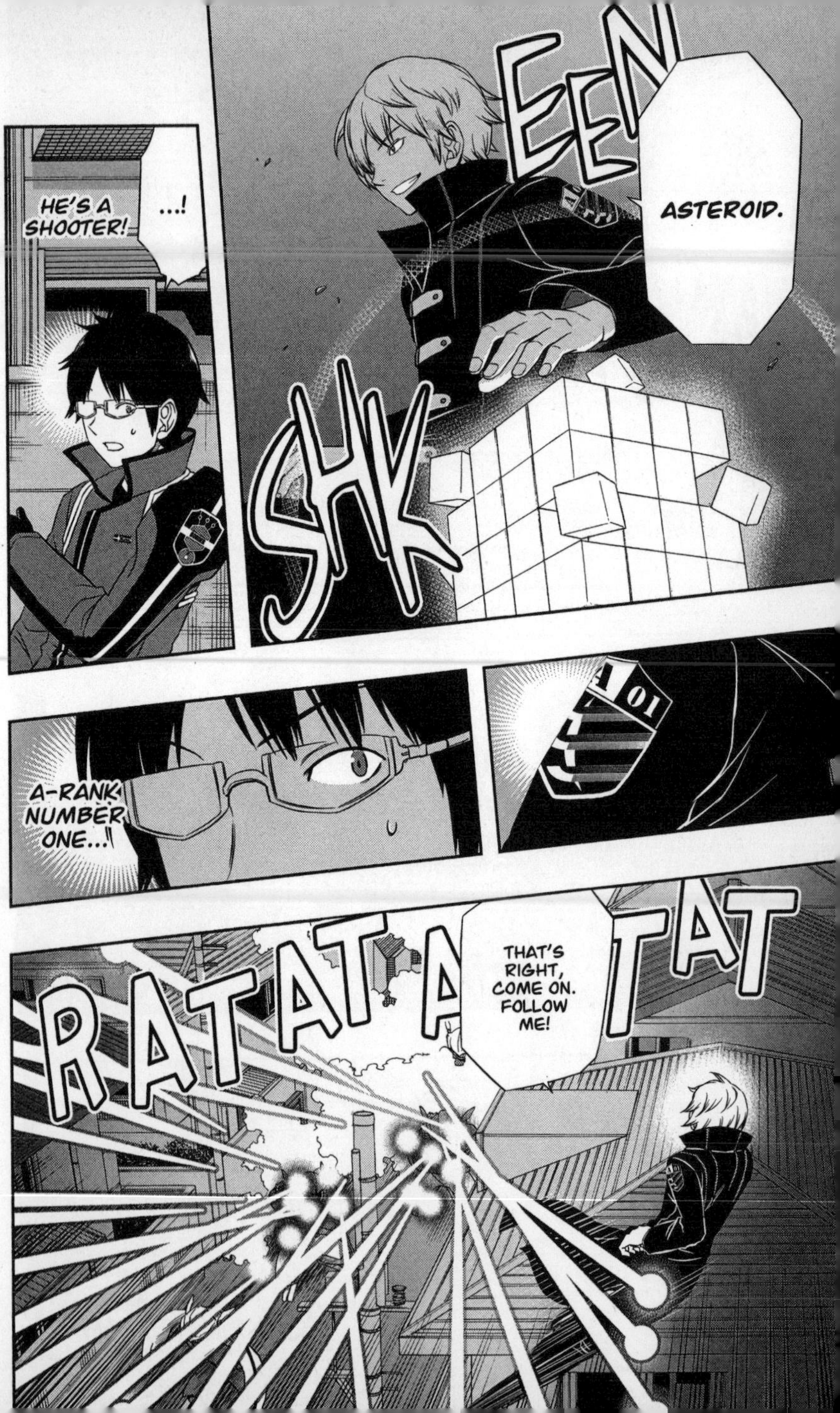
EEN
ASTEROID.
SHK
...!
HE'S A SHOOTER!
A-RANK NUMBER ONE...!
RATATATAT
THAT'S RIGHT, COME ON. FOLLOW ME!

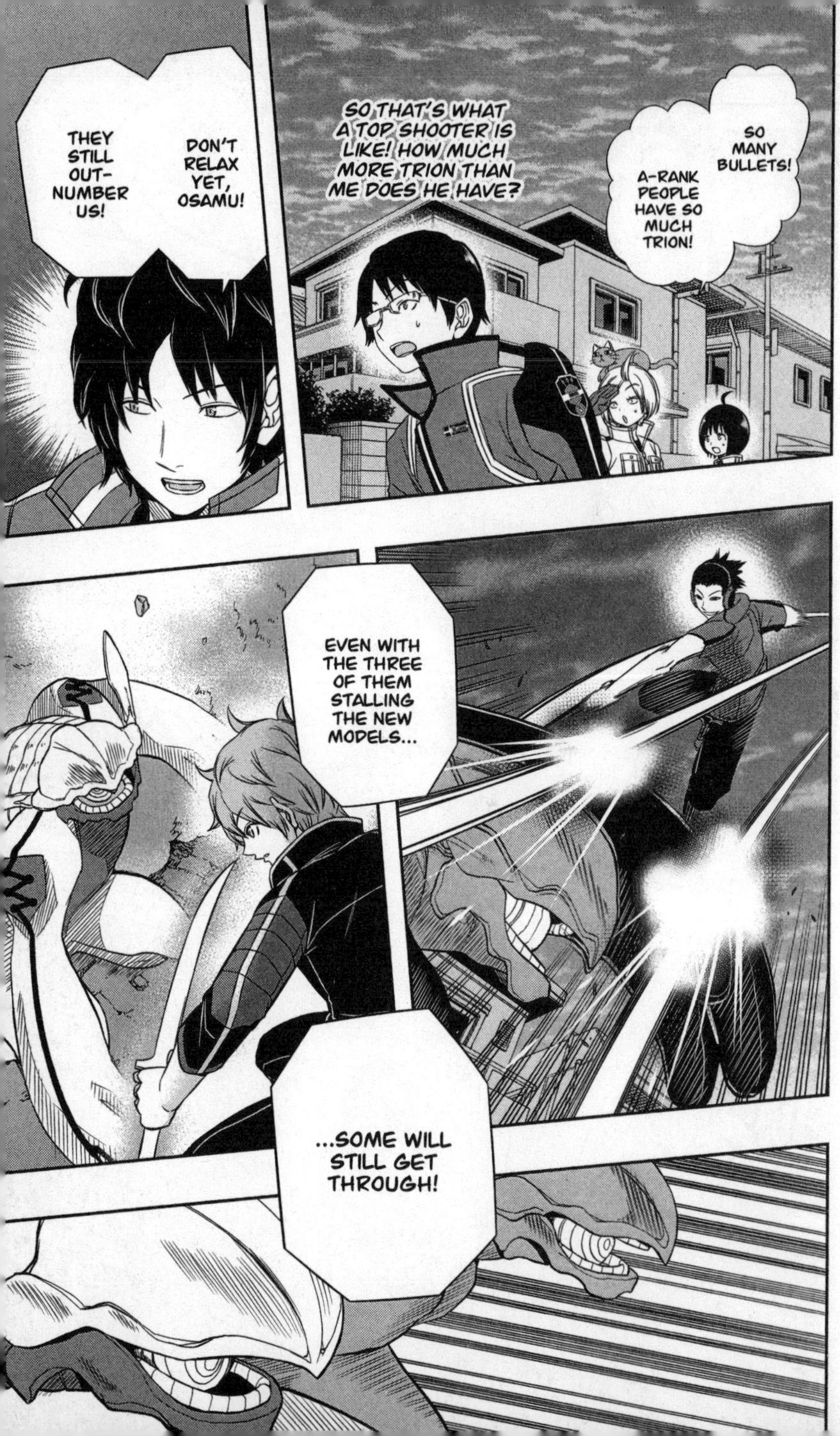
SO MANY BULLETS!
A-RANK PEOPLE HAVE SO MUCH TRION!
SO THAT'S WHAT A TOP SHOOTER IS LIKE! HOW MUCH MORE TRION THAN ME DOES HE HAVE?
DON'T RELAX YET, OSAMU!
THEY STILL OUT-NUMBER US!
EVEN WITH THE THREE OF THEM STALLING THE NEW MODELS...
...SOME WILL STILL GET THROUGH!

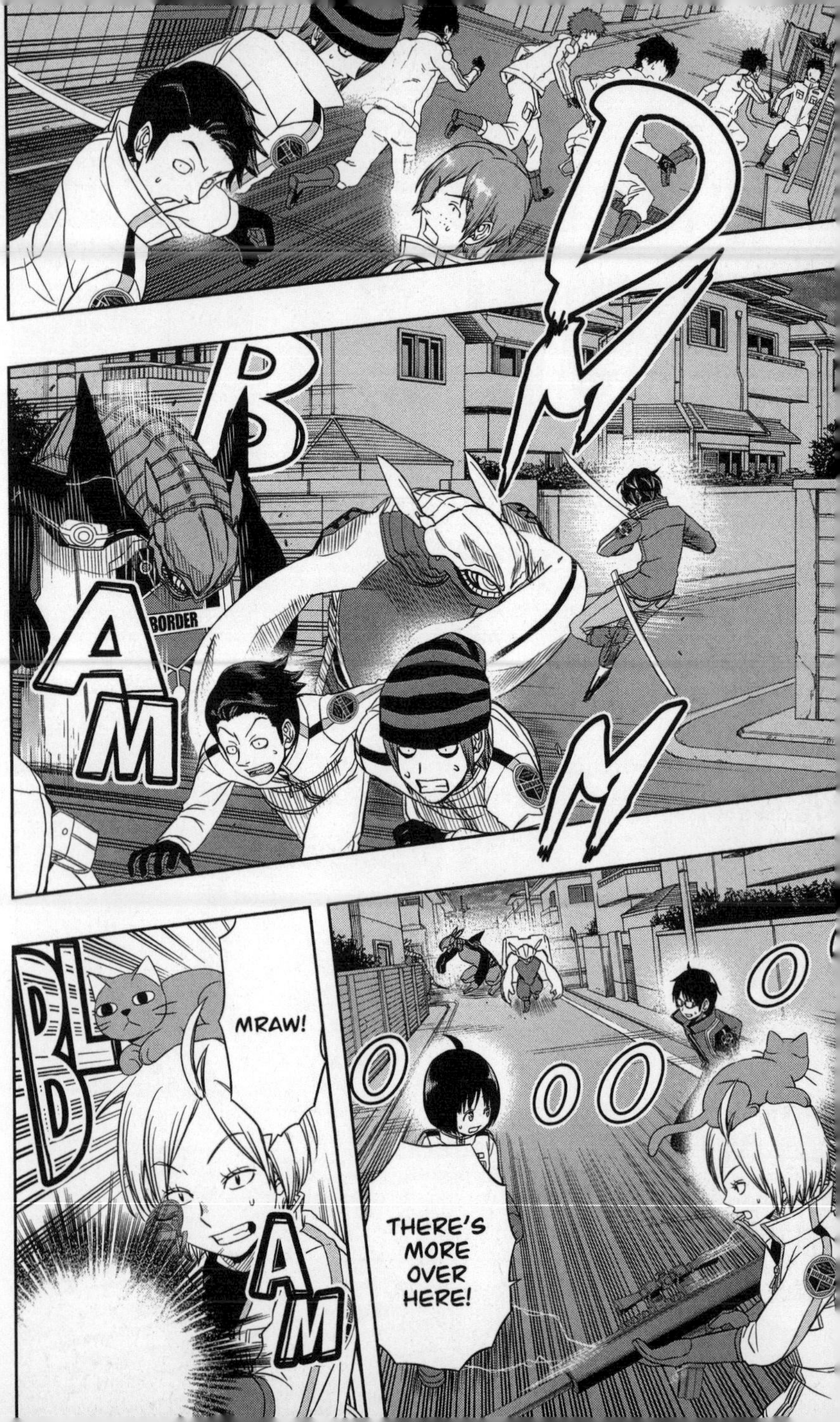

DMM
BAM
OOOOO
THERE'S MORE OVER HERE!
MRAW!
BLAM

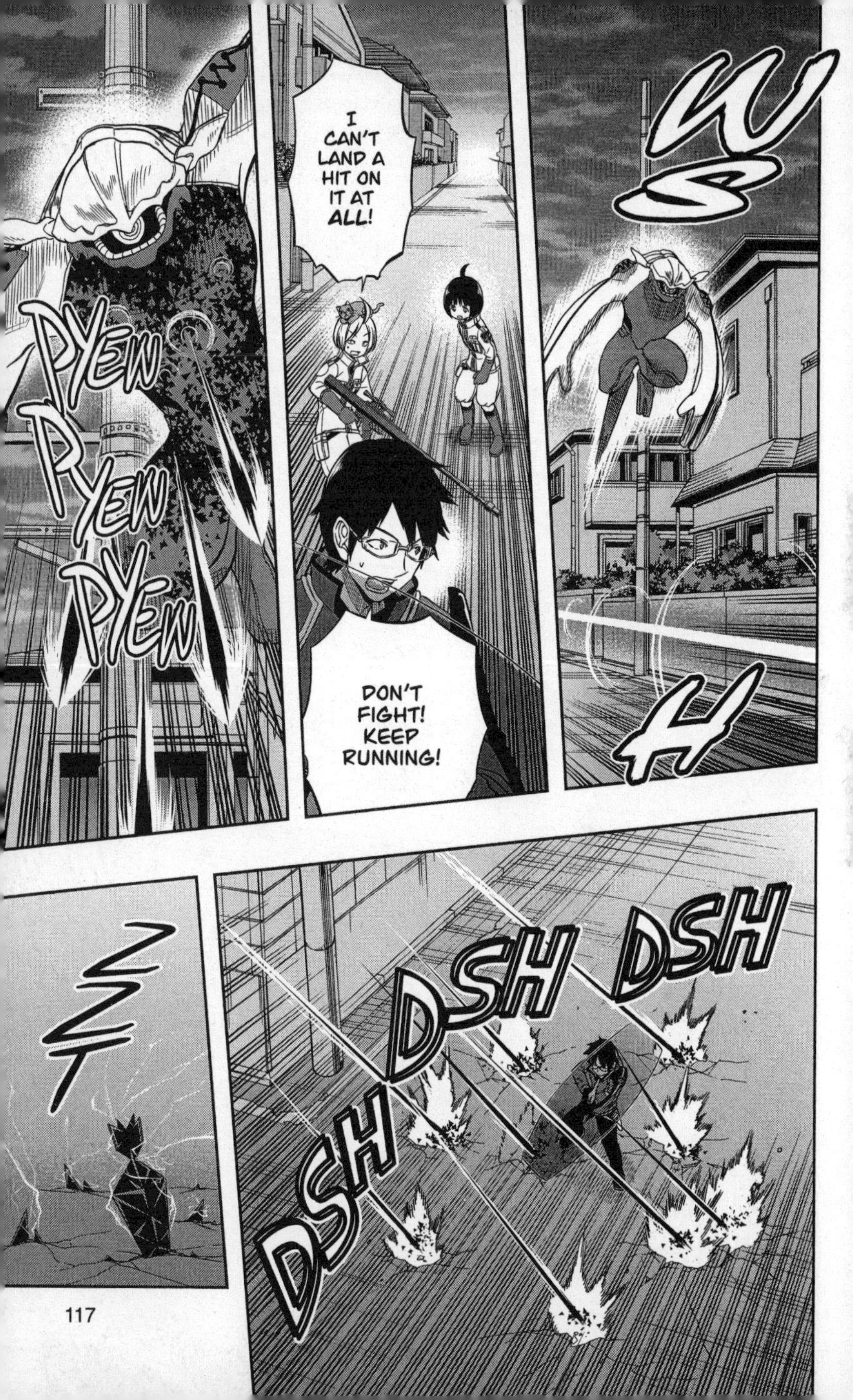
WUSH
H
I CAN'T LAND A HIT ON IT AT ALL!
DON'T FIGHT! KEEP RUNNING!
PYEW
PYEW
PYEW
PYEW
DSH DSH DSH DSH
ZZT

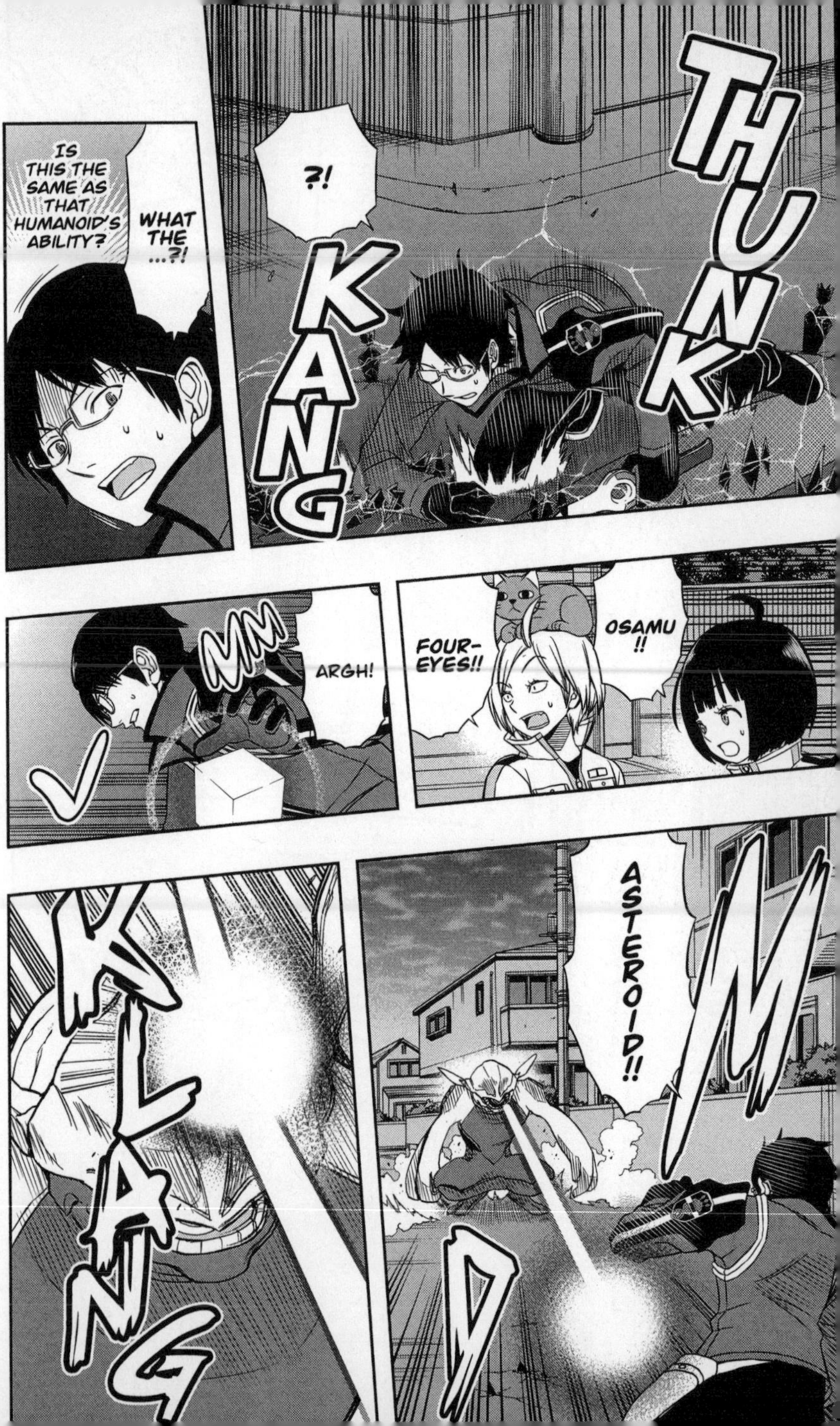
THUNK
?!
KANG
WHAT THE ...?!
IS THIS THE SAME AS THAT HUMANOID'S ABILITY?
OSAMU!!
FOUR-EYES!!
ARGH!
MM
ASTEROID!!
KLANG

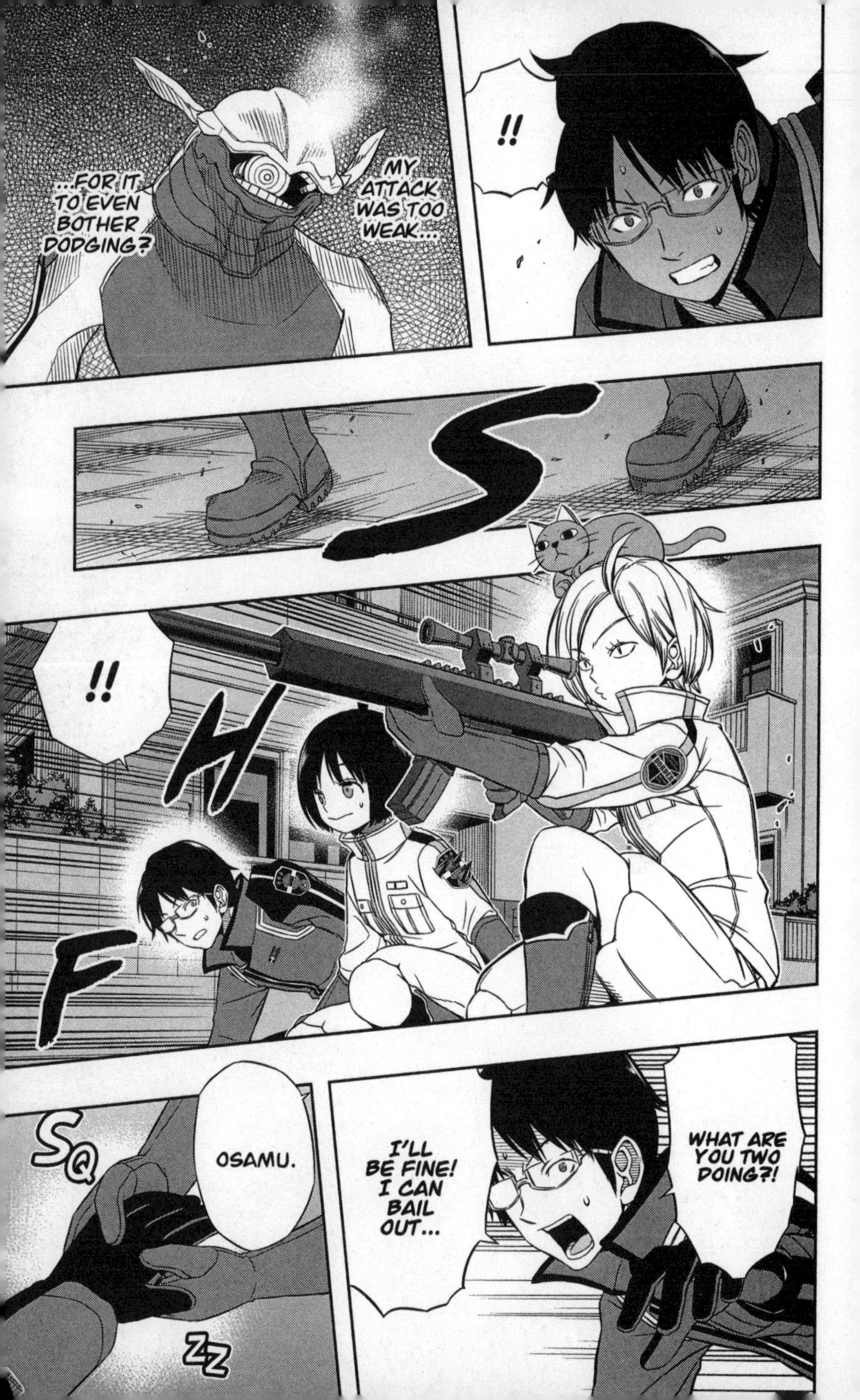
!!
MY ATTACK WAS TOO WEAK...
...FOR IT TO EVEN BOTHER DODGING?
S
!!
H
F
WHAT ARE YOU TWO DOING?!
I'LL BE FINE! I CAN BAIL OUT...
OSAMU.
SQ
ZZ

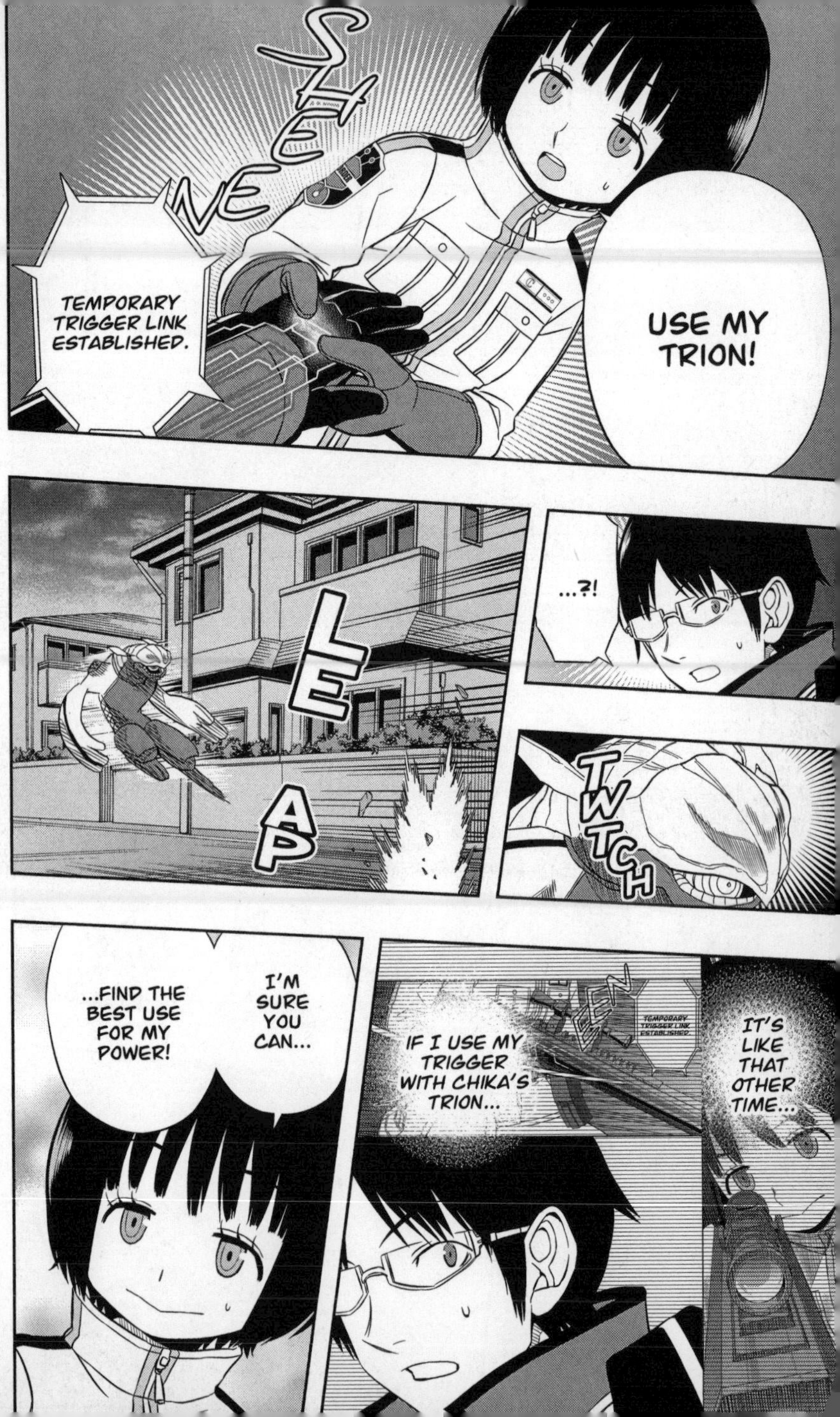
USE MY TRION!
SHEENE
TEMPORARY TRIGGER LINK ESTABLISHED.
...?!
TWTCH
LEAP
TEMPORARY TRIGGER LINK ESTABLISHED.
IT'S LIKE THAT OTHER TIME...
IF I USE MY TRIGGER WITH CHIKA'S TRION...
I'M SURE YOU CAN...
...FIND THE BEST USE FOR MY POWER!

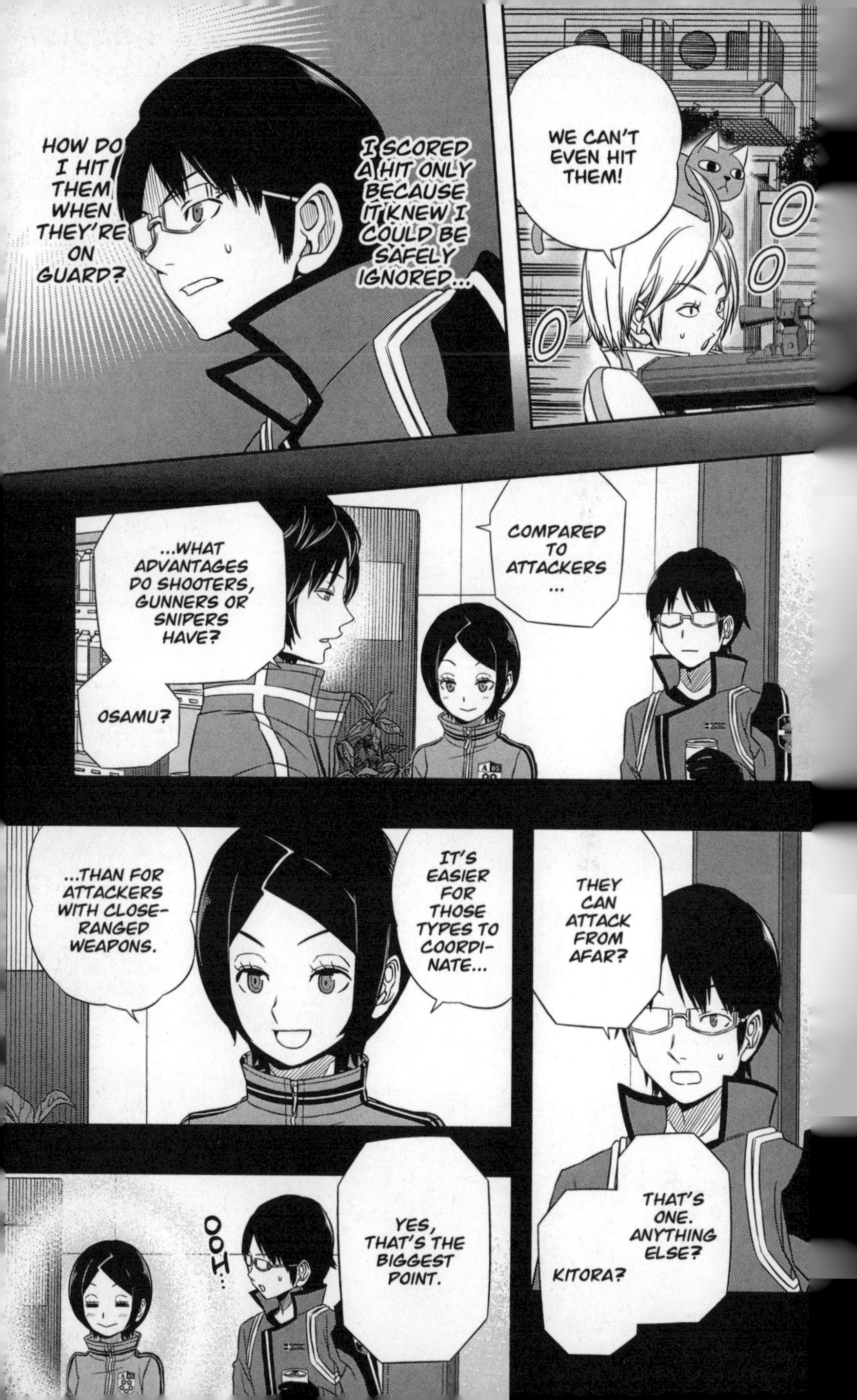
WE CAN'T EVEN HIT THEM!
I SCORED A HIT ONLY BECAUSE IT KNEW I COULD BE SAFELY IGNORED...
HOW DO I HIT THEM WHEN THEY'RE ON GUARD?
COMPARED TO ATTACKERS...
...WHAT ADVANTAGES DO SHOOTERS, GUNNERS OR SNIPERS HAVE?
OSAMU?
THEY CAN ATTACK FROM AFAR?
YES, THAT'S THE BIGGEST POINT.
OOH...
THAT'S ONE. ANYTHING ELSE?
KITORA?
IT'S EASIER FOR THOSE TYPES TO COORDINATE...
...THAN FOR ATTACKERS WITH CLOSE-RANGED WEAPONS.

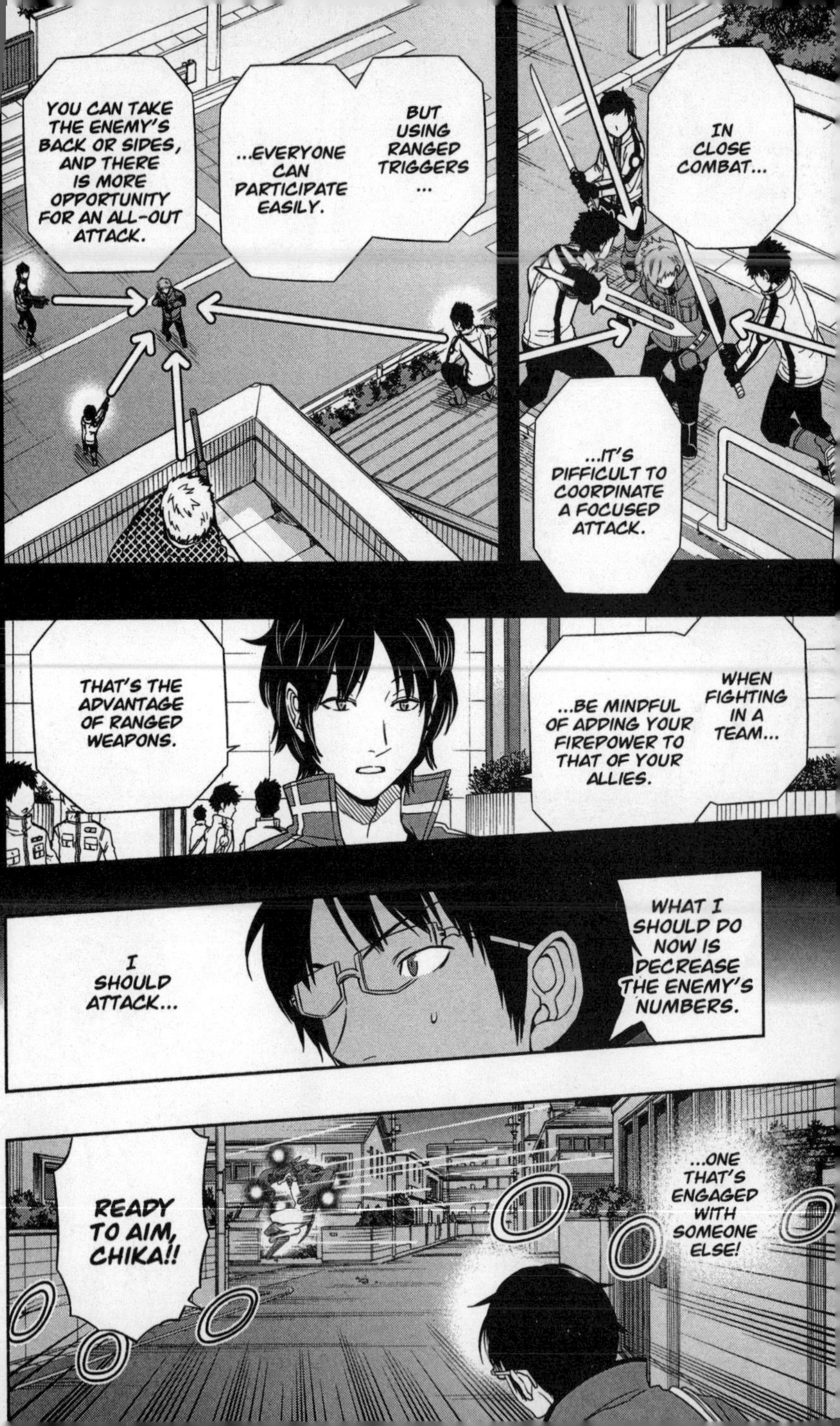
IN CLOSE COMBAT...
...IT'S DIFFICULT TO COORDINATE A FOCUSED ATTACK.
BUT USING RANGED TRIGGERS...
...EVERYONE CAN PARTICIPATE EASILY.
YOU CAN TAKE THE ENEMY'S BACK OR SIDES, AND THERE IS MORE OPPORTUNITY FOR AN ALL-OUT ATTACK.
WHEN FIGHTING IN A TEAM...
...BE MINDFUL OF ADDING YOUR FIREPOWER TO THAT OF YOUR ALLIES.
THAT'S THE ADVANTAGE OF RANGED WEAPONS.
WHAT I SHOULD DO NOW IS DECREASE THE ENEMY'S NUMBERS.
I SHOULD ATTACK...
...ONE THAT'S ENGAGED WITH SOMEONE ELSE!
READY TO AIM, CHIKA!!

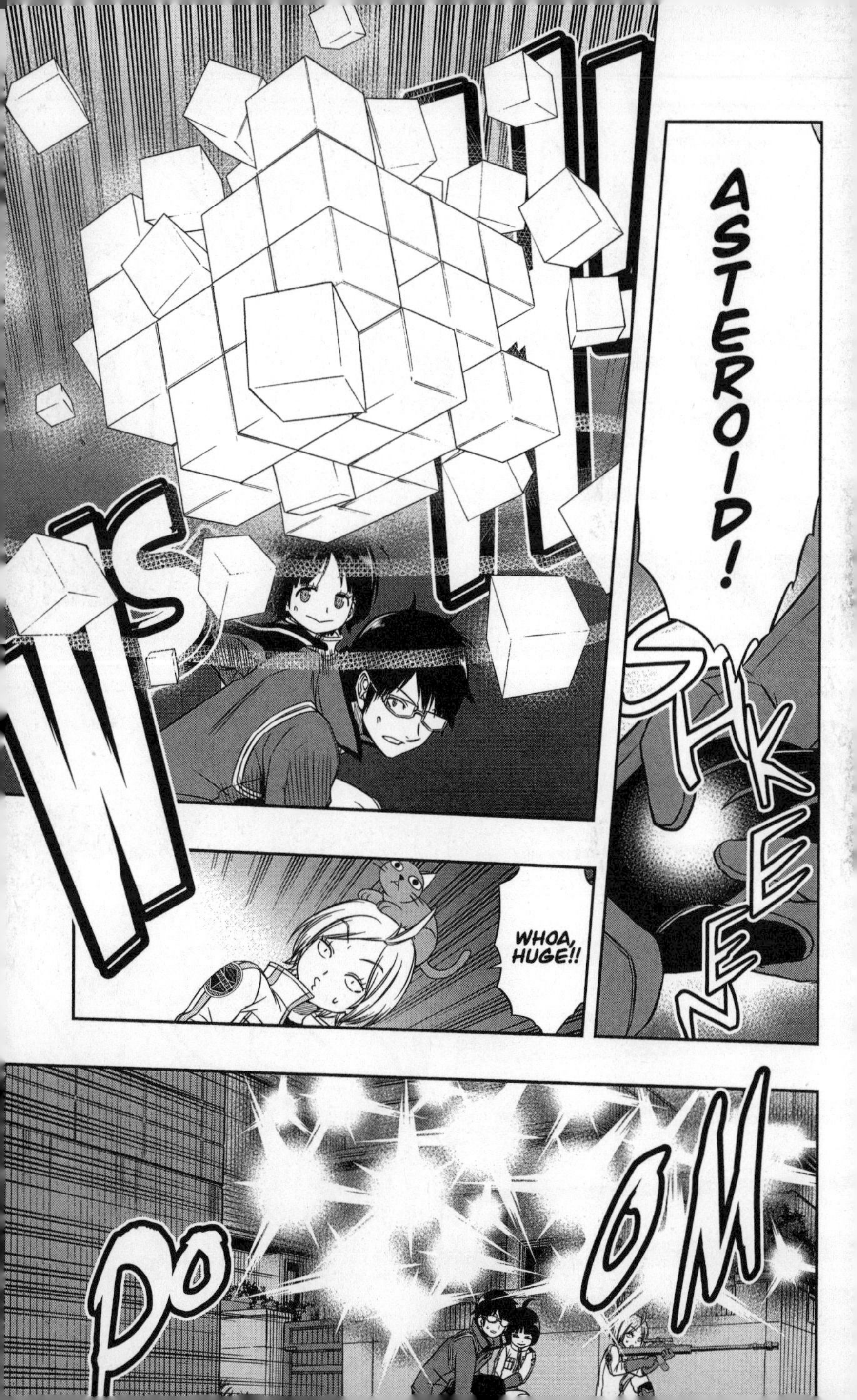
ASTEROID!
SHKEEN
WHOA, HUGE!!
DOOM

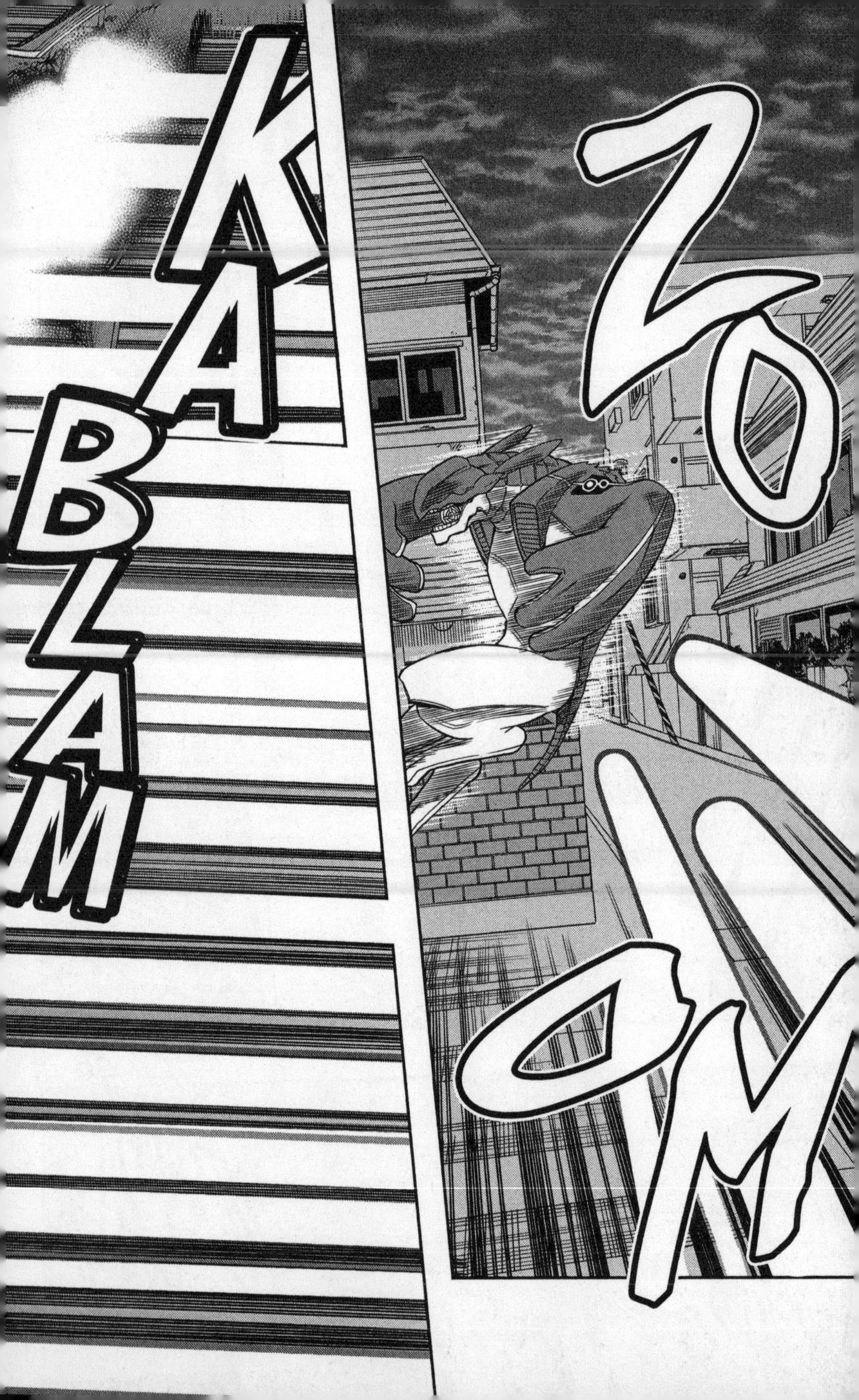
ZOOM
KABLAM

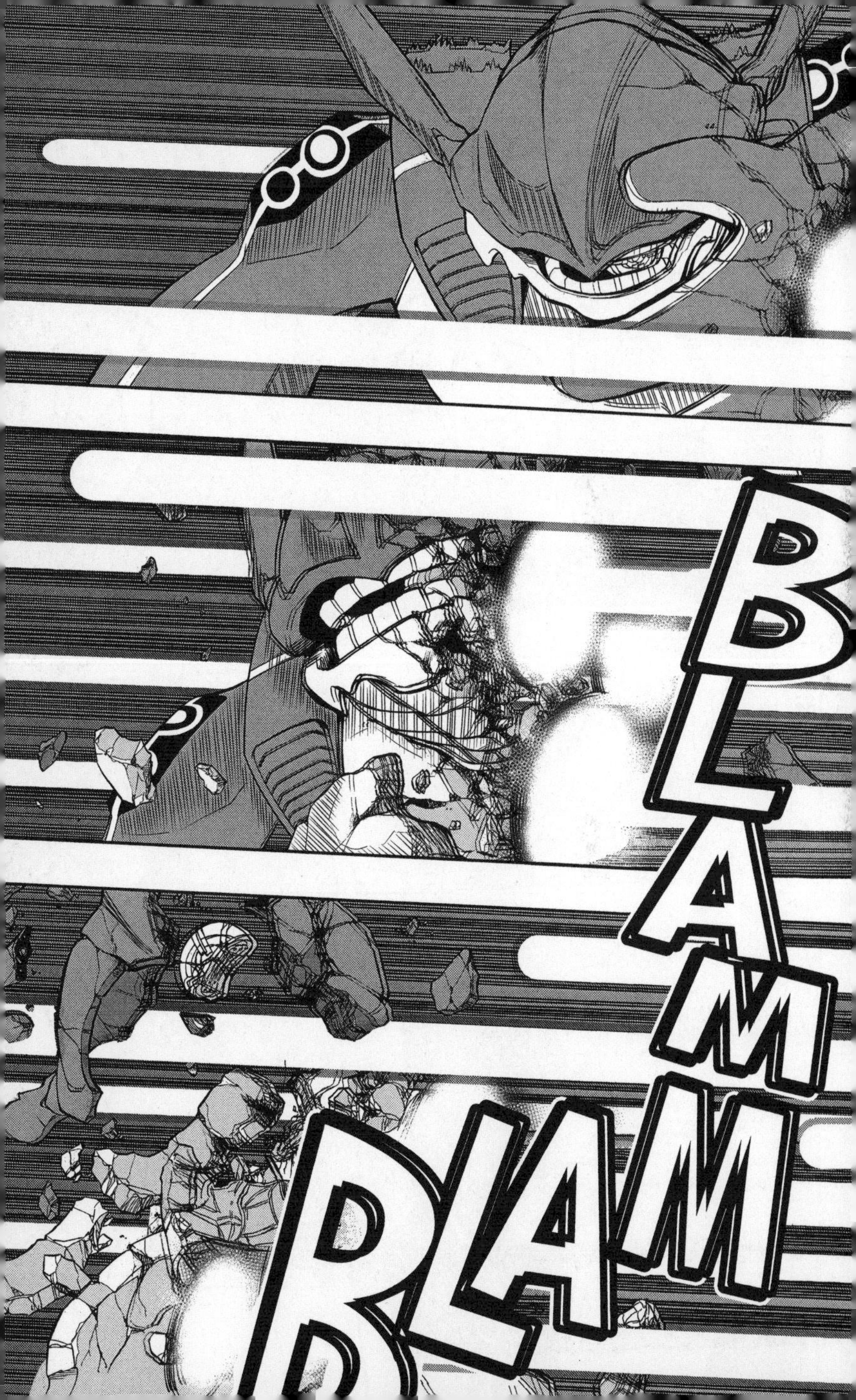
BLAM
BLAM

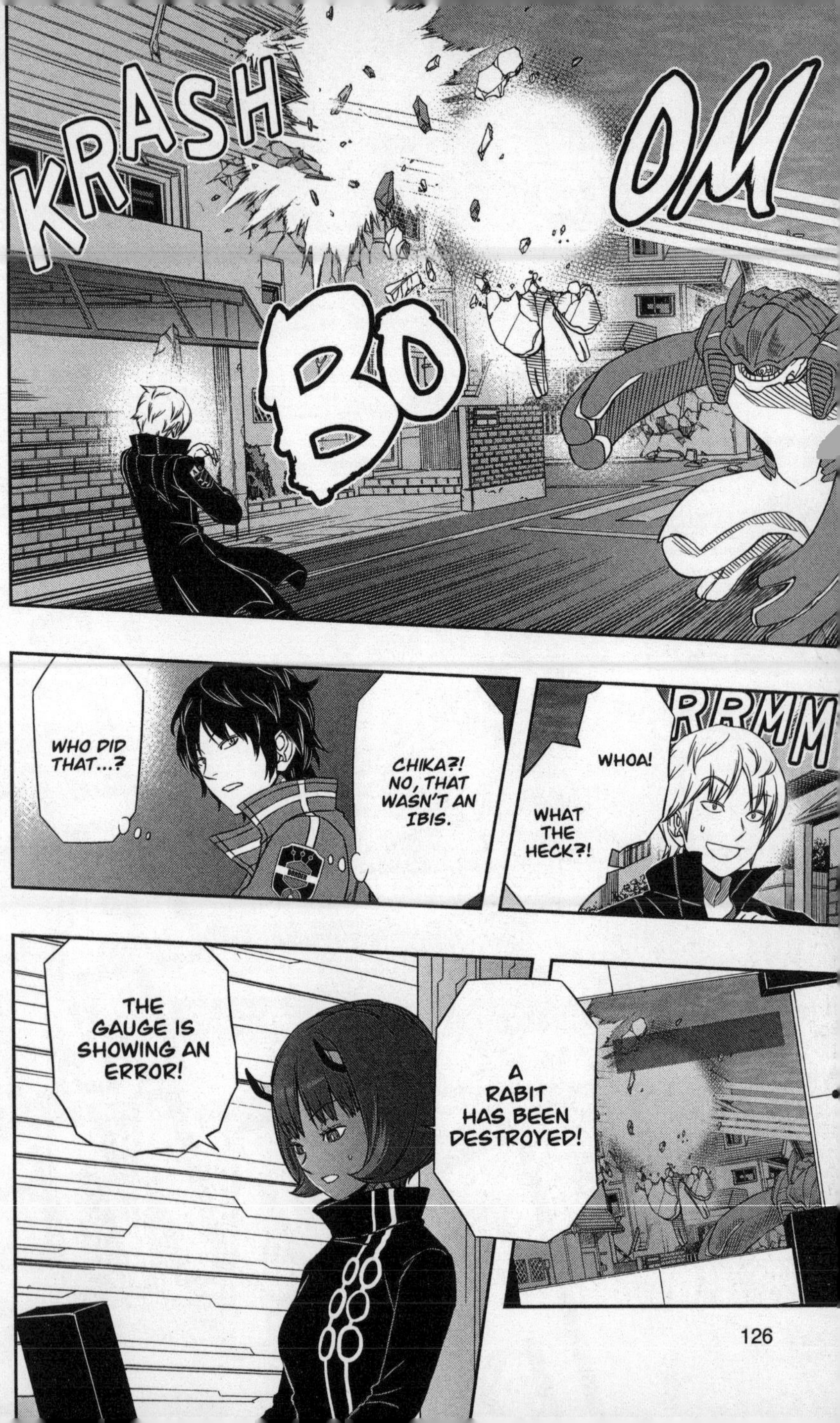
BOOM
KRASH
RRMM
WHOA!
WHAT THE HECK?!
CHIKA?! NO, THAT WASN'T AN IBIS.
WHO DID THAT...?
A RABIT HAS BEEN DESTROYED!
THE GAUGE IS SHOWING AN ERROR!

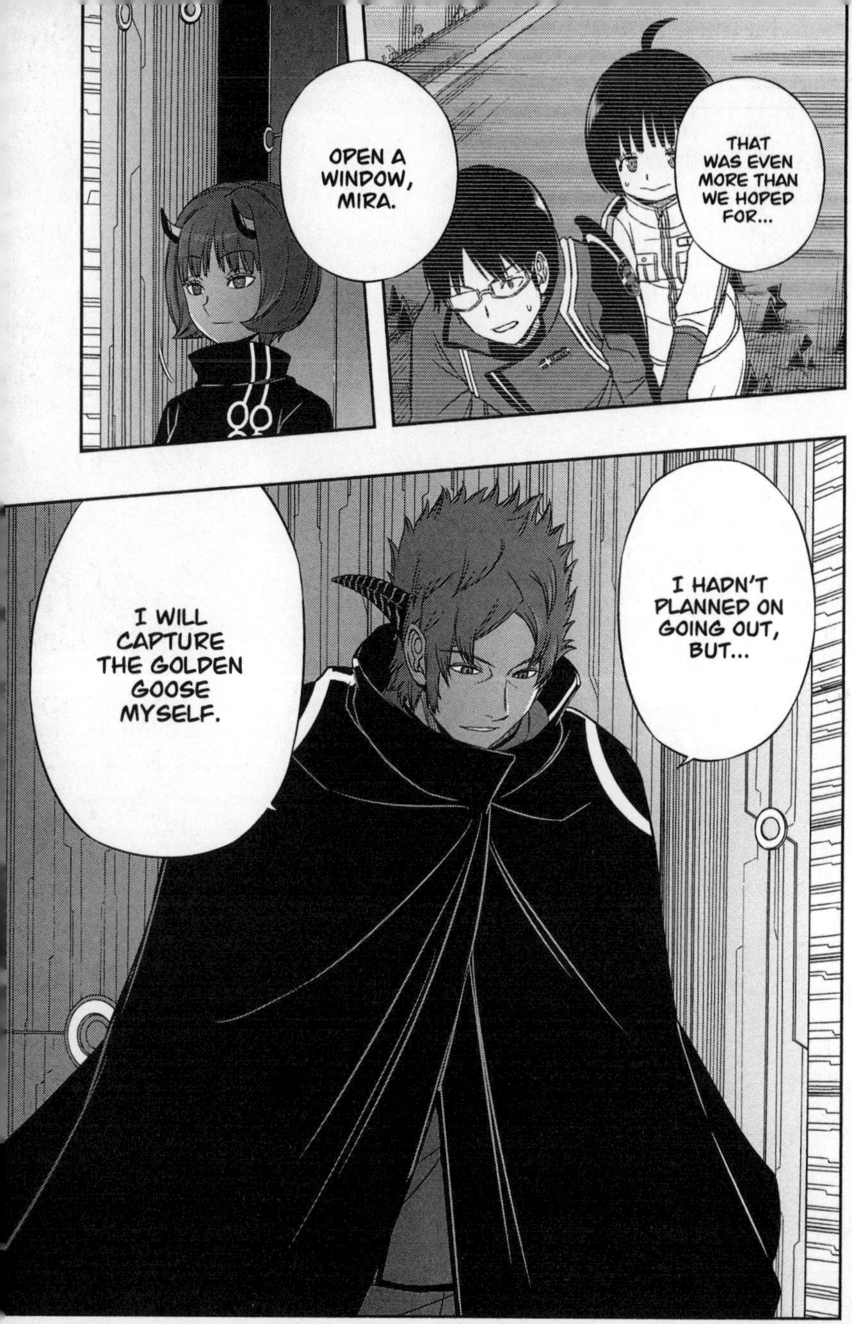
THAT WAS EVEN MORE THAN WE HOPED FOR...
OPEN A WINDOW, MIRA.
I HADN'T PLANNED ON GOING OUT, BUT...
I WILL CAPTURE THE GOLDEN GOOSE MYSELF.

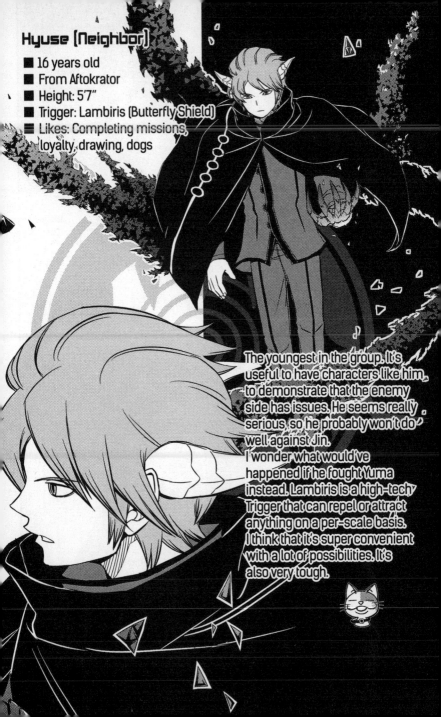

Hyuse [Neighbor]

- ■ 16 years old
- ■ From Aftokrator
- ■ Height: 5'7"
- ■ Trigger: Lambiris (Butterfly Shield)
- ⊟ Likes: Completing missions, loyalty, drawing, dogs

The youngest in the group. It's useful to have characters like him to demonstrate that the enemy side has issues. He seems really serious, so he probably won't do well against Jin.
I wonder what would've happened if he fought Yuma instead. Lambiris is a high-tech Trigger that can repel or attract anything on a per-scale basis. I think that it's super convenient with a lot of possibilities. It's also very tough.

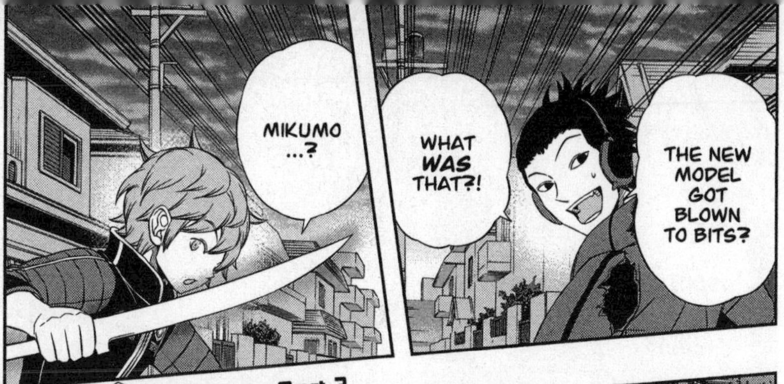
THE NEW MODEL GOT BLOWN TO BITS?
WHAT WAS THAT?!
MIKUMO ...?

Chapter 68 Aftokrator: Part 3

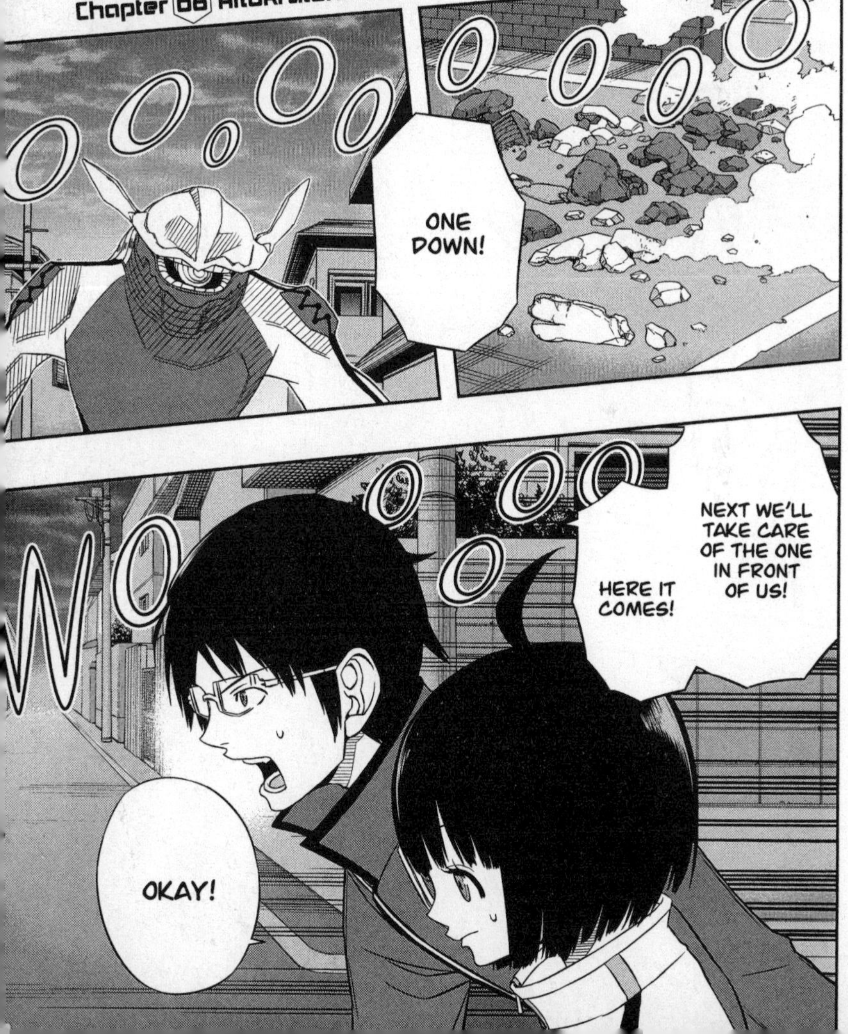
ONE DOWN!
NEXT WE'LL TAKE CARE OF THE ONE IN FRONT OF US!
HERE IT COMES!
OKAY!

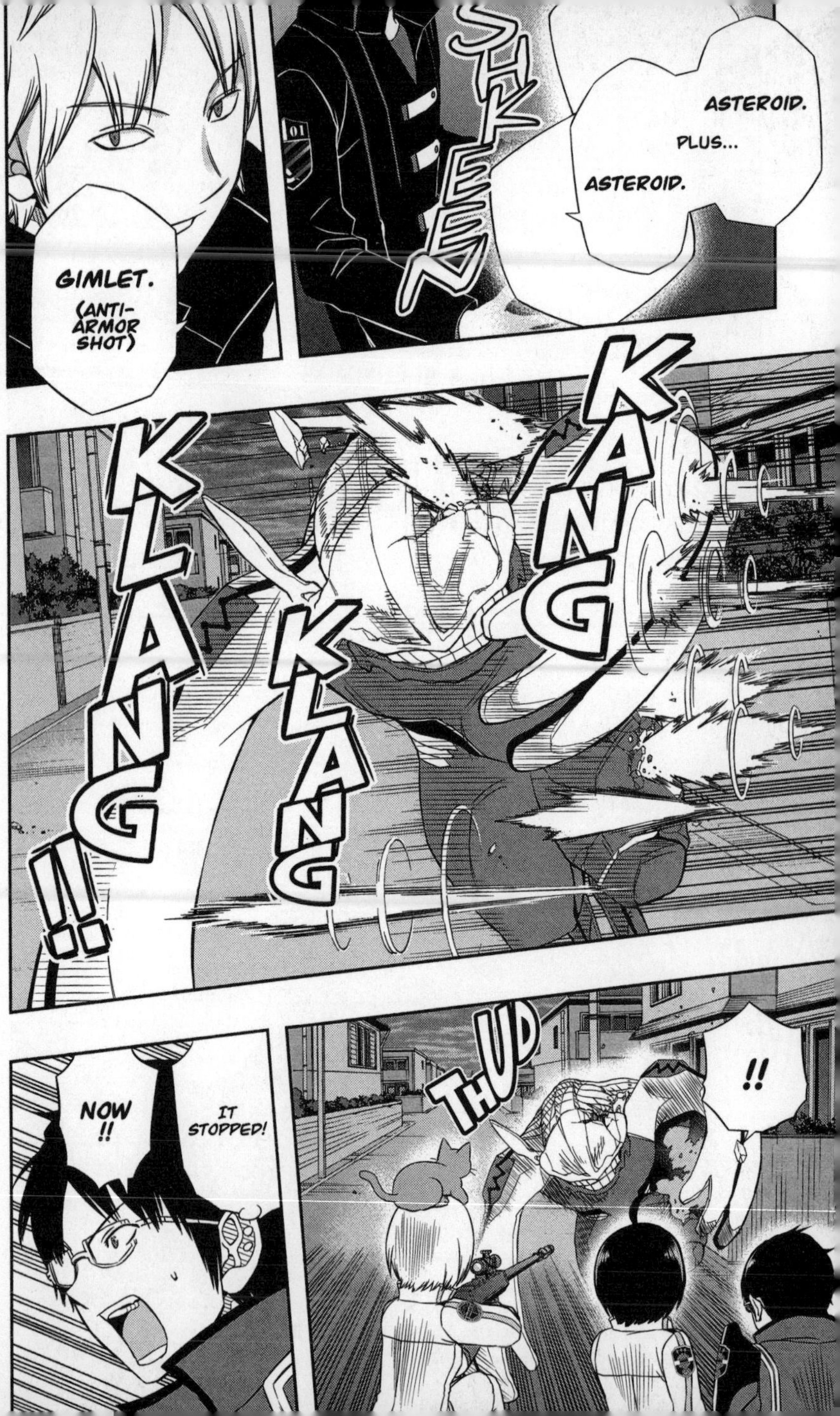
ASTEROID.
PLUS...
ASTEROID.
SHKEEEN
GIMLET.
(ANTI-ARMOR SHOT)
KANG
KLANG
KLANG!!
THUD
!!
NOW!!
IT STOPPED!

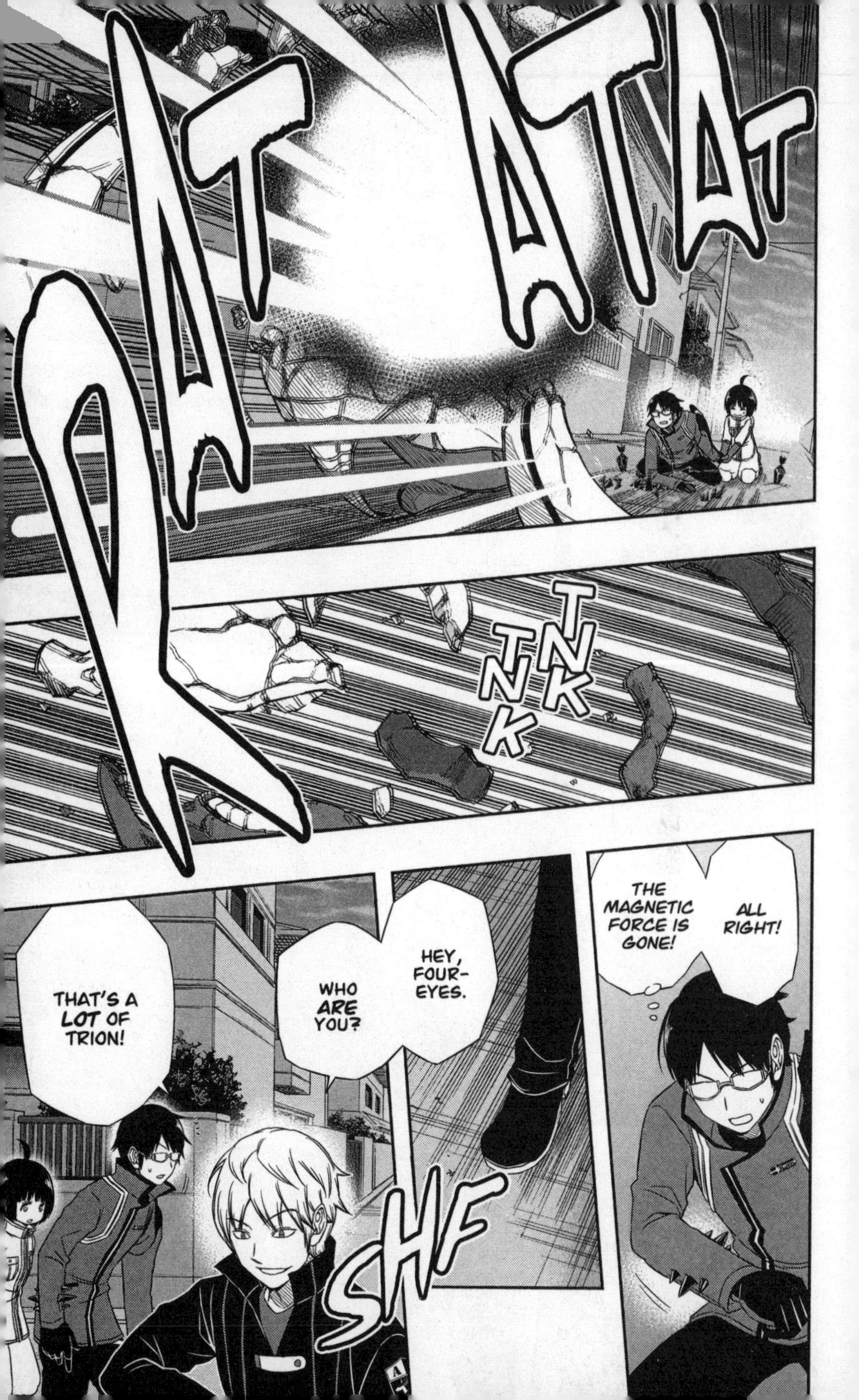
DAT ATATAT
TNK TNK
ALL RIGHT!
THE MAGNETIC FORCE IS GONE!
SHF
HEY, FOUR-EYES.
WHO ARE YOU?
THAT'S A LOT OF TRION!

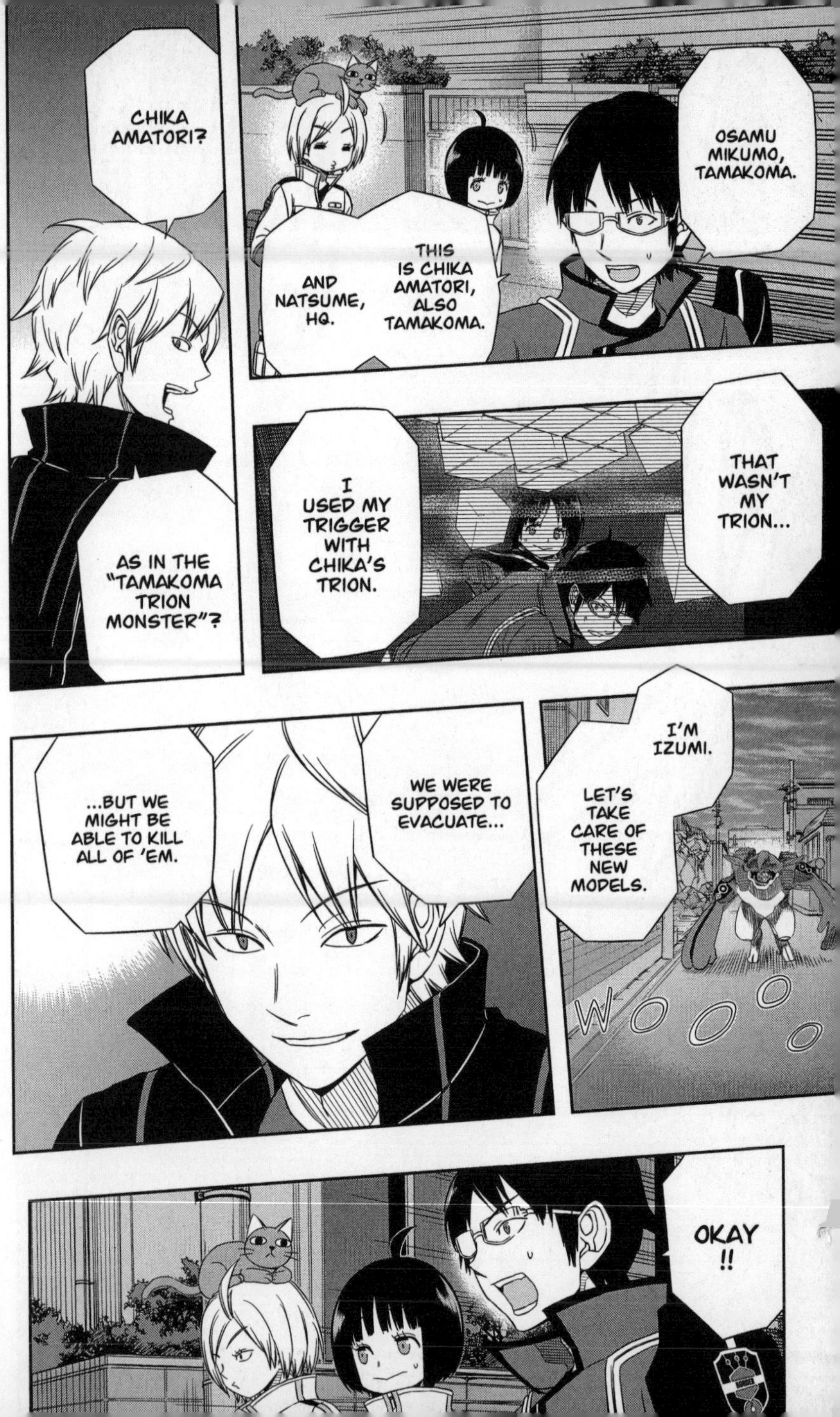
OSAMU MIKUMO, TAMAKOMA.
THIS IS CHIKA AMATORI, ALSO TAMAKOMA.
AND NATSUME, HQ.
THAT WASN'T MY TRION...
I USED MY TRIGGER WITH CHIKA'S TRION.
CHIKA AMATORI?
AS IN THE "TAMAKOMA TRION MONSTER"?
I'M IZUMI.
LET'S TAKE CARE OF THESE NEW MODELS.
WOOOO
WE WERE SUPPOSED TO EVACUATE...
...BUT WE MIGHT BE ABLE TO KILL ALL OF 'EM.
OKAY!!

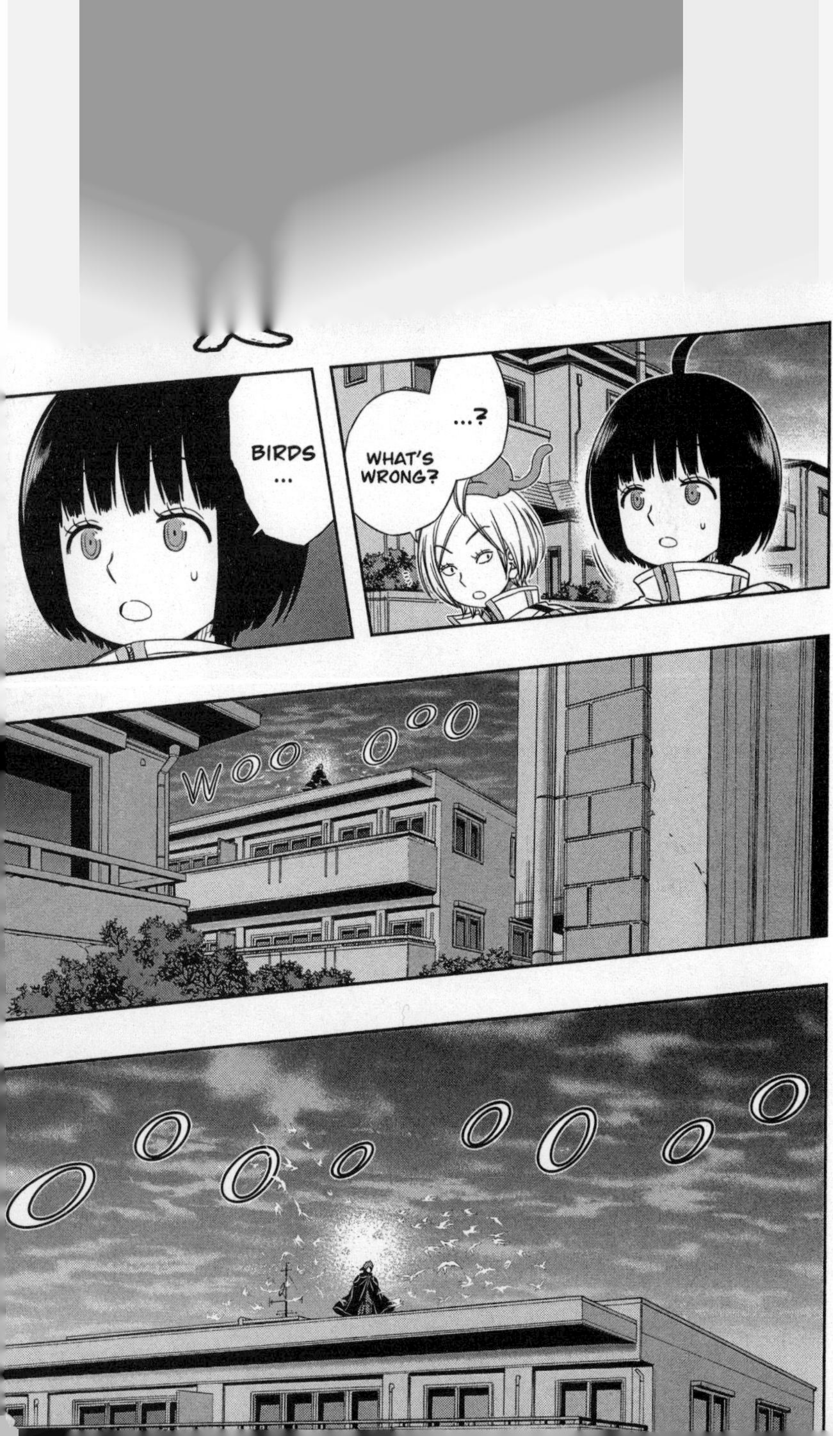

WHAT'S WRONG?
...?
BIRDS ...
WOOOOO
OOOOOOOOOO

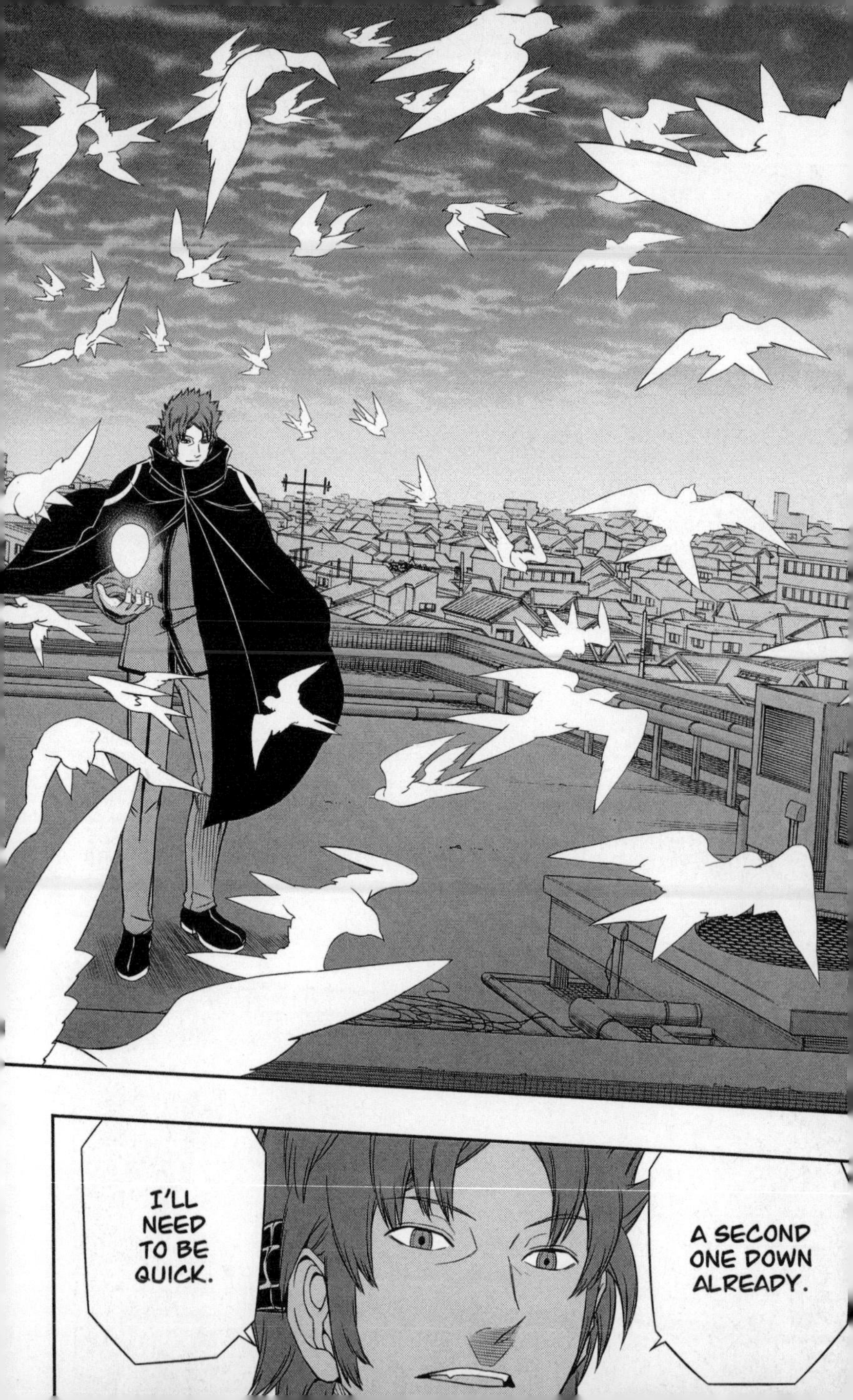
A SECOND ONE DOWN ALREADY.
I'LL NEED TO BE QUICK.

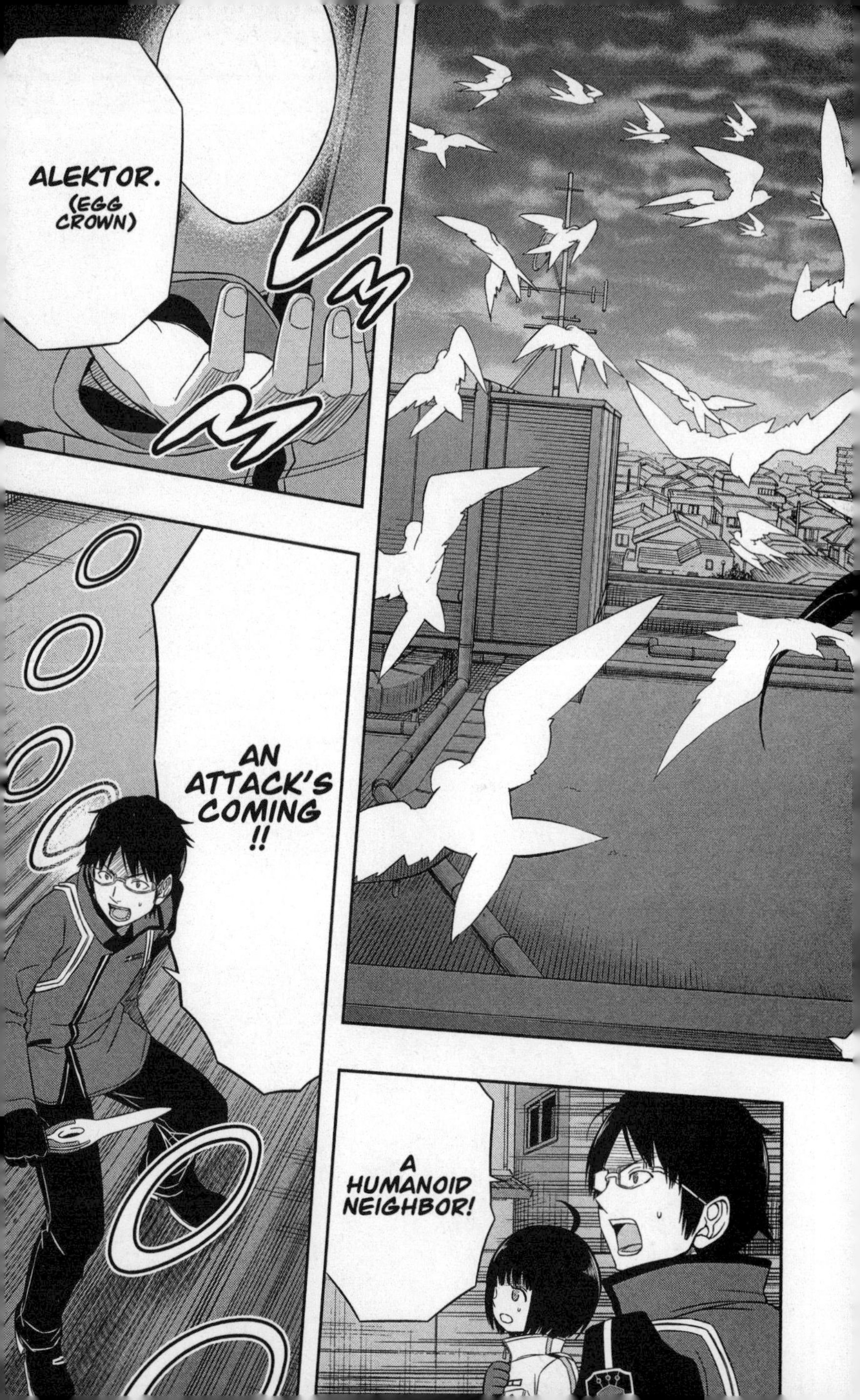

ALEKTOR.
(EGG CROWN)
VMM
AN ATTACK'S COMING!!
A HUMANOID NEIGHBOR!

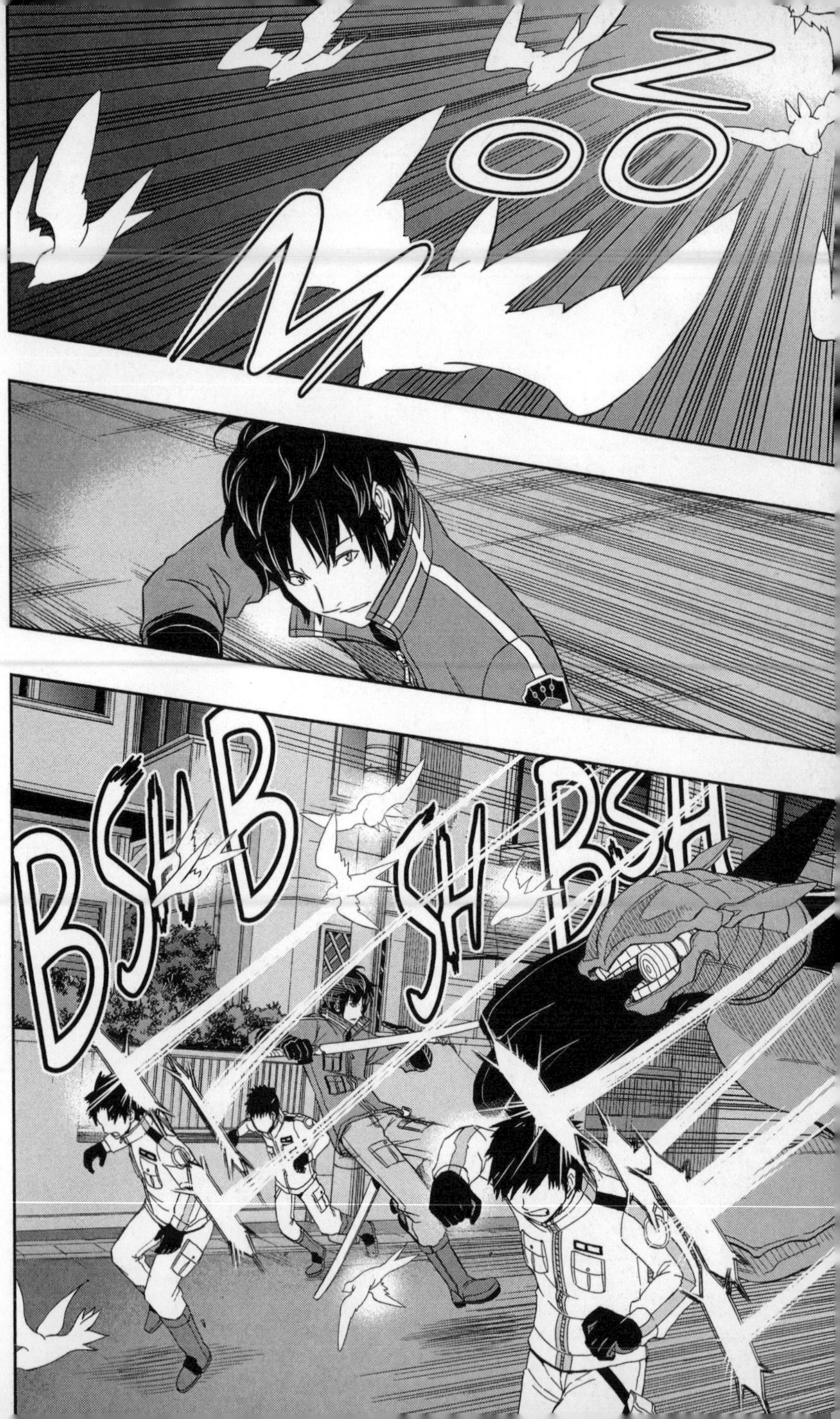
ZOOM
BSH BSH BSH

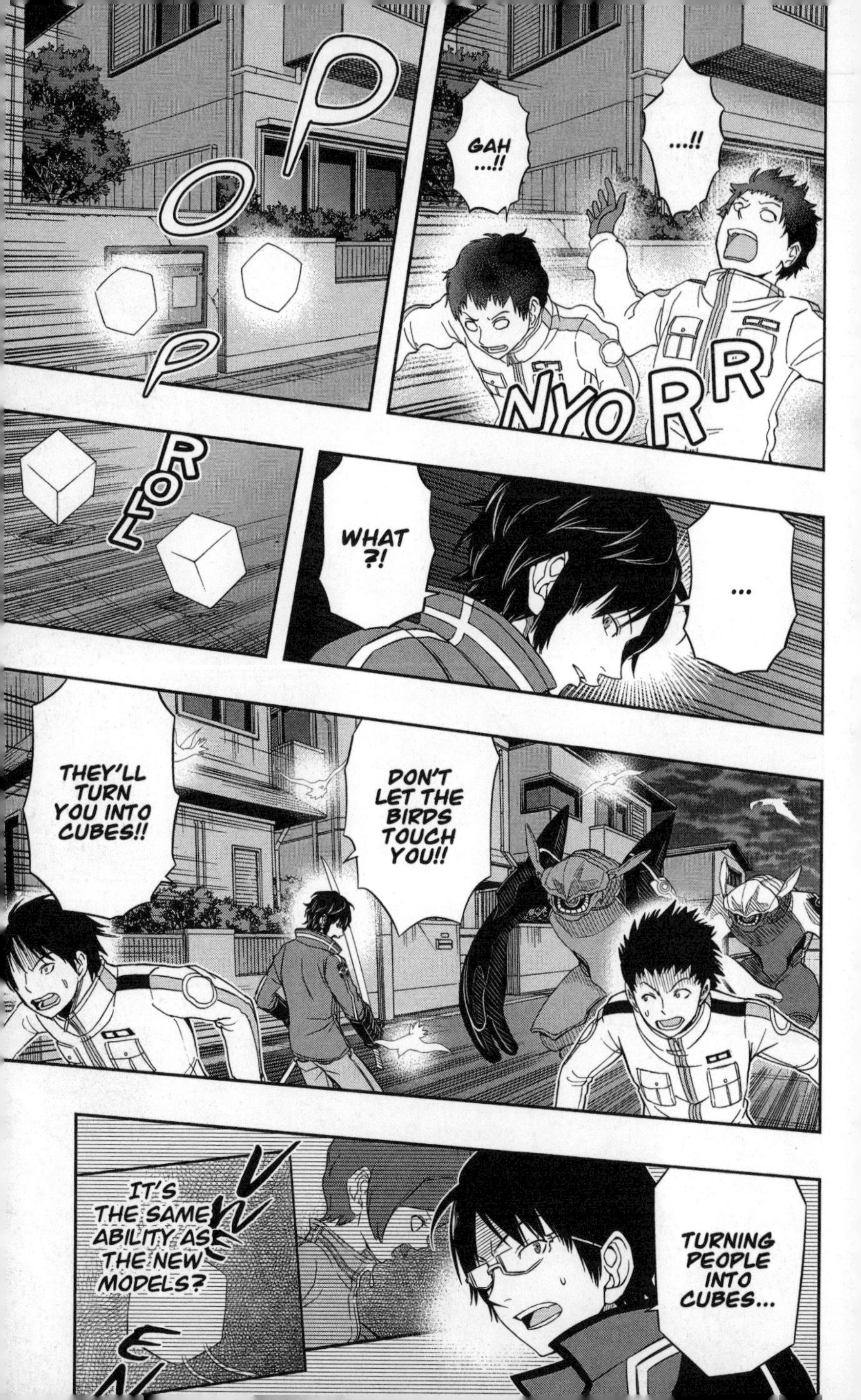
...!!
GAH ...!!
NYORR
POP
...
WHAT?!
ROLL
DON'T LET THE BIRDS TOUCH YOU!!
THEY'LL TURN YOU INTO CUBES!!
TURNING PEOPLE INTO CUBES...
IT'S THE SAME ABILITY AS THE NEW MODELS?

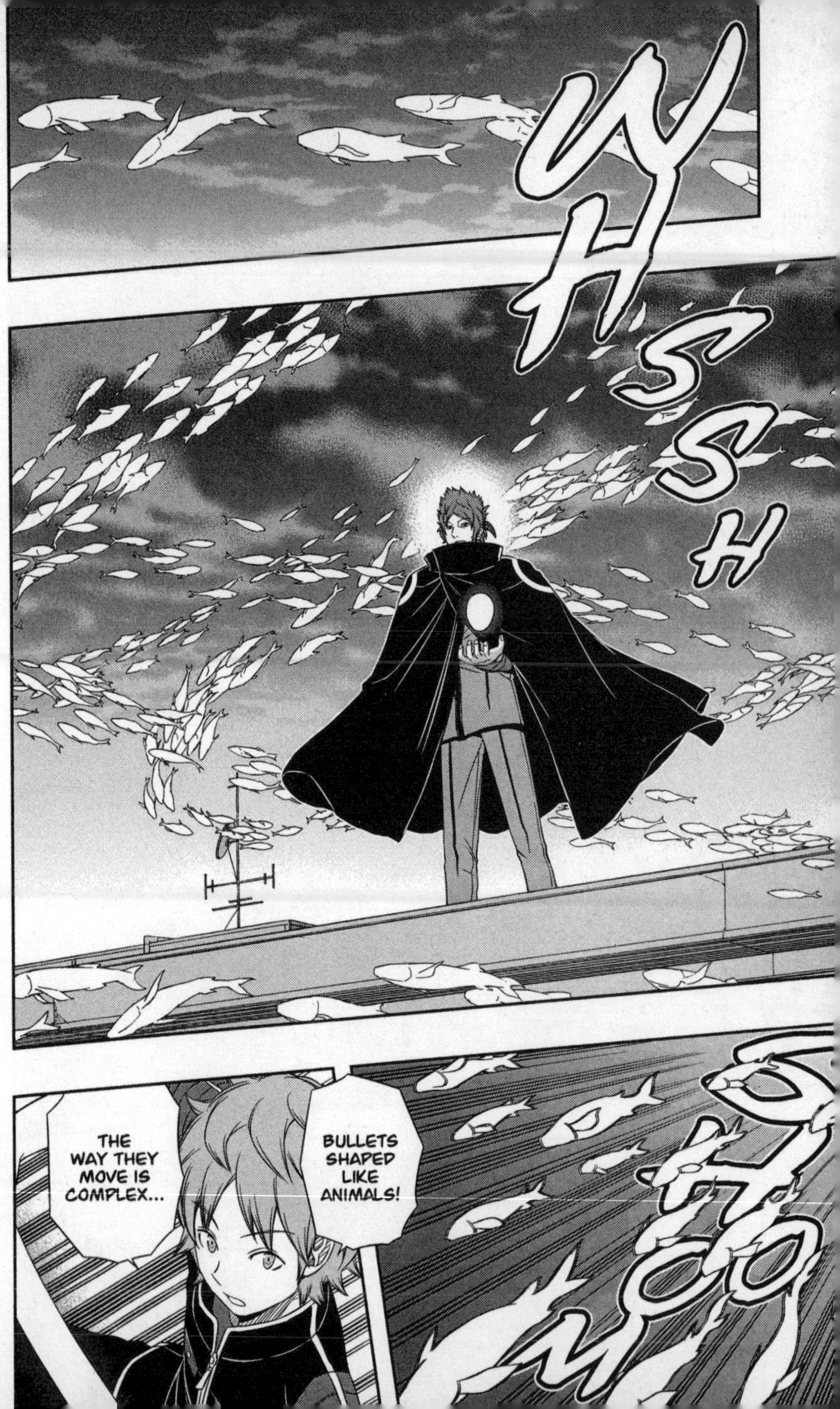
WHSSH
SHOOM
BULLETS SHAPED LIKE ANIMALS!
THE WAY THEY MOVE IS COMPLEX...

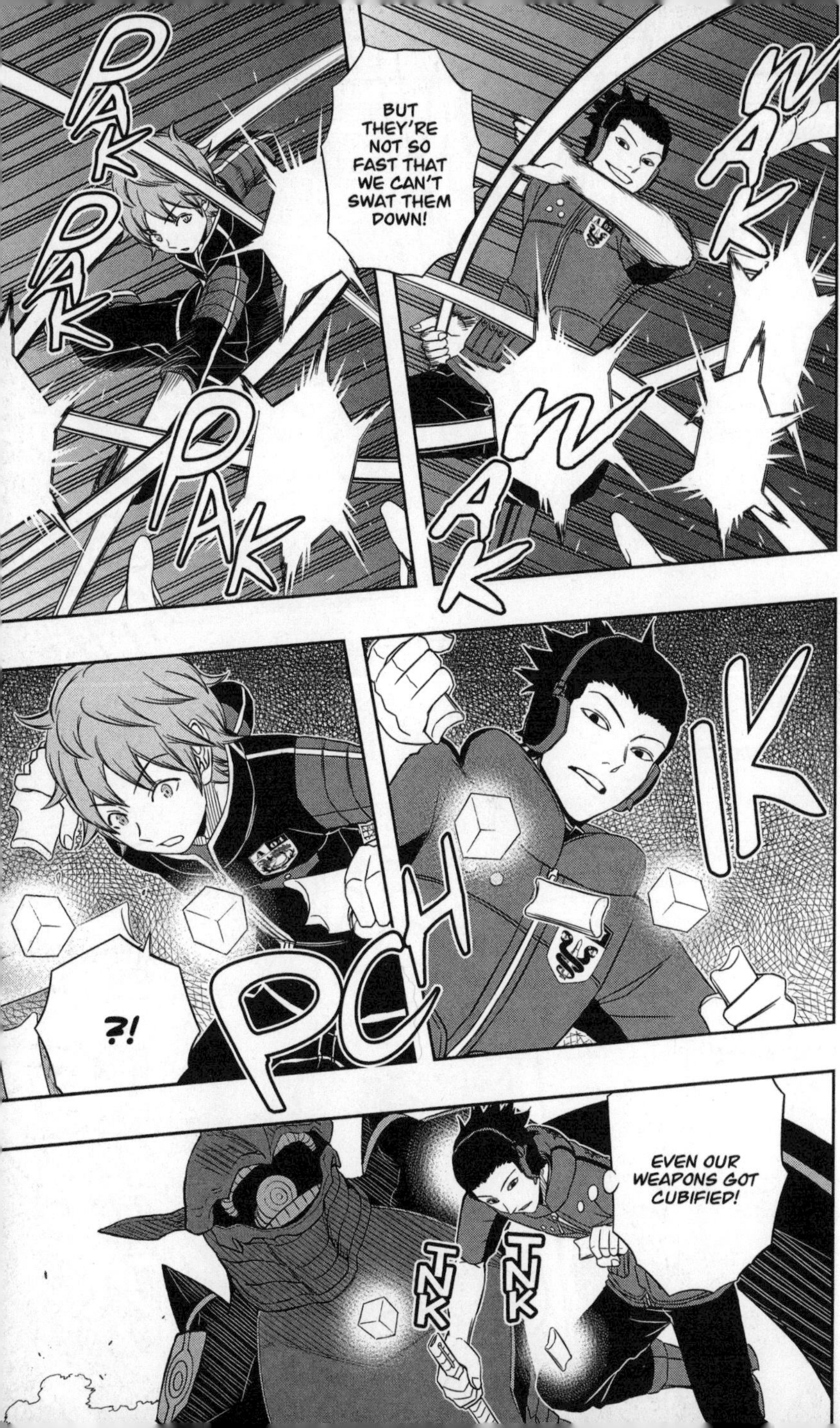

BUT THEY'RE NOT SO FAST THAT WE CAN'T SWAT THEM DOWN!
WAK
WAK
PAK
PAK
PAK
PCHIK
?!
EVEN OUR WEAPONS GOT CUBIFIED!
TNK
TNK

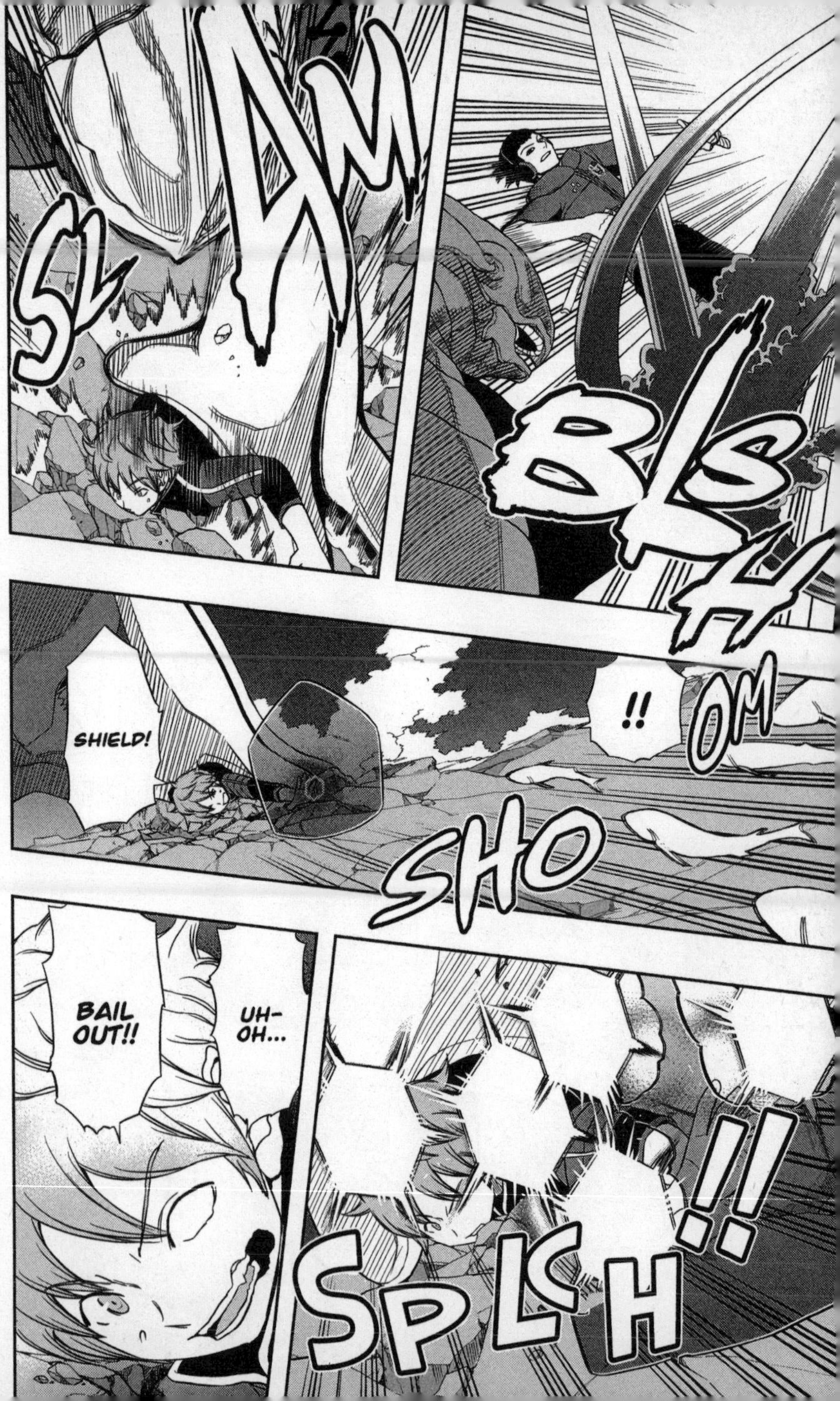
BLSH
SLAM
!!
SHOOM
SHIELD!
SPLCH!!
UH-OH...
BAIL OUT!!

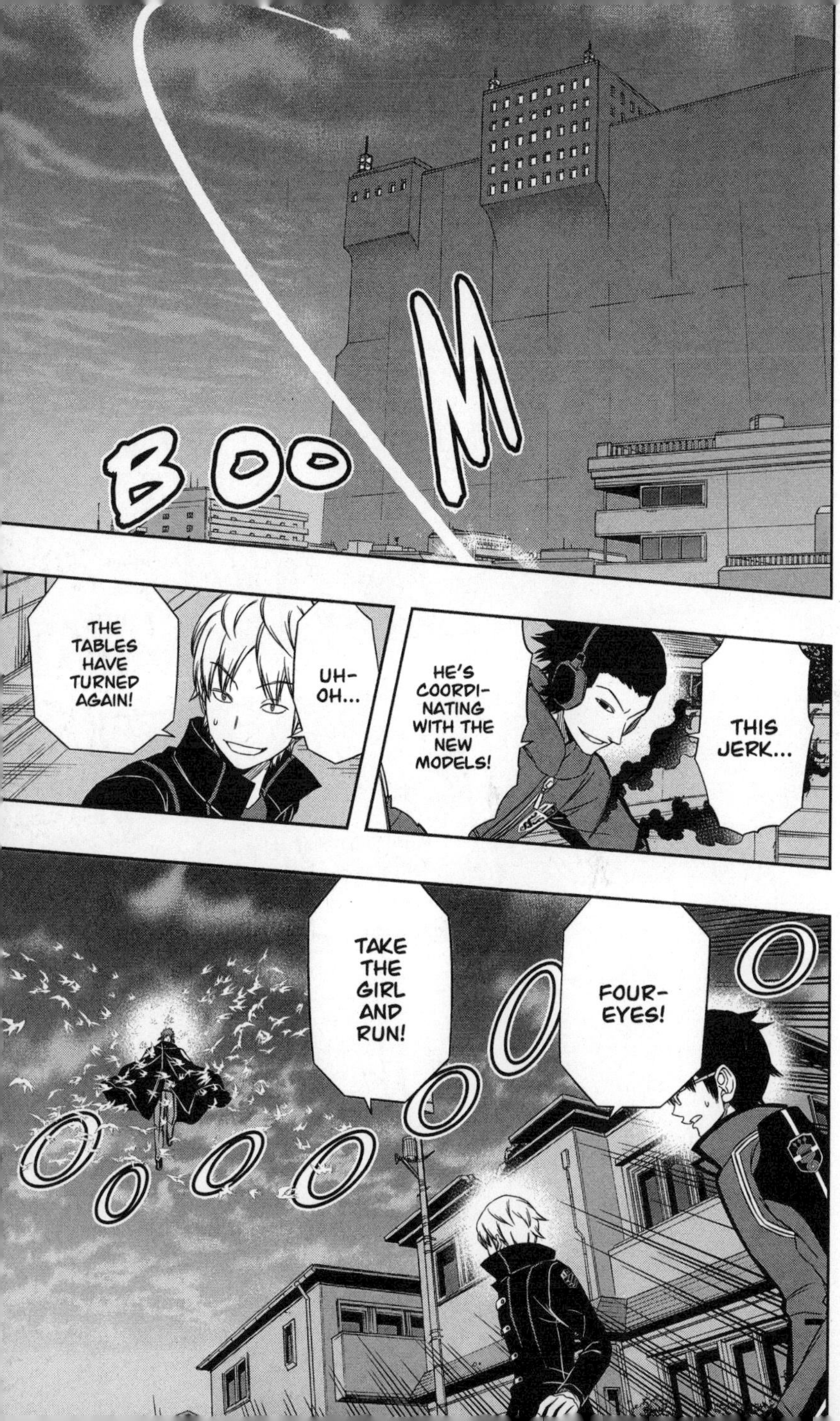
BOOM
THIS JERK...
HE'S COORDI-NATING WITH THE NEW MODELS!
UH-OH...
THE TABLES HAVE TURNED AGAIN!
FOUR-EYES!
TAKE THE GIRL AND RUN!

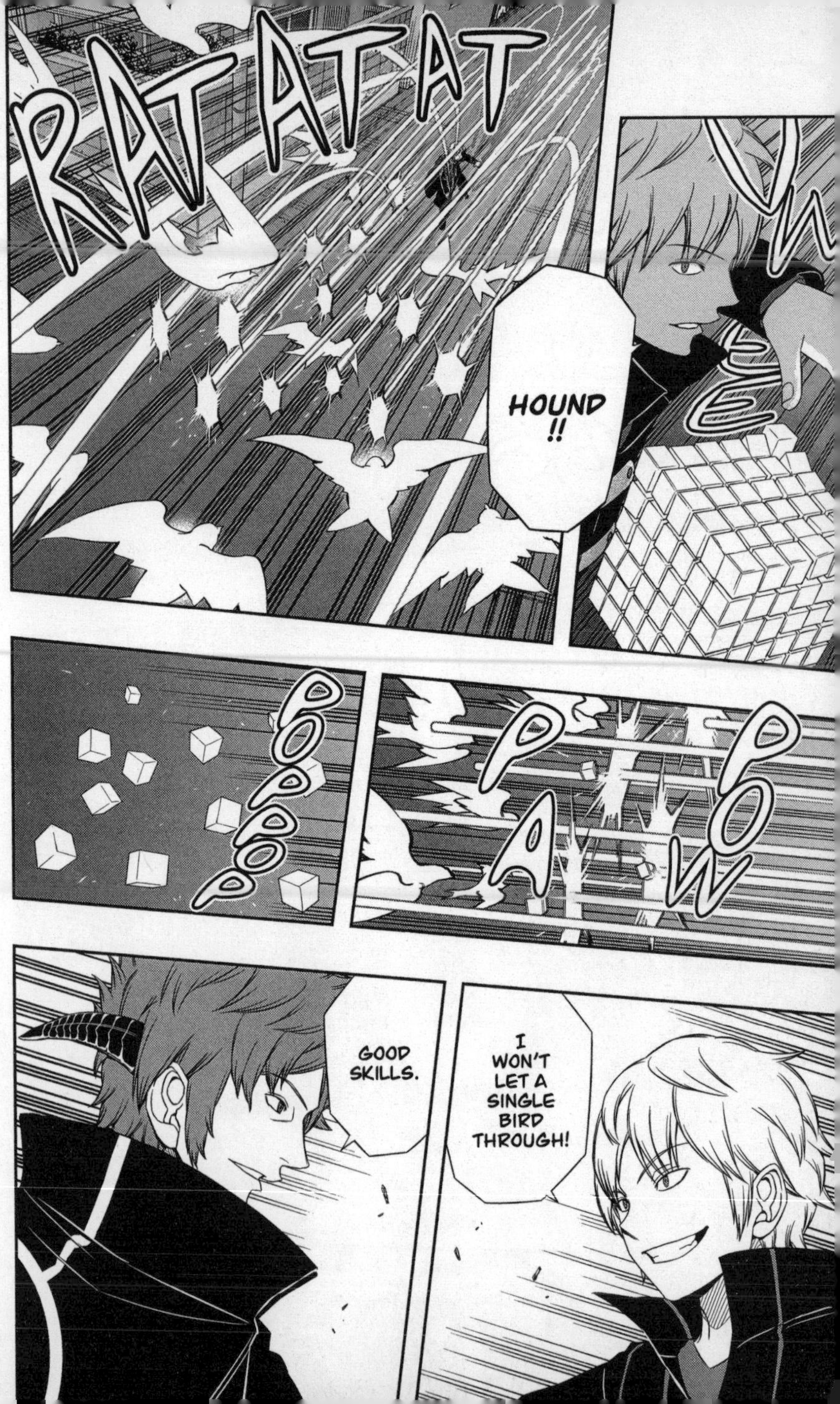
HOUND!!
RATATAT
POW
PA
POPOPOP
I WON'T LET A SINGLE BIRD THROUGH!
GOOD SKILLS.

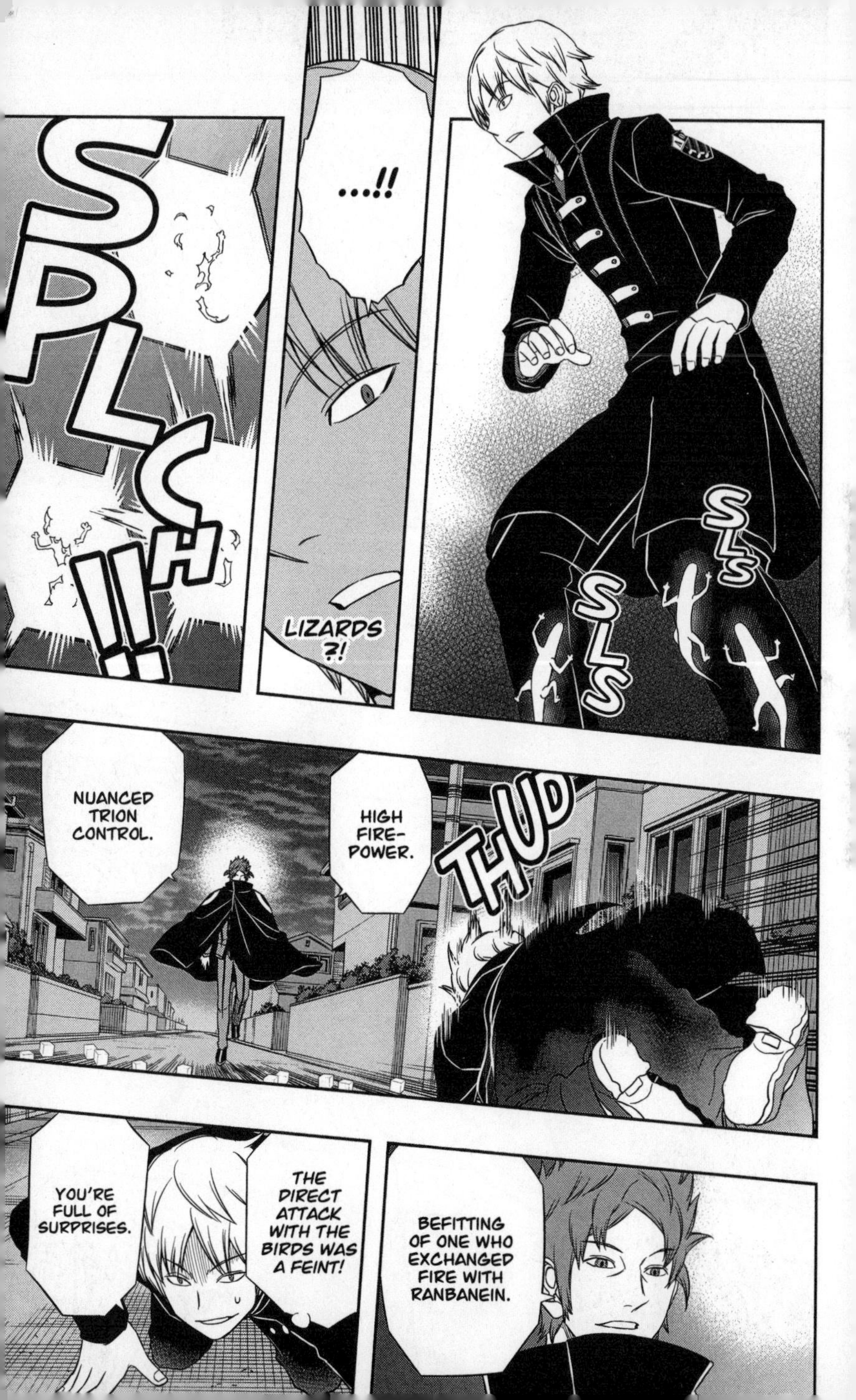
SLS
SLS
...!!
LIZARDS ?!
SPLCH!!
THUD
HIGH FIRE-POWER.
NUANCED TRION CONTROL.
BEFITTING OF ONE WHO EXCHANGED FIRE WITH RANBANEIN.
THE DIRECT ATTACK WITH THE BIRDS WAS A FEINT!
YOU'RE FULL OF SURPRISES.

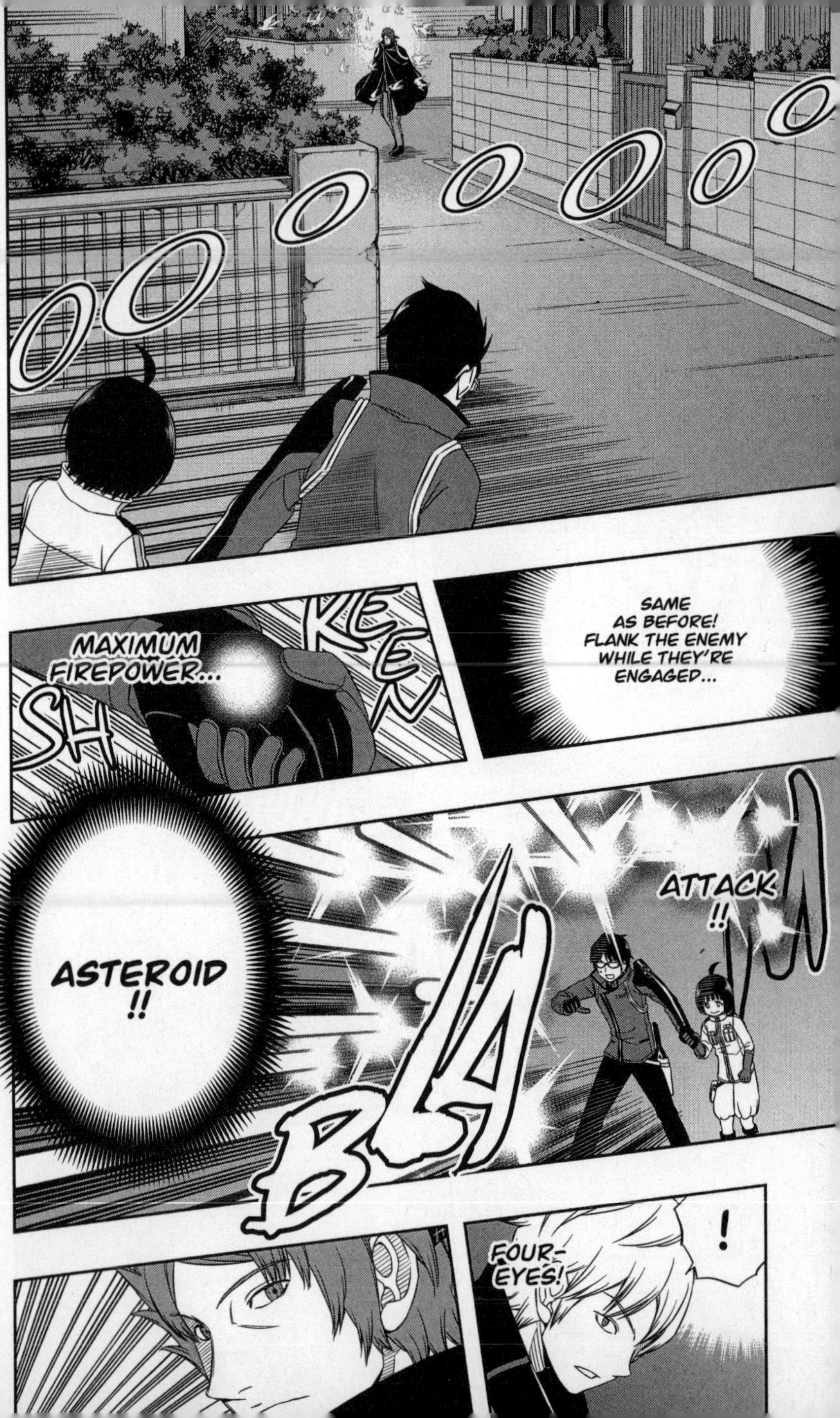

SAME AS BEFORE! FLANK THE ENEMY WHILE THEY'RE ENGAGED...
KEEN
MAXIMUM FIREPOWER...
SH
ATTACK!!
ASTEROID!!
BLAM
!
FOUR-EYES!

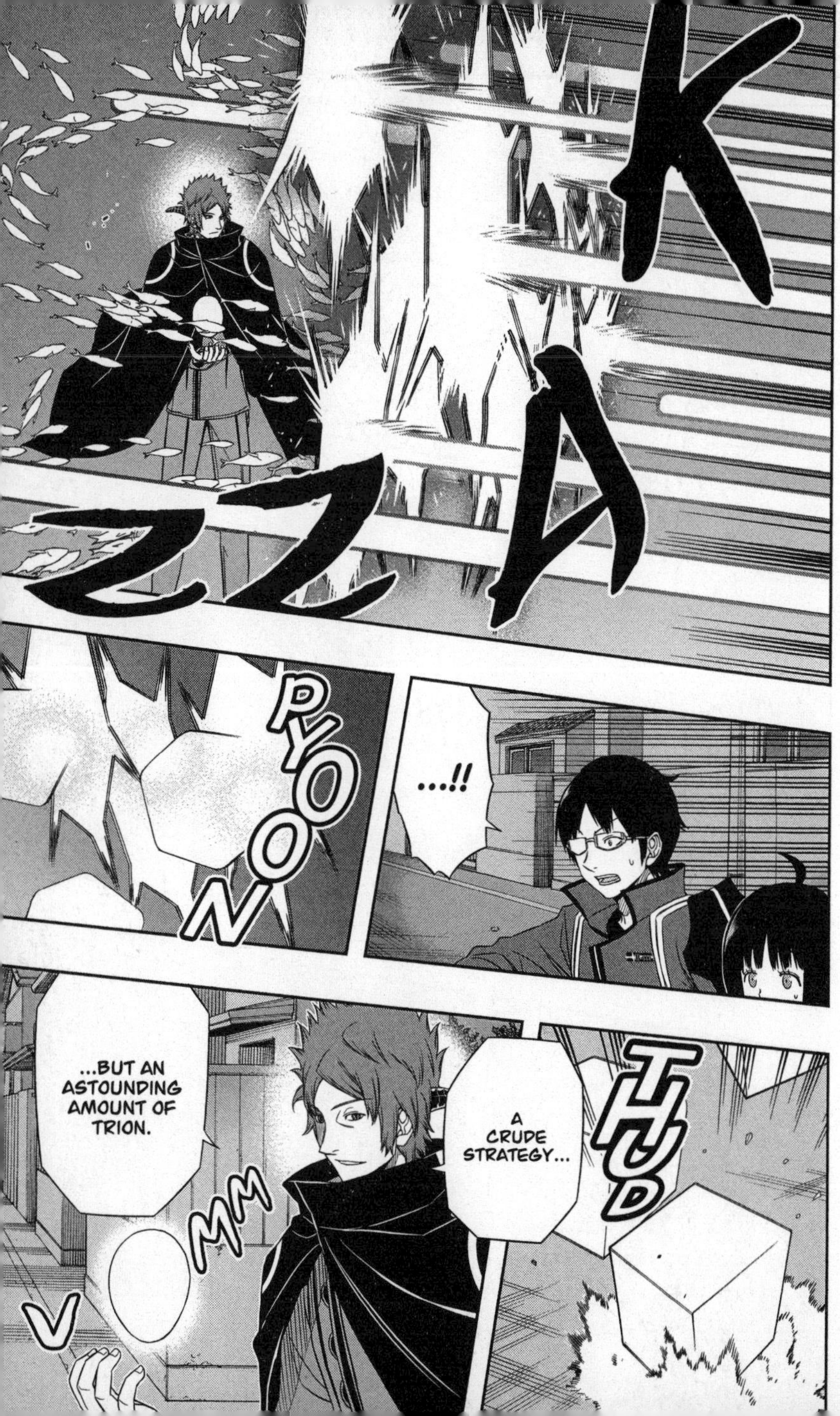
...!!
PYOON
THUD
A CRUDE STRATEGY...
...BUT AN ASTOUNDING AMOUNT OF TRION.
VMM

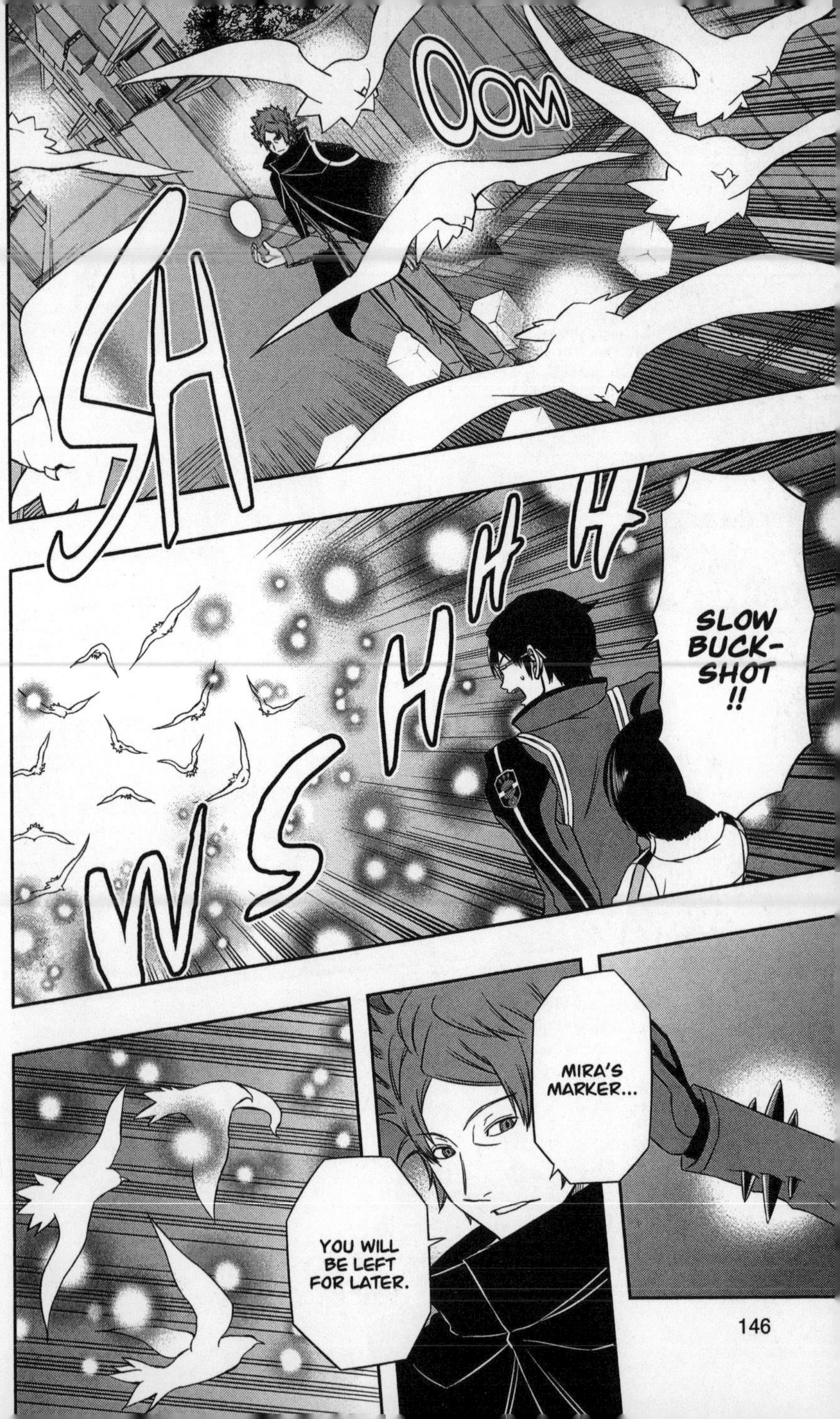
OOM
SH
SLOW BUCK-SHOT!!
WSHHH
MIRA'S MARKER...
YOU WILL BE LEFT FOR LATER.

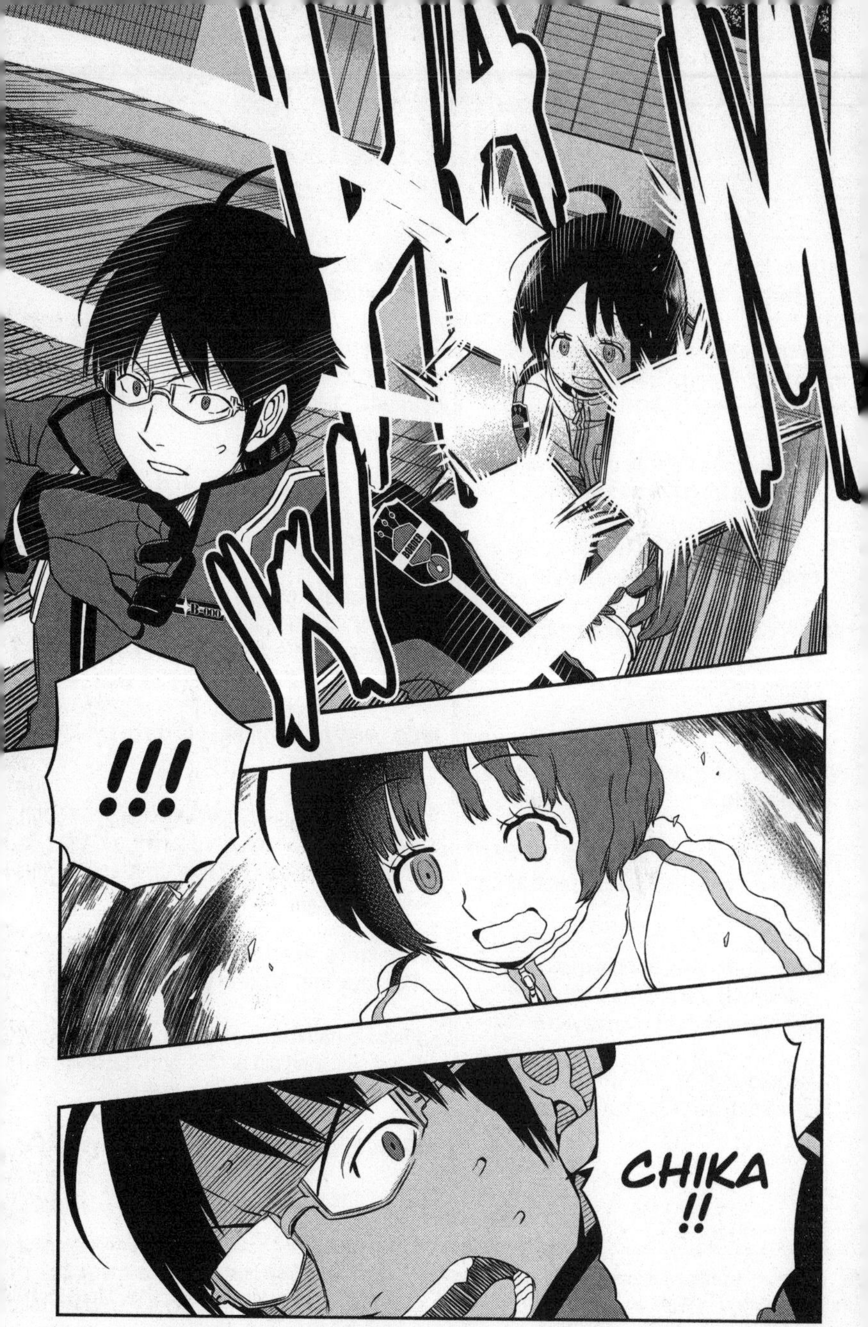
!!!
CHIKA !!

Q&A: Part 7

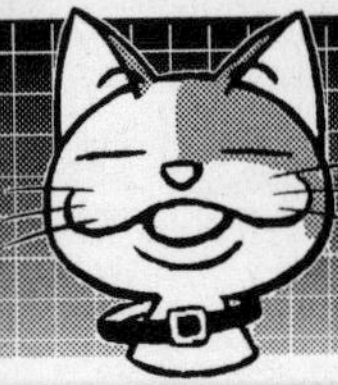

Inquiring minds are inexhaustible.

■Does Konami's battle mode have short hair to conserve Trion?

It's most likely so her hair doesn't get in the way during a battle. It's her old hairstyle.

■Tokieda lists cats as one of his likes, but does he have any at home?

He has two. Arthur, a brown tabby, and a black and white cat named Tomio.

■Why does Yotaro wear a helmet?

Because he's always in battle mode. Reiji made it for him.

■Who is the main character, Yuma or Osamu?

Either one. I personally consider the four people I drew on the first title page as the main characters.

■If you were to eat Bonchi fried rice crackers in Jin's room without asking him, would he get mad at you?

You would start to get shipments of Bonchi fried rice crackers sent to your room.

■Do Gates open only in Mikado City or do they also open elsewhere?

They open around the world and people secretly get kidnapped. But since a big one opened in Mikado, the world thinks that they only open in Mikado.

■Why is Tachikawa affiliated with Kido when Shinoda taught him how to use a sword?

The Kido faction prioritizes away missions, and the Shinoda faction prioritizes defense. Tachikawa is interested in away missions. It's not because he disagrees with Shinoda.

■Do away mission agents try to avoid detection?

They sneak in to get Trigger technology through trades or negotiations. If a country is in the middle of a war, they will fight off Attackers and take their triggers.

■Konami and Arashiyama are related. Did they join around the same time?

Konami joined much earlier. Konami has been around since the old Border, and Arashiyama joined after the current base was built.

■Does Kikuchihara actually like anything?

Friends and colleagues.

■ I sometimes answer questions I get in my fan mail on my official Twitter feed. My editor mumbles, "They're coming..." when I get more followers. **World Trigger official Twitter account: @W_Trigger_off**

Chapter 69 Osamu Mikumo: Part 8

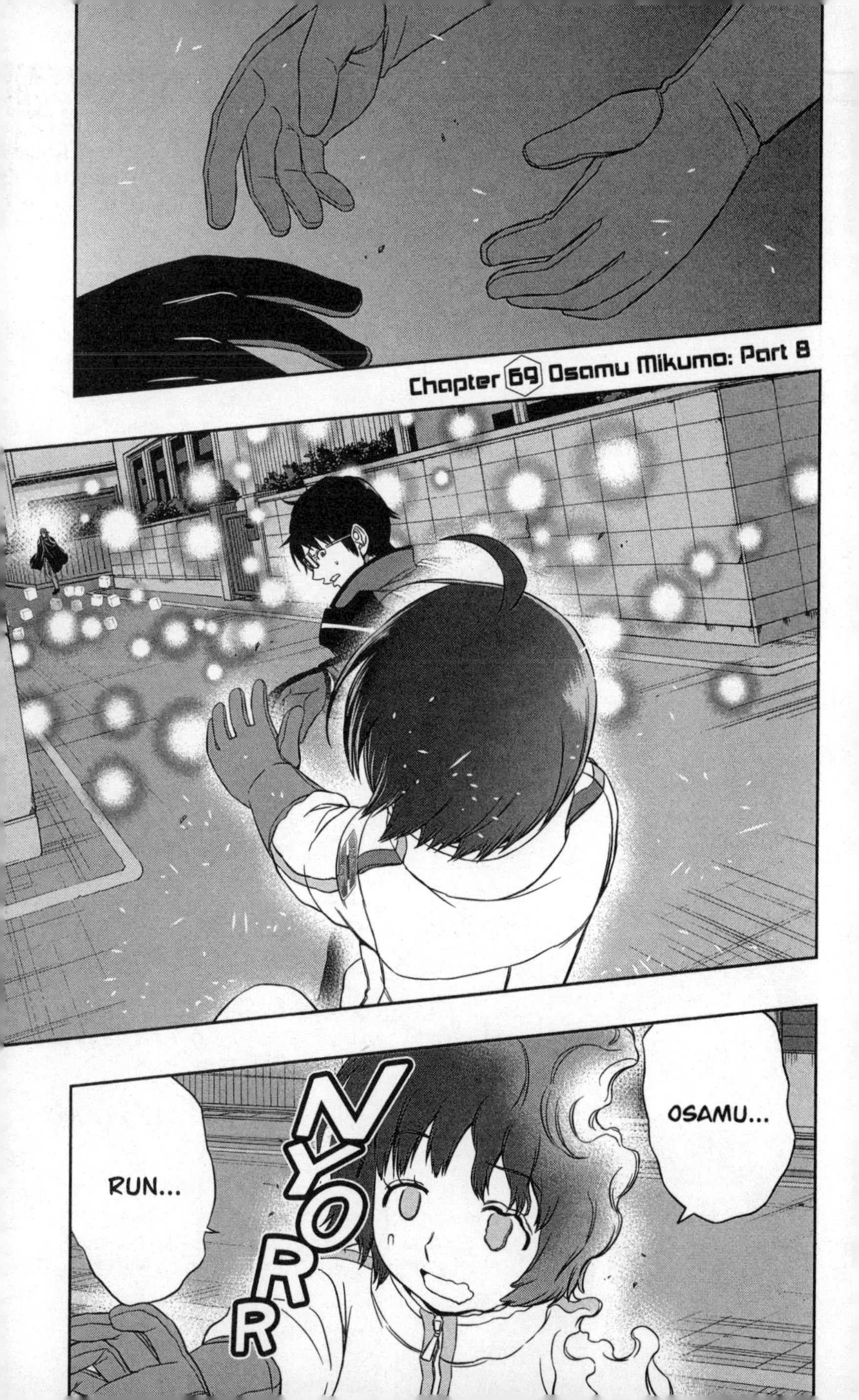
OSAMU...
NYORR
RUN...

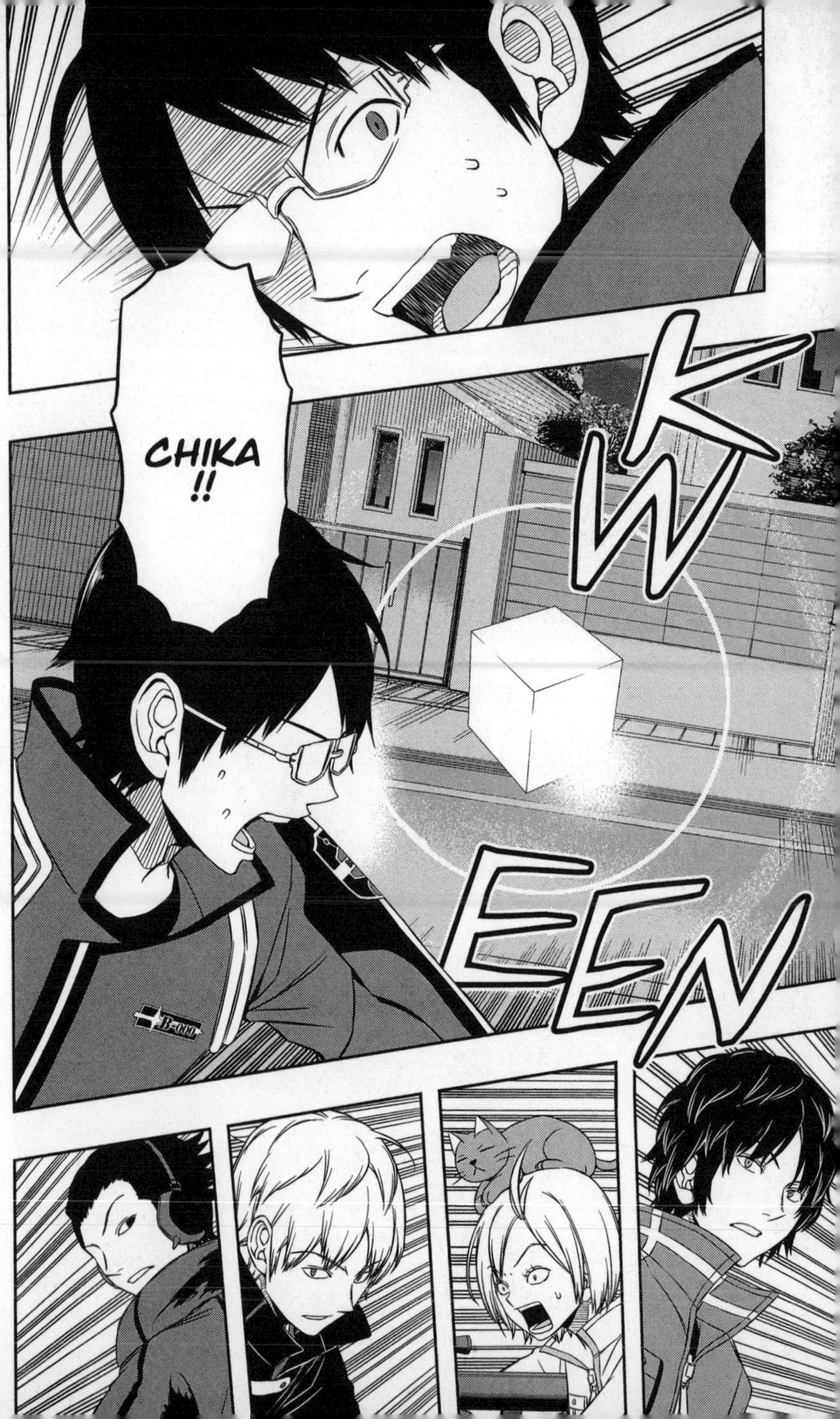
CHIKA !!
KWEEN

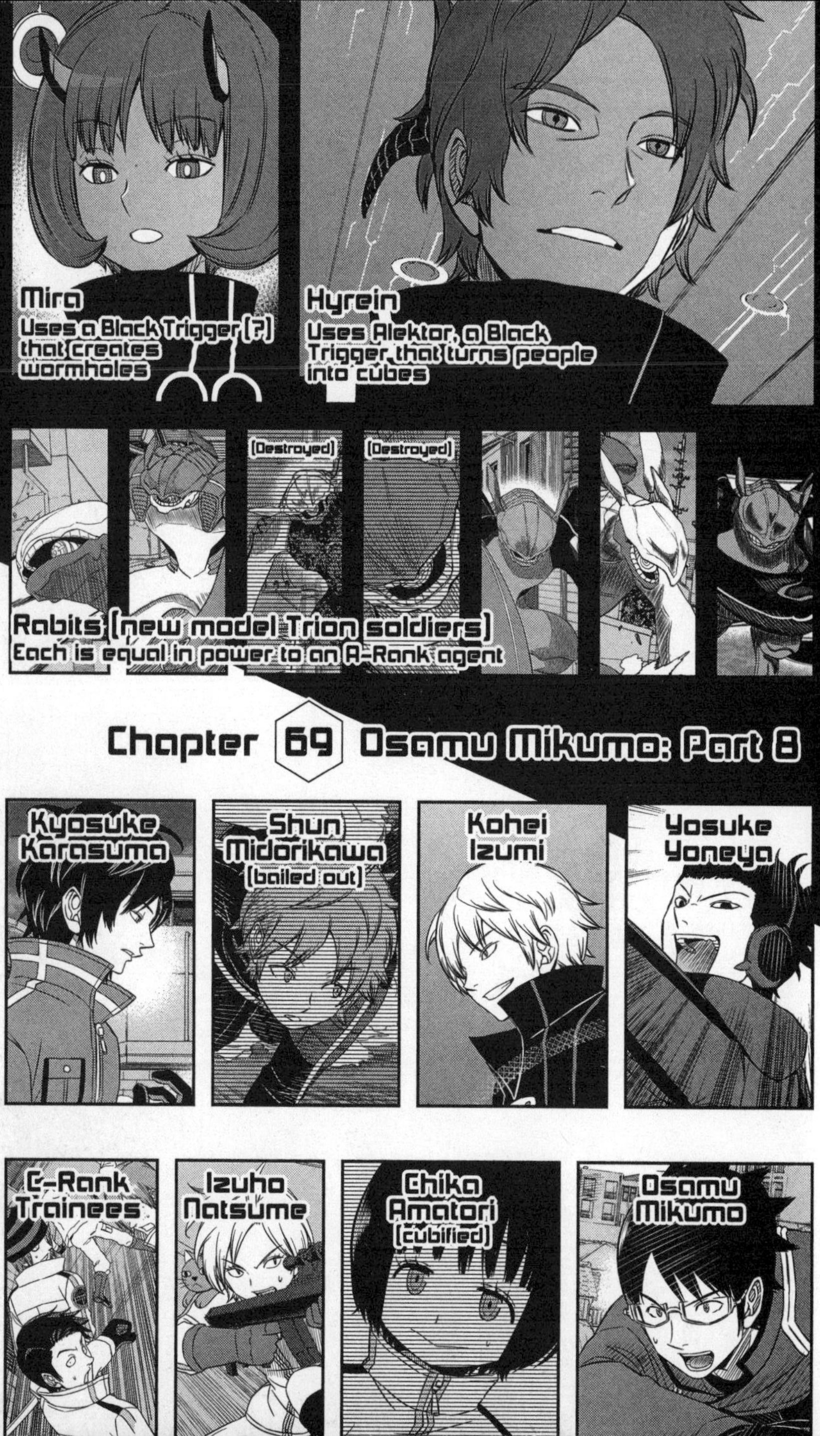
Hyrein
Uses Alektor, a Black Trigger that turns people into cubes
Mira
Uses a Black Trigger (?) that creates wormholes
(Destroyed)
(Destroyed)
Rabits (new model Trion soldiers)
Each is equal in power to an A-Rank agent
Chapter 69 Osamu Mikumo: Part 8
Yosuke Yoneya
Kohei Izumi
Shun Midorikawa
(bailed out)
Kyosuke Karasuma
Osamu Mikumo
Chika Amatori
(cubified)
Izuho Natsume
C-Rank Trainees

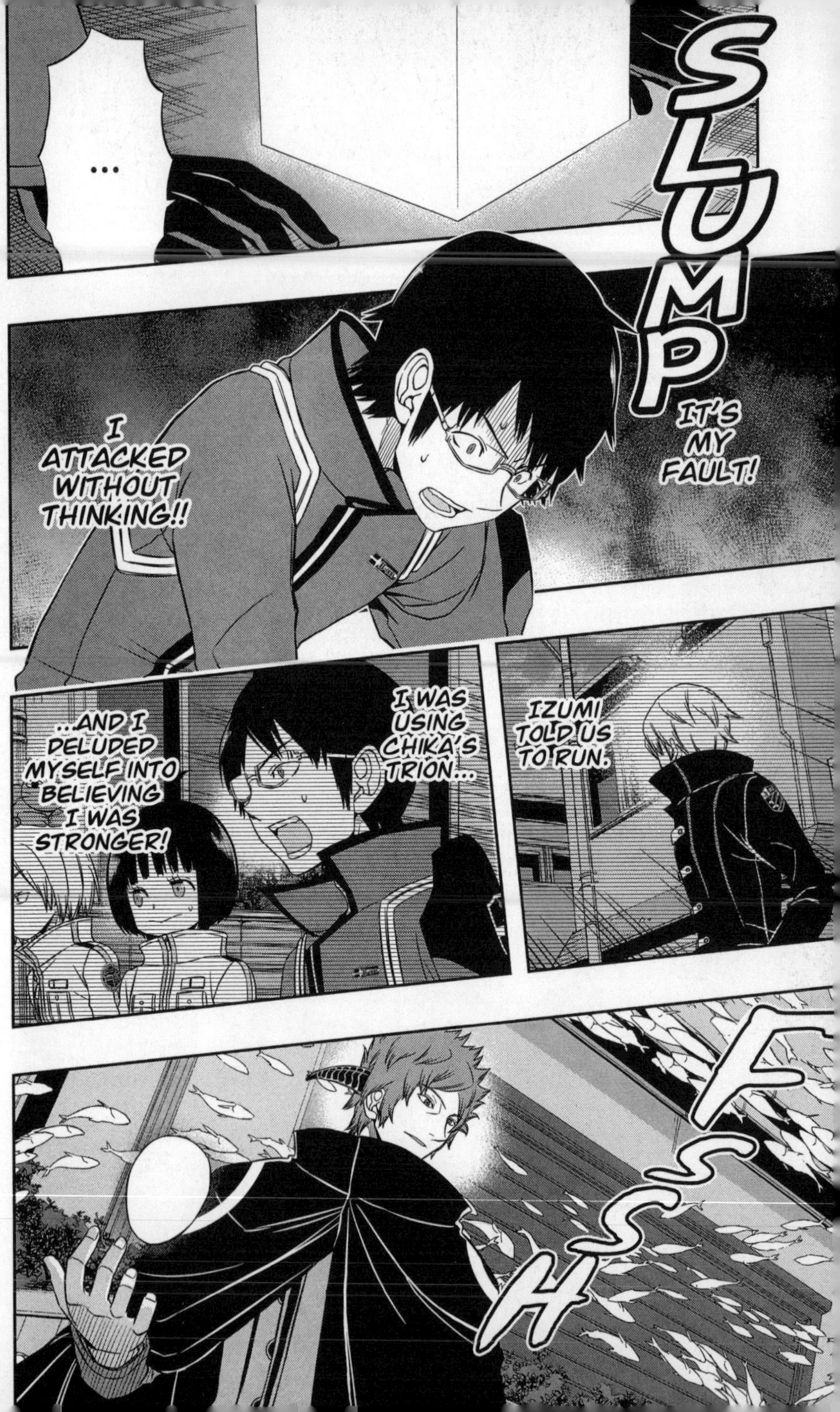
...
SLUMP
IT'S MY FAULT!
I ATTACKED WITHOUT THINKING!!
IZUMI TOLD US TO RUN.
I WAS USING CHIKA'S TRION...
...AND I DELUDED MYSELF INTO BELIEVING I WAS STRONGER!
FSSSH

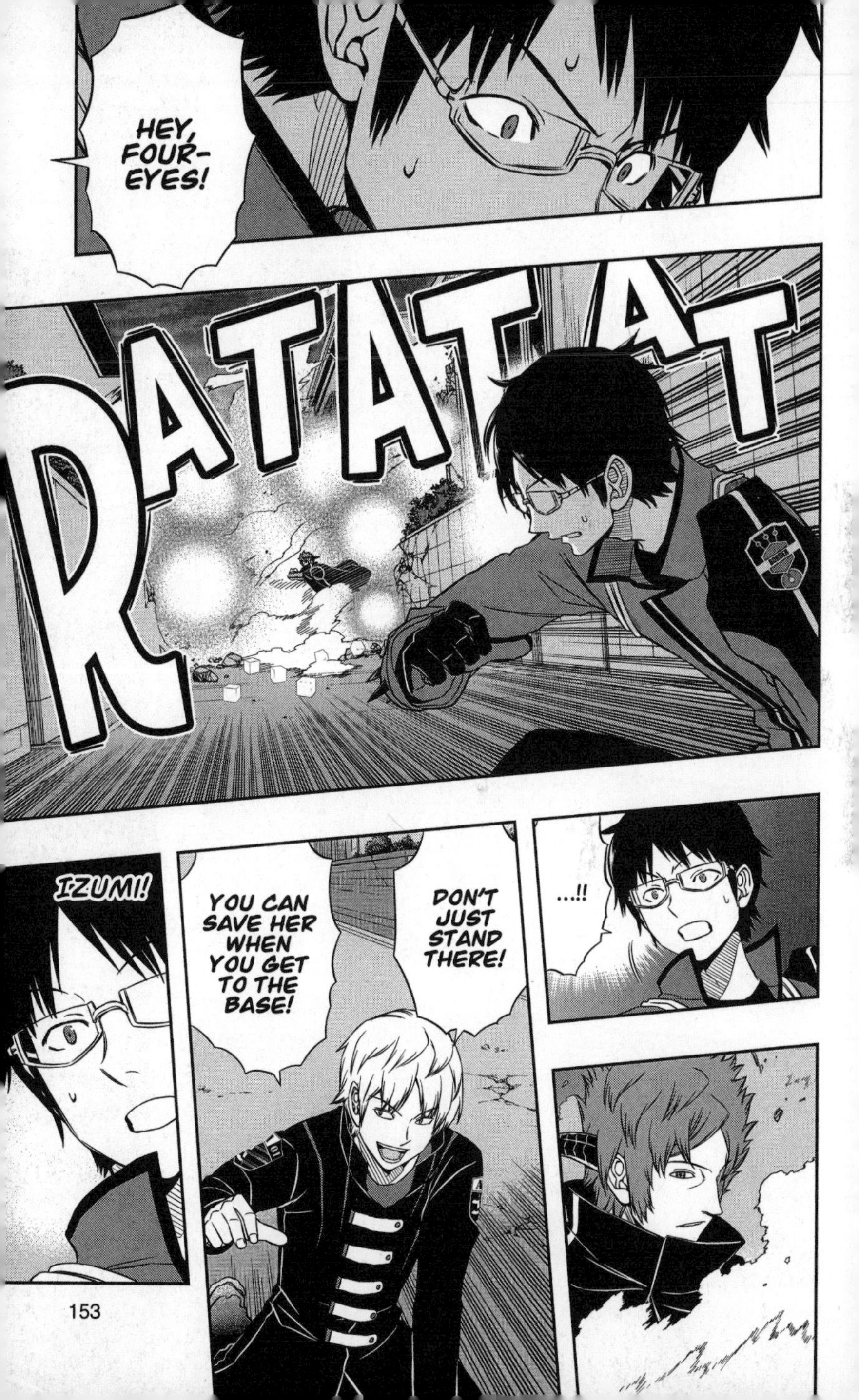
HEY, FOUR-EYES!
RATATAT
...!!
DON'T JUST STAND THERE!
YOU CAN SAVE HER WHEN YOU GET TO THE BASE!
IZUMI!

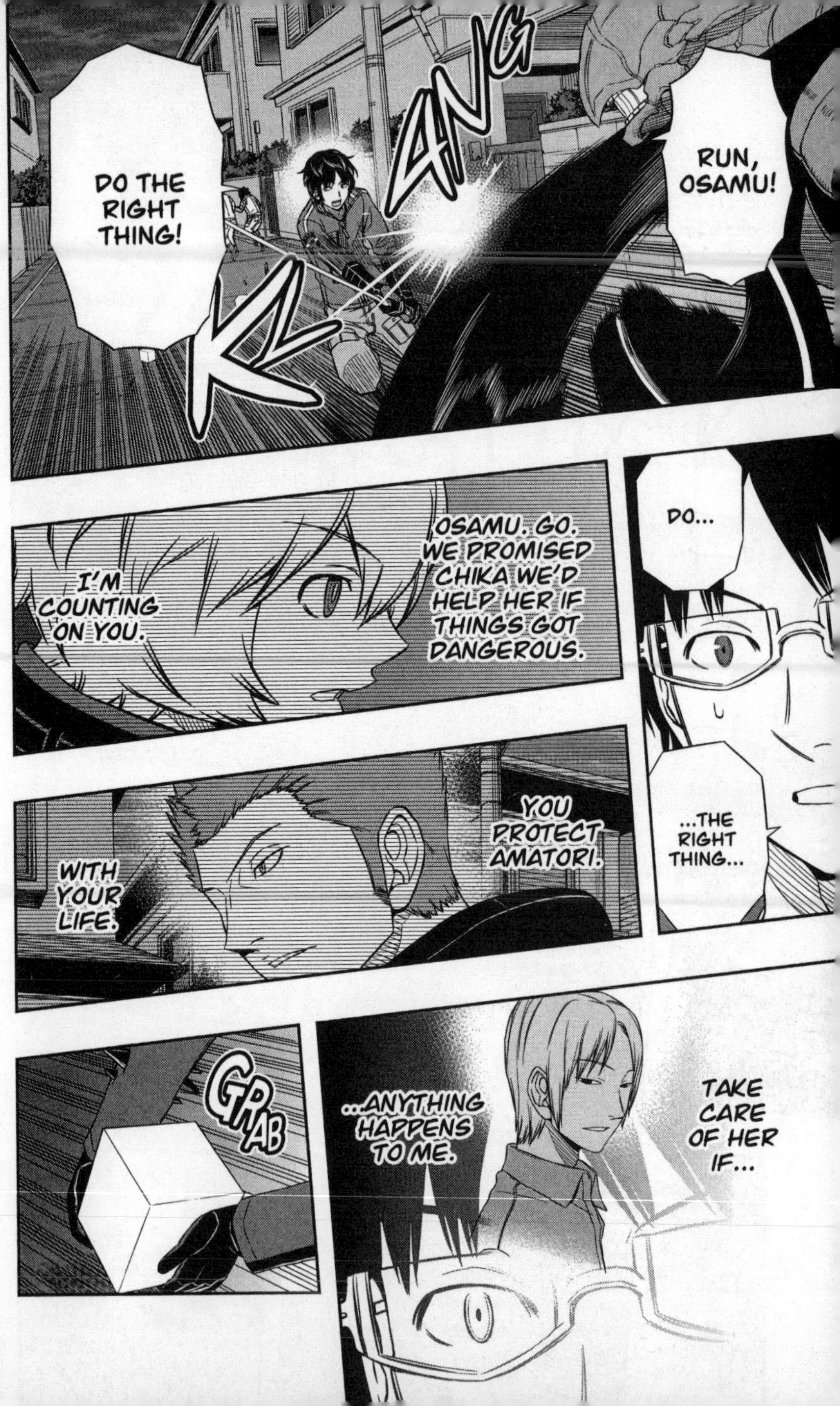
RUN, OSAMU!
DO THE RIGHT THING!
KLANG
DO...
...THE RIGHT THING...
OSAMU. GO. WE PROMISED CHIKA WE'D HELP HER IF THINGS GOT DANGEROUS.
I'M COUNTING ON YOU.
YOU PROTECT AMATORI.
WITH YOUR LIFE.
TAKE CARE OF HER IF...
...ANYTHING HAPPENS TO ME.
GRAB

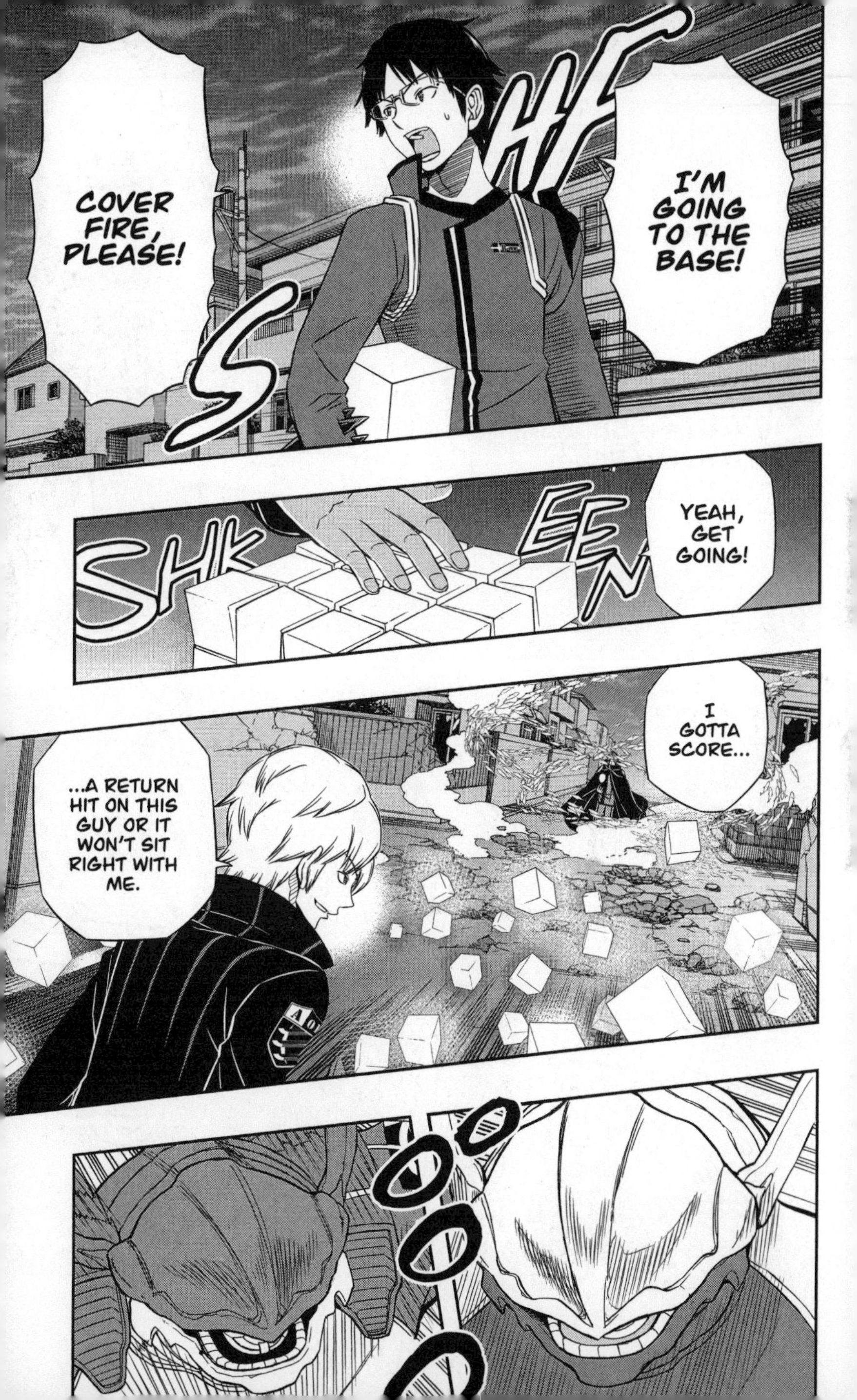
I'M GOING TO THE BASE!
SHF
S
COVER FIRE, PLEASE!
YEAH, GET GOING!
EEN
SHK
I GOTTA SCORE...
...A RETURN HIT ON THIS GUY OR IT WON'T SIT RIGHT WITH ME.

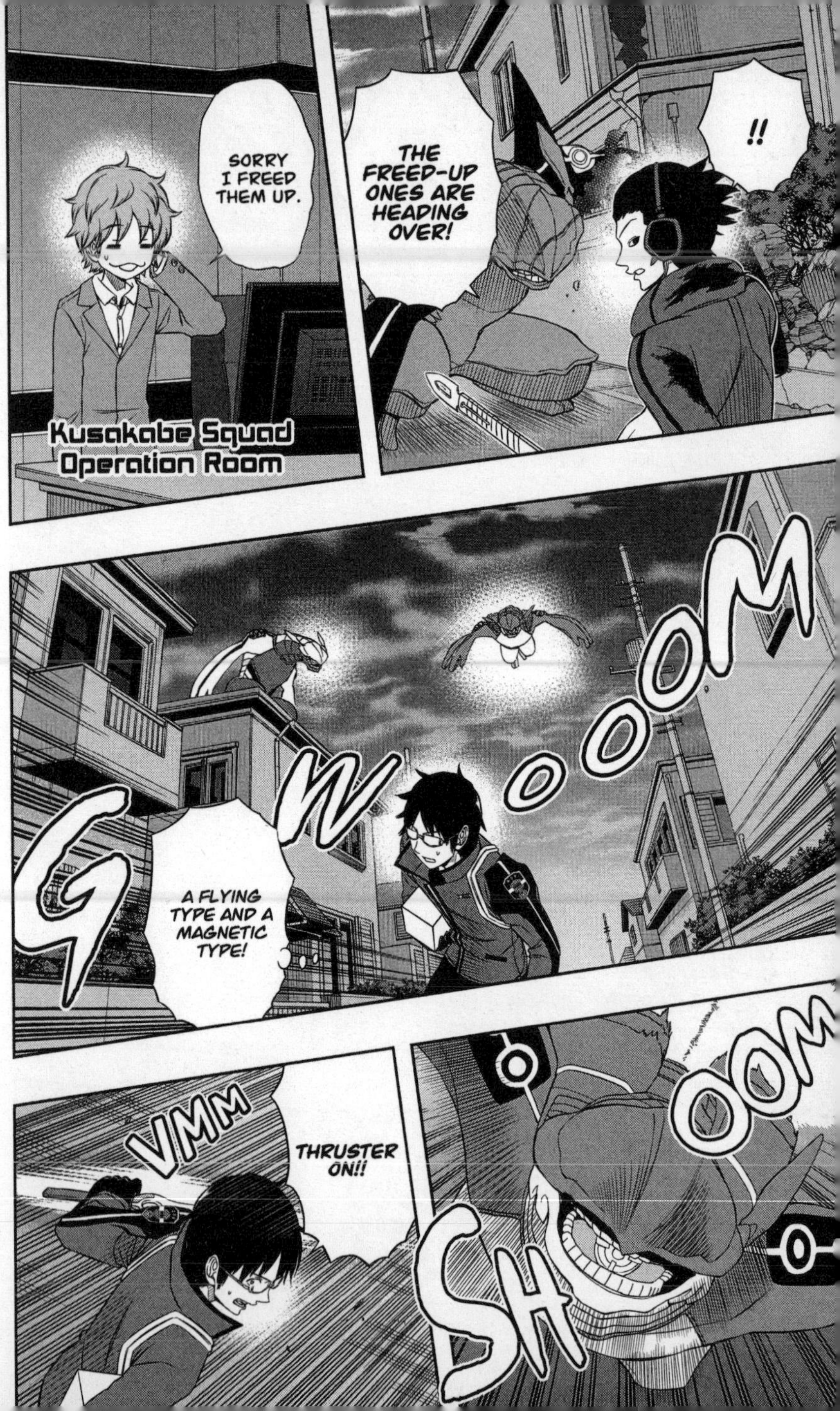
!!
THE FREED-UP ONES ARE HEADING OVER!
SORRY I FREED THEM UP.
Kusakabe Squad Operation Room
GWOOOOM
A FLYING TYPE AND A MAGNETIC TYPE!
SHOOOM
VMM
THRUSTER ON!!

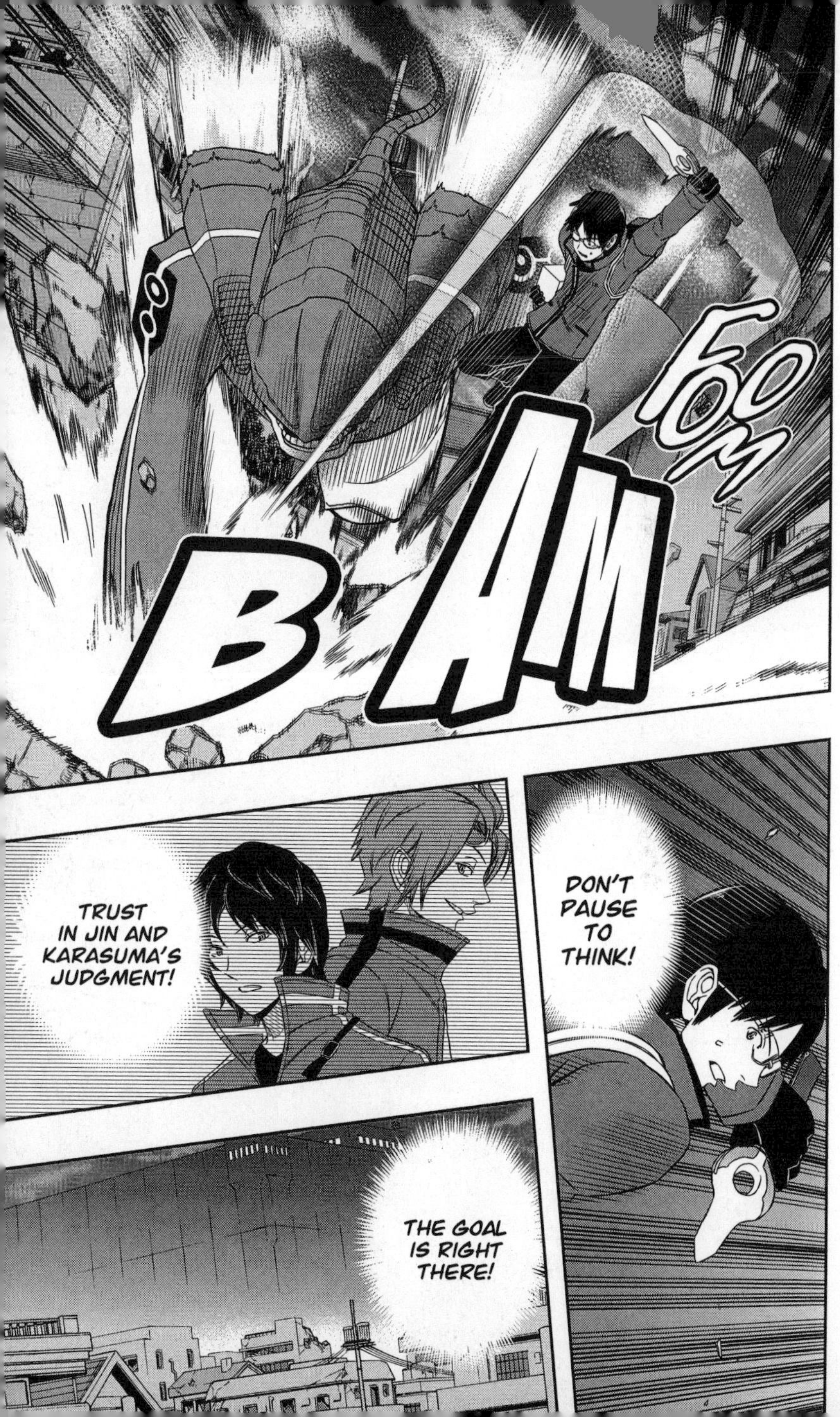
FOOM
BAM
DON'T PAUSE TO THINK!
TRUST IN JIN AND KARASUMA'S JUDGMENT!
THE GOAL IS RIGHT THERE!

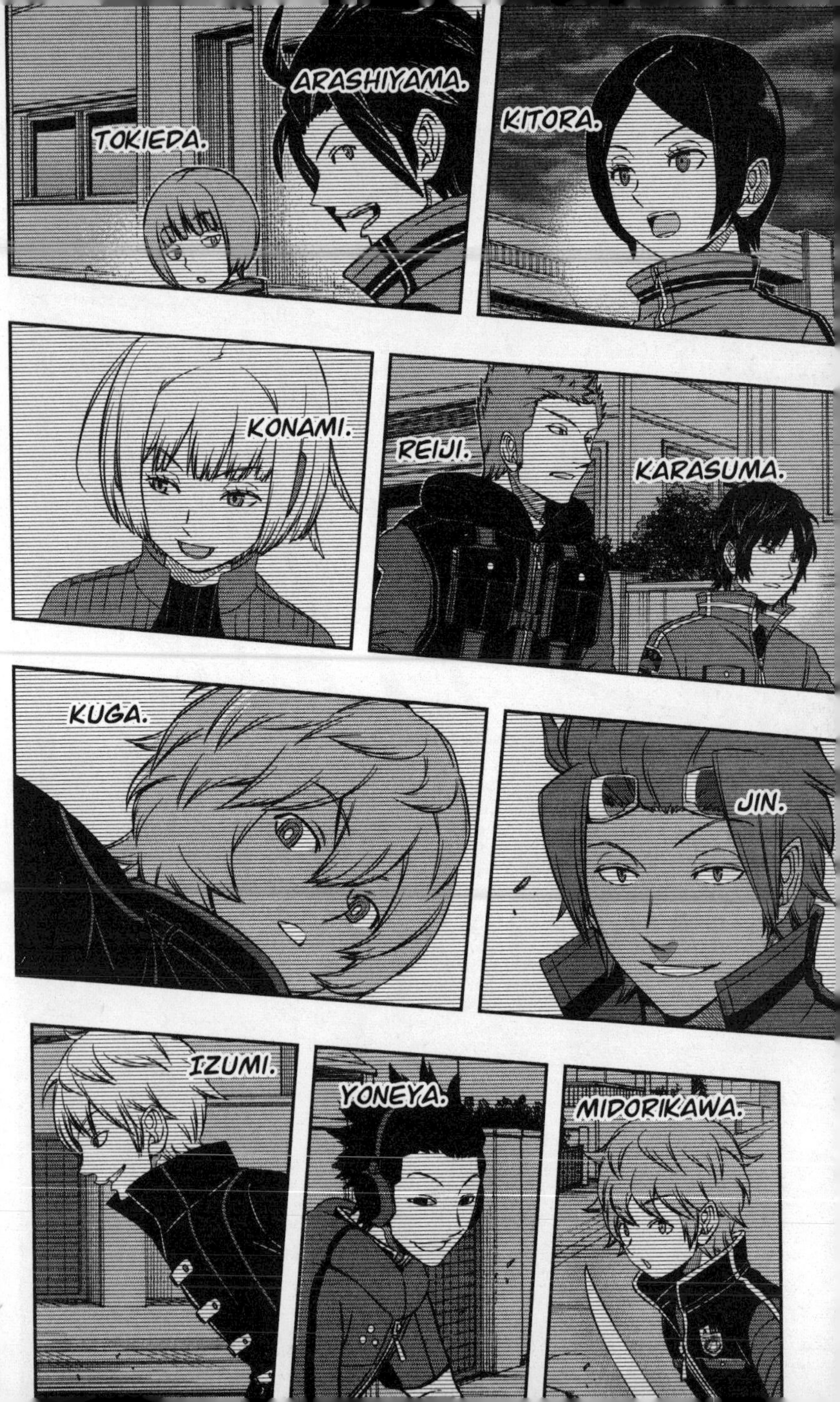
KITORA.
ARASHIYAMA.
TOKIEDA.
KARASUMA.
REIJI.
KONAMI.
JIN.
KUGA.
MIDORIKAWA.
YONEYA.
IZUMI.

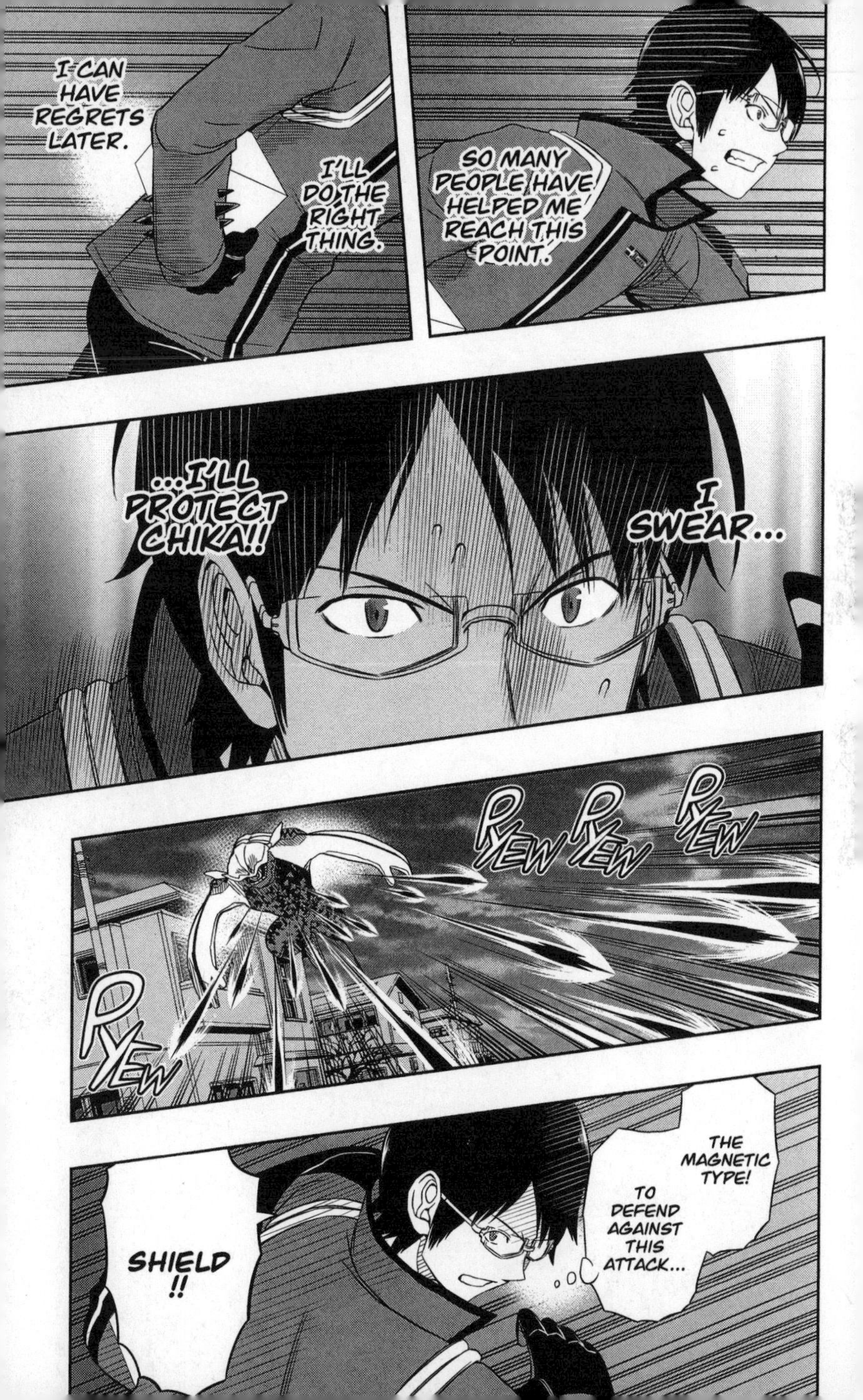
SO MANY PEOPLE HAVE HELPED ME REACH THIS POINT.
I'LL DO THE RIGHT THING.
I CAN HAVE REGRETS LATER.
I SWEAR...
...I'LL PROTECT CHIKA!!
PYEW
PYEW
PYEW
PYEW
THE MAGNETIC TYPE!
TO DEFEND AGAINST THIS ATTACK...
SHIELD!!

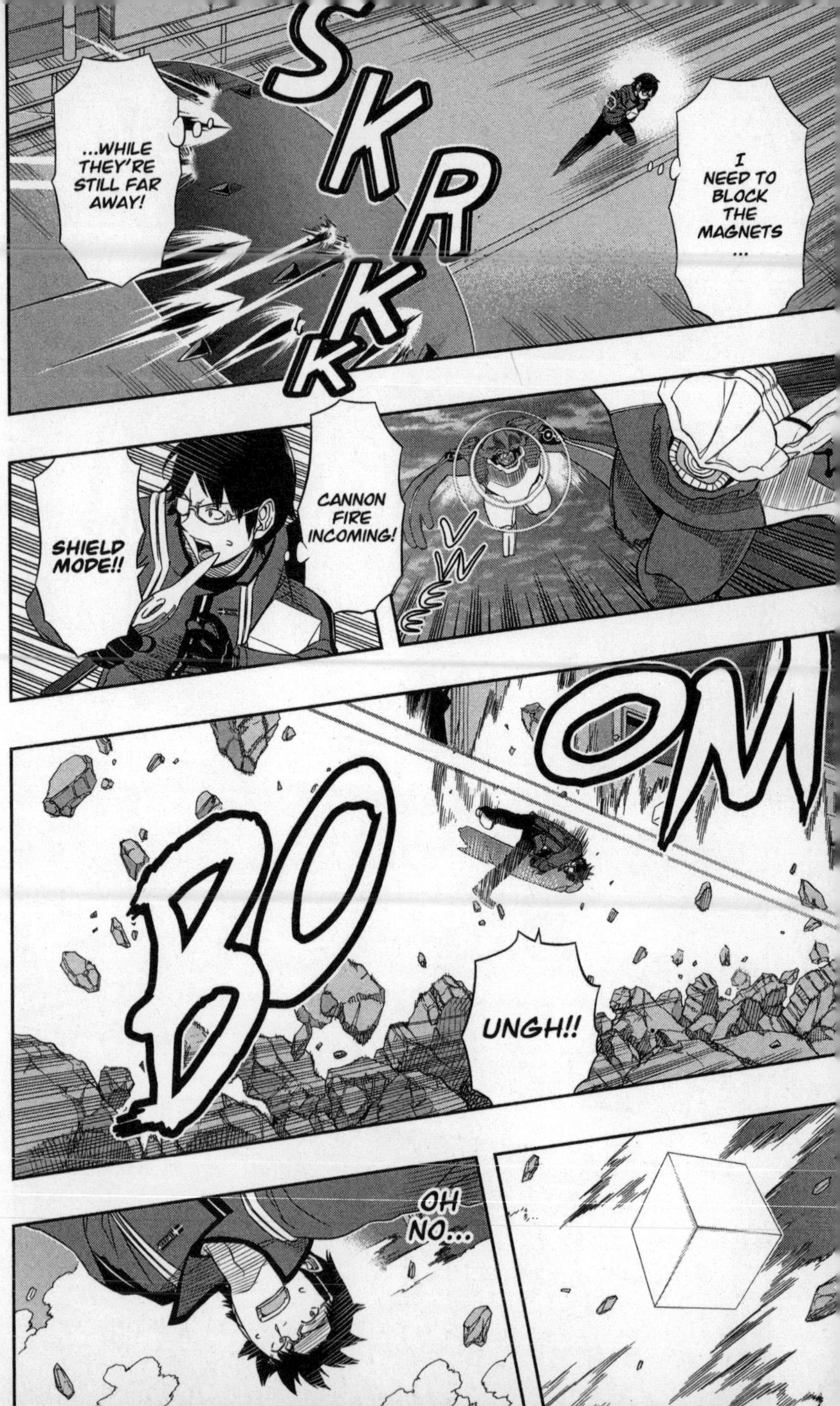
I NEED TO BLOCK THE MAGNETS ...
...WHILE THEY'RE STILL FAR AWAY!
SKRKK
CANNON FIRE INCOMING!
VWEE
SHIELD MODE!!
BOOM
UNGH!!
OH NO...

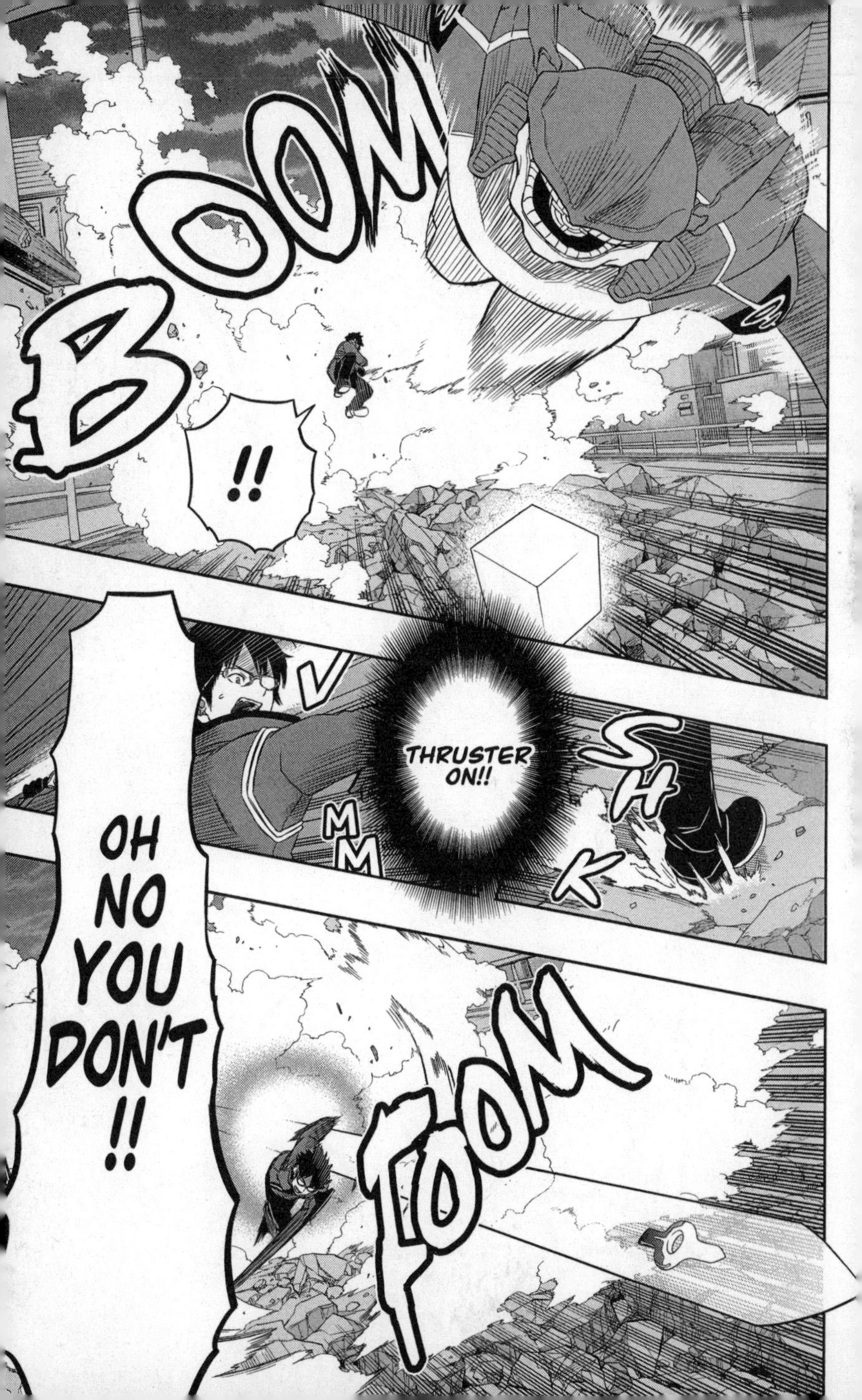
BOOM
!!
SHK
THRUSTER ON!!
OH NO YOU DON'T!!
TOOM

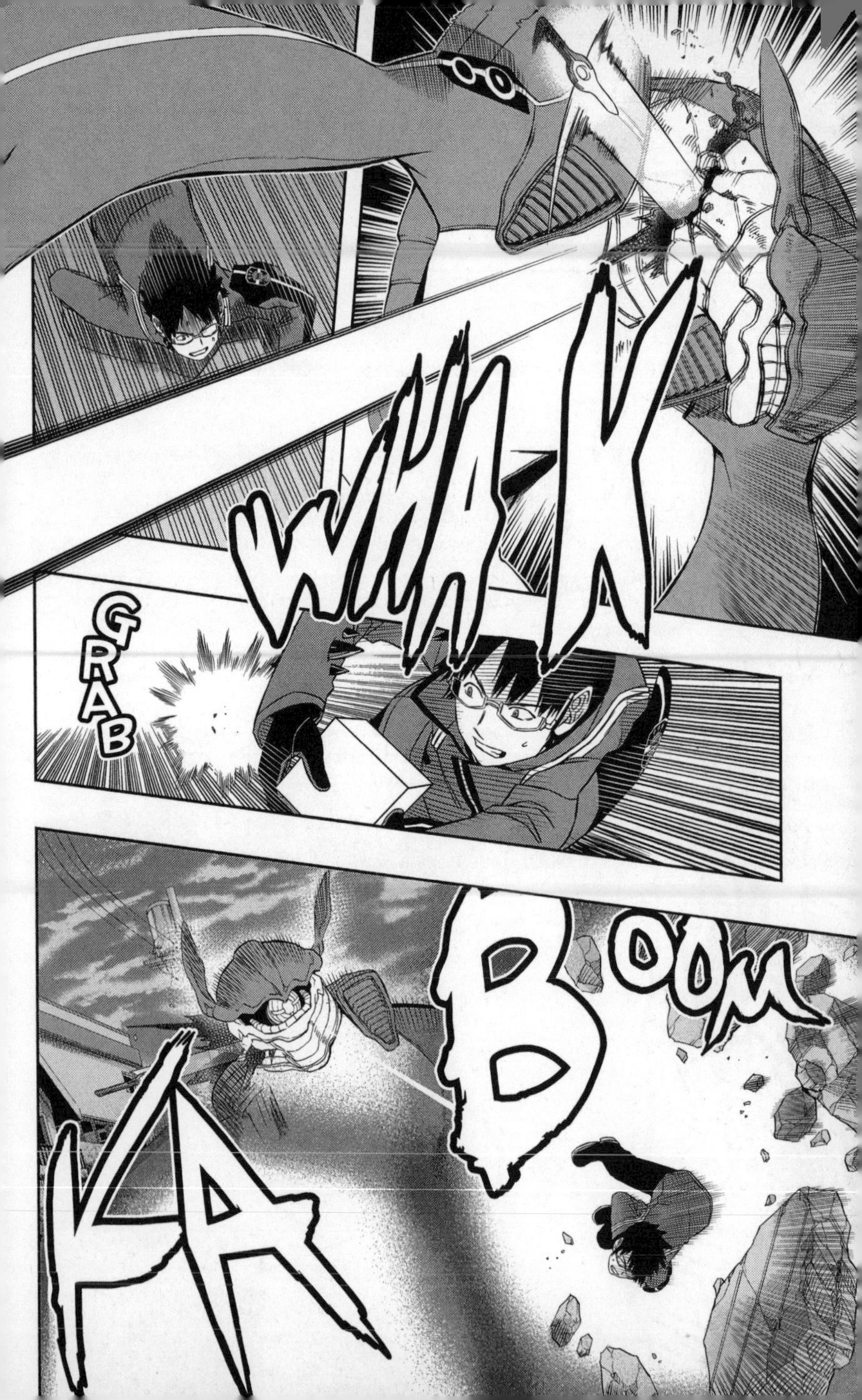
WHAK
GRAB
KA
BOOM

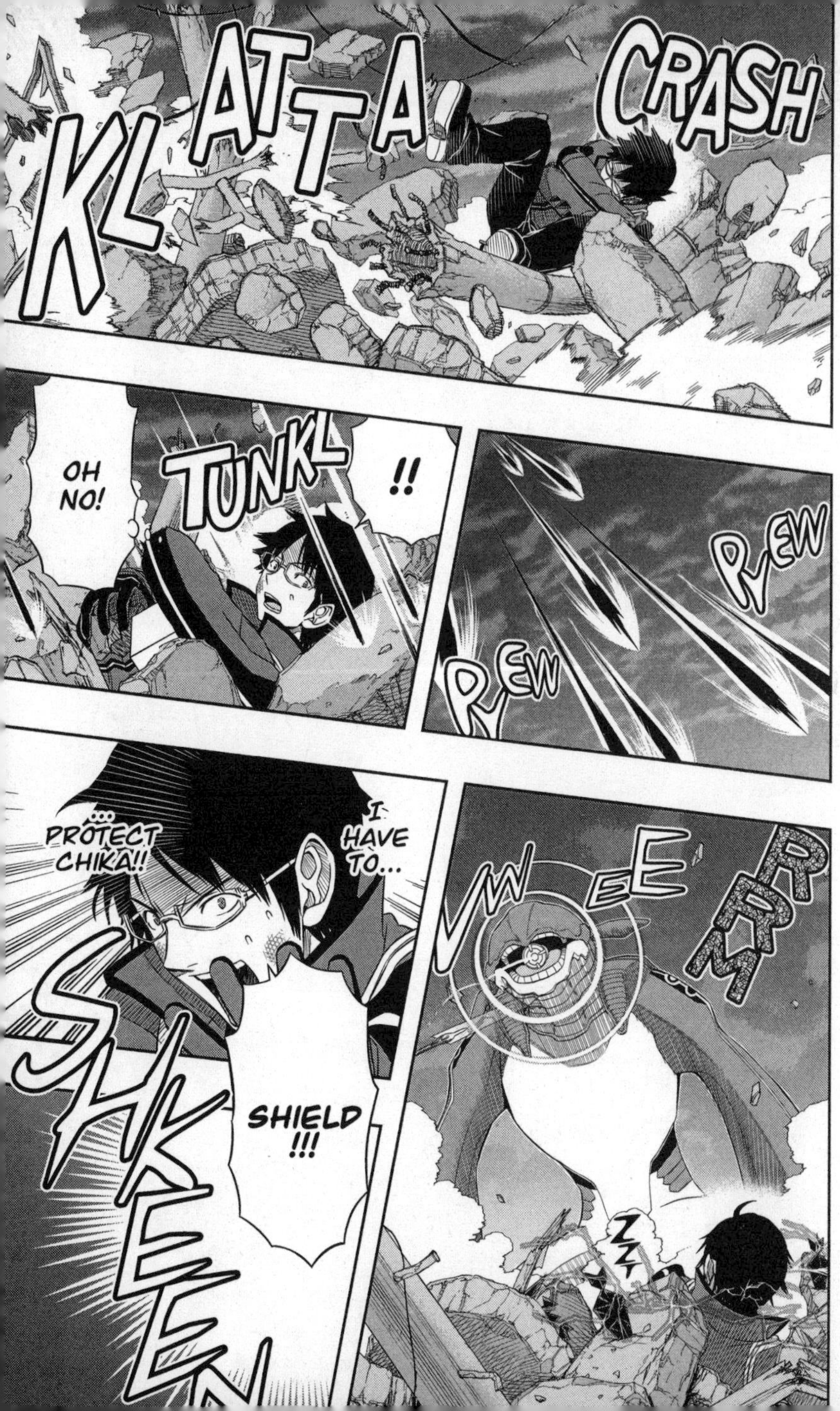
CRASH
KLATTA
PEW
PEW
!!
TUNKL
OH NO!
VWEERRRM
ZZT
I HAVE TO...
...PROTECT CHIKA!!
SHIELD!!!
SHKEEEN

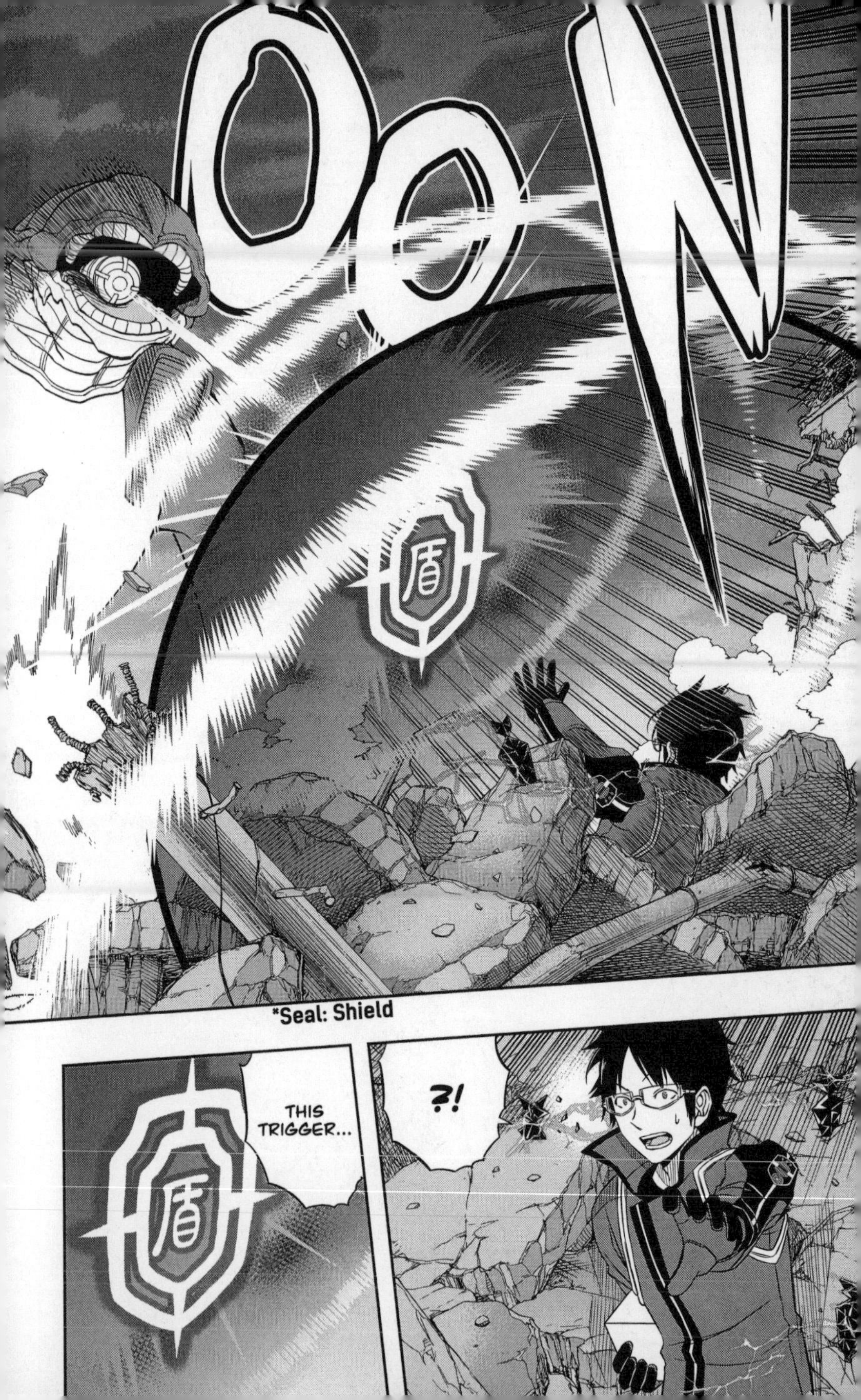
OON
盾
*Seal: Shield
?!
盾
THIS TRIGGER...

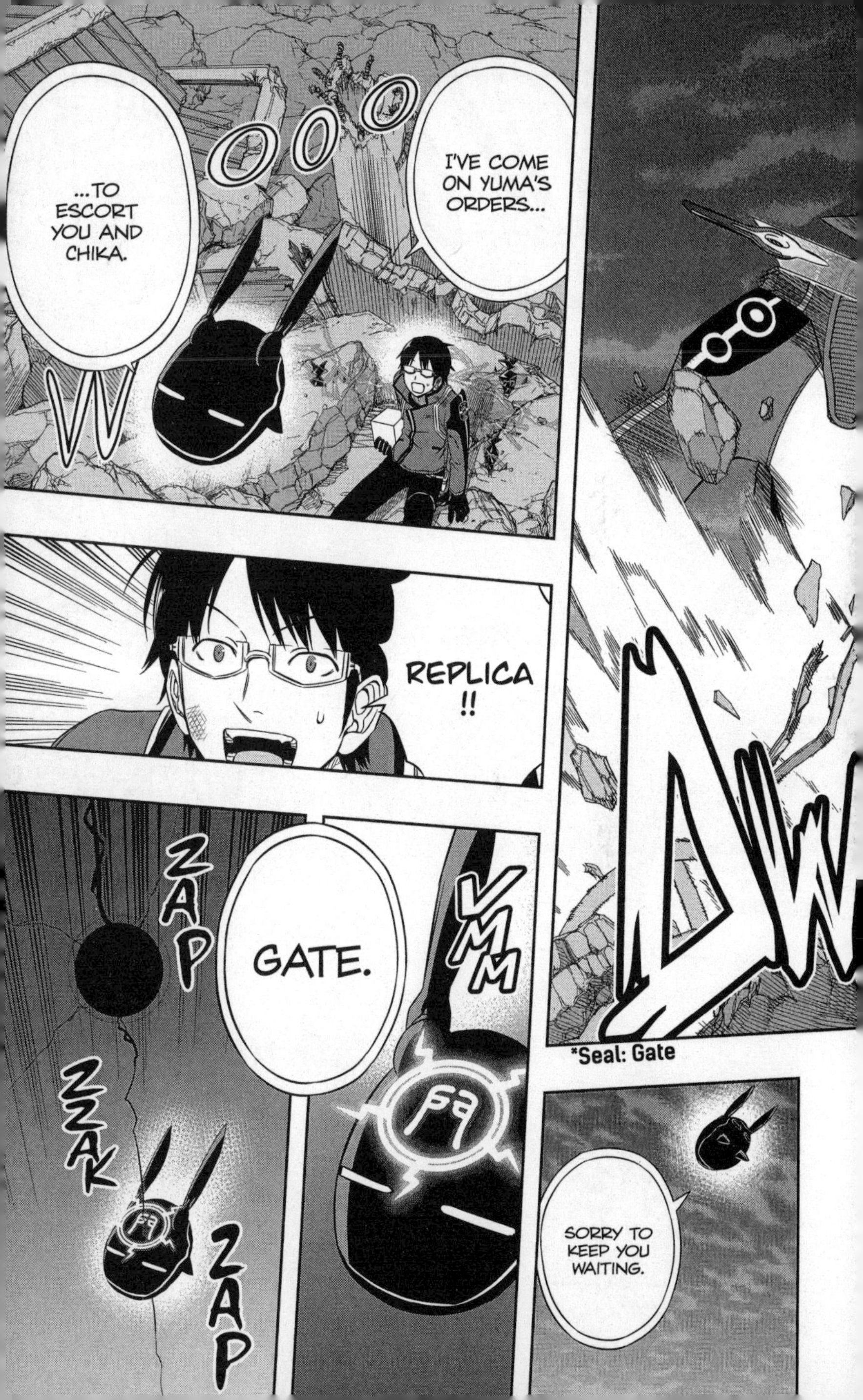
DW
I'VE COME ON YUMA'S ORDERS...
OOOO
...TO ESCORT YOU AND CHIKA.
VV
REPLICA !!
SORRY TO KEEP YOU WAITING.
VMM
GATE.
ZAP
ZZZAK
ZAP
*Seal: Gate

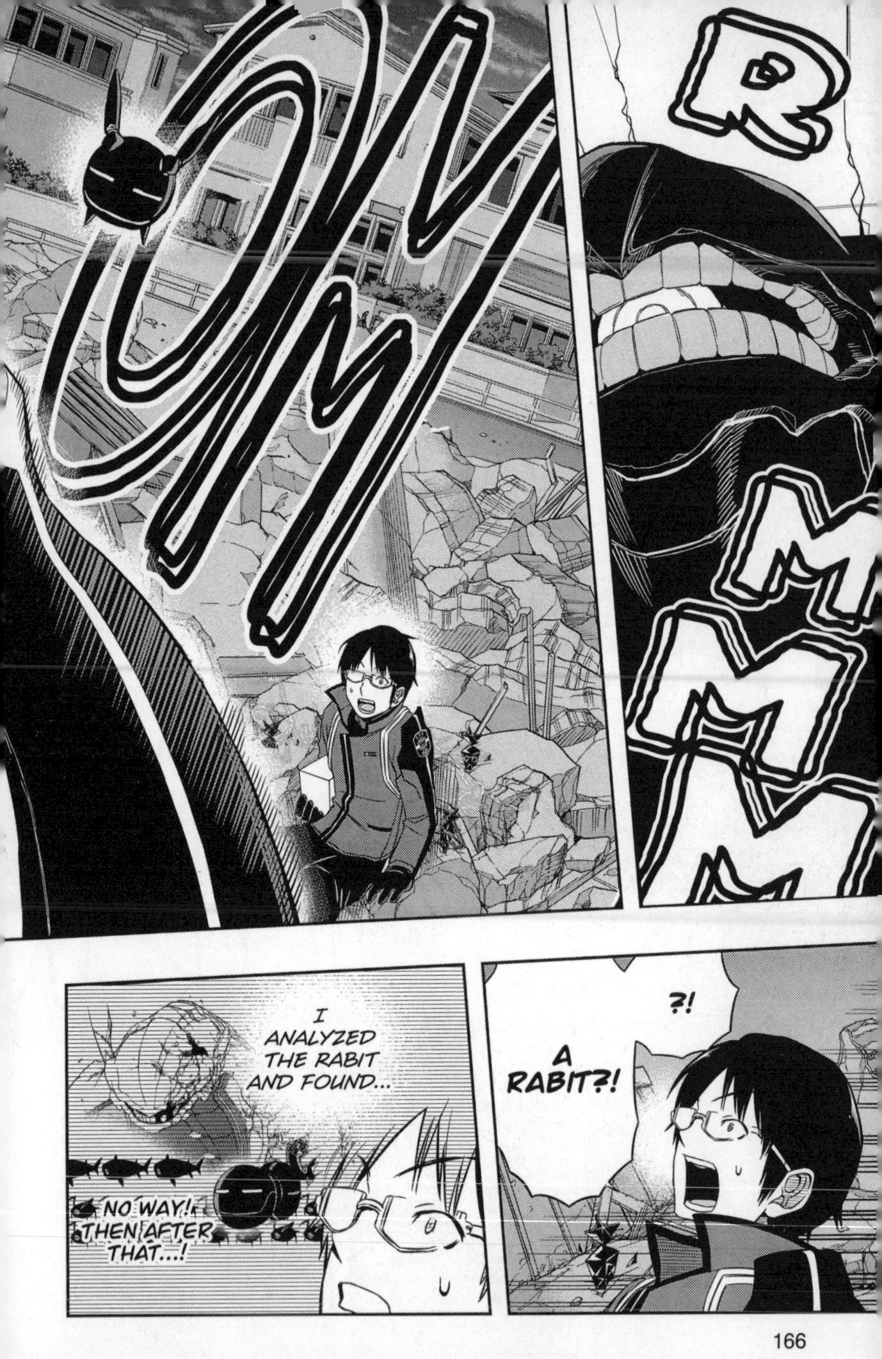
RMMM
?!
A RABIT?!
I ANALYZED THE RABIT AND FOUND...
NO WAY! THEN AFTER THAT...!

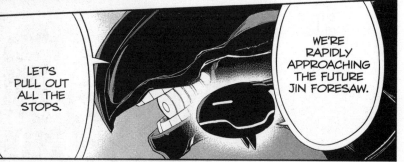

WE'RE RAPIDLY APPROACHING THE FUTURE JIN FORESAW.

LET'S PULL OUT ALL THE STOPS.

WORLD TRIGGER

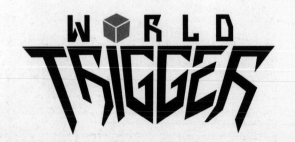

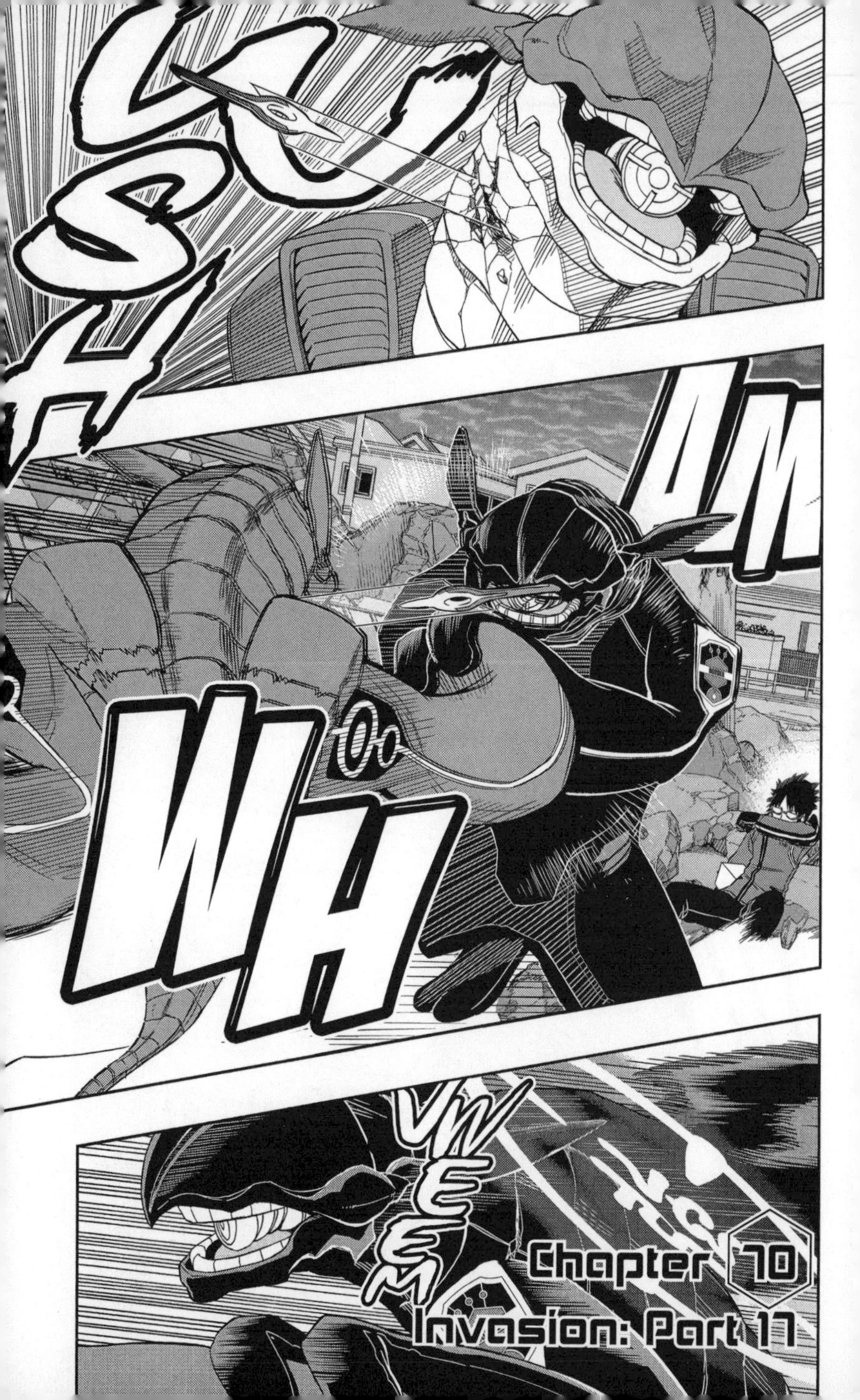
Chapter 10
Invasion: Part 11

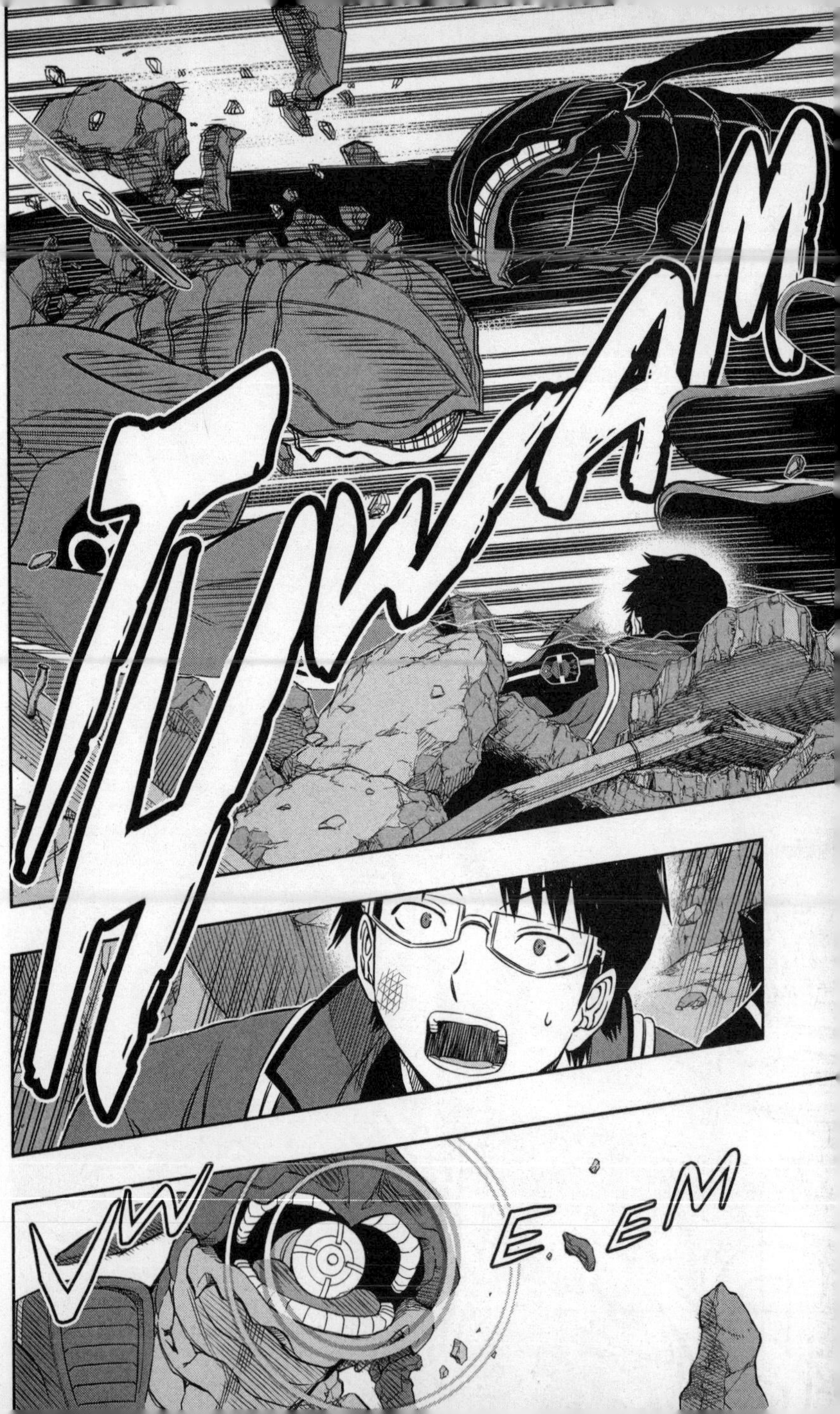
THWAM
VWEEEM

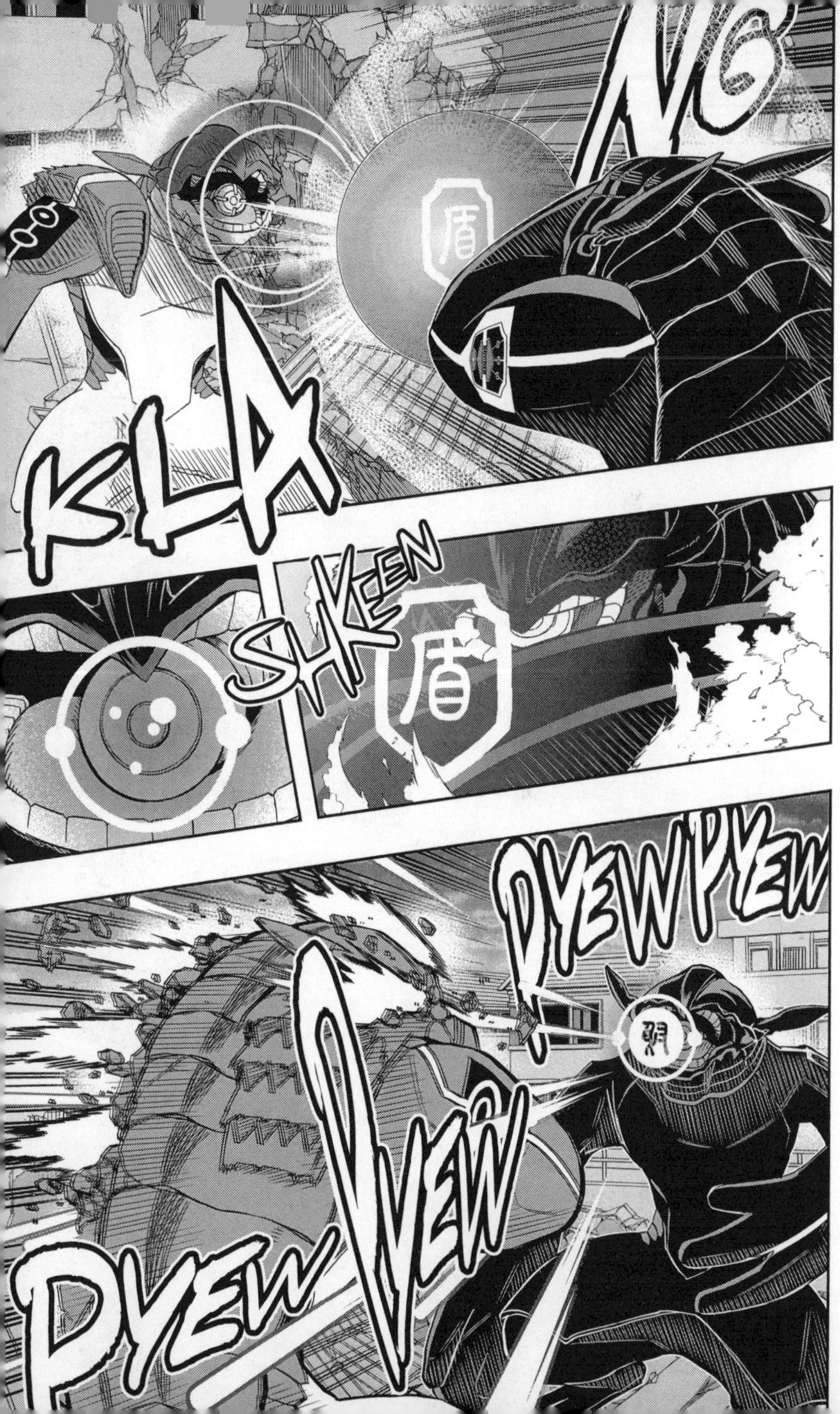
NG
盾
KLA
SHKEEN
盾
PYEW PYEW
VEW
PYEW

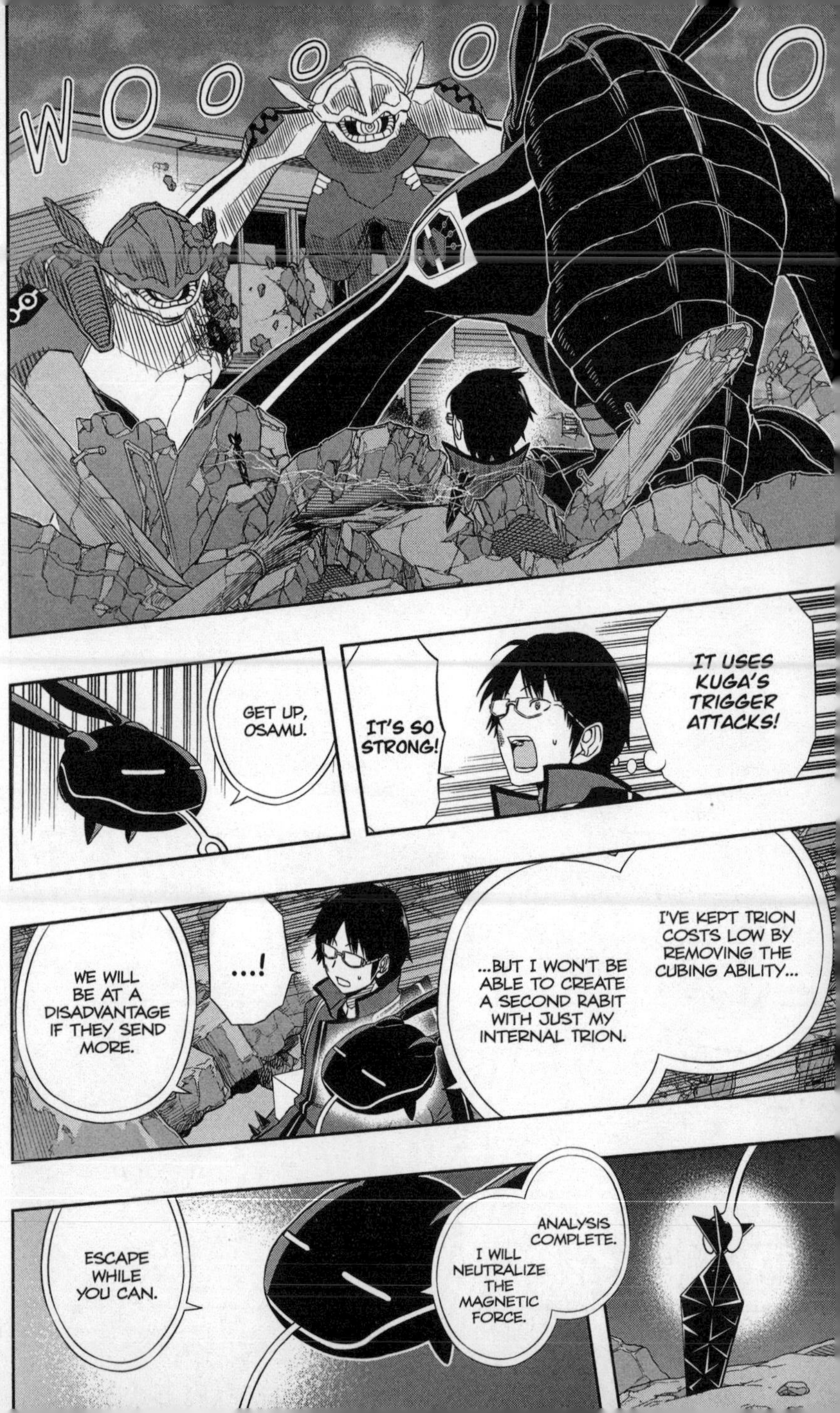
WOOOOO
IT USES KUGA'S TRIGGER ATTACKS!
IT'S SO STRONG!
GET UP, OSAMU.
I'VE KEPT TRION COSTS LOW BY REMOVING THE CUBING ABILITY...
...BUT I WON'T BE ABLE TO CREATE A SECOND RABIT WITH JUST MY INTERNAL TRION.
...!
WE WILL BE AT A DISADVANTAGE IF THEY SEND MORE.
ANALYSIS COMPLETE.
I WILL NEUTRALIZE THE MAGNETIC FORCE.
ESCAPE WHILE YOU CAN.

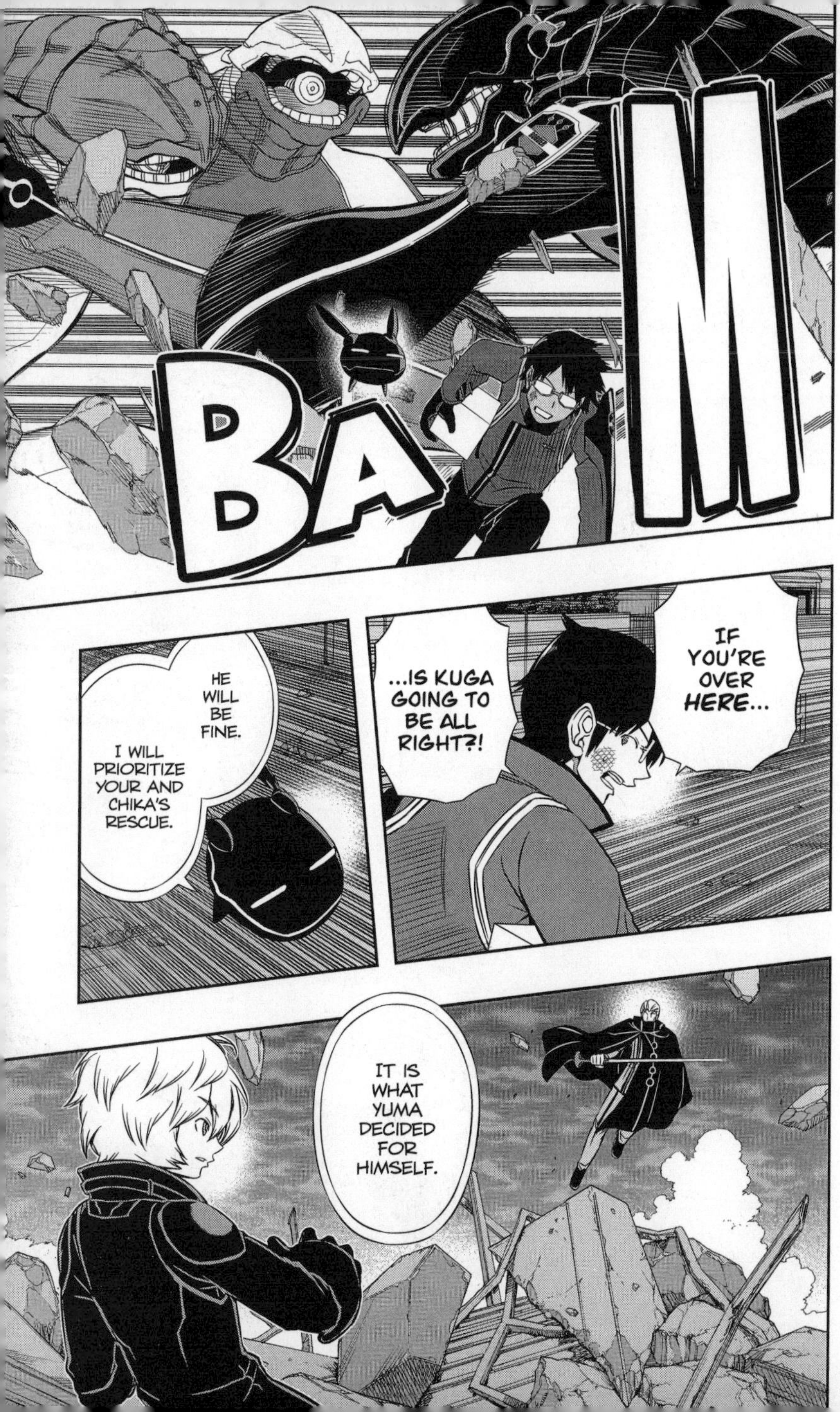
BAM
IF YOU'RE OVER HERE...
...IS KUGA GOING TO BE ALL RIGHT?!
HE WILL BE FINE.
I WILL PRIORITIZE YOUR AND CHIKA'S RESCUE.
IT IS WHAT YUMA DECIDED FOR HIMSELF.

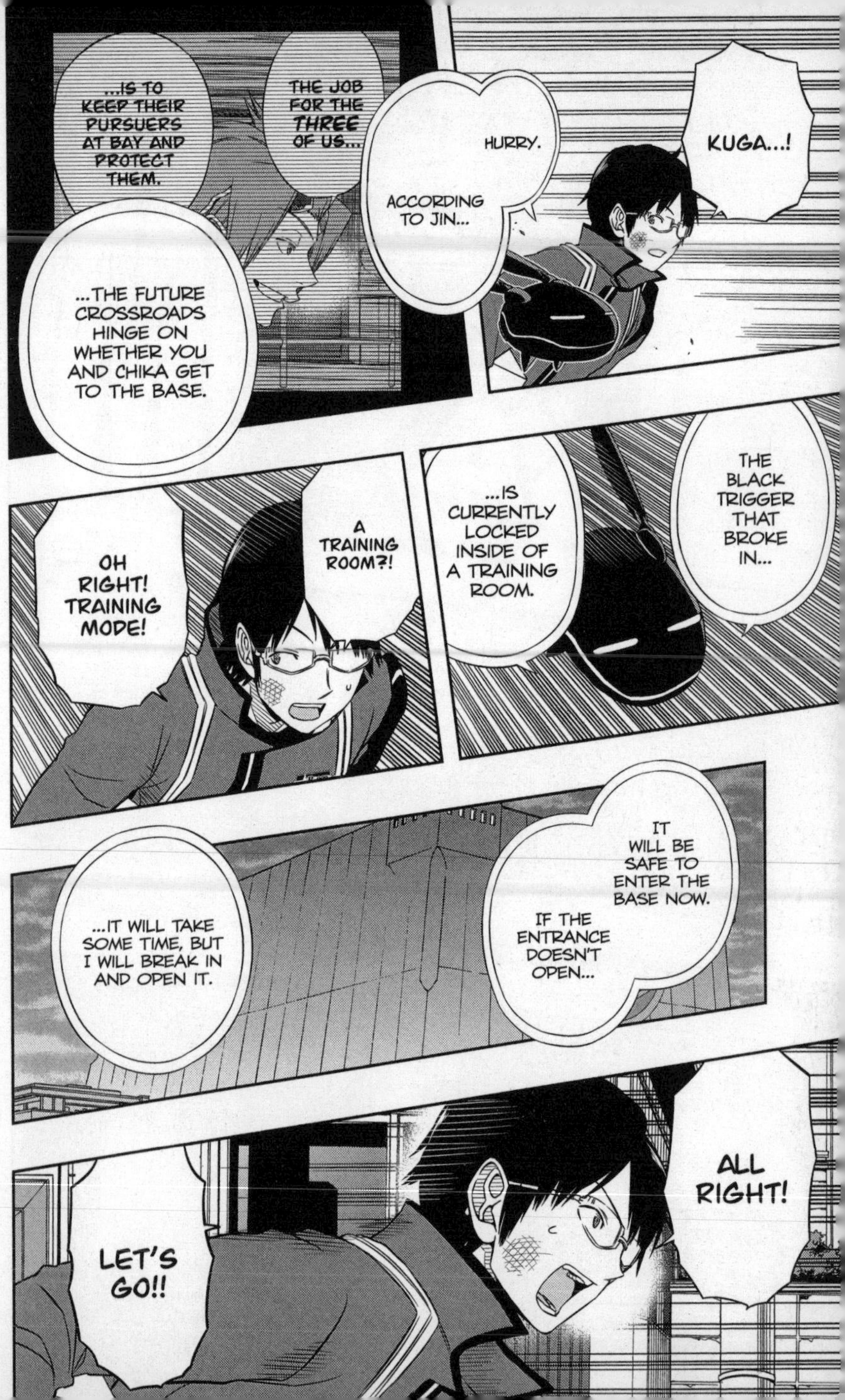
KUGA...!
HURRY.
ACCORDING TO JIN...
...THE FUTURE CROSSROADS HINGE ON WHETHER YOU AND CHIKA GET TO THE BASE.
THE JOB FOR THE THREE OF US...
...IS TO KEEP THEIR PURSUERS AT BAY AND PROTECT THEM.
THE BLACK TRIGGER THAT BROKE IN...
...IS CURRENTLY LOCKED INSIDE OF A TRAINING ROOM.
A TRAINING ROOM?!
OH RIGHT! TRAINING MODE!
IT WILL BE SAFE TO ENTER THE BASE NOW.
IF THE ENTRANCE DOESN'T OPEN...
...IT WILL TAKE SOME TIME, BUT I WILL BREAK IN AND OPEN IT.
ALL RIGHT!
LET'S GO!!

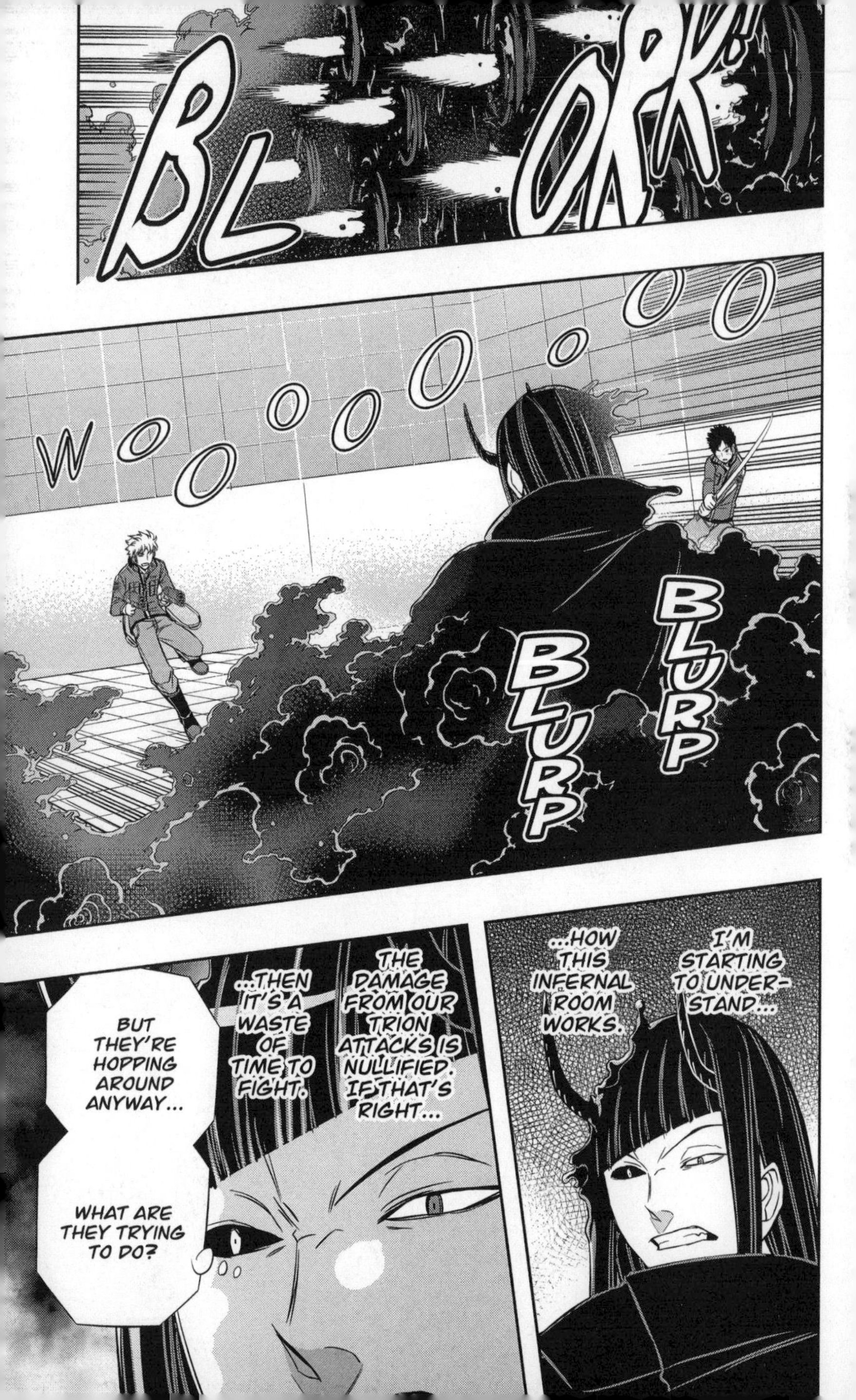
BLORK
WOOOOOOOOO
BLURP
BLURP
I'M STARTING TO UNDER-STAND...
...HOW THIS INFERNAL ROOM WORKS.
THE DAMAGE FROM OUR TRION ATTACKS IS NULLIFIED. IF THAT'S RIGHT...
...THEN IT'S A WASTE OF TIME TO FIGHT.
BUT THEY'RE HOPPING AROUND ANYWAY...
WHAT ARE THEY TRYING TO DO?

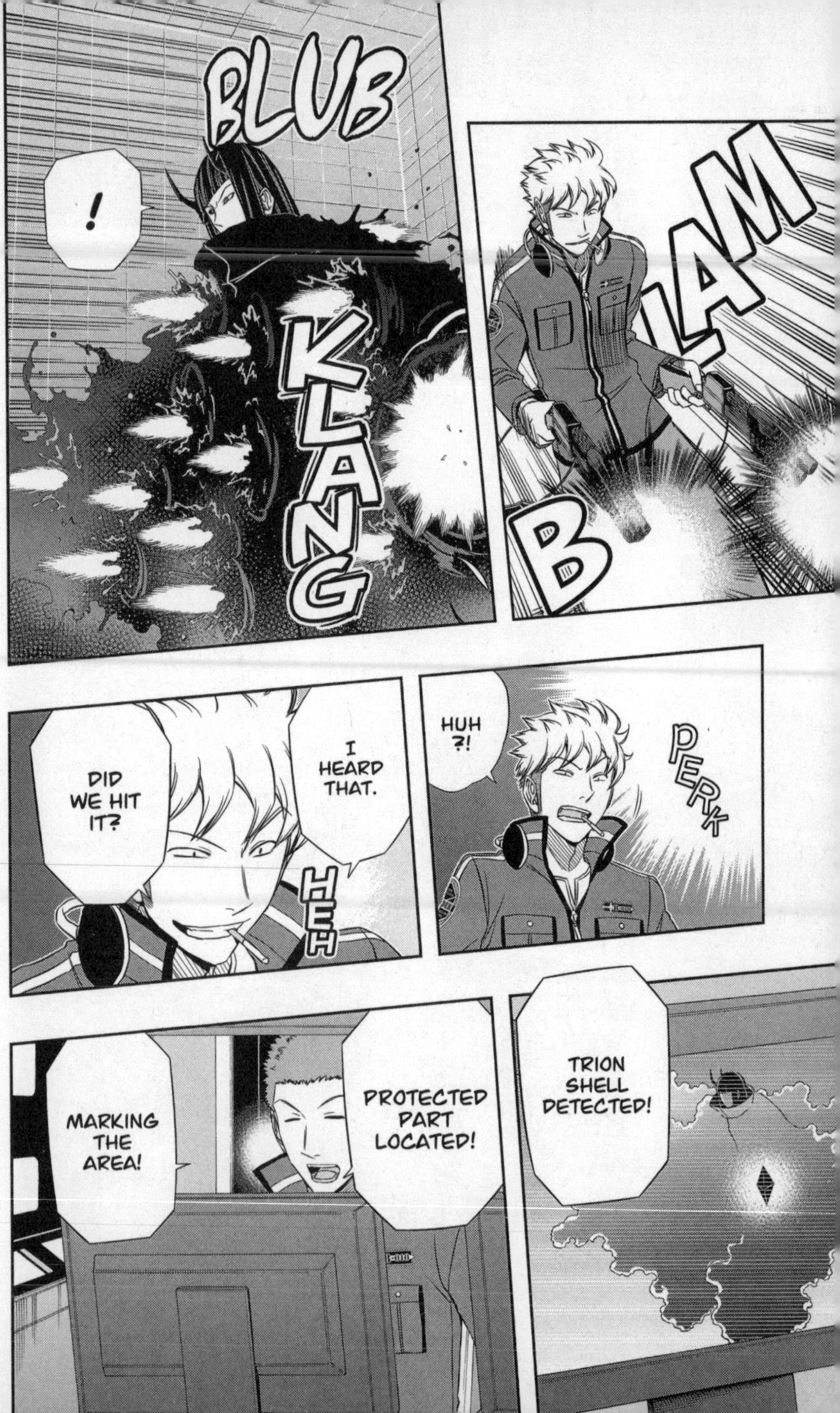
BLAM
BLUB
!
KLANG
HUH?!
PERK
I HEARD THAT.
DID WE HIT IT?
HEH
TRION SHELL DETECTED!
PROTECTED PART LOCATED!
MARKING THE AREA!

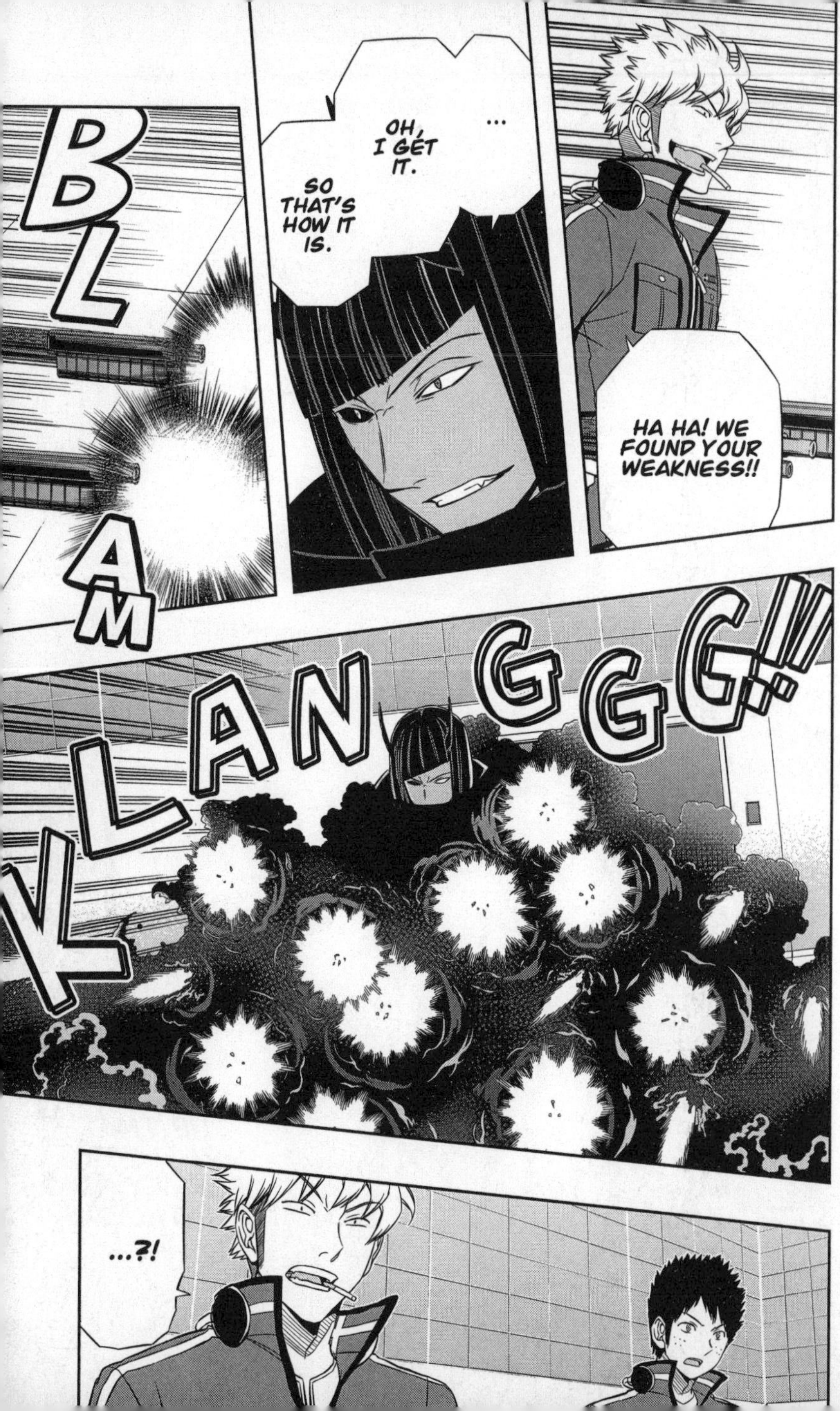
HA HA! WE FOUND YOUR WEAKNESS!!
...
OH, I GET IT.
SO THAT'S HOW IT IS.
BLAM
KLANGGG!!!
...?!

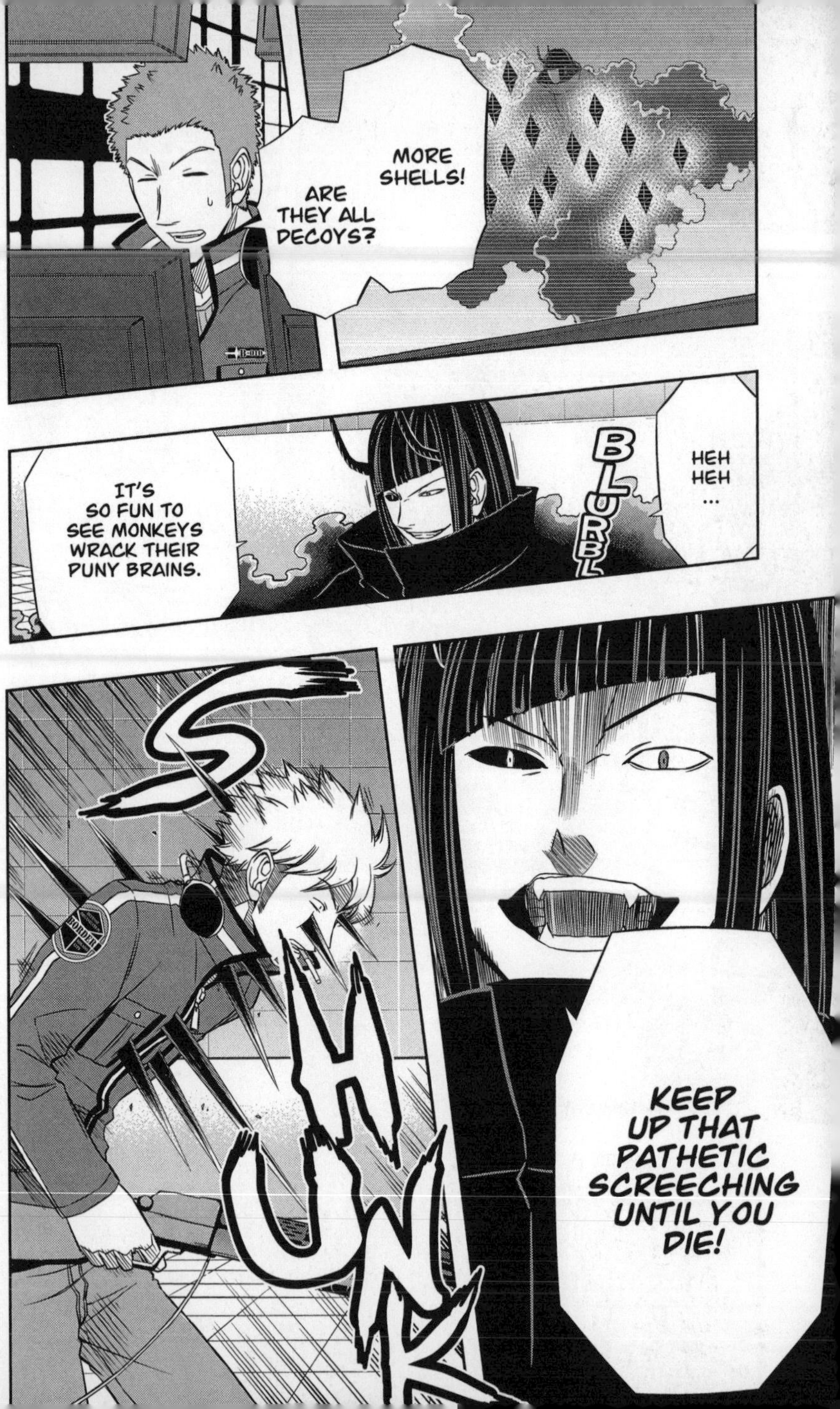
MORE SHELLS!
ARE THEY ALL DECOYS?
HEH HEH ...
BLURBL
IT'S SO FUN TO SEE MONKEYS WRACK THEIR PUNY BRAINS.
KEEP UP THAT PATHETIC SCREECHING UNTIL YOU DIE!
SHUNK

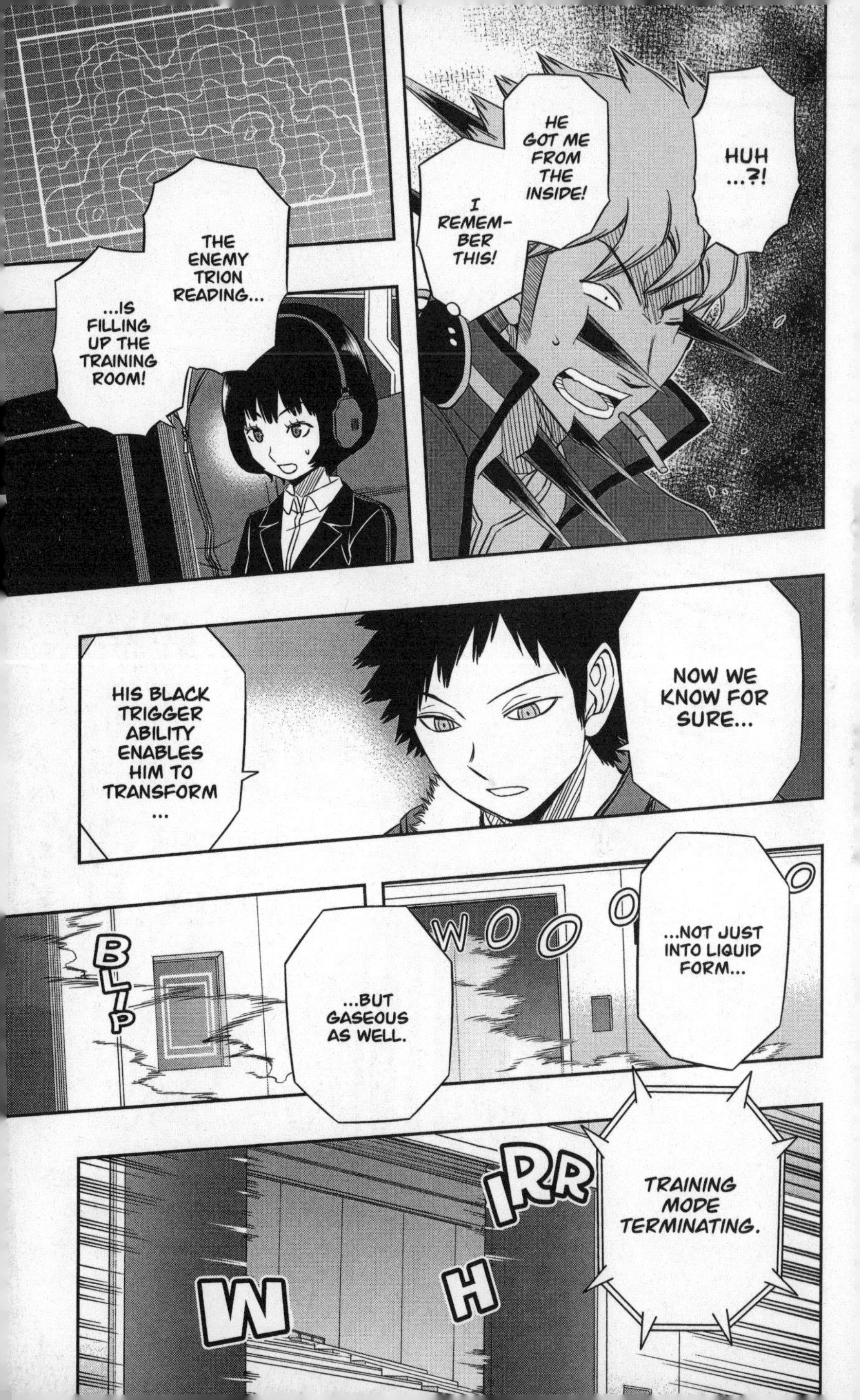
HUH ...?!
HE GOT ME FROM THE INSIDE!
I REMEMBER THIS!
THE ENEMY TRION READING...
...IS FILLING UP THE TRAINING ROOM!
NOW WE KNOW FOR SURE...
HIS BLACK TRIGGER ABILITY ENABLES HIM TO TRANSFORM ...
WOOOO
...NOT JUST INTO LIQUID FORM...
...BUT GASEOUS AS WELL.
BLIP
TRAINING MODE TERMINATING.
WHIRR

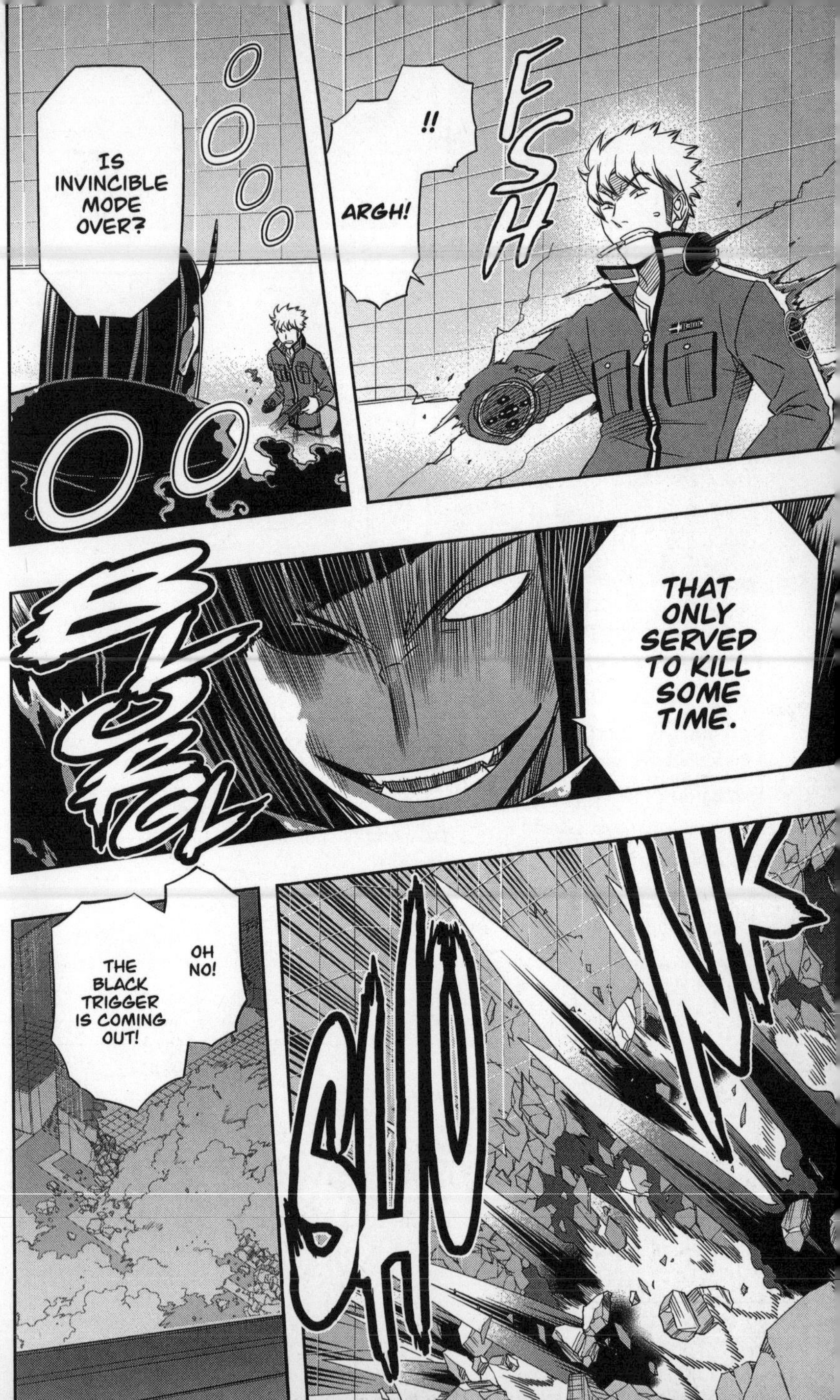
FSH
!!
ARGH!
IS INVINCIBLE MODE OVER?
OOOOOO
THAT ONLY SERVED TO KILL SOME TIME.
OH NO!
THE BLACK TRIGGER IS COMING OUT!

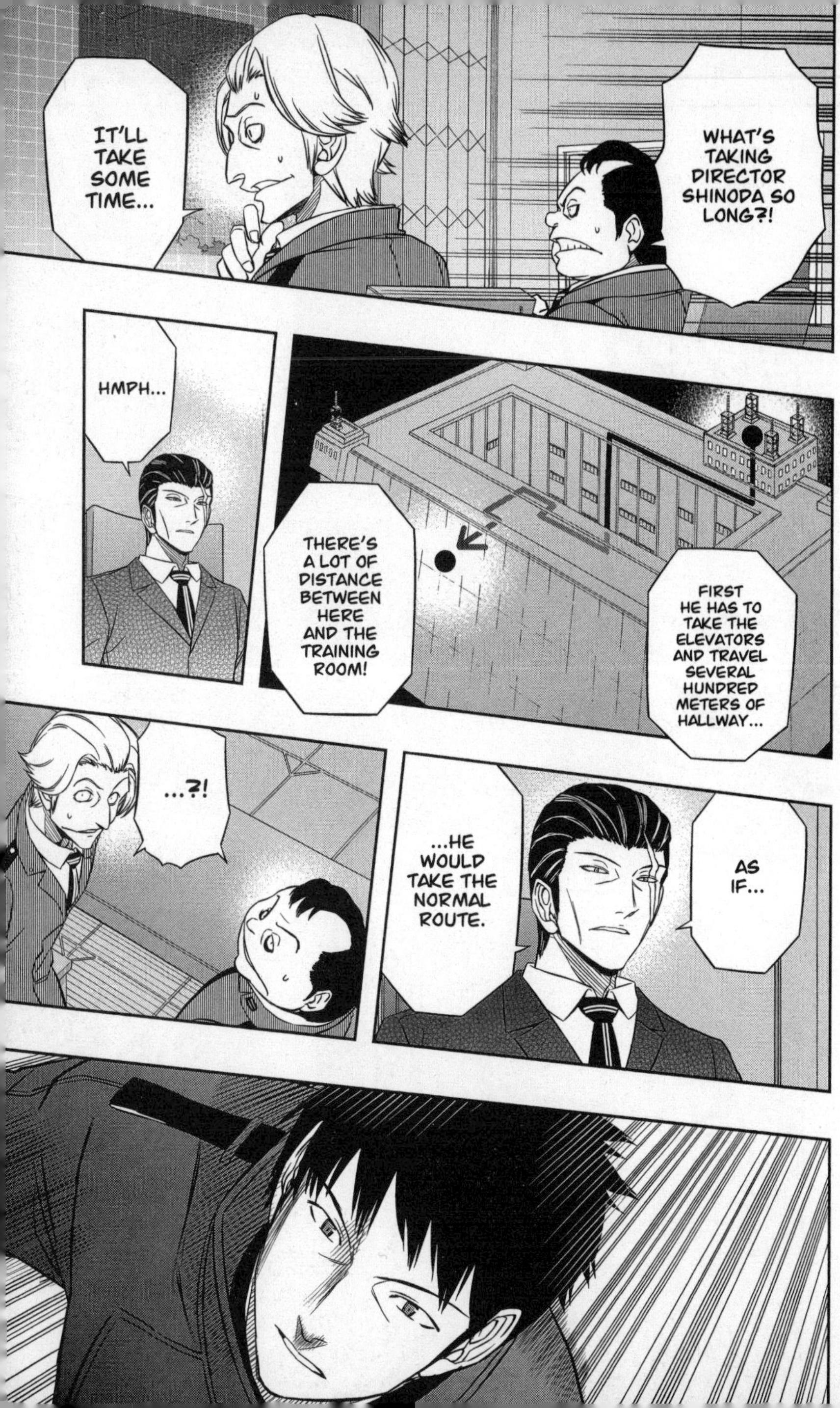
WHAT'S TAKING DIRECTOR SHINODA SO LONG?!
IT'LL TAKE SOME TIME...
THERE'S A LOT OF DISTANCE BETWEEN HERE AND THE TRAINING ROOM!
FIRST HE HAS TO TAKE THE ELEVATORS AND TRAVEL SEVERAL HUNDRED METERS OF HALLWAY...
HMPH...
AS IF...
...HE WOULD TAKE THE NORMAL ROUTE.
...?!

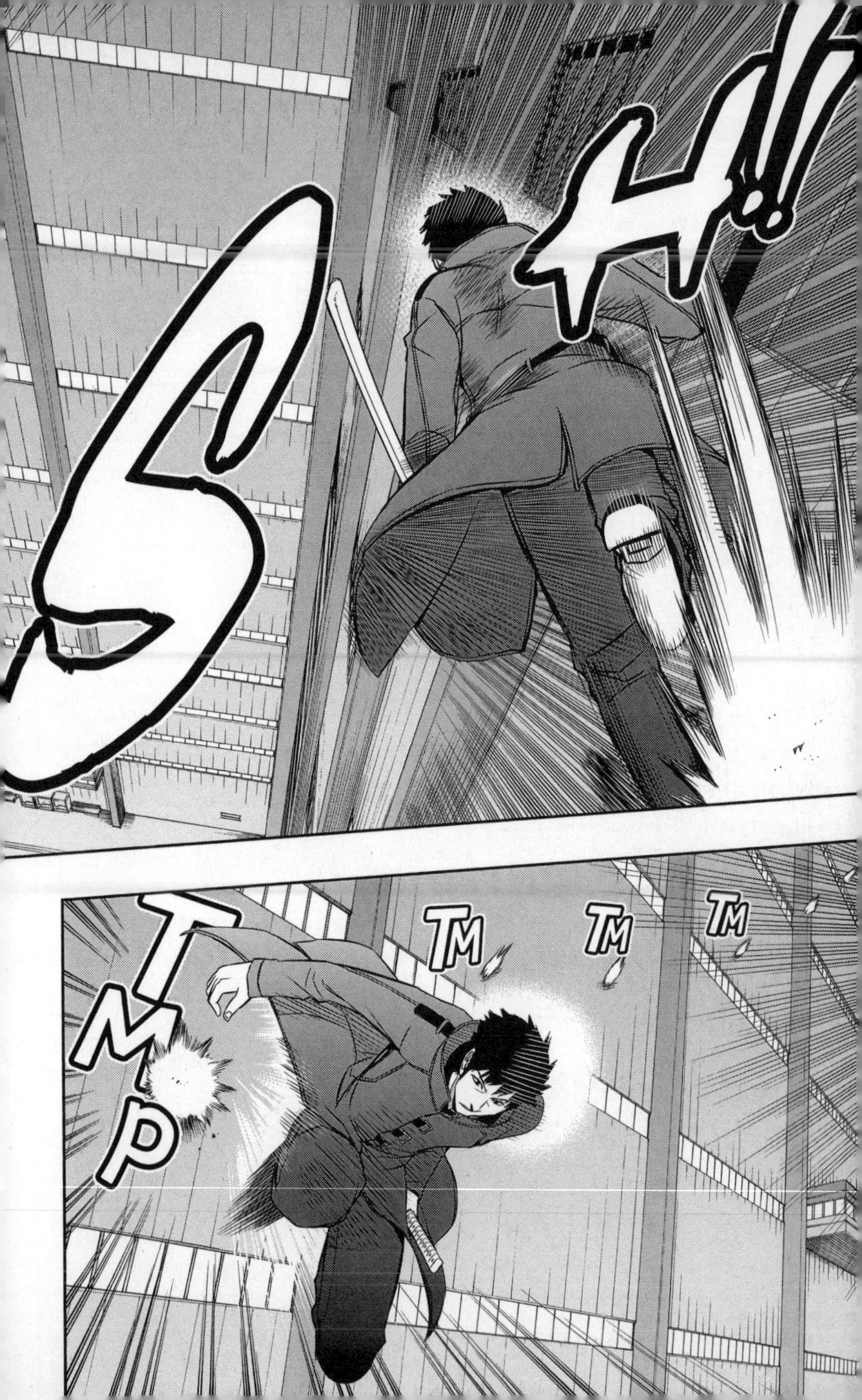
SH!!
TM
TM
TM
TMP

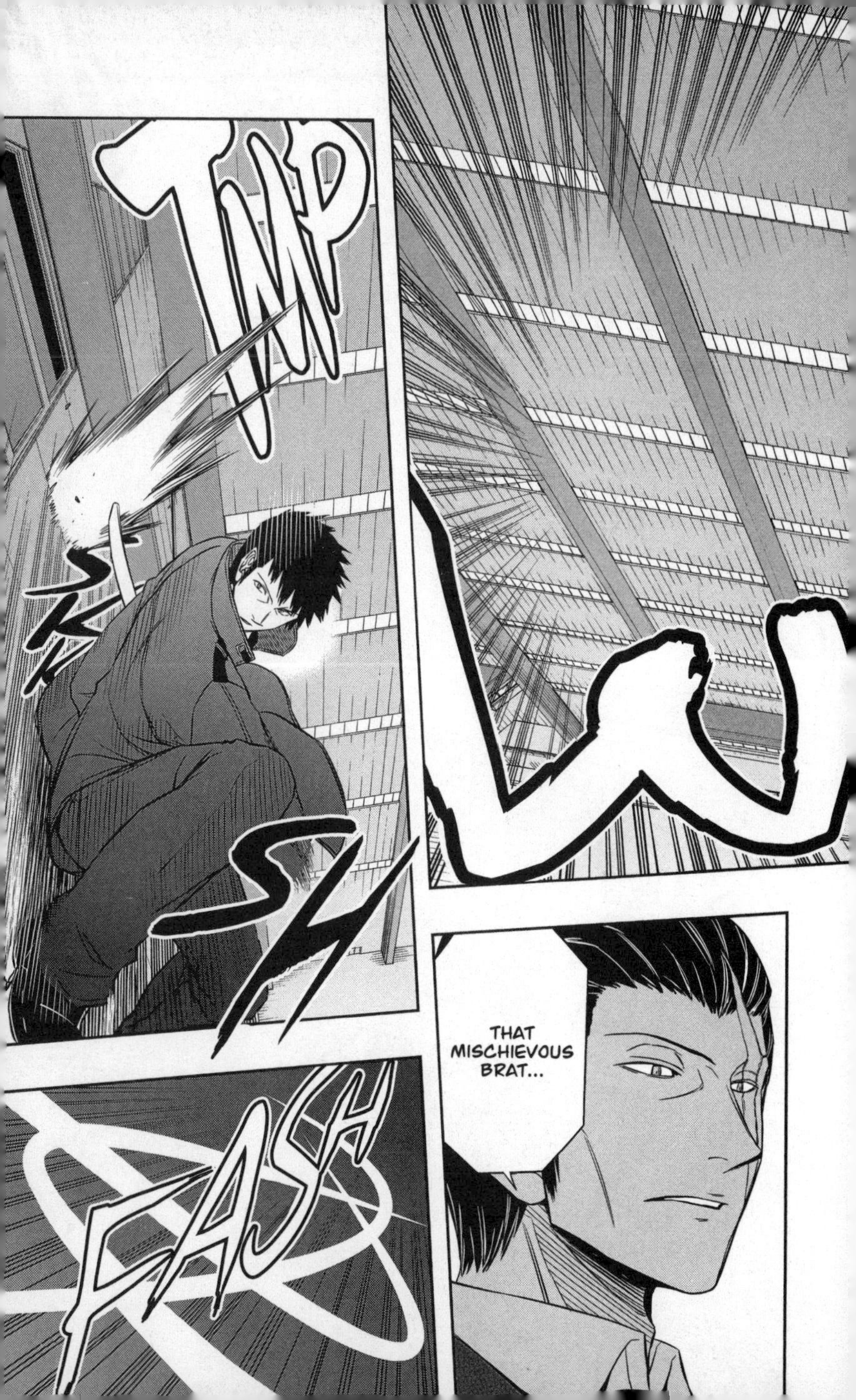
TMP
SH
THAT MISCHIEVOUS BRAT...
FASH

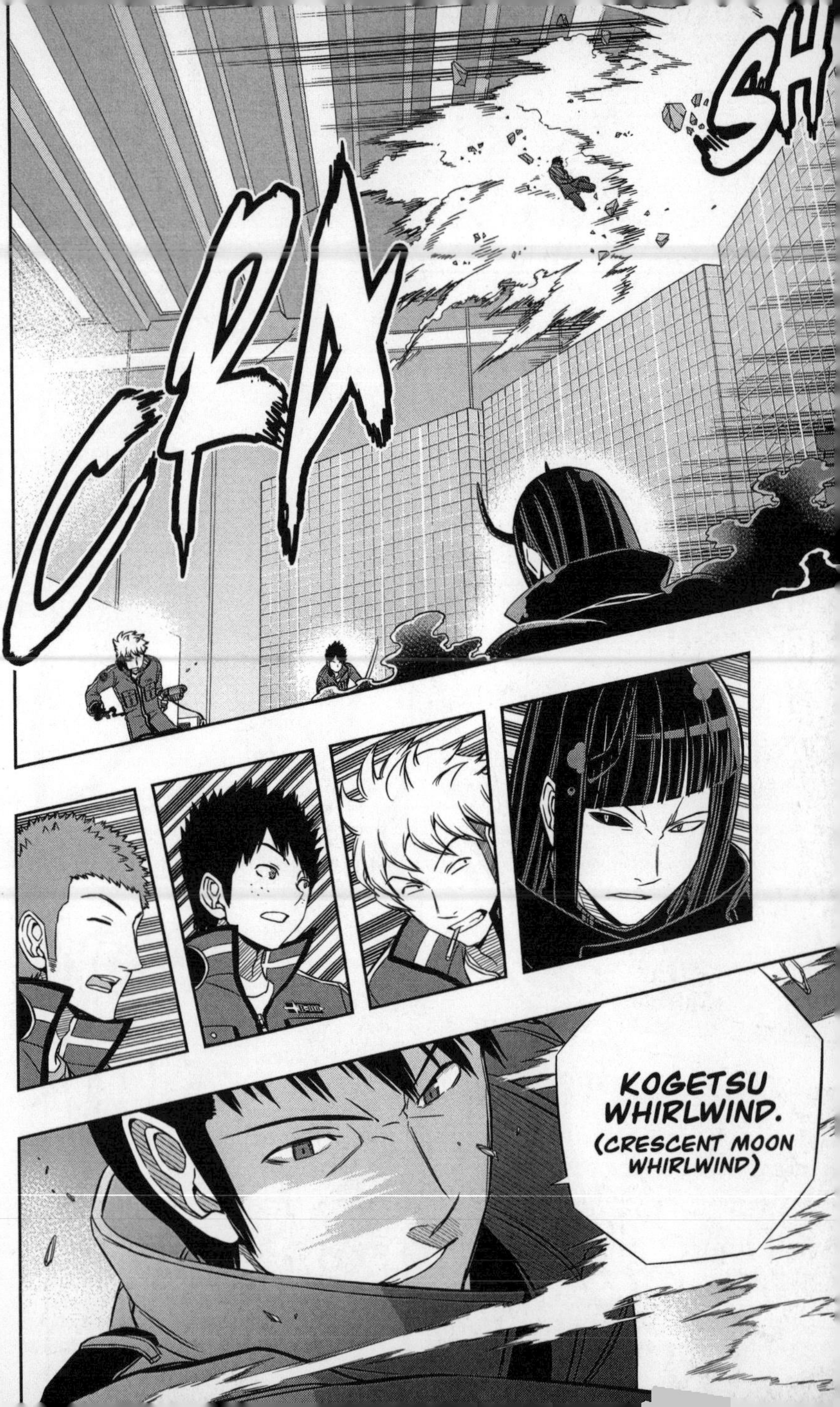
SH
CRA
KOGETSU WHIRLWIND.
(CRESCENT MOON WHIRLWIND)

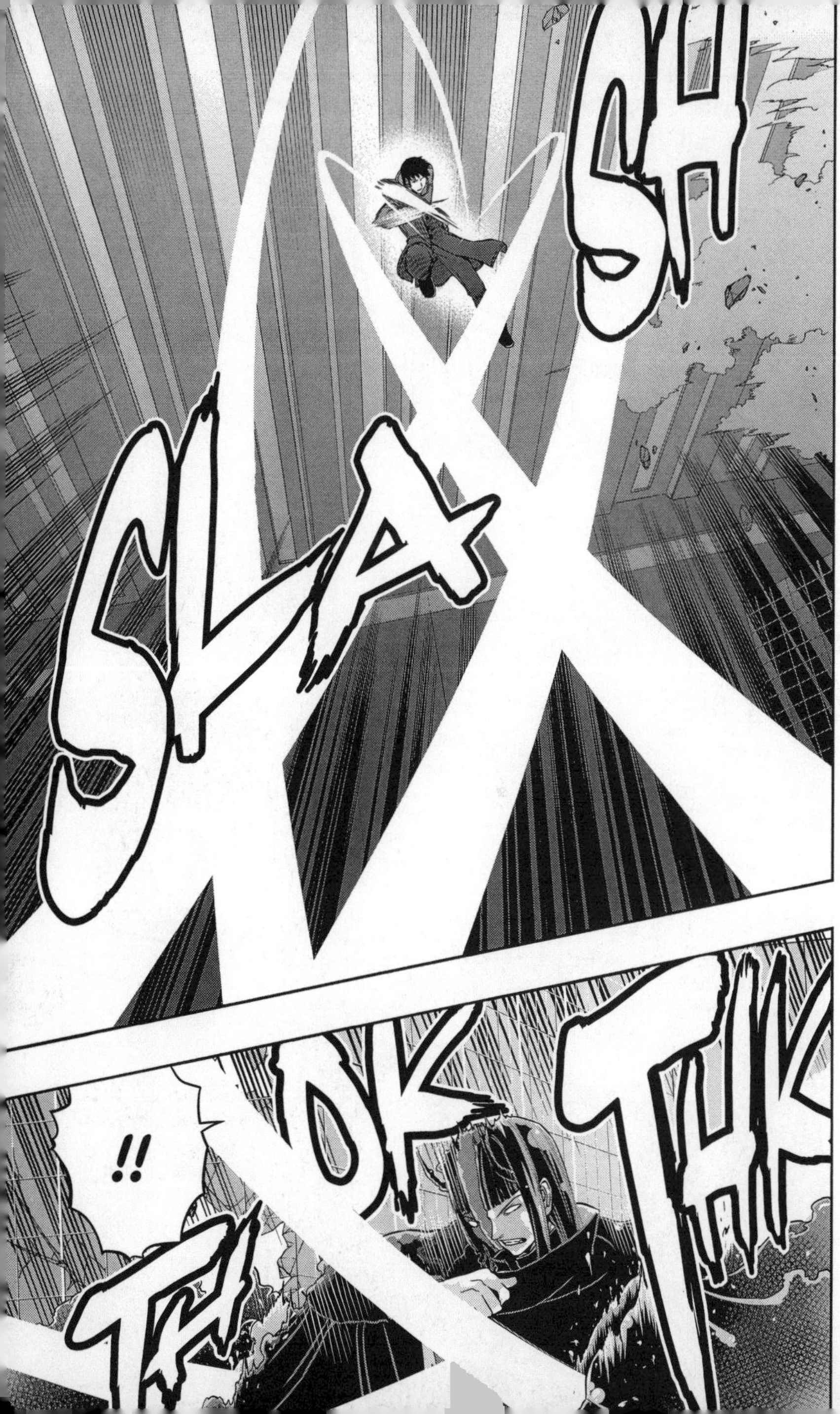
SLASH
THK
!!

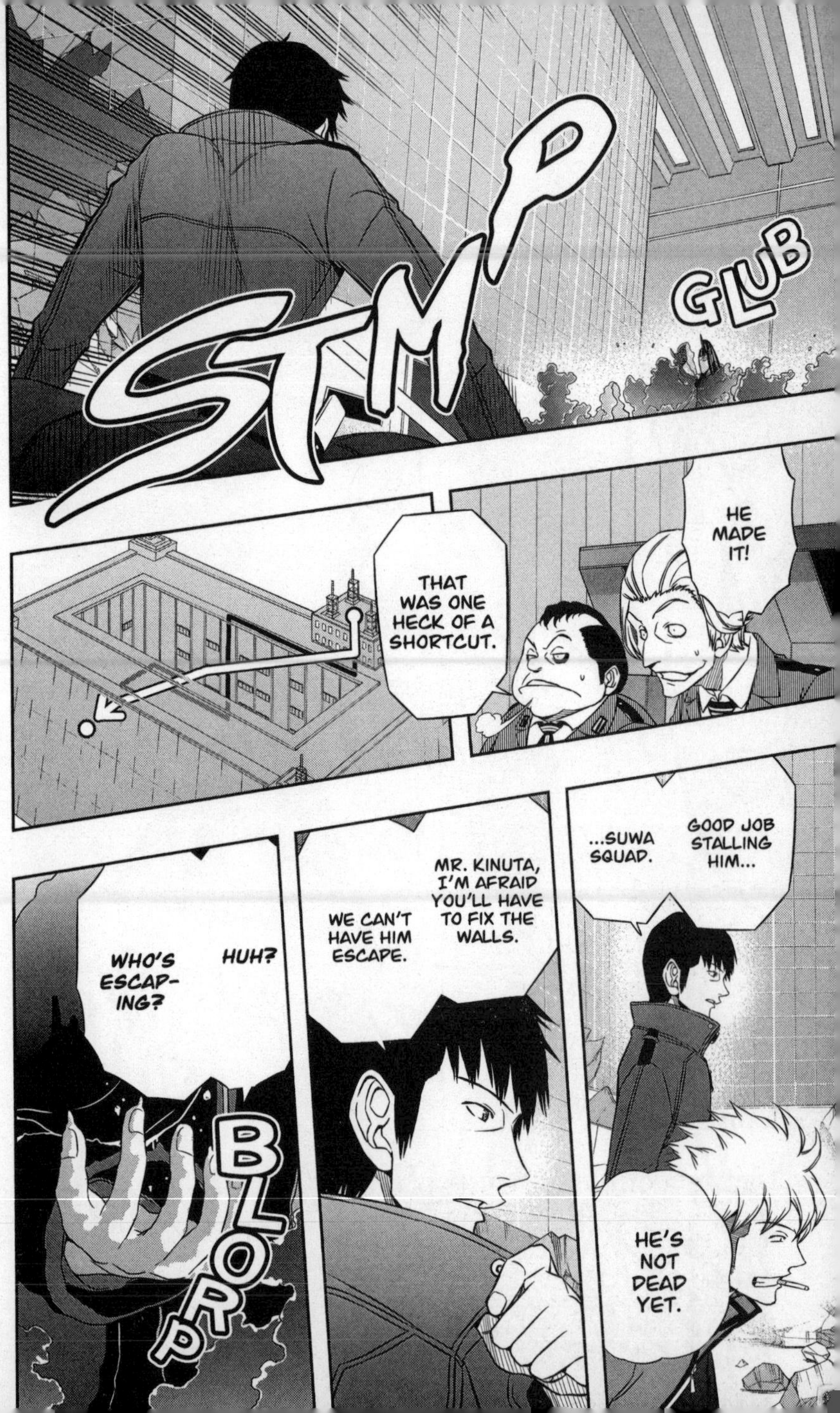
GLUB
STMP
HE MADE IT!
THAT WAS ONE HECK OF A SHORTCUT.
GOOD JOB STALLING HIM...
...SUWA SQUAD.
HE'S NOT DEAD YET.
MR. KINUTA, I'M AFRAID YOU'LL HAVE TO FIX THE WALLS.
WE CAN'T HAVE HIM ESCAPE.
HUH?
WHO'S ESCAP-ING?
BLORP

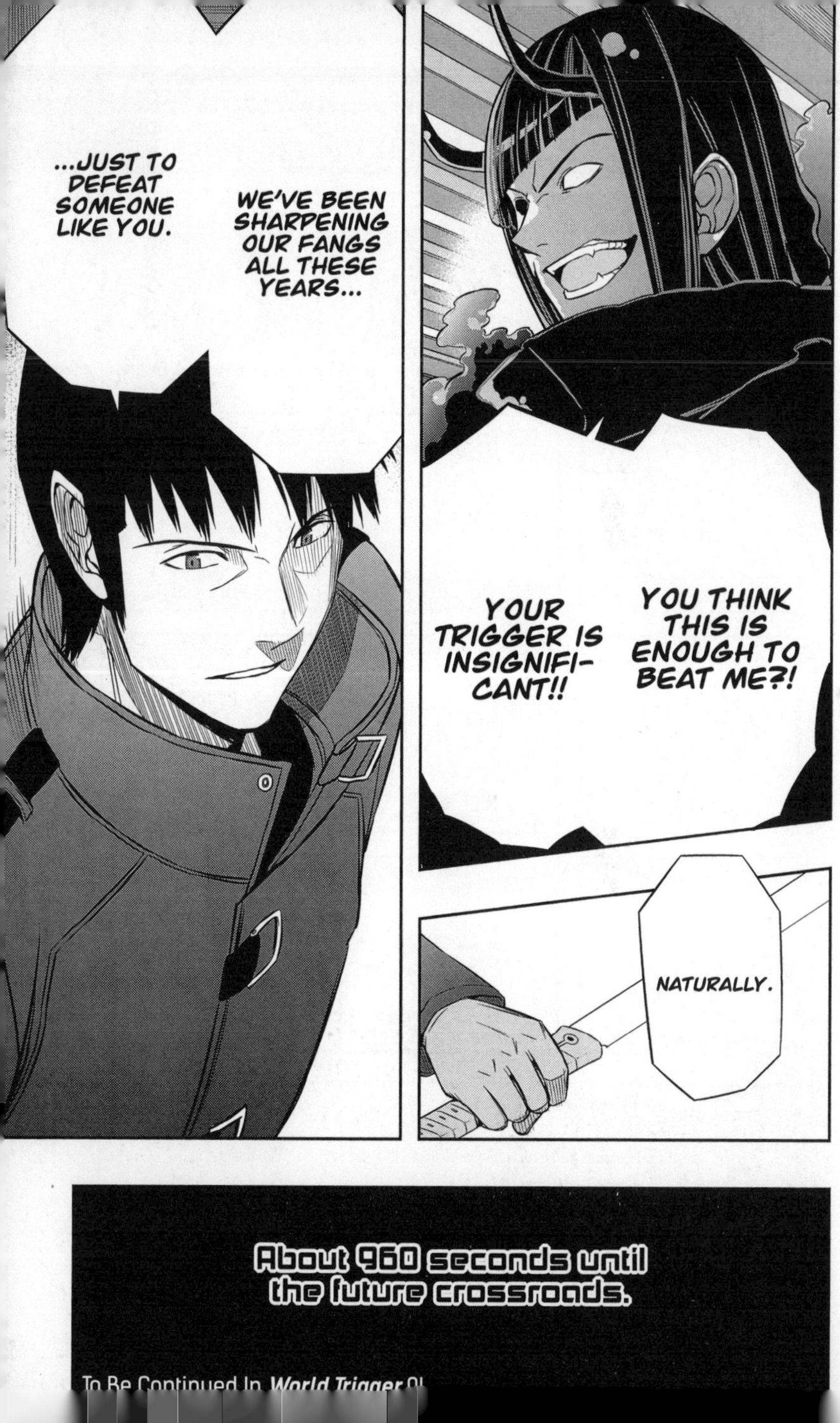
YOU THINK THIS IS ENOUGH TO BEAT ME?!
YOUR TRIGGER IS INSIGNIFI-CANT!!
NATURALLY.
WE'VE BEEN SHARPENING OUR FANGS ALL THESE YEARS...
...JUST TO DEFEAT SOMEONE LIKE YOU.

About 960 seconds until the future crossroads.

To Be Continued In *World Trigger* 9!

First Popularity Poll Contest Results: 18th and below

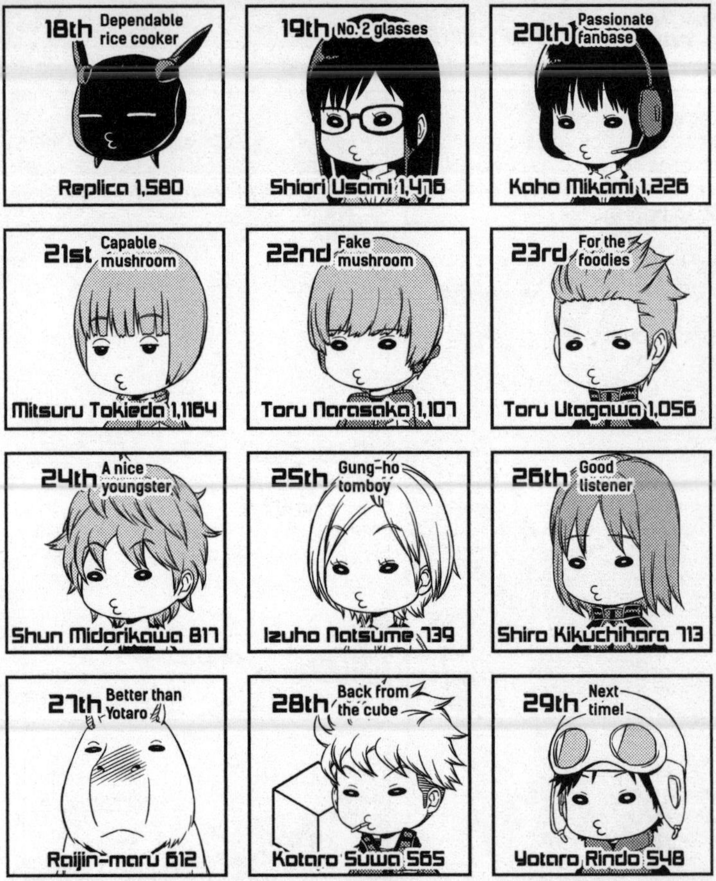

18th
Dependable rice cooker
Replica 1,580
19th
No. 2 glasses
Shiori Usami 1,476
20th
Passionate fanbase
Kaho Mikami 1,226
21st
Capable mushroom
Mitsuru Tokieda 1,1164
22nd
Fake mushroom
Toru Narasaka 1,107
23rd
For the foodies
Toru Utagawa 1,056
24th
A nice youngster
Shun Midorikawa 817
25th
Gung-ho tomboy
Izuho Natsume 739
26th
Good listener
Shiro Kikuchihara 713
27th
Better than Yotaro
Raijin-maru 612
28th
Back from the cube
Kotaro Suwa 565
29th
Next time!
Yotaro Rindo 548

30th

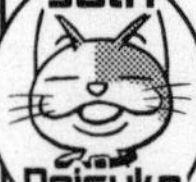

Daisuke Ashihara

31: Shohei Kodera
32: Hyuse
33: Haruaki Azuma
34: Katsumi Karasawa
35: Masamune Kido
36: Ms. Mizunuma
37: Ko Murakami
38: Tsukihiko Amo
39: Ranbanein
40: Isami Toma
41: Ren Tsukimi
42: Hyrein
43: Motokichi Kinuta
44: Rinji Amatori
45: Takumi Rindo
46: Yugo Kuga
47: Mira
48: Makoto Chano
49: Enedora
50: Ichinose
51: Hisato Sasamori
52: Kyoko Sawamura
53: Rilienthal
54: Itsuki Fujisawa
55: Tatsuya Kuruma
56: Taichi Betsuyaku
57: Bonchi crackers
58 (tie): Eizo Netsuki, Viza
60: Izukacha

First Popularity Poll Contest (analysis)

Before the poll started, we got so many letters that said, "I can't pick one favorite character! I'll send multiple postcards!" So the rule became that you could vote for three characters in order of preference. There were still plenty of enthusiastic fans who sent multiple postcards. We tallied a version that didn't count the multiple votes (one postcard per person), which resulted in a lot of fluctuations, such as Satori ranking 12th, Kitora in ninth, Replica in eighth, and so on. I wonder what makes the difference between one character getting passionate support from a few fans vs. a character who gets wide-spread support from many fans. I wish I could have figured that out from the data.

The top without counting multiple votes:
1: Yuma, narrowly beating 2: Osamu, 3: Jin, 4: Konami, 5: Chika, 6: Kazama, 7: Torimaru.

Thank you so much to everyone who voted. I can't really remember, but they were accepting votes around Chapter 51 for a four- to five-week period (I think that's right because people voted for characters that appeared in Chapter 55). If the poll were to be conducted now, I bet Yoneya, Izumi, Midorikawa and Azuma would rank higher along with the Aftokrator crew.

This was the first popularity poll of my career as a manga artist. It was very interesting getting a feel for character popularity in *Shonen Jump*. I felt the principal factors for the rankings were talent, being allies with the main characters, having a long history with the main characters, flashy action scenes and star combat power. Of course, there are other reasons such as being sympathetic, someone to cheer for, a role model or having visual appeal.

Thank you for all your votes!
Number of votes: 77,943
Number of postcards: 25,981

WORLD TRIGGER

Bonus Character Pages

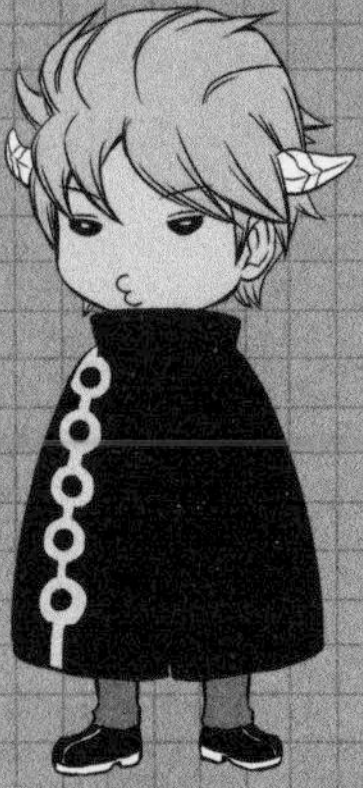

HYUSE

Magnetic Youth

An elite fighter with the most modern Trigger, he was chosen at a young age for the away team so he should have been awesome. Unfortunately, he was matched against Jin and ended up looking like cannon fodder. He is from the most recent generation of horned fighters to be deployed, which in terms of stability and Trion augmentation is one of the best in history. But he has the terrible burden of only being able to sleep on his stomach. Live on!

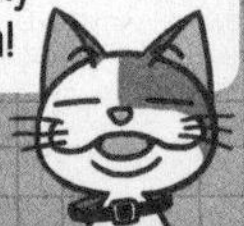

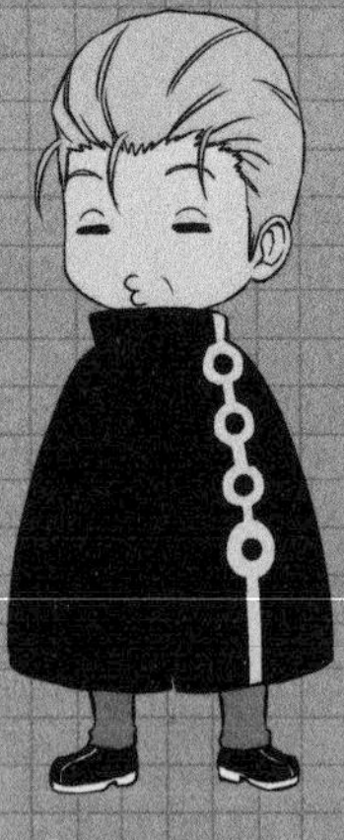

VIZA

Building-Slashing Grandpa

He wields a brutal Black Trigger with a wide-ranged, indiscriminate, insta-kill slashing attack. As an expert swordsman with loads of experience, he can influence an entire war from afar. He has the makings of a true hero. He is definitely one of the most powerful characters in *World Trigger*. He has probably brought down entire regimes by himself. He was definitely even more dangerous when he was younger. I'd really like to try drawing his past.

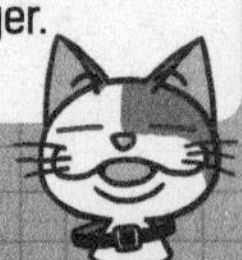

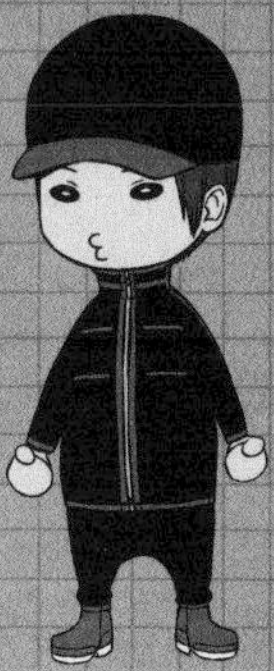

ARAFUNE

Hollywood Action Hero

He is a show-off sniper, always featured in scenes of jumping off the top of buildings. He most likely picks rooftops just so he can jump off of them. He goes to a prep school and has good grades, which is rare for a B-Rank agent. Maybe the academic pressure is fueling the flashy action. His weaknesses are his inability to swim and his fear of dogs.

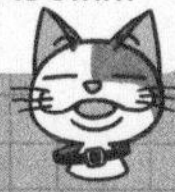

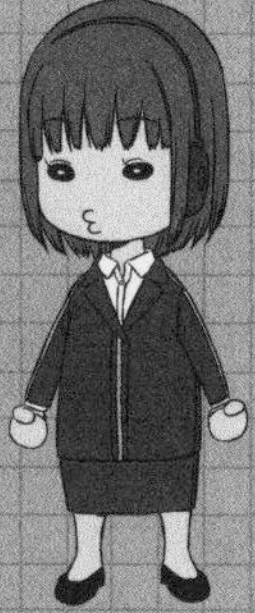

AYATSUJI

The Epitome of a Model Student

The one everyone looks up to, both in and out of Border. She has the looks and the smarts, but is disastrous at the arts. While she is a perfect being in every other way, legend has it that her atrocious singing amused Commander Kido and made Karasawa break out in a cold sweat. Additionally, she is the iron-fortress C-cup who is the student council vice president at her prep school.

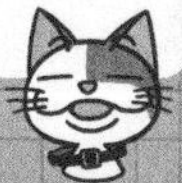

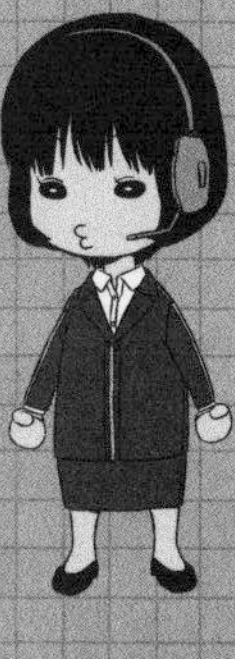

KAHO MIKAMI

Mika-Mika

A competent Operator who, just like Kazama, is the embodiment of "small but effective." As the eldest of four, she has been cultivated into a motherly figure with a caring personality and is thus especially popular with other women. Konami, Shiori, Ayatsuji, Kunichika and Sawamura all admire her. She is an A-cup who wishes that someone would take care of her sometimes.

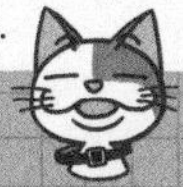

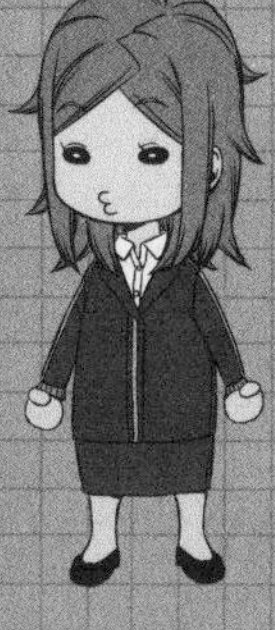

KUNICHIKA

From Spelunker to FPS

Border's top gamer. Her days consist of eating, sleeping and gaming. Unlike the other two women, she goes to an average school and her grades are only so-so. But she's a number one A-Rank agent! Both her and Tachikawa are proof that grades aren't everything. She is a E-cup who will strangle her opponent with tears in her eyes whenever she loses a match.

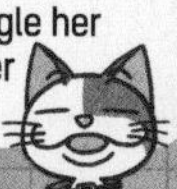

YOU'RE READING THE WRONG WAY!

World Trigger reads from right to left, starting in the upper-right corner. Japanese is read from right to left, meaning that action, sound effects, and word-balloon order are completely reversed from the English order.

142